Gandhian Nonviolent Struggle and
Untouchability in South India

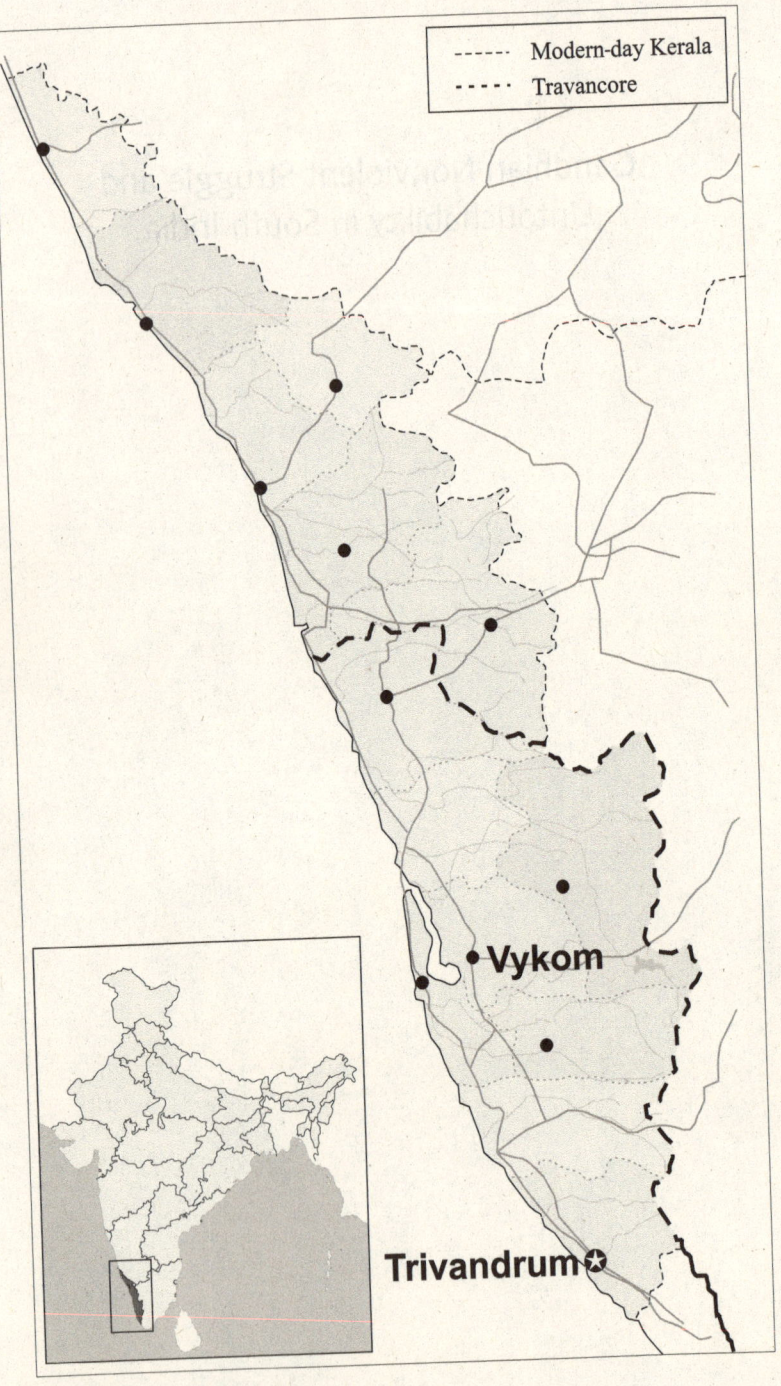

Map 1 Vykom, Travancore

Source: Author

Gandhian Nonviolent Struggle and Untouchability in South India

The 1924–25 Vykom Satyagraha and the Mechanisms of Change

Mary Elizabeth King

OXFORD
UNIVERSITY PRESS

OXFORD
UNIVERSITY PRESS

Oxford University Press is a department of the University of Oxford.
It furthers the University's objective of excellence in research, scholarship,
and education by publishing worldwide. Oxford is a registered trademark of
Oxford University Press in the UK and in certain other countries

Published in India by
Oxford University Press
YMCA Library Building, 1 Jai Singh Road, New Delhi 110001, India

© Oxford University Press 2015

The moral rights of the author have been asserted

First Edition published in 2015

ISBN-13: 978-0-19-945266-8
ISBN-10: 0-19-945266-0

Typeset in ITC Giovanni Std 9.5/13
by Zaza Eunice, Hosur, India

In Memoriam: K. K. Kusuman (1943–2007)

This study is dedicated to the memory of Professor Kusuman who, despite the inconvenient moment of my first arrival in Trivandrum, generously dropped everything he was doing to help my research. Making certain that I had critical and obligatory materials, he lent me his personal copies in some instances. I treasure his discernments.

Kalathilparambil Kumaran Kusuman was born to Kumaran and Kunjulakshmi on April 27, 1943, at S. L. Puram, in the Alleppey district of the one-time princely State of Travancore. Hailing from a prominent ancestry that had made literary and cultural contributions to modern Kerala, he was orphaned at an early age and reared by his maternal uncle, S. L. Puram Sadanandan, a cultural and political figure in Kerala. After excelling at school and college, he joined the Department of History at the University of Kerala as a research scholar under the supervision of Professor T. K. Ravindran, who would later become Vice-Chancellor of Calicut University. His doctoral thesis was on "The History of Trade in Travancore (1600–1805)." In 1978, he joined the history faculty at Kerala University as lecturer. After a short period at the University of Calicut, Professor Kusuman returned to Kerala University and headed the history department there until his retirement in 2004. His published works include *Slavery in Travancore, The Abstention Movement, The Extremist Movement in Kerala, English Trade in Travancore*, and *A History of Trade and Commerce in Travancore (1600–1805)*. He was the editor of the *Journal of Indian History* and *Journal of Kerala Studies*. He met an untimely death in an automobile accident on March 18, 2007, at Trivandrum.

Contents

Figures and Maps

Figures

Maps

Foreword

Confronted with various kinds of injustices during his long political life, Gandhi wondered how best to fight against them. Since rational discussion had its limits and violence was morally unacceptable, he developed what he called the science of satyagraha (nonviolent struggle) and experimented with various forms of action.

His science of satyagraha contained an ambiguity. Convinced that every human being had an *atman* or spark of the divine, and hence the capacity to recognize and respond to truth or justice and feel with and for others, Gandhi argued that the best way to win over the opponent was through the power of suffering love. This involved taking a stand against injustice and undergoing such suffering as this entailed in a spirit of love. Gandhi thought that this was bound to break through the "wall of prejudice," trigger in one's opponent a process of self-examination, and get him or her to see the justice of one's cause or to "convert." If it did not, that could only be because one's suffering was not pure or persistent enough, and one then needed to make oneself a purer person and one's suffering untainted by base considerations.

Gandhi's experiences convinced him that this view was deeply problematic. His satyagraha against the Transvaal Registration Act 1907 went on for months without desired results. That against the Natal Immigration Bills and others in South Africa and India fared no better. Gandhi therefore introduced new forms of pressure such as mobilizing neutral public opinion, boycotts, strikes, fasts, nonpayment of taxes, civil disobedience, and various forms of noncooperation. While these were effective in various degrees, they sat ill at ease with his belief in the irresistible power of suffering love. He continued to hold that belief and seems to have thought that these forms of action became necessary because the *satyagrahis* were unlikely to possess the required degree of purity of character.

While most satyagrahas by Gandhi and his followers were mixed in character and involved varying combinations of both suffering love and nonmoral pressure, that in Vykom was and is often seen differently. It was mounted by the untouchables to secure the right of access to the roads encircling the outer walls of a temple that had long been closed to them by the orthodox Brahmins on grounds of pollution. In small groups, representatives of the untouchables, later joined by caste Hindus, kept vigil, sang devotional songs, and braved the monsoon when they stood in waist-deep icy waters and faced cold blasts of wind. The satyagraha, which attracted national attention and brought Gandhi's involvement, lasted just over twenty months and resulted in a settlement that met most, though not all, of its demands. A long line of distinguished Gandhi scholars, including Richard Gregg, Krishnalal Shridharani, Joan Bondurant, and Gene Sharp, has accepted a narrative of conversion and quoted in support a remark allegedly made by the orthodox Brahmins that they "cannot any longer resist the prayers that have been made to us." Though other commentators have taken a different view, the idealized version has enjoyed greater prominence.

Mary King, an academician and a civil rights activist, challenges it. Drawing on an extensive range of primary and secondary sources and interviews, she convincingly shows that the reality was different. Although the suffering of the satyagrahis influenced neutral public opinion, attracted the attention of the country at large, and provided an additional motive for action to well-disposed caste Hindus, it had little impact on the orthodox Brahmins, who remained firm in their beliefs. Not their "conversion" but other factors played a part in securing the final settlement, such as the wider anti-untouchability movement, spread of liberal and egalitarian ideas, the royal intervention, and the fear of the untouchables converting to other religions.

As King points out, the suffering love reaches its limits when there is a clash of fundamental interests and beliefs or the social distance between the two parties is too great to allow empathy with the protesters. She is also right to make the more general point that an uncritical belief in it can prove unacceptably costly in terms of human lives and suffering, and lead to a misguided emphasis on the moral purity of the satyagrahis rather than the forms of action needed to alter the wider structure of power, climate of ideas, and play of interests.

King's book is remarkable for its quality of research, fairness of approach, and depth of analysis. I know no other work on the Vykom satyagraha that comes anywhere near it. Its value is not limited to that particular historical event as it offers powerful theoretical and practical insights into Gandhi's science of satyagraha. Probing him from a novel perspective and highlighting both the strengths and limitations of his religious approach to political issues, it is a most welcome addition to the large and growing literature on Gandhi and deserves to be widely read and discussed.

Bhikhu Parekh
House of Lords

Preface

A twenty-month nonviolent struggle took place during 1924–5 against the Hindu caste system's practice of untouchability in Vykom (now in the state of Kerala in India). Reports that spread beyond Kerala and India, starting in the 1930s, affected the understanding of nonviolent civil resistance worldwide. In interpreting the meaning of India's momentous nonviolent struggles for Western readers, authors writing in the mid-twentieth century did not have access to archival materials, which often disclose the thoughts and actions of authorities and other participants in this drama. In part, these missing pieces led to idealized accounts of this 604-day struggle, spreading the belief that a solution was reached to this particular conflict that stemmed from conversion of the high-caste Brahmins—in other words reaching the hearts and minds of the target group—to the extent that they accepted the viewpoint of the outcastes and untouchables, and therefore changed their behavior.

By the 1970s, in the body of international theoretical work explaining nonviolent civil resistance, one analytical tool had incorporated an interpretation of conversion as the first of several mechanisms of change. This construal was based on Gandhi's frequent refrain on the necessity to convert, not coerce. The mechanisms developed as a useful tool for scholars and practitioners, because they help to answer two questions that can be applied to specific struggles either for planning or in retrospective assessment: How does nonviolent action work? How can its strategy be aimed? The perceived conversion in the case of

Vykom was often cited as evidence of effective nonviolent action. Conversion was never said to be common, but writings on it were frequently based wholly or partially on erroneous assessments of the Vykom struggle. The other three mechanisms are accommodation, nonviolent coercion, and nonviolent disintegration, as analyzed by the scholars Clarence Marsh Case, Richard Gregg, George Lakey, and Gene Sharp. Of these, accommodation is far and away the most frequent.

Comprehension of how to employ strategies in applying nonviolent sanctions and how they work has been skewed by exuberant accounts of this particular struggle and, therefore, may at times have affected the perceived validity and employment of nonviolent strategic action as a method for social change. In other words, the mistaken impression was created, in the parlance of nonviolent action, that the actions of the civil resisters brought about the Brahmins' "conversion." Joan Bondurant, for example, claims that the struggle instituted a major turning point in India's battle against untouchability.[1]

Revisiting the historical record of the Vykom campaign can help to clarify how the technique of civil resistance utilizes nonviolent sanctions to bring about results and thus make this form of struggle more valuable for current and future practitioners. In addition to substantiating a narrative of what happened, this work is an examination of Gandhi's concept of conversion through self-imposed suffering, which is the way he insisted that social change would occur.

The chronicle here of the 1924–5 Vykom satyagraha is based on an examination of primary sources in repositories, archives, and newspaper morgues; secondary sources; and formal interviews of Indian historians, scholars, and journalists. As a political scientist, I have adopted a methodology based on attempting to confirm events and assertions through three sources, preferably from varying types of resources. As this particular research took place long after the actual events, I have not always been able to find three informants or documents, much less sources that concur. Instances where I have noted conflicting information in this case study reflect the historical analysis and archival records.

A verifiable account is helpful for those wanting to know about the practicalities of intentionally fighting for social and political change

---

[1] Joan V. Bondurant, *Conquest of Violence: The Gandhian Philosophy of Conflict* (Berkeley: University of California Press, 1965), 50.

without violence. It can broaden appreciation of how, in the modern history of one of the world's most ancient civilizations, an important social struggle came about through individuals taking action over a social justice issue that also questioned the basis of social power—the caste system. This case study seeks to correct misunderstandings about what happened in the twenty-month Vykom struggle, addresses the rarity of conversion as a mechanism, and brings out the shortcomings of Gandhi's actual leadership, which in this instance was based on certain faulty principles.

In the course of the research, the questions I asked myself about the struggle arose from practical knowledge, my previous research, and my teaching peace and conflict studies to instructors and graduate students. The attraction of the Vykom campaign arose from my range of experiences—including as a participant in a mass nonviolent movement and years of work that have taken me to more than 120 developing countries—along with my study of the phenomenon of nonviolent action. All of these elements have helped to shape my narrative and historical approach.

My involvement with civil resistance began when I worked for four years in the vortex of the U.S. civil rights movement. Immersion in the theories and methods of nonviolent struggle in the Deep South of the United States in the 1960s is the defining experience of my life, the grounding for my previous books, and the basis of the international pedagogical work that led to my being awarded the Jamnalal Bajaj International Prize in 2003 and the El-Hibri Peace Education Prize in 2009.

It is my hope that this work will not only serve as a correction to a long-told tale, but will also be of practical value to scholars, practitioners, and trainers involved in civil resistance worldwide; instructors and students in peace and conflict studies; and social scientists specializing in various related fields where nonviolent resistance intersects with their primary studies. Careful and studious use of nonviolent methods and strategies increases the possibilities of transforming conflict without violence, while recognizing the accomplishments (and failures) of their application helps in understanding the past so as to improve theory and practice in the future.

M.E.K.

Acknowledgments

The undertaking of this project was first suggested to me in 2000 by theoretician Gene Sharp, senior scholar in Boston at the Albert Einstein Institution. He said that the events of Vykom needed to be reinterpreted and encouraged me to embark on this major research endeavor.

I am grateful to Christopher A. Miller for sketching an initial draft chronology of the Vykom satyagraha, while working for the Albert Einstein Institution, mainly from secondary sources. Chris subsequently acted as my research assistant for four years and has my deep appreciation for his help on this project while we were both in Oxford.

This venture could not have been carried out without the assistance of the University of Oxford's Rothermere American Institute (RAI) in Britain. During 2004–5, as the resident senior fellow, I was able to review British colonial records and secondary sources in the Bodleian Library, and to view archival records. The RAI recognized the worth of this research by providing Chris Miller with an office so that he could assist me during 2004–5. In 2005, the RAI gave me a grant to travel to Kerala. There, in Vykom, thanks to the kind help of P. Sanal Mohan, Mahatma Gandhi University, Kottayam, I walked the environs to grasp the social organization, roads, human settlements, ponds, and waterways. I took photographs, developed raw notes, and interviewed N. K. Jose, who remembered hearing firsthand accounts from volunteers in the events of the 1920s. I also conducted formal interviews of a number of historians.

Over the years, M. S. Swaminathan in Chennai and historian B. R. Nanda in New Delhi gave me assistance and encouragement, for which

I remain grateful. At New Delhi's Institute of Social Sciences, I enjoyed the backing of its founder, sociologist George Mathew. In more ways than can be enumerated here, he has contributed to the substance of this project. I would like to thank the historian David Hardiman for his astute assistance.

I devoted to this research the funds that were awarded to me in 2003 in Mumbai, as the winner of the Jamnalal Bajaj International Prize, and I thank the Bajaj family and Venkat R. Chary, IAS (Ret.) for acknowledging my work.

I wish in particular to extend appreciation to Dinoo Anna Mathew, candidate for a doctorate from the University for Peace, who is based in New Delhi at the Institute of Social Sciences. Her proficient assistance has been of inestimable value for more than five years. A native of Trivandrum, of all the individuals who have helped me on this project, she deserves special thanks for her support, particularly for her translations from the Malayalam language in the Kerala State Archives, enabling me to complete my review of pertinent documents there.

Thanks go to Sundarannadar Raimon, the director of the Kerala State Archives in Trivandrum in 2005, who expedited my access to the archives. From that initial time, I drafted memos that helped shape the account.

In 2005, in Kerala, in the morgue of the nationalist newspaper *Mathrubhumi* (Motherland) in Kozhikode, I made orienting memos and laid out a chronology with the expert assistance of Vasu Thilleri, historian at Pocker Sahib Memorial Orphanage College, Calicut. He provided running translations from the Malayalam language of the newspaper's reports from Vykom for 1924–5.

While visiting Calicut, Kottayam, Vykom, and Trivandrum in both 2005 and 2009, I was able to interview seven historians from a protocol of questions and later made verbatim transcriptions from the resulting cassette-tape recordings. It is impossible adequately to express my appreciation for the generosity of spirit expressed by each of them. They included M. G. S. Narayanan, former head of the Department of History, University of Calicut, and former chairman of the Indian Council for Historical Research. K. N. Panikkar, chairman of the Indian Council for Historical Research and former dean and professor, School of Social Sciences, Jawaharlal Nehru University, welcomed me to his home for our interview. The late historian K. K. Kusuman, University of

Kerala, was most kind to me in Trivandrum. I also thank the following academicians and scholars for sharing their knowledge with me: J. Devika and Suresh Jnaneswaran in Kerala; and N. N. Pillai, A. K. Ramakrishnan, and Gilbert Sebastian in New Delhi. I also thank the journalists A. J. Philip and Joseph Maliakan for sharing their viewpoints with me in New Delhi. I thank Professor K. Gopalankutty, Calicut University, who greatly aided my perspective.

The United States Institute of Peace (USIP) provided a research grant in 2008, making it possible for me to return to spend time in libraries and research institutes in New Delhi, such as the Nehru Memorial Library and Indian Council for Historical Research. I thank my USIP program officer, Steven M. Riskin, for his counsel. With gratitude to the USIP for its support, I returned to Trivandrum in 2009 and revisited the morgue of the *Mathrubhumi*, again helped by Vasu Thillari, intensifying my search in the repository of *Mathrubhumi* reports, with their contemporaneous firsthand evidence and eyewitness accounts.

I thank Reji Kumar, who succeeded Raimon as director for the Kerala State Archives and enabled my work in the archives, accompanied by Dinoo Mathew. P. Cherian, director of the Institute for Kerala History in Trivandrum, who also gave assistance.

My appreciation goes to A. Shaji for his clarifications. I would like to thank Qurban Ali, for his kindness in searching for material from Rammanohar Lohia. As I approached the completion of the case study, I benefited from the viewpoint of Justin Mathew, Department of History, Hans Raj College, Delhi University, who, as a specialist on Kerala's history, contributed important perspectives.

As I neared completion of the study at the University of Oxford in recent years, I received invaluable help from the director of the RAI, Nigel Bowles, whom I specifically thank. The head librarian of the Vere Harmsworth Library, Jane Rawson, gave me valued help. Suggestions from the historian of modern India, Professor Judith M. Brown, were useful. Ross Baird and Jen Kyle have my appreciation for their research assistance. I thank Robin Surratt for her editorial assistance.

I offer the art director of the *Mathrubhumi* newspaper, Madanan Pv, my special and sincere appreciation for his unique sketches, included in this volume.

M. E. K.
Fredericksburg, Virginia

Introduction

From April 1924 to November 1925, upper-caste Hindus and others led a nonviolent struggle in the small town of Vykom, India, to gain access for untouchables to the roads encircling the outer walls of the Brahmin temple there. The campaign against the severe conditions affecting untouchables stemmed from discontent with social and civic inequalities particular to the princely state of Travancore, but as it proceeded, it gripped the attention of British India and beyond. Within the decade after the Vykom campaign concluded, accounts began to appear that would establish a narrative in which all the Vykom temple roads were opened to outcastes as a result of the upper castes' conversion and change of heart, thereby resolving the struggle. This narrative has persisted to this day. Yet these portrayals are not borne out by assessment of the available documentary evidence.

Richard Gregg's 1934 description was the most influential of the accounts establishing the false narrative:

> The endurance and consistent nonviolence of the reformers was finally too much for the Brahmans. In the autumn of 1925, after a year and four months, their obstinacy broke down, and they said, "We cannot any longer resist the prayers that have been made to us, and we are ready to receive the untouchables." The Brahmans opened the road to all comers and the low-caste people were allowed to walk at any time past the temple and past the Brahman quarters.[1]

---

[1] Richard B. Gregg, *The Power of Nonviolence*, 3rd ed. (1934; New York: Schocken Books; London: James Clarke and Company Ltd., 1960), 20.

Krishnalal Shridharani in 1939 described the conclusion in Vykom as follows:

> The suffering of the Satyagrahis had its visible effect on the orthodox Brahmins . . . . Finally the Brahmins gave in, saying; "We cannot resist any longer the prayers that have been made to us, and we are ready to receive the untouchables." Thus the Satyagraha won for the untouchables their civic rights. The repercussions of the victory were felt all over the country, and the cause of social reform was materially boosted.[2]

R. R. Diwakar claims:

> Ultimately [Travancore authorities] were persuaded to withdraw the police pickets and remove the barricades. In the autumn of 1925, after a year and four months of satyāgraha the road was cleared and the opposition of the brahmins broke down. Possibly if the State had not gone to the aid of the priests, the problem would have been solved much earlier.[3]

Joan Bondurant, classifying the response of the upper castes as capitulation, wrote, "In the autumn of 1925, the Brahmans declared: 'We cannot any longer resist the prayers that have been made to us, and we are ready to receive the untouchables.'" The "roads opened to all comers," she asserts. "The immediate objective of the satyagraha had been fully achieved . . . . Before terminating their action, *satyagrahis* insisted upon and secured full agreement with the opponent."[4] The same quotation and similar iterations from unnamed Brahmins are offered in Sharp's influential, three-volume *Politics of Nonviolent Action* (1973).[5] Mark Juergensmeyer states that after sixteen months of Gandhi-directed prayer vigils in front of the police cordon that prevented their passage, "the opposition relented and the policy was changed."[6]

[2] Krishnalal Shridharani, *War without Violence: A Study of Gandhi's Method and Its Accomplishments* (New York: Harcourt Brace and Company, 1939; rev. ed., Bombay: Bharatiya Vidya Bhavan, 1962), cited here, 94, 95.

[3] Ranganath Ramachandra Diwaker, *Saga of Satyagraha* (1956; New Delhi, Bombay: Gandhi Peace Foundation, 1969), 132. Diwaker chaired the Gandhi Peace Foundation and was an editor of *Gandhi Marg*.

[4] Joan V. Bondurant, *Conquest of Violence: The Gandhian Philosophy of Conflict* (Berkeley: University of California Press, 1965), 50, 52.

[5] Gene Sharp, *Power and Struggle*, vol. 1 of *The Politics of Nonviolent Action* (Boston: Porter Sargent Publishers, 1973), 83.

[6] Mark Juergensmeyer, *Gandhi's Way: A Handbook of Conflict Resolution* (New Delhi, Oxford, New York: Oxford University Press, 2003), 61.

In reality, the Vykom struggle lasted for 20 months, and the opposition did not relent. The Global Nonviolent Action Database, an online compendium of nonviolent civil resistance campaigns established in 2011 by George Lakey, offers a similarly magnified view of Vykom, again based on Gregg and Bondurant.[7] The author of this very book in an earlier work wrote, based on Shridharani, Bondurant, and Sharp, "As the satyagrahis restrained themselves through self-discipline, the upper-caste Indians were thrown off balance and won over."[8]

Other authors also bent the facts. Regarding Vykom's settlement, a biography of Gandhi claims, "The police . . . threw a cordon across the road. The volunteers took their stand in front of it, day after day, month after month, in an attitude of prayer . . . . At last after sixteen months, the Brahmins gave way and highways were opened to untouchables, not only there, but all over Travancore."[9] K. Ramachandran Nair contends that as a result of a compromise, "the approach roads to the Vaikom Temple were thrown open to all and the display boards indicating the bar on the entry of avarnas were removed."[10] While Louise Ouwerkerk prudently notes that "most of the social reform of Hinduism was carried out by numerous community organizations," because the social structures effectively forced reformers to start within their own group, she, too, embellishes the outcome of the struggle: "the whole episode was regarded locally as a victory for everybody except the obscurantists."[11] Until 2005, the Kerala Department of Public Relations

[7] The database is a project of Swarthmore College in Pennsylvania and is overseen by the Peace and Conflict Studies program, the Peace Collection, and the Lang Center for Civic and Social Responsibility. See nvdatabase.swarthmore.edu (accessed on July 11, 2014).

[8] Mary King, *Mahatma Gandhi and Martin Luther King Jr: The Power of Nonviolent Action*, 2nd ed. (New Delhi: Indian Council for Cultural Relations and Mehta Publishers, 2002), 53.

[9] H. S. L. Polak, H. N. Brailsford, and Lord Pethick-Lawrence, *Mahatma Gandhi: The Father of Modern India* (New Delhi: Anmol Publications, 1986), 185, as cited in George Gheverghese Joseph, *George Joseph: The Life and Times of a Kerala Christian Nationalist* (Hyderabad: Orient Longman, 2003), 158.

[10] K. Ramachandran Nair, *The History of the Trade Union Movement in Kerala* (Thiruvananthapuram: Kerala Institute of Labour and Employment, 2006), 14.

[11] Louise Ouwerkerk, *No Elephants for the Maharaja: Social and Political Change in the Princely State of Travancore, 1921–1947* (New Delhi: Manohar, 1994), 58, 57.

rhapsodized online, under "Socio-Religious Reform Movement," that "[p]ublic opinion in the state was so favourable that the government threw open the approach roads to the 'Avarnas [those without caste].'"

This is not to say that solely idealized accounts were published. Despite the flawed conclusion earlier studies attached to the Vykom struggle, a number of interpretations helpfully describe the contradictions and incongruities of the campaign and the so-called settlement of the struggle, with supporting verification from public and official sources.

Examples include Mahadev Desai's *Epic of Travancore*, Robin Jeffrey's chapter in *People, Princes and Paramount Power: Society and Politics in the Indian Princely States*, Koji Kawashima's *Missionaries and a Hindu State*, P. K. Karunakara Menon's *History of the Freedom Movement in Kerala*, and M. S. A. Rao's *Social Movements and Social Transformation*. A half century after the events, T. K. Ravindran undertook *Vaikkam Satyagraha and Gandhi* as "a refutation" of the prevalent notion that the struggle succeeded in achieving its objectives.[12] His account was overlooked internationally and never received the attention it deserved.

The chronicle offered in the following pages rests on searching through evidentiary materials that have survived, but until now had not been thoroughly mined, thus providing another reason for probing the enduring significance of the Vykom struggle. While granting the resoluteness and resilience of the campaign's local and regional leaders, any evaluation of it deserves to be tempered by the realization that there remains greater knowledge to be found in probing Vykom's perplexities and predicaments, including periods of ineptitude and flawed reasoning by Gandhi. The conversion of hearts and minds for which Gandhi had hoped simply did not occur in Vykom, unless considered in an elliptical and attenuated sense spanning twelve years after the campaign's conclusion, when in 1936 the maharaja issued a proclamation opening all of the princely state's temple roads and the temples themselves to any worshipper.

Nevertheless, the unvarnished story of the problems encountered during the Vykom campaign—a major and early effort to develop a practical technique for groups collectively to fight for justice without violence—discloses insights more useful than the enthusiastic, roseate tale that mistakenly spread to North America, Europe, and elsewhere.

---

[12] M. P. Shreekumaran Nair, review of T. K. Ravindran, *Vaikkam Satyagraha and Gandhi, Journal of Indian History* 54 (April 1, 1976): 761.

1 Travancore Society
Early Stirrings of Organized Opposition against Caste

*We received blows and suffered punishment for having ventured to tread
on the road through which cats, cows and dogs are allowed to pass.*

—From a song sung at Vykom, 1924

For centuries, Travancore society was ruled by strong caste distinctions that can be traced in their modern form back to the twelfth century, although some fluidity probably was permitted within the hierarchical system of roughly the southern half of the modern Indian state of Kerala.[1] Generations before the British arrived, the Malayali people who lived in the area were speaking and writing a tongue identifiable as their own, and Kerala today continues to be characterized by the Malayalam language.

---

[1] Kerala, created in 1956, hugs the southwestern coast of India. In the colonial era, the territory of today's Kerala consisted of Travancore and Cochin states, the British district of Malabar, and the southernmost section of the British district of South Kanara. It is a slender, verdant coastal state 174 miles in length from north to south and 75 miles wide. Its area contains three geographical sections: the coastal strip, distinguished by numerous lagoons and lakes, connected by canals and backwaters, offering virtually continuous navigability from north to south; the central heartland, comprising rounded hills traversed by narrow valleys and small rivers; and the eastern flank, where the Western Ghat Mountains physically differentiated Travancore from British India. Travancore comprised most of Kerala's southern portion.

In 1600, Queen Elizabeth I granted a charter for trade to the East India Company. During the eighteenth century, the company began to involve itself in local politics and even in wars, transforming itself from a commercial enterprise into a territorial political power in India. When Maharaja Martanda Varma forged the state of Travancore from unruly chieftaincies after the 1730s, he had the support and assistance of the East India Company. In 1795, the maharajas of Travancore and Cochin entered into alliances with the company.[2]

Travancore had a "feudal, militaristic, and ruthless system of custom-ridden government," in the words of cultural anthropologist Ayinipalli Aiyappan.[3] To this, the British and the East India Company brought Western bureaucratic structures of administration and law and sought to formalize relations with the princes of the states to bring about a stable, tranquil, and pacified India under their control. They generally honored the treaties that they wrote and signed with local rulers. By the mid-nineteenth century a variety of economic, political, and social forces had begun to alter the organization of society.

Vykom, a sprawling small town in the former Travancore, lies among a network of creeks and lagoons.[4] Mohandas Karamchand Gandhi would later call Travancore a "golden garden" because of the impression left by the expansive fields and gardens between the interspersed houses of residents.[5] The area had come under British suzerainty by

[2] The maharaja was the traditional, hereditary ruler of a princely state. *Raja*, meaning "king," with the appendage *maha* means "great king."

[3] Ayinipalli Aiyappan, *Social Revolution in a Kerala Village: A Study in Culture* (London: Asia Publishing House, 1965), 106.

[4] Variations in transliteration from the Malayalam language include Vykom, Vaikkam, Vycome, Vycombe, and others. The name is said to derive from Vyghralaya, which means "the residence of the sage Vyaghrapada." V. Nagam Aiya, *Travancore State Manual*, 2: 87, as cited in V. Balambal, "E. V. R. and Vaikom Satyagraha," *Journal of Kerala Studies* 7 (March, June, September, December 1980): 246n4.

[5] Gandhi writes in 1925, "Travancore is like a beautiful garden or an orchard. . . . One can travel in boats by way of canals and backwaters or by road in a car. . . . The view on the backwaters is magnificent. . . . [A]ll the year round, as far as the eye can see, there stretches an endless garden on both shores." Mohandas K. Gandhi, "A Golden Garden," *Navajivan* [Gujarati], March 29, 1925, in *Collected Works of Mahatma Gandhi* (hereafter *CWMG*, 100 vols., ed. K. Swaminathan (New Delhi: Ministry of Information and Broadcasting, Government of India, 1958–84), 31: 76.

1788.[6] Violent peasant rebellions in nearby districts further prized open the door for the British, who by 1800 had made it compulsory for Travancore to have a political resident. More than a diplomat, the political resident represented and acted for the British empire. B. Sobhanan calls him an "uncrowned king."[7] The power of the maharaja and the political resident represented two different sovereign authorities, creating dual contradictory structures of government.

What the British called "native" states, or Indian states, are also referred to as princely states. These nominally sovereign units during the era of British colonialism in India were not directly administered by the British; instead, they remained under a traditional heriditary Indian ruler in a form of indirect rule under the British crown. Approximately 600 of these "states" existed at the turn of the twentieth century. The term "British India" refers to areas under direct control of the British, through the viceroy, aided by a large British-trained civil service comprised mainly of Indians. Approximately two-fifths of India's landmass would remain under the "rule" of the maharajas (and Muslim nawabs) until abolished in 1947–8 by the newly installed government of the Congress party. They were allowed to retain their titles and privy purses as a concession until 1971, when Prime Minister Indira Gandhi ended these allowances. During the period of this account, the princely states represented a surviving political expression of pre-colonial epochs.

Travancore was a princely state, not part of British India, and for six decades, the British intervened relatively little in Travancore's society or politics. The resident, acting indirectly, introduced a number of administrative reforms to bring the princely state into line with the administration in British India. The effects of colonialism on Travancore can be characterized as catalytic in the sense that they provided impetus for social alterations, including amelioration of some of the inequalities inherent in the caste system, a primary feature in the southern part of Kerala, and the use of slave and bonded labor. They also produced new models of management and ushered in elements of modernity.

[6] Vanaja Rangaswami, *The Story of Integration: A New Interpretation in the Context of the Democratic Movements in the Princely States of Mysore, Travancore and Cochin, 1900–1947* (New Delhi: Manohar, 1981), 1.

[7] B. Sobhanan, *Dewan Velu Tampi and the British* (Trivandrum: Kerala Historical Society, 1978), 2. Sobhanan was formerly Dean of Social Sciences, University of Kerala.

In 1749, Maharaja Utram Thirunal Marthanda Varma had dedicated the princely state of Travancore to the deity Padmanabha (also transliterated Padmanabhan), the god of the great temple in Trivandrum, capital of Travancore and now of Kerala.[8] The rulers of Travancore designated themselves as Padmanabha *dasa* (servant of Padmanabha) and devoted both funds and activities to maintaining the happiness of the Brahmins, the priestly class.[9] Travancore had 1,300 Hindu temples, most of which had come under the maharajas' control by 1875.[10] Travancore was, in a disclosure by the Maharaja Visakham Thirunal Rama Varma (1880–5), "perhaps the most priest-ridden . . . in the whole of India. . . . [T]he ruler himself is not his own master in religious matters."[11]

The reign of Swati Thirunal (1829–47) as maharaja was considered a golden age in modern Travancore, with the introduction of reforms in the judicial system and the beginnings of education in English. An English school opened in 1834 in Trivandrum, along with a charity hospital. His ascendance to the *gaddi*, the cushioned stool-throne, was marked by administrative enlightenment and economic progress. His successor, Utram Thirunal Marthanda Varma (1847–60), continued

---

[8] Trivandrum was one of four districts and the largest administrative unit in the princely state of Travancore. The other three in the nineteenth and early twentieth centuries were Kottayam, Padmanabhapuram, and Quilon. Among the 14 districts in Kerala, Kottayam district encompassed Vykom, occasionally mentioned here. Trivandrum is also called Thiruvananthapuram, its earlier name.

[9] Experts appointed by India's Supreme Court have documented treasure troves of inestimable value in the Sri Padmanabhaswamy temple in Trivandrum. A. Srivathsan, "Panel to Seek National Geographic Society's Help for Inventory of Temple Treasure," *Hindu* (Chennai), April 13, 2013.

[10] Robin Jeffrey, "Travancore: Status, Class and the Growth of Radical Politics, 1860–1940, the Temple-Entry Movement," in *People, Princes and Paramount Power: Society and Politics in the Indian Princely States*, ed. Robin Jeffrey (New Delhi: Oxford University Press, 1978), 139. Hindu is a Persian word that means "India." R. C. Zaehner, *Hinduism*, 2nd ed. (Oxford: Oxford University Press, 1966), 1.

[11] Visakham Thirunal Rama Varma (1837–85), in "A Native Statesman," *Calcutta Review* 55 (1872): 251, as cited in Jeffrey, "Travancore: Status, Temple-Entry Movement," in *People, Princes and Paramount Power*, 139, 165n5.

these trends. In 1853, he issued a royal proclamation to emancipate all future offspring of slaves who served the maharaja's government. In 1859 another proclamation abolished customary restrictions that had forced lower-caste women to leave their upper bodies unclothed. The maharaja opened a school for girls that same year. The first post office began operating at Alleppey in 1857.

In Travancore, although the sovereign was required by treaty to rule with British "advice," delivered through the British resident, its maharaja and regent exercised substantial autonomy. From the 1820s onward, Travancore's princes were educated in English, and by 1855, English had been designated the language of governmental administration. The princely states were being inexorably pulled toward the imperial system.

In 1860, Ayilyam Thirunal, a young and well-educated maharaja (1860–80), came to the throne. At that time, the British appointed a new resident, and the *dewan*, T. Madhava Rao, undertook a program of reform.[12] The dewan acted as the chief executive minister, functioning as a prime minister for the maharaja, who was head of state. The maharaja was forced to appoint a dewan chosen by the British, and the length of tenure and security of the dewan's office depended upon his ability to please the British officers.[13] Rao had come into office in the last years of Ayilyam Thirunal's government as it began to centralize, creating a modern bureaucracy, structuring government schools, eliminating commercial monopolies, instituting land reform, opening a public postal service, establishing a public works department, founding an arts college, and introducing competitive examinations for government service.[14] The administration opened several hospitals. Travancore came to be regarded as a modernizing and progressive princely state. Even so, at every rung of society, Travancoreans could not conceive of altering orthodox Hinduism, of which the maharaja was custodian.

---

[12] *Dewan* is originally a Persian word that can also be spelled *diwan*. In Travancore it was usually spelled dewan, although other variations are also found.

[13] Sobhanan, *Dewan Velu Tampi and the British*, 2.

[14] Jeffrey, "'Travancore: Status, Temple-Entry Movement," in *People, Princes and Paramount Powe*, 140; Jeffrey, "The Social Origins of a Caste Association, 1875–1905: The Founding of the SNDP Yogam," *South Asia* 4 (October 1974): 43.

The government of Mulam Thirunal Varma (1885–1924) continued the advancements of his predecessors and improved irrigation and communications; built bridges, canals, and roads; broadened access to qualified physicians and surgeons; and implemented vaccination programs. Mulam Thirunal's reign brought expansion in education, as the principle of free primary education was recognized, and government schools were opened for the lower strata of society. By the mid-1870s, a thousand miles of roads had been constructed, whereas in the 1850s no roads had existed.[15] Meanwhile, more missionaries from Britain and Europe were in Travancore than in any similar area of India, and they were intensifying their educational and evangelical work among low-caste Hindus.

Measured by the way that the British imposed their command and dominance in India, or as they termed it, their paramountcy, Travancore was in 1867 allotted a nineteen-gun salute from the paramount power. Only Hyderabad and Mysore among the traditional rulerships had larger populations. The Travancore Legislative Council was formed by the maharaja on March 10, 1888, making it the first of its kind in an Indian state.[16]

On October 22, 1904, the Sri Mulam Popular Assembly (Praja Sabha, SMPA) was created, comprising members chosen by the government to represent various Travancore constituencies and tap into public opinion in a limited sense. V. P. Madhava Rao set up the Sri Mulam Popular Assembly in an effort to counter the influence of palace factions. The aim was to furnish the dewan with popular support against those who possessed preferential privileges and to bring political problems and disgruntlement into an open, formal sphere, thus ameliorating disputes in the corridors of the palace and spread in the columns of an opinionated

[15] Jeffrey, "Temple-Entry Movement in Travancore, 1860–1940," *Social Scientist* 4, no. 8 (March 1976): 5.

[16] Chaired by the dewan, the council was not a representative body. Its six officials and two non-officials were nominated by the maharaja, who could accept or decline its recommendations. It, however, provided a foundation for representative bodies in Kerala. Over a period of years, it went from eight members, with the dewan presiding, to fifteen members; during 1919–20 membership was fixed at twenty-five, of which two-fifths could not be government officials; in 1921–2, the council was expanded to fifty members, of whom thirty-five were non-officials.

local press.[17] The principle of elections began to be recognized, including the right of women to vote, but this entitlement amounted to
approximately 2.5 percent of the population casting ballots.[18]

State by princely state, these little kingdoms and traditional rulerships were drawn into the superimposed imperial administration, but
generally did not develop a nationalist viewpoint. People who lived in
Travancore did not express a vision of themselves as Travancoreans.
Nationalism was spreading from British India to the princely states, yet
it was an all-India perspective rather than state nationalism. As it developed in British India, nationalism at the outset manifested itself among
members of the service castes who first received Western education,
where they had encountered the snares and insults of bigotry. Travancore
probably had a higher ratio of government servants to general population than any other state in British-controlled India.

By the 1920s, the influence of the British resident was on the wane, but
his interventions could still be felt in economic matters and in tempering
any potential democratic surges. The resident was concerned that the
states not become seedbeds for spreading sedition from British India.
Continual jockeying had once characterized relations between the British
and the traditional rulers, yet by the early twentieth century, the chances
of a maharaja leading insurrections against British rule had long passed.
The princes had become convenient to the British for protecting the native
states from the spread of rebellion from British India and had also become
reliable ornamental figures for imperial and international display.

Travancore: Land, Education, and Reverence

The area of the former Travancore was historically unlike other regions
of India, in part because of its location on the Arabian Sea. What is now
Kerala is a narrow strip of land bounded by the Western Ghat mountains

[17] Robin Jeffrey, *The Decline of Nayar Dominance: Society and Politics in
Travancore, 1847–1908* (New Delhi: Vikas Publishing House, 1976), 243. *Sabha*
means assembly, association, meeting, or society. The caste sabha differs from a
jati, or caste group, in that one must be born into the pertinent caste grouping
and also choose to participate, for example, by paying fees. Caste sabhas led the
way with conscious mobilization around caste identity.

[18] A. Sreedhara Menon, *A Survey of Kerala History* (Kottayam: Sahitya
Pravarthaka Co-operative Society, 1967), 332–4.

and the sea, into which its sixty-odd rivers flow. Monsoons, called trade winds, blow from West to East for about three or four months of the year with regularity. They bring clouds, causing precipitation upon reaching the mountains, meaning that Kerala has three or four months of rainy season, after which the wind alternatively blows from East to West.

By the 1890s, Travancore had an elite, a large number of whom had been educated in English and through a Western approach. In the early twentieth century, Travancore's literacy was the highest of any province or state in India. By the end of World War I, Travancore had a perceptible middle class and expanding working class. The newly developing classes cracked the mold of the traditional hierarchy, in which caste Hindus had owned most of the land and wielded the economic and political power that usually accompanied it. With time, growing numbers of the lower castes were moving into the ranks of the educated.

Syrian Christians probably accounted for the largest proportion of people among the ranks of the educated and wealthy. They believe themselves to be the descendants of the early Middle Eastern Christian communities in Antioch and Aleppo that emigrated and trace their origins to Thomas the Apostle. The oral traditions of the ancient Syrian Christian congregations in Kerala hold that Doubting Thomas of the New Testament arrived at the port of Kodungallur in 52 C.E. Old, intact Syrian Christian families maintain that they have descended from Nambudiri Brahmins who were converted by Thomas.

According to M. G. S. Narayan:

> Jews *must* have been here in Kerala in the early centuries, but in the case of the Syrian Christians the earliest document that we have is from the ninth century. The earliest written document that we have for the Jews is at the end of the tenth century. By the ninth and tenth centuries, these Christian and Jewish documents are written in the local language. Chieftains and kings are giving the Christians and Jews certain privileges, making them part of the Kerala aristocracy. That much integration had taken place by the ninth and tenth centuries.[19]

It is traditionally surmised that Jews fleeing the Romans ended up in India in the first century C.E. Arab traders later found patronage among

---

[19] M. G. S. Narayanan, interview (Kozhikode [Calicut], August 12, 2005). Narayanan formerly chaired the Department of History, University of Calicut, Kerala, and the Indian Council of Historical Research.

local chieftains and introduced Islam in the centuries after the death of the Prophet Muhammad in 632.

In a rapidly shifting situation of incipient conflict, Brahmin ideology had long granted certain entitlements and privileges to caste Hindus by virtue of their birth. This remained relatively unchanged, despite the fact that the economic and social conditions that had given rise to it were swiftly vanishing. Among the ideologically justified prerogatives were temples for their sole use; lower castes and outcastes were not allowed to approach the exterior walls or touch them. They could not drink from the village well. Denied access to the main village, they lived outside it.

The British resident in Travancore and Cochin from 1810 to 1819 was Col. John Munro, who had close ties with Christian missionary societies and facilitated their work, which was often geared toward the Syrian Christians. "Munro's game plan was to transform these ancient Christians into a loyal client population."[20] The London Mission Society at Nagercoil, founded in 1816, was given patronage by the maharani of Travancore with a grant of 5,000 rupees per year and a bungalow. Beginning in 1806, these and other Protestant missionaries began establishing schools, promoting the study of English, and pioneering the education of women. The Church Missionary Society (CMS) set up printing presses and in 1816 founded a college. According to historian R. N. Yesudas:

> The system of education established by [CMS], with a college at [the] top, where higher and theological education was imparted, a parochial school attached to each church, a grammar school serving as a place of intermediate instruction and schools for girls, was an efficient instrument for the educational uplift of the Syrians [Christian] and others. . . . All of these efforts of the CMS Missionaries led to the social awakening of the Syrians, and later of the backward classes in Central Kerala.[21]

With their emphasis on the equality of all the children of God, the widening educational opportunities that the missionaries provided created self-awareness, individual consciousness, and a tentative perception of rights among the population.

[20] George Gheverghese Joseph, *George Joseph: The Life and Times of a Kerala Christian Nationalist* (Hyderabad: Orient Longman, 2003), 35.

[21] R. N. Yesudas, "Christian Missionaries and Social Awakening in Kerala," *Journal of Kerala Studies*, no. 4 (1980): 197–8.

Abolition of slavery was a critical step taken in Malabar, Travancore, and Cochin toward altering society. In 1847, the missionaries began a concerted drive to persuade the Travancore government to end the practice and improve severe aspects of the social hierarchy. In 1852, they began to broadcast the status of Travancore slaves throughout India and in Britain.[22] A royal proclamation brought an end to slavery in 1855, when slave or serf castes were perhaps 15 percent of Travancore's population. By the 1860s, so-called untouchables and members of the formerly serf castes were in recurring contact with Christian missionaries and able to obtain basic education from their schools. After the schools were opened to all, the Travancore government resolved in 1904 to bear the costs of educating children from lower-caste and out-caste families.[23] In Travancore, even the poor had access to education, helping to explain its being the state or province in India with the highest literacy.

The recently educated and thriving among the lower castes chafed against the debasements of a theocracy in which they were constrained from birth. The focal point of their desires and ambitions was the right to enter temples and thus become respected Hindus. In Travancore, this entitlement fell under the domain of the Hindu maharaja, the earthly steward for the deity, and could never have been granted by the British government. Furthermore, Mahadev Desai explains:

> The great esteem, bordering on reverence, in which these Maharajahs and Maharanis were held by their loyal people made the problem of untouchability more difficult, rather than easy, of solution, because [the

[22] Jeffrey, *Decline of Nayar Dominance*, 46, esp. 44–50, on the anti-slavery fight.

[23] *Travancore Government Gazette*, August 16, 1904, 8, no. 29: 180, as cited in Yesudas (1980), 201. In 1904, the Travancore government began to absorb the cost of primary education of "backward castes"; the principle of education for all children being the responsibility of the government was accepted in the same year. In 1911, restrictions on the admission to departmental schools of children whose families were formerly slaves or serfs were eliminated. Complete removal of caste exclusions on admissions to primary schools would await the late 1920s. Steps toward compulsory primary education would not be taken until 1945. Kerala today has nearly universal literacy rates. P. R. Gopinathan Nair, "Education and Socio-Economic Change in Kerala, 1793–1947," *Social Scientist* 4, no. 8 (March 1976): 33–4, 37.

untouchables] were believed by the orthodox to be supporting the evil in all its forms, and the reformers [who sought the abatement of untouch-ability] had not the courage to displease sovereigns so popularly esteemed.[24]

The Caste System

The Hindu caste system developed over thousands of years. Slowly instituted around 500 B.C.E., it took centuries for it to grow into the prominent method of social demarcation based on a hierarchy whose placement related to theoretical degrees of purity. The structural distance between varying castes was identified in terms of pollution versus purity. Higher castes are at all times "pure" in relation to lower castes, and to preserve their higher status, they should refrain from specific forms of contact with the lower castes. Hindus also link kinship to concepts of pollution, which was considered to be contagious.[25]

Hindus are said to seek release from the self and absorption into the ground of all being through successive lives. Each is born into a system of hierarchically ordered strata that determines facets of an individual's life, particularly one's occupational and social status. Caste became joined with the Hindu Law of Karma, resulting in the idea that one's thoughts, words, or deeds establish one's status in the rebirths associated with reincarnation. Thus, karma came to be understood as justification for what was occurring in one's current life, and an ethical justification was bestowed on the misery of those considered the least pure.

Over time, the main castes subdivided. By the turn of the twentieth century, more than 2,000 Hindu castes determined which lines of inter-marriage and association could or could not be crossed. Intricate delineation among the multitudes of varying jatis (caste groups) grew, although lacking strict classification. In villages, jatis were structured

---

[24] Mahadev Haribhai Desai, *The Epic of Travancore* (Ahmedabad: Navajivan Karyalaya, 1937), 8. Desai served as Gandhi's secretary, and also as editor and interpreter.

[25] Those that could "pollute" caste members were referred to as *teendal*, *theendal*, or *tindal jati*.

along convoluted subdivisions and oftentimes highly complex local variations according to religious requirements of purity and pollution. These groupings divided eventually into myriad subcastes, with almost endless variation such that nearly every occupation came to be associated with a singular caste.

Caste differentiations prohibited marriage, dining, and other social familiarities across caste lines. Such distinctions also had the outcome of defining some people as having little worth in society. The lower-caste status of these people obliged them to take menial jobs that offered meager pay, but were nonetheless indispensable, such as the toil of laundry and sanitation. Among employment categories, those relating to manual work—which might entail the handling of soiled or polluting substances, such as human waste or dead animals—ranked lower than non-manual work. At the lowest level are those whose manual or non-manual work is considered sinful or polluting or both.

The Sanskrit word for caste is *varna*, meaning color. The main basis of division in Hindu society was between the members of the four main castes, collectively referred to as the *savarna*s, and those who fell outside these groups and were called the *avarna*s, in Sanskrit meaning those who do not have a *varn*, or "outcastes." Members of this latter group are familiar to many as the people formerly called the "untouchables," or Dalits.[26] The savarnas consisted of the Brahmins, sweepingly

---

[26] Avarna was used to mean "unclean," referring to those who were below the caste system and would "pollute" savarnas. They are sometimes referred to as *panchama*, or the fifth caste. The terms "untouchable" and "depressed class" were generally used prior to the Government of India Act of 1935, when the term "scheduled caste" came into use. Other terms were "Harijans" (of Sanskrit derivation, literally, "children of God," coined by Gandhi), "backward communities," and "non-caste Hindus." Generally, Dalit refers to erstwhile untouchables, or those defined as "scheduled castes," under the classification dating to the British Raj of the 1930s and 1940s, and associated with a vast apparatus for designating assistance to castes across India whose ritual status, impoverishment, or lack of opportunity weighed them down with disabilities. "Backward" groups were scheduled by the government to obtain access to reserved seats in the electoral system. Today, "Dalit" may be used to mean oppressed, or downtrodden, and by some globalizing social movements to convey solidarity with the economically disadvantaged, not considering caste.

called the priestly caste and customarily considered the most pure; the Kshatriyas, the ruler, warrior, or military caste; the Vaisyas (also Vaishyas), the merchant caste; and the Sudras, laborers and artisans.[27] The thousands of subcastes and castes referred to above fall under these four main categories.

The avarnas, who were not among the four main castes and were also called outcastes, held no caste and had little hope of rising in the social ranking (unless they had been only temporarily outcasted for violating caste rules and anticipating restitution after suitable atonement for offenses). Since no one with caste would take polluting jobs, such as removal of human waste or work involving dead animals, these fell to the avarnas to perform. People without caste were considered lower than members of the lowest caste. Sometimes they found themselves in a condition of indentured servitude, a status that would not be legally abolished until 1976. Some of the categories of outcastes were once referred to as the slave or serf castes. The distinctive rigidity of caste structures in what is now Kerala, with their extreme intricacies of behavior, was without parallel elsewhere in India, where even slaves might have more rights than the untouchables. A missionary in Travancore, William Saunders Hunt, wrote in 1924, "The distinction between 'outcast' and 'outcaste' should be noted. The latter have not, like 'social outcasts,' been cast out of society; they were never in, though some claim they once were." He quotes another missionary: "The outcaste had fallen, not *to* the bottom, but on *through* the bottom of the social order."[28]

---

[27] Aiyappan, *Social Revolution in a Kerala Village*, 115. Based on fieldwork, Ayinipalli Aiyappan writes of a village he studied, hypothetically called Mayur, in nearby British Malabar.

While Brahmin conveys both status (varna) and jati (caste group), Ksatriya solely denotes status. Gail Omvedt, *Dalits and the Democratic Revolution: Dr. Ambedkar and the Dalit Movement in Colonial India* (New Delhi, Thousand Oaks, and London: SAGE Publications, 1994), 44.

[28] William Saunders Hunt, *India's Outcastes: A New Era* (London: Church Missionary Society, 1924), 32n1. The British may have coined "outcaste." The first use cited by the *Oxford English Dictionary* is W. H. Sykes, "Statistics of the Educational Institutions of the East India Company in India," *Journal of the Statistical Society of London* 8, no. 2 (June 1845): 111.

Anthropologist Louis Dumont asserts that the use of the term "untouchable" as a category is English rather than indigenous.[29] In other words, "untouchable" is not an Indian expression. Within one's caste, one did what one was supposed to do, but did not think of one-self as untouchable or use this term toward others. Early usage of the word *achut* or *achchuta* (untouchable) referred more to things than human beings.

Bhimrao Ramji (Babasaheb) Ambedkar (1891–1956), the untouch-able lawyer who would become the spokesperson and exemplar for the Dalits, visualized caste as separating communities "in a graded order one above the other in social status" but also as a "notion" or state of mind. The latter to him, therefore, meant the destruction of caste would not simply mean the elimination of physical or locational barriers.[30] In the Marathi language of Maharashtra, Ambedkar's place of origin, Dalits, as another name for untouchables, means "broken men."[31]

Marxist analysts contributed to a fuller comprehension of the caste system by relating caste to class and feudal tenure. Mainstream

---

[29] Louis Dumont, *Homo Hierarchicus: Essay sur le Système Des Castes* (Paris: Gallimard, 1966), 69, trans. for author by Emily F. Henderson. Dumont has been accused of romanticizing the caste system, suggesting that untouchables accepted their position and the hegemony of the upper castes because it provided stability and order in their lives. Dalit activists strongly challenge this viewpoint.

[30] Babasaheb B. Ambedkar, "Caste in India," *Caste and Democractic Politics in India*, in Essential Writings in Politics series, ed. Rajeev Bhargava and Partha Chatterjee, 104, 88, 102: extract from Ambedkar, *Writings and Speeches* (Bombay: Government of Maharashtra, 1987), 3: 99–111.

[31] Ambedkar says the Broken Men result from "continuous tribal warfare which was the normal life of the tribes in their primitive condition"; "instead of being completely annihilated," a tribe was defeated and "broken into bits." Thus, in primitive times, a floating population of "broken tribesmen" roamed. In the transition from nomadic to settled life, the Broken Men lived in separate quarters beyond the settled tribes in villages, because they were from a different tribe and not "of the same blood." Living at the edge of villages, they could guard them and face any raids from hostile nomadic tribes. Although they lived outside the village, that is not the origin of untouchability. Ambedkar judges that "when the stigma of Untouchability fell on them they were prohibited from coming into the village." Ambedkar, *Writings and Speeches*, vol. 7, ed. Vasant Moon (Education Department, Government of Maharashtra, 1990), 272, 275–6.

historians and social scientists in contemporary Kerala have in recent decades been influenced by Marxist analyses of the caste system, introducing such factors as landholdings and economic production, which had previously been missing from what had been heavily religious scrutiny.

By the middle of the nineteenth century, Travancore's government owned 80 percent of the cultivated land and most wasteland, a consequence of a policy of annexing the lands owned by local chieftains, a practice lingering from earlier periods. What remained was mainly in the possession of a small class of landlords, who were mostly Brahmins, in Travancore called Nambudiris, and concentrated in the districts of Travancore, Cochin, and Malabar. Land was also owned by high-caste temples and descendants of local chieftains, who had an absolute right to the land or paid a small tax to the government. This was a claim to ultimate ownership, giving the right of taxation. The British created the concept of state ownership and then imposed it on India, particularly in the case of supposed "wastelands" (including former common property resources). In practice, many groups had ancestral rights on cultivated land, being in effect "owners" paying taxes to the state. The state of Travancore thus maintained a direct relationship between the state and the cultivators and users of common-land resources in 80 percent of its territory. In the remaining 20 percent, they dealt with landlords and temples that held various property rights.

For millennia, land has been the most consequential asset in India. In an agricultural subsistence economy, where cash was relatively unimportant, land was the most coveted possession. The majority of landholders controlled the land by grace of governmentally granted tenure, and of these, the Nambudiris and the Nairs (also Nayars), who were below the Nambudiris in varna, exercised the most control over land that had not been put under direct governmental jurisdiction. Nambudiris were the largest landlords, while Nairs—who in Travancore were the warrior, militiamen, and chieftain caste—were the largest body of landholders and non-laboring land managers. Generally speaking, Nairs, who comprised approximately one-fifth of the population, supervised the land owned by Nambudiris as well as their own, which was cultivated by low-caste laborers and slaves. Decisions regarding much of temple land were made by Nambudiris as custodians. By 1865, Travancore had instituted land reforms and declared all *sarkar*

pattam, government-tenure lands, to be transferred to private ownership, allowing 75 percent of the land to be privatized.[32]

The avarnas were typically allotted work in occupations of agricultural labor, fishing, and handicrafts.[33] The part of south India discussed
here had more avarnas than any other region of India, with the nature
and structure of its caste relationships in the early twentieth century
being exceedingly complex. The majority of the upper so-called polluting castes were landless laborers; the still lower groups, having shortly
before been living in a state of semi-serfdom, were reserved the most
grueling tasks. Travancore's first "scientific" census, in 1875, recorded a
population of 2,311,000, of which 74 percent were Hindu, 20 percent
Christian, and 6 percent Muslim. It identified 420 "sub-divisions of
Hindu castes"; the formal report notes 75 general subdivisions. The
biggest group among the caste Hindus were the Nairs, at 19 percent of
the population; its members were further divided by the census taker
into 35 subcastes. The census counted approximately 25 percent as
savarna and 40 percent of the total population as avarna.[34] This represented a revision of earlier tallies that had counted savarnas in excess of
avarnas. The Nambudiris comprised only 2 percent of Travancore's
population.

Travancore Brahmins

In the families of the Nambudiris, the eldest male traditionally married
within his own caste, to continue the lineage, while other sons had
informal carnal alliances with Nair women. Any offspring of the latter
were considered Nair. Marriage between and among Nambudiris and
Nairs was not marriage in a conventional or religious sense. In matrilineal Nair society, marriage was a matter of convenience for both parties.
Women had the freedom to reject a prospective husband, and if she
accepted him, she could later reject him.

The Nairs formed matrilineal joint families, in which the women of
the family lived together, with their husbands visiting periodically.
They followed *Marumakkathayam*, or matrilineal law, in which property

[32] Rangaswami, *Story of Integration*, 12.

[33] See J. H. Hutton, *Caste in India* (Bombay: Oxford University Press, 1969).

[34] Jeffrey, "Temple-Entry Movement," *Social Scientist*, 6.

passed from mother to daughter. The senior-most male member of a matrilineal family customarily administered matters for the family and was often the brother or maternal uncle to the woman who headed the family, not her husband. Uncles, rather than fathers, usually reared the children.

Although apparently dating to the tenth or eleventh century, matriliny had unquestionably been established by the fourteenth century.[35] The Nairs' extended matrilineal and matrilocal system was hypergamous, that is, one usually married a partner with higher social status, meaning that Nair women had liaisons with Nambudiri men, who were above them. A Nair woman could have several husbands at the same time, but none of them had rights over her or her children. It was also the case that Brahmin men could have more than one woman. Paradoxically, between Nambudiris and Nair women, caste inflexibility and considerations of pollution and purity did not stand in the way of sexual relationships. Nair women had liaisons with Nambudiri Brahmins, Malayali Kshatriyas, Brahmins from Tamil Nadu, and Nairs of higher subcastes. Divorce was simple and uncomplicated.[36]

The majority of Nambudiri Brahmins were not priests, with the exception being a small group within the Brahmin community. In Travancore most Brahmins were landlords.[37] The Nambudiris had several subdivisions, with non-priestly subgroups that could be superior to the priestly groups.[38] Nairs and their allied caste superiors possessed the land and the power to exact the subservience that they expected from the lower rungs of society. What gave the social grievances of the underprivileged classes their economic and political overtones was the ubiquity of the Nair monopoly, which also dominated the composition of the legislature. Although by tradition Nairs would have served in the militias of feudal nobles, by the nineteenth century, they held the largest number of posts in the civil service. They shared names, dress,

[35] Jeffrey, *Politics, Women and Well-Being: How Kerala Became "A Model"* (Houndsmill, Basingstoke, Hampshire: Macmillan Press Limited, 1992), 24–5.

[36] "[The] woman had only to place the sandals of her former husband … outside the door and the husband knew that he had to retire." Louise Ouwerkerk, *No Elephants for the Maharaja: Social and Political Change in the Princely State of Travancore, 1921–1947* (New Delhi: Manohar, 1994), 41.

[37] Narayanan, interview (August 12, 2005).

[38] Menon, *Survey of Kerala History*, 373.

and privileges or restrictions of castes. Recognizable caste names for Nairs included Menon, Nayanar, Panicker (also transliterated as Panikkar), and Pillai.

Nairs filled 60 percent of government service positions in Travancore, while Christians, overall one-fifth of the population, and avarna Hindus were excluded.[39] In addition, the close association between the ruler and the Nairs meant that officials and servants in the maharaja's palace were customarily Nairs. The raja usually married a Nair; the relatives of the consort to the raja could wield great influence. British colonialism did not mitigate this structure. If anything, the British amplified the prerogative of the upper-caste rulers and elites, because they wanted these groups' full support in upholding their dominion. The Syrian Christians were the sole community that approximated the Nairs in standing, numbers, and economic clout. Concentrated in central and northern Travancore, they, too, owned land and were traders. Moreover, they adopted many of the Hindu practices for keeping avarna Hindus in segregation.

Within the ranks of avarna Hindus, the largest group of the so-called untouchables was the Ezhavas.[40] They made up 16 percent of the total population of 2.31 million in the 1875 census. They were regarded as "polluting" and had in the census been officially written off as being not distinguishable by any attributes worth mentioning. The Ezhavas were the highest ranking of the excluded castes, putting them midway in the overall caste hierarchy. They followed a matrilineal descent system similar to the Nairs. In the four or five centuries prior, the share of the Ezhavas' political power had decreased to very nearly zero. Their only delegated authority was the limited control that they exercised over the artisan castes and the untouchable washer–launderer caste. Although not mentioned in medieval documents upon which fragmentary histories are based, the tradition is unambiguous that some artisan castes were controlled by the Ezhavas.[41] So, although regarded as

[39] Jeffrey, "Social Origins of a Caste Association," 42.

[40] Ezhava is pronounced and sometimes transliterated as "Irava" or "Erhava." "Izhava," "Elava," or "Ilava" are also recognized spellings. In north Travancore and Cochin, Ezhavas were also known as Chogans or Chovans. In British Malabar, they were called Tiyyans, Tiyas, or Tiyyas. Variations in name reflected internal divisions during the nineteenth century.

[41] Aiyappan, *Social Revolution in a Kerala Village*, 106, 161.

"polluting" by caste Hindus, the Ezhavas nonetheless enjoyed a status superior to that of former slave castes, such as the Pulayas and Parayas. Among the untouchables were, in descending status, the Ezhavas, Channans, Cherumas, Pulayas, Parayas, and Nayadis.[42]

The Pulayas, Purayas, Panans, and others who lived in out-of-the-way places and ditches, according to Yesudas, were not considered as human beings, and were "bought and sold like cattle."[43] They had to move about at night, emerging from their abodes after dark to remain unseen. Although identification was weakly defined, Pulayas carried out the most grueling chores of agricultural cultivation for upper-caste masters. The Parayas were primarily manual laborers. These formerly slave castes tallied perhaps 15 percent of the total population.[44] The English word *pariah* is derived from the serf caste Parayas.

Writing in 1924, William Saunders Hunt described outcastes as "desperately, unbelievably poor" and recorded a scene he had witnessed involving them:

> During an afternoon drive in Travancore we come upon a group of people whom we now recognize as outcastes. A dozen of them, some standing and some squatting, are in the middle of the road facing a very humble shop. . . . The shop-keeper lolls against the door-post. . . . From time to time one or other of the group on the road calls out in a whining tone, occasionally the shopkeeper tosses a scornful reply. . . . The outcaste people are would-be purchasers, and a bargain is in [the] process of being struck between them and the shopkeeper. At length it is completed. The outcastes deposit a few coins on the road and back away. The shopkeeper comes leisurely forward, picks up the coins, puts down in their place the articles bargained for, and returns to his shop. Then the purchasers advance, take up their purchases with muttered grumblings at their smallness, and trot off with them, single file, along the edge of the road.[45]

---

[42] Nayadis were a nomadic tribe and often dwelled in jungles. Tiyas, particularly in Malabar, were practically on a par with Ezhavas. Both Tiyas and Ezhavas are understood to have migrated to India from Sri Lanka.

[43] R. N. Yesudas, "Pulappedi in Kerala," *Journal of Kerala Studies* 2 (March 1975): 44.

[44] *Travancore Census Report* (1875), 188–9, as cited in Jeffrey, "Social Origins of a Caste Association," 42.

[45] Hunt, *India's Outcastes*, 14–15, 36.

The gap between the Nambudiris, who were but a minute fraction of the population, and the rest of the society was great. Venerated, wealthy, and remote, the Nambudiris would until the twentieth century prevail, oblivious to emergent alterations around them. The slave castes were so circumscribed and restricted that they were ill-positioned to take advantage of shifts that were beginning to occur. Travancore's system of government in the nineteenth century, in the words of historian T. K. Ravindran, had become

> the worst form of feudalism which reduced most of the people to the condition of hewers of wood and drawers of water to their lords. The lower castes who formed the majority of the people, were subjected to ignominious treatment and . . . suffered to live in hovels and work for upper-caste masters. They enjoyed no right to personal safety and freedom of any kind.[46]

V. Balambal condemns the system of taxation as capricious and unscientific: "The underprivileged classes were heavily taxed and the higher strata enjoyed concessions. Poll tax, marriage tax and hut tax [*kuppakazhcha*, a tax on habitation] were collected from them. They had to pay tax for the hair they grew and for the breast of the ladies."[47]

Yet this way of life survived essentially intact until approximately 1860, when the well-educated maharaja Ayilyam Thirunal, the young dewan T. Madhava Rao, and a new British resident took up their respective offices. By 1884, the Ezhavas in Travancore were submitting petitions to British officials protesting the grievances forced upon them. Between the 1875 census and the one in 1891, literacy among Ezhava men rose from 3.15 percent to 12.10 percent, even though the number attending government schools continued to be small.[48]

Educator N. N. Pillai recalled cruel discrimination resulting from the caste system as it had evolved in Kerala:

> When I was age five or six and on vacation—normally I lived in my father's place, but on vacations I lived at my mother's place, three miles

[46] T. K. Ravindran, *Asan and Social Revolution in Kerala: A Study of His Assembly Speeches* (Trivandrum: Kerala Historical Society, 1973), v.

[47] Samuel Mateer, *Native Life in Travancore* (London: 1883), 292, as cited in V. Balambal, "E.V.R. and Vaikom Satyagraha," *Journal of Kerala Studies* 7 (1980): 246, 246n3.

[48] Jeffrey, "Social Origins of a Caste Association," 49.

away. An Ezhava girl who worked in my father's home would accompany me to my mother's place, and take me back again. As we walked from one house to the other, along the way there were many vegetables, one of which had umbrella-like leaves. One day, walking through the fields, with her following me, I was carrying one of the umbrella-like leaves. A bull was attracted by my waving leaf and charged. She cried, "run, run." The bull hit me. The girl lay down on me to take the blows from the bull. Someone came and tossed away the leaf, and the bull went after the leaf.

As we were about one mile away from reaching my father's place, a Nair leader went to my mother and told her that her son had been "polluted" by an Ezhava. She was in the kitchen and turned on the Nair, saying, "Do you want me to punish her for saving my son?" Instead, my mother gave both of us food. It is very cruel and hard to remember now, but "pollution" came from touching.[49]

P. Chandramohan, a scholar at New Delhi's Nehru Memorial Library, relates a story about Aloommootil Channar, an Ezhava, who was one of two persons in Travancore who owned a car. His driver was Muslim. When the automobile reached a point in the road where the Ezhavas were not allowed to pass, Channar had to get out of his vehicle and take another route on foot, rejoining the road a mile or so later. Since the driver was Muslim, however, he could drive on the road prohibited to his employer and would be waiting at the wheel for Channar to rejoin him.[50] As Aiyappan wrote, "Social, political, and economic forces all worked in an integrated manner to keep each caste in its place and to enable the multi-caste local community to function smoothly without their understanding the inequity of a social system which made a minority behave … as though they themselves were gods and the others mere vermin."[51]

---

[49] N. N. Pillai, interview (New Delhi, March 12, 2009). Pillai, originally from Vykom, is the principal at the Post-Graduate College of Communication and Management, and director of the Jawaharlal Nehru Academy of Languages, New Delhi.

[50] P. Chandramohan, "Social and Political Protest in Travancore: A Study of the Sree Narayana Dharma Paripalana Yogam (1900–1938)" (M.A. diss., Centre for Historical Studies, School of Social Sciences, Jawaharlal Nehru University, 1981), as cited on p. 234, note 1, C. Kesavan, *Jeevithasamarm* [autobiography] (Kottayam, Kerala: 1968), 302.

[51] Aiyappan, *Social Revolution in a Kerala Village*, 124.

Untouchability, Unapproachability, and Unseeability in Travancore

Caste, particularly in Travancore, was often a localized matter. Although untouchability and caste were at the heart of social life, P. Chandramohan contends that in Travancore "caste rules [were] practiced in the most irrational manner with the triple social evils of untouchability, unapproachability and unseeability."[52] Extreme forms of caste prohibitions had evolved in Travancore with the dominance of the Nambudiris, due to both the operational procedures and ideological justifications required for maintaining a severely segregated society. Historian K. N. Panikkar dates such extreme forms of exclusion as emerging only in the ninth and tenth centuries: "With the dominance of the Brahmin Nambudiris, it was important to organize the society on the basis of the functional requirements of a mode of control. Land and hierarchies became one."[53] The Nambudiris acquired the highest status in part because of the power that came with their significant landholdings.

Travancore's caste exclusions came to be practiced with particularly precise and pronounced customs that were rigidly drawn and strictly enforceable in a way not found in the rest of India. "Untouchability was in all of India, but unseeability was practiced in Kerala alone; the unseeable people were hated," historian K. K. Kusuman recalled. He further said:

> When we get up in the morning, we must see something that is auspicious—that is the belief of some [in Kerala] even now. To see a Harijan [untouchable] is an ill omen. A Harijan is not expected to be seen by a caste Hindu in the morning. This was the belief of the Nambudiris. In Malayalam, you would say "po po," meaning go away, get out, get away. By saying "po po," one could get the untouchables to move along the path—"get away, get away."[54]

An originary tale thought to date to the seventeenth century holds that the god, Parasurama, gave Travancore's land to the Nambudiri

[52] Chandramohan, "Social and Political Protest in Travancore," 229.

[53] K. N. Panikkar, interview (Trivandrum, Kerala, August, 15, 2005). Panikkar chairs the Indian Council for Historical Research and is former dean and professor at the School of Social Sciences, Jaawaharlal Nehru University, New Delhi.

[54] K. K. Kusuman, interview (Trivandrum, August 16, 2005). On Kusuman, see Dedication here.

Brahmins by virtue of *janmam* (birth or nativity), which brought with it absolute, tax-free ownership. By inference, the legend excuses the humiliations visited upon the avarnas. Ravindran judges that the predominance of the Nambudiris had created a form of pervasive degradation:

> Moral torpor and social malaise bedevilled the Hindu population in Kerala and produced intellectual, cultural and economic stagnation. ... [The] caste system, in all its severity and rigidity, divided Hindu society into innumerable exclusive groups mutually hating and cooperating only to degrade the other. The debasing quality of this institution made the higher classes to despise the lower strata and push them out of the pale of civilized society.[55]

The dewan in 1870 describes restrictions on the personal liberties of outcastes: a proportion lived in "avowed slavery," which included being "attached to land like chattels, and were bought and sold." They could not carry out trade and were restricted to playing or listening to certain music. They could wear nothing but coarse cloth and were not allowed to wear shoes or use umbrellas. The roads prohibited for them consisted not simply of bypaths but also included portions of the direct main routes passing within the requisite distance of a temple or a high-caste eating establishment or dwelling. This meant that untouchables were forbidden from entering the courts of justice and public offices. Thus, they had no chance of obtaining justice under any circumstance or countering their oppression. Were an avarna acting as a witness, he could not come to court; rather, "the court must go to him, not too near in any case." His evidence was taken by an "intermediate peon," but "owing to the distance involved neither the question nor the answer would be audible or intelligible." P. K. K. Menon also notes "that a large portion of the community who contributed their quota to the State revenues from which the schools were mainly supported were debarred from attending them."[56]

All castes but the highest were considered ritually polluting. Foodstuffs, garments, houses, temples, ponds, and wells, in addition to

---

[55] Ravindran, *Asan and Social Revolution in Kerala*, 10.

[56] Dewan's letter, ref. no. 1357, reply to Resident, Government of Madras, March 9, 1870, as cited in P. K. Karunakara Menon, *The History of the Freedom Movement in Kerala*, vols. 1 and 2 (1600–1938), compiled by the Regional Records Survey Committee, Kerala State (Trivandrum: Government Press, 1970), 280n7, 281, 281n9. Hereafter, P. K. Karunakara Menon, who was convener of the Regional Records Survey Committee, is referred to as P. K. K. Menon.

human beings, were "defiled" by the touch or proximity of the polluting castes. Caste Hindus could be polluted if an outcaste's shadow fell
upon them. If untouchables were admitted to a village, it should be at
high noon, when a shadow is at its slightest, covering the feet.[57] The
prohibitions imposed on untouchables increased in severity based on
rank: "The greater the social distance the greater also was the polluting
distance."[58] To avoid polluting the upper castes, distances between the
various groups were manifested in "pollution" rules, literally the
number of paces to be maintained between them, traditionally fixed
and prescribed by contact taboos with precise measurements. "While
the belief in human beings as carriers of graded degrees of ritual impurity is common to all Hindus," Aiyappan notes, "its manifestations are
nowhere so hypertrophied [excessively developed] as in Kerala."[59] The
indignities to which outcastes were subjected by practices associated
with untouchability of an extreme sort were especially irritating for
Ezhavas who had received Western forms of education.

The harsh practices that evolved in Travancore's theocracy had created a system of rigid status and stigmatization of select subgroups
among the untouchables, among which were the "unapproachable"
and "unseeable." With singular complexity, caste stratification specified
that the unapproachables, from an inferior caste cluster, were expected
to step off the road or footpath as members from a superior cluster
approached to avoid inadvertently polluting them. Kusuman recalled,

> The lowest caste people had to stay at a distance of 64 feet, as the pre-
> scribed distance. For others, there was a prescribed distance of 32 feet.

[57] Eleanor Zelliot, *From Untouchable to Dalit: Essays on the Ambedkar Movement* (New Delhi: Manohar, 2001), 315n20.

[58] Aiyappan, *Social Revolution in a Kerala Village*, 79.

[59] In the Malayalam language, the word for ritual pollution is *ayittam* (*asud-ham*), meaning impurity. Malayalam has an abundant vocabulary of terms for the caste inferior to use with the caste superior in conversing and written docu-ments. When addressing a superior, caste honorifics were to be used, not a personal name (Aiyappan, *Social Revolution in a Kerala Village*, 79, 132). This was also true of the high castes. A Nair when speaking with a Nambudiri exhibited inferiority by calling himself a foot-servant and referring to his house as a dung-pit. Edgar Thurston, with K. Rangachari, *Castes and Tribes of Southern India*, vol. 5 (Madras: Government Press, 1909), 196.

Even the Nairs, who were also upper caste, had to keep away from the Nambudiri at a distance of 6 paces. The Parayas and others had to be at 64 feet from the Nambudiri.[60]

In varying accounts, an Ezhava was regarded as polluting a Nair from 12 paces and a Nambudiri Brahmin from 36 paces. A Pulaya was regarded as polluting a Nambudiri from 96 paces away.[61] An approaching Pulaya had to announce his proximity with loud, frequent shouts. Pollution was removable by the polluted high-caste person immersing himself and his clothes in water.[62]

Additional forms of identification were part of the system for preventing pollution. As with other groups, obligatory appearances made them readily identifiable. An Ezhava man's clothing immediately revealed his status; a cloth that did not hang below the knees or rise above the waist told anyone at a distance of his rank. An Ezhava man could not wear a shoulder cloth to cover his torso, or wrap his lower legs. He had to have a tuft of hair at the front of his head. Outcaste women were required to expose their breasts in the presence of caste Hindus and were unable to move about at liberty in society. During times of famine, impoverished parents would sell their children for the sake of their own survival. "Caste restrictions made the major section of the people mere slaves of the caste Hindus. All properties, including women, became Parasurama's gift to the Nambudiris. . . . The caste Hindus made laws for their convenience and pleasure. They enjoyed the right 'to put any one to death on the spot who should resist their brutal demands.'"[63] Ravindran contends, "Absolute

---

[60] Kusuman, interview (August 16, 2005).

[61] See Hutton, *Caste in India*, esp. 79–81, for a digest of distances to be maintained to prevent distance pollution.

[62] Aiyappan, *Social Revolution in a Kerala Village*, 79.

The Portuguese explorer, Duarte Barbosa, wrote in approximately 1516, after arriving in India, "When they walk along a street or road, they shout to the low caste folk to get out of their way; ... if one will not, the Nayre may kill him without punishment. . . . They say that they do this that their blood may not be tainted." Duarte Barbosa, *The Book of Duarte Barbosa*, trans. Mansel Longworth Dames (London: Hakluyt Society, 1921), 2: 49, 50.

[63] Yesudas, "Christian Missionaries and Social Awakening in Kerala," 195–6.

freedom in sexual life was the right of every male Brahmin and absolute surrender was ordained for female[s]."[64] Gilbert Sebastian
phrased an exception to pollution thusly: "With rape, there was no
distance!"[65]

By 1870, clothing restrictions for untouchables and the style of
referring to themselves in disparaging language were no longer
enforced by the Travancore government, but the upper castes nonetheless effectively maintained these customs. Roads near high-caste temples were public pathways, but announced as being closed to Ezhavas
and other untouchable Hindus by *teendal palakas*, notice boards maintained by the government to display prominently the prohibitions
against the polluting castes entering onto them. As late as the early
twentieth century, excluded castes could in some instances pray and
make offerings from distances of between fifty and one hundred yards
from the outer gates of temples, while Christians, Jews, and Muslims
could go to the outer gates. Upper-caste temples had trees specifically
planted or flagstones inserted to mark the points up to which the lower
castes were permitted to proceed. Worshippers in the banned categories would put their cash offerings into the prescribed place, step away
to let temple servants remove the moneys, and then wait for the sancti-
fied contributions of food or flowers, called *prasadams*.[66] The coins and
currency of the untouchables were apparently not polluted by their
touch.

Syrian Christian communities (and doubtless others) absorbed
many of the hierarchies, stratifications, practices, and conventions of
the caste system. Narayanan offered as evidence the Synod Diamper, an
Anglicized canon from 1599 recording decisions taken by the Syrian
Christians in Udayamperur, near Cochin. Narayanan explained:

> Unable to pronounce "Udayamperur," a place name, they called it
> Diamper. The Synod Diamper shows that the Portuguese Roman
> Catholics wanted the local Christians [Syrian Christians] to follow their

---

[64] Ravindran, *Asan and Social Revolution in Kerala*, xii.

[65] Gilbert Sebastian, interview (New Delhi, March 12, 2009). Sebastian is a
fellow at the Council for Social Development, New Delhi.

[66] Aiyappan, *Social Revolution in a Kerala Village*, 135.

methods. One of the charges the Catholics made was that the Syrian Christians had Hindu names, not Christian names; they observed the caste system, and pollution. They continued to worship the Hindu gods and goddesses, although they claim to be Christians. By that time, 1599, the Syrian type of Christianity in Kerala had become very much like Hinduism.[67]

George Gheverghese Joseph cites the 1599 church synod meeting at Udayamperur and apparently quotes from it, without attribution, corroborating the mixture of Hindu with Syrian Christian practices. For example, strict rules pertained to food preparation and with whom one could eat, part of a convoluted system concerning ritual pollution, which the Syrian Christians inherited from high-caste Hindus. The Syrians also observed distance pollution.[68] Among their own, they did not recognize ritual purity, but they were deliberate and careful in managing their relationships with outcastes so that they themselves would not be blamed for polluting the Nambudiris and Nairs.

James Hough depicts representatives of the Church of Rome in the early seventeenth century as also adopting Brahminical customs. The Jesuits "had to imitate the brahmins in their outward appearance, and adopt their habits of life," by wearing the yellow cloth worn by Indian religious scholars and penitents, adopting their ablutions, never appearing publicly without wearing on their foreheads a wafer made of

---

[67] Narayanan, interview (August 12, 2005). In 1503, Cochin was occupied by the Portuguese, the first European colonial settlement in India, later to come under Dutch and British colonialism. For the Synod Diamper, see Appendix A: "A Dioscesan Synod of the Church and Bishoprick of Angamale belonging to the Ancient Christians of St. Thomas in the Serra or Mountains of Malabar, 1599, Church of All Saints, in the town and kingdom of Diamper, subject to the King of Cochin, ...," in James Hough, *History of Christianity in India from the Commencement of the Christian Era* (London: R. B. Seeley and W. Burnside, 1839), 2: 511–683. Hough was chaplain to the East India Company at Madras.

[68] Joseph, *George Joseph: Life and Times*, 32, 29. George Gheverghese Joseph is the great grandson of the barrister and Syrian Christian nationalist leader, George Joseph (1887–1938), who figures in Chapters 3 and 4.

sandalwood powder as worn by Brahmins, and abstaining from eating meat. "Regardless of the Christian teacher's imperative duty to preach the Gospel to the poor, they paid exclusive attention to the rich," Hough notes, showing contempt of the lower castes, whom they kept "at a distance with true brahminical arrogance."[69]

[69] Hough, *History of Christianity in India*, 2: 244–5.

2 The Ezhava Community Awakens

The Ezhavas were both tappers and purveyors of toddy, the palm wine made from coconut, sago, and palmyra trees. The toddy tappers customarily scaled palm trees to tap the bud at the top and draw the sap for fermentation into palm wine or distilled arrack. They then sold these products, except in southern Travancore, where weaving also differentiated their occupation. Folklore, legends, and songs portray the Ezhavas as having introduced the coconut palm from Ceylon, before the Common Era. Considering available historical and legendary information, the Ezhavas appear to have been the first settled agriculturists in what would become Kerala. Aiyappan notes, "The four artisan castes, carpenter, blacksmith, bronze-smith, and goldsmith, are also closely linked in legendary history with the Iravas[,] who are said to be their protectors."[1]

In the evolving but traditional economies, the Ezhavas were often subtenants of Nambudiri, Nair, or Syrian landlords, or were workers paid in grain. The liquor trade was among the few profitable and independent professions (even if stigmatized by the high castes) that Ezhavas could pursue with little capital and minimal training. Until the British began to farm out the selling and manufacture of toddy, any Ezhava could produce and sell it with the payment of a small tax to the

---

[1] Ayinipalli Aiyappan, *Social Revolution in a Kerala Village: A Study in Culture* (London: Asia Publishing House, 1965), 116, 119.

ruler's local representative.[2] In the main, most Ezhavas were tenant farmers, free laborers, or small business owners; only a small percentage of Ezhavas actually engaged in tapping toddy, perhaps 3 percent in some areas (in 1921). Ezhavas of higher economic status claimed that only the poorer of their ranks were tappers. Some leaders of the Ezhavas, including Sri Narayana Guru, held the view that the making and selling of liquor was among the factors that contributed to the lower-caste status of the Ezhavas. Some went so far as to say that alcohol was poison and that their hereditary profession must be abandoned.[3]

The Ezhavas may have been Buddhist immigrants centuries ago from what is now Sri Lanka, particularly since the name Ezhava, or Irava, means people from Ceylon (although today's Sri Lankans, excluding Tamils, are called Singhala or Singhalese). A folk song in Malayalam concerning a sixteenth-century Ezhava hero, Aromar Chevakar (also Aromal Chevakar), alludes to the ancestry of the Ezhavas:

Our ancestors of old

Had their homes in the land of Iram [Ceylon].

To the lord of Ceylon, an *ola* [letter on palm leaf] was sent

By the king of Kerala.

The lord of Ceylon got the letter.

Then said the king of Ceylon

"I shall send seven soldiers from here."

The same song mentions that the newcomers were treated as honored people and given insignia of high standing by a royal charter.[4] Chevakar's sister, Unni Archa, was famed for her fencing and ability to wield a

---

[2] Aiyappan, *Social Revolution in a Kerala Village*, 155. At least in Malabar, the British continued the traditional tax on those who drew toddy and distilled arrack, called the knife and still tax. As India moved toward national independence, the Indian National Congress would make prohibition part of its social welfare program.

[3] Aiyappan, *Social Revolution in a Kerala Village*, 117, 154. Aiyappan notes that traditional folk values in Kerala held no stigma attached to the consumption of toddy.

[4] As cited in Aiyappan, *Social Revolution in a Kerala Village*, 119.

sword such that she could fight singlehandedly against a Muslim chief and his companions who were said to have insulted her. Over the centuries, the Ezhavas were absorbed in south India as an inferior stratum of Hindus, explained by the supposition that their status as relative newcomers in an ancient land meant they had no caste.

While Nambudiris might move about freely and learn about the larger world, an Ezhava was constrained; even knowledge of his fellow Ezhavas a few miles away was limited. The yearning to move up in the hierarchy culturally through imitating the norms of the higher castes must have been felt even prior to any British influence on the political and economic structures of Travancore's social system, Aiyappan notes, writing of nearby British Malabar district and suggesting that however slight such assertions might have been, they expressed an "unconscious dissatisfaction with the *status quo*."[5] Despite being ensconced in the social structure as agricultural laborers and toddy tappers, the Ezhavas eventually emerged as one of the best educated, most progressive, and well-organized untouchable communities in India.

The Lure of Religious Conversion and Education

Little tangible evidence can be found of active proselytization by the Christian and Muslim traders from the Middle East and Arabian Peninsula respectively, who had introduced their faiths centuries earlier to Travancore. For the casteless or formerly slave castes, however, conversion to Christianity arose as a means of social advancement. With caste division endorsed by religious laws, the as yet unformed revolt of the lower castes and casteless expressed itself in the attraction and founding of novel religious denominations. According to E. M. S. Namboodiripad:

> [D]issident sects like those of the Jains, the Buddhists, etc., gave expression to the protest against Brahmin domination over society. Later on, when caste division with its superior–inferior relationships came to be consolidated, nobody within the Hindu fold being permitted to go out of the caste or sub-caste into which one was born, foreign religious denominations that made their appearance, either through the Muslim conquerors in the North or through the Jewish, Christian and Muslim

---

[5] Aiyappan, *Social Revolution in a Kerala Village*, 124–5.

traders who came to the coastal towns, ... [and they] became so many ways of escape for the "lower" and "untouchable" Hindu castes; here were doors open before them to escape the sufferings imposed on them by the rigorous caste system, ... [through] large-scale conversion from Hindu to other religions.[6]

The status of those who had converted to another religion rose in the seventeenth century as the influence of the Portuguese, Dutch, and British expanded. In the eighteenth century, as the East India Company inserted itself into governance, its officials took care not to disrupt the customary prerogatives of the higher castes. By the Victorian era, as members of the lower castes became government functionaries, the Indian penal code changed to call for observing equality in the eyes of British administrators, so caste was not observed in certain public spaces. Some feudal characteristics of the Hindu social system began to bend, affecting other alterations in social life. Although in some areas Christians were viewed as polluting to the upper castes, nonetheless the Christians, Jews, and Muslims who had arrived in Travancore from other climes centuries earlier offered fresh means for reordering interactive relationships.

As societal changes began to accelerate, from the 1860s onward, increasing numbers of Ezhavas and Pulayas came into contact with European missionaries, many of them receiving an education at mission schools. The Protestants had been the first to offer education in the early nineteenth century, to be followed by Roman Catholics.[7] Travancore's Christians consisted primarily of three main groups (excluding those who had converted to escape untouchability): Syrian Christians, Latin (Roman) Catholics, and Protestants. As noted previously, old Syrian Christian families claimed to have been Nambudiri Brahmins who converted in the first century. Most Catholics were descendants of those who became Christian when the Portuguese were most influential at the end of the sixteenth century. The educational work of the Protestant Lutherans would later be significant.

---

[6] E. M. S. Namboodiripad, *Kerala Society and Politics: In Historical Survey*, rev. ed. (New Delhi: National Book Centre, 1984), 18. Namboodiripad was a communist leader, theoretician, and historian who was elected to be the first chief minister of Kerala, after it became a state.

[7] Francois Houtart and Genevieve Lemercinier, "Socio-Religious Movements in Kerala: A Reaction to the Capitalist Mode of Production," *Social Scientist* 6, no. 11, part 1 (June 1978): 9.

Indian society was generally tolerant on religious matters, so differing religious traditions enjoyed relative freedom in advancing their articles of faith. "Although Christianization was not on the colonial agenda, a nexus between government officials and missionaries came to be established during [the nineteenth century]." Regardless, Panikkar notes, "The colonial system of education itself was viewed as an attempt to indirectly help Christianization. . . . The influence of colonial education which drew upon the elements of an alien culture and upon the historical experience of a different civilization was primarily denationalizing, as it alienated the members of the educated middle class from their cultural moorings."[8]

From research in nineteenth-century family histories and diaries in the Malayalam language, Aiyappan found that "the far-sighted among the Iravas [Ezhavas] were anxious to get English education, to grow cash crops, the trade in which was expanding, to earn more money by investing savings productively, and try in other ways to fall in line with the higher castes."[9] Although converting to Christianity lingered as an expedient option, an implicit threat to caste Hindus that Ezhavas could make, the acquiring of subordinate standing among Christians became a less appealing alternative as the potential for achieving reputability among Hindus became more feasible. Conversion was not necessarily a solution. In 1924, Hunt writes of how the converts were viewed by others: "Outcastes do not cease to be untouchable when they become Christian."[10]

In response to pressures from British officials, Europeans working for Travancore's government service, and residents of Travancore who had been Western-educated, Ezhavas began to be admitted to Travancore's government schools and were being graduated from the Trivandrum college by the 1870s. Although some Ezhavas successfully pursued education as a portal to advancement, overall it offered little

[8] K. N. Panikkar, *Culture, Ideology and Hegemony: Intellectuals and Social Consciousness in Colonial India* (New Delhi: Tulika, 1995), 102, 105.

[9] Aiyappan, *Social Revolution in a Kerala Village*, 130–1.

[10] William Saunders Hunt, *India's Outcastes: A New Era* (London: Church Missionary Society, 1924), 65–6. No precise figures are available, but Namboodiripad notes that in Kerala, by the 1960s, more than 40 percent of the population was non-Hindu and all of them did not emigrate or descend from those who arrived from elsewhere. Many, therefore, must have been religious converts. Namboodiripad, *Kerala Society and Politics*, 19.

help in obtaining jobs in the government service, because such posts were reserved for members of the upper castes. Indeed, in the nineteenth century, most significant appointments in the government of the princely state went to Brahmins from outside Travancore.[11]

Despite their treatment as untouchables, many in the Ezhava community were becoming socially and politically active by the end of the nineteenth century. Educated Ezhavas were entering trading and small industries, generally held in contempt by caste Hindus; by the end of the nineteenth century, the Ezhavas had become the mainstay of these local industries. Remarkably, for untouchables who had not converted to Christianity by the standards of the day, by 1891, 24,996 Ezhavas, 858 Parayas, and 4,031 Pulayas had become literate, and by 1921, 4,529 Ezhavas had become literate in English.[12] Yet not until the second decade of the twentieth century would the Ezhavas and other *avarnas* be able to take their places in the public services. From 1911 to 1921, literacy in the Malayalam language among Ezhava males rose from 11 percent to 36 percent.[13] Progress for Ezhavas in the nearby British Malabar district came more quickly than in the native state of Travancore.

Early Ezhava Socio-Religious Reform Efforts: Persuasive Nonviolent Methods

In the late nineteenth century, exertions to overcome caste disabilities acquired at birth were being made in two ways: pursuit of socio-religious reform and use of elementary nonviolent methods, such as petitioning. Travancore's rulers had long honored an ancient entitlement of the ruled to have access to the raja by presenting petitions and supplications before him. In 1891, P. Velayudhan and Padmanabhan Palpu, Travancore's only Ezhava graduates at the time, began working

[11] K. N. Panikkar, "Vaikkam Satyagraha: The Struggle against Untouchability," in *We Fought Together for Freedom: Chapters from the Indian National Movement*, ed. Ravi Dayal (Delhi, Bombay, Calcutta, Madras: Oxford University Press and Indian Council of Historical Research, 1995), 126.

[12] Panikkar, "Vaikkam Satyagraha," 126.

[13] Robin Jeffrey, "Travancore: Status, Class and the Growth of Radical Politics, 1860–1940, the Temple-Entry Movement," in *People, Princes and Paramount Power: Society and Politics in the Indian Princely States*, ed. Robin Jeffrey (New Delhi: Oxford University Press), 144.

together, associating themselves with a petition of rights called the Malayali Memorial. Palpu was a physician who, because of his untouchability, had been unable to study or practice medicine in Travancore; as a consequence, he attended medical school in Madras. Rejected by Travancore for employment, he joined the British civil service in around 1890 and became a local government official in Mysore the following year. Palpu's father had learned English from missionaries, and part of his family had converted to Christianity.

The petition effort was organized by young Nair officials in the government to press specific issues, mainly to end the government practice of hiring "foreigners," particularly Brahmins who hailed not from Travancore but from the neighboring Tamil-speaking Madras presidency (now the adjacent state of Tamil Nadu). The petition written by K. P. Sankara Menon, a member of the Madras bar, was signed by 10,000 Nairs, Ezhavas, and Christians, and presented to the maharaja on January 1, 1891.[14] It pointed out that non-Malayali Brahmins were being given the best jobs in government service, and one paragraph noted the government's discrimination against Ezhavas. The signatories wanted the Travancore administration to pass an act that "would restrict the giving of appointments, as much as possible, to none but natives irrespective of class, caste, or creed."[15] The government had singled out the Ezhavas for condemnation as unfit for work in the government, because they were "confirmed social inferiors."[16] Although the government took no action, Palpu had found an approach for campaigns to come.

[14] Ramachandran K. Nair, *The History of the Trade Union Movement in Kerala* (Thiruvananthapuram: Kerala Institute of Labour and Employment), 9.

[15] As cited in T. K. Ravindran, *Vaikkam Satyagraha and Gandhi* (Trichur: Sri Narayana Institute of Social and Cultural Development, 1975), 26. Ravindran's account appeared precisely 50 years after the events he analyzes, and is cited as the first "critical and full-length study of this major event that happened in the Gandhian era of India's struggle for freedom." Shreekumaran Nair, review, Ravindran, *Vaikkam Satyagraha and Gandhi*, 761. Ravindran was professor and head of the Department of History, University of Kerala, Trivandrum, and served as editor of the *Journal of Kerala Studies* and the *Journal of Indian History*. On the Malayali Memorial, see also Robin Jeffrey, "The Social Origins of a Caste Association, 1875–1905: The Founding of the SNDP Yogam," *South Asia* 4 (October): 49.

[16] *Endorsement to the Travancore Memorial*, file no. 1899/M. 884, English records, Government Secretariat, Trivandrum, as cited in Ravindran, *Vaikkam Satyagraha and Gandhi*, 27n2.

In 1895 Palpu sent his long petition, written in English, to S. Sankara Soobiar (also Shungarasoobyer), *dewan* to Maharaja Mulam Thirunal Rama Varma. After eight months without a reply, Palpu took leave of his job in Mysore, went to Trivandrum, and received the assurance of the dewan that qualified Ezhavas would be considered for departmental jobs, except in the revenue department. When some applied, however, they found that there were no jobs. In response, the dewan said that Ezhavas were too insufficiently educated to be employed in the government. He dismissively proclaimed that in 1891 only a mere two Ezhavas out of 387,176 males held university degrees—a rejoinder that infuriated the Ezhava community, of which, according to the 1891 census, 25,000 had become middle class, working as shopkeepers, practitioners of ayurvedic medicine, weavers, and astrologers.[17]

Later, Palpu left his job again to return to Travancore to organize another petition. Addressed to the maharaja on behalf of Ezhavas, its slogan was "The Chovas have had enough!"[18] "Chova" was a derogatory term for Ezhavas. Only Ezhavas signed the document, and within months, 13,176 had attached their names to it.[19] Palpu presented the petition—called the Ezhava Memorial, or Community Memorial—on September 3, 1896; he also released it to Madras newspapers.[20] The document reminded the maharaja that the Ezhavas were numerically the second largest community in the state. Nearly half of the signatories paid land taxes.[21]

The memorial described the indignities faced by Ezhavas, asserted that Ezhavas paid more taxes than other communities, complained that government schools were closed to them, and noted that Ezhavas were denied the incentive to education that government service offered.

[17] Houtart and Lemercinier, "Socio-Religious Movements in Kerala," 12; Robin Jeffrey, *The Decline of Nayar Dominance: Society and Politics in Travancore, 1847–1908* (New Delhi: Manohar Publications), 188.

[18] Houtart and Lemercinier, "Socio-Religious Movements in Kerala," 12.

[19] Ezhava Memorial, file no. C. 1231, English Records, Government Secretariat, as cited in Ravindran, *Vaikkam Satyagraha and Gandhi*, 27n3.

[20] Ezhava Memorial, Bangalore, May 12, 1895, file no. C. 1231, English Records, Government Secretariat, as cited in Ravindran, *Vaikkam Satyagraha and Gandhi*, 27n3; Jeffrey, "Social Origins of a Caste Association," 49.

[21] Jeffrey, "Social Origins of a Caste Association," 49; Houtart and Lemercinier, "Socio-Religious Movements in Kerala," 12.

Those Ezhavas with English education had, like Palpu, left the state. It pointed out that Syrian Christians were already being hired and that conversion to other religions seemed the only alternative:

> Even low places, such as those of peons, police constables, public work maistries [construction workers], and hospital and jail warders are denied [Ezhavas] on the score of their caste, even though they possess more than necessary qualifications. At present, no qualification can secure ... any of these appointments in his own native land unless he becomes a convert to Christianity or Mohamedanism or at least takes shelter under mere Christian or Mahomedan [*sic*] name.[22]

Given a petition of more than 13,000 signatures, the threat of converting to another faith wielded some weight, though few Ezhavas were actually among the already converted.[23] While converting to another faith had very limited effects on the social order of south India, the perceived threat of such alterations was noticed by the government. The central concern of the government involved potential disruptions of the economic order, which never materialized.[24] The risk of conversions remained a factor in the background.

---

[22] Izhava Memorial, or Ezhava Memorial, 1895, file no. C. 1231, English Records, Government Secretariat, as cited in Ravindran, *Vaikkam Satyagraha and Gandhi*, 27n5.

[23] Robin Jeffrey, "Temple-Entry Movement in Travancore, 1860–1940," *Social Scientist* 4, no. 8 (March): 8. Christian missionaries insisted on consecrated marriage, which would cause property losses for Ezhavas living in the flexible joint-family system of matrilineal law where property passed through the females. Jeffrey "Social Origins of a Caste Association," 47–8.

[24] See Koji Kawashima, *Missionaries and a Hindu State: Travancore, 1858–1936* (New Delhi: Oxford University Press, [1965] 1998), 153–71. The political threats associated with converting to another faith were most likely exaggerated by the government. Among those who had converted to Christianity, the caste system was still practiced by Christians, with only slight alterations. On this point, see D. R. Mankekar, *The Red Riddle of Kerala* (Bombay: Manaktalas, 1965), 56. Converts did not show any greater likelihood of social organization or activism for reforms. Although the 1875 census had shown Travancore's population to be 20 percent Christian, by 1901 conversions to Christianity had resulted in 24 percent of the population identifying themselves as Christian, with nearly 45 percent of the populace lower-caste Hindus. Jeffrey, "Travancore: Status, Class and the Growth of Radical Politics," 142–3.

In these petitions, the Ezhavas essentially sought two demands: access to public institutions without differentiation of caste or creed and appointment of Ezhavas in government service, from which they had been virtually totally excluded. The dewan's aloof reply—that Ezhavas were not adequately educated for employment in the government—and trivializing comment that in 1891 only two Ezhavas had university degrees were received as evasive and offensive. Placing the blame for any lack of eligibility for government service on the Ezhavas, the dewan also claimed that public opinion was unfavorable to them, an attitude mainly shaped by governmental policies.

With no official actions forthcoming to redress their objections, the Ezhavas began to swing the arc of their efforts away from the elementary persuasive nonviolent methods of petition and documentation and toward the organizing of nonviolent direct action—which for them signified assertive protest actions to consolidate community support and media awareness while broadening popular backing for their demands. Nonviolent direct action refers to the claimants taking action directly to the source of the grievance, and not working through representatives, agencies, or agents of government in institutionalized politics. The principal figures involved in leading these public campaigns, through newspaper coverage and civic forums, were Palpu, Kumaran Asan, C. V. Kunjuraman, and T. K. Madhavan. These leaders used the demands that had been articulated in the memorial petitions to sharpen their articulation of grievances and press for attendant constitutional reforms.

On October 22, 1904, the Sri Mulam Popular Assembly was established, named for Mulam Thirunal, Travancore's maharaja who would remain on the throne through the first eight months of 1924. Members consisted of landholders chosen to participate in the body, though without lawmaking responsibilities.[25] The following year, it was

---

[25] The assembly was unique in India and its purpose was to familiarize the government with popular wishes. Its members were initially not elected, but were nominated by various constituencies, district heads, municipalities, and representative groups; the government nominated ten of the members. The original powers of the members consisted solely of putting questions to the *durbar*, with each member accorded two questions. The durbar (from Persian and Urdu) was the court of an Indian ruler or raja, the executive government for a princely state, and also referred to an audience or reception. Ouwerkerk, *No Elephants for the Maharaja*, 67–8.

expanded so that two-thirds were elected from the male population. Election was reliant on property ownership, but this was sufficient for the Ezhavas to acquire formal representation for their views. At its October 21, 1905, meeting, when seventy-seven of its one hundred members were elected and others nominated, an Ezhava from Karthikappalli named Kochu Kunju Channar raised the question of the *teendal palakas*, the sign boards giving notice to polluting castes that they could not enter temple roads. Christian members joined in attacking the exclusions.[26] Even though the government remained unmoved by the remonstrances voiced in the assembly, the Ezhavas had begun to use public forums to challenge openly the social practices associated with untouchability and obtain support for their position from members of the assembly.[27]

The emblematic teendal palakas were not the actual issue. Panikkar says:

> That some public roads were closed to a section of society was seen as an expression of a serious malaise, represented by untouchability and unapproachability. The untouchables were not permitted to use the roads because temples were out of bounds for them. Demanding the right to enter temples irrespective of caste was, therefore, tantamount to questioning the practice of untouchability itself.[28]

In 1896, Palpu, who sponsored the education of Kumaran Asan, one of the aforementioned leaders, founded the Ezhava Mahajana Sabha, the Ezhava people's assembly, at the time that he was organizing petitions in the early stages of broadening public mobilization. The *sabha* was a forerunner of caste associations that, by the turn of the century, would become salient in Hindu social caste-reform movements. The sabhas sought to develop and improve the standing of outcastes in reaching more elevated status in caste hierarchies, in part by emulating the customs of higher castes, such as Sri Narayana Dharma Paripalana Yogam (SNDP Yogam), to be catalyzed by Sri Narayana Guru shortly after the turn of the century. A wave of rising

---

[26] Ravindran, *Vaikkam Satyagraha and Gandhi*, 39.

[27] *Vaikom Satyagraha Commemoration Volume*, 54, as cited in Panikkar, "Vaikkam Satyagraha," 127, 136n4.

[28] Panikkar, "Vaikkam Satyagraha," 127–8.

consciousness of the excluded castes was starting to crest. Ravindran expressed it as follows:

> Dr. Palpu's spirit for social reform together with Kumaran Asan's supreme poetical power made a conjunction with Sri Narayana Guru's spiritual influence and from that confluence in 1903 emerged a socio-religious organization Sri Narayana Dharma Paripalana Yogam, which, in the course of a decade or two, brought about a metamorphosis in the pattern of life in the Irava community throughout Kerala.[29]

Sri Narayana Guru and Sri Narayana Dharma Paripalana Yogam

The SNDP Yogam was an association for the propagation of dharma (Sanskrit for knowing and obeying the law [of God], faithfulness to duty, virtue, piety) as understood through moral or sacred law for Hindus and interpreted by Sri Narayana Guru (1854–1928).[30] It soon became a driving force behind Ezhava activism and one of India's best known caste organizations. Such associations took on particular relevance, confronting the need for reform, and frequently worked to upgrade the standing of a local caste or imitate the social and ritual conduct of a higher caste. In Travancore, although formal education was essential to understanding vigorous Malayali politics, caste associations worked to lobby for the social recognition that only princely liberalizing could bestow. For example, at nearly every meeting from 1917 to 1920, the SNDP Yogam would pass resolutions demanding temple entry.[31]

Originating in Travancore and at its strongest there, the SNDP Yogam sought for the first two decades of the twentieth century to improve the conditions of life for Ezhavas. It spearheaded the fight for the rights of the offspring of the Ezhava middle class to attend government schools and subsequently to enter public service in Travancore and Cochin. With caste differences compulsorily enforced by the government, Ezhavas throughout Travancore had a collective identity forced upon them, but their chafing at it also had a unifying effect by aiding in overcoming subcaste distinctions among them. The SNDP

[29] Ravindran, *Vaikkam Satyagraha and Gandhi*, 37–8.

[30] The guru's exact date of birth is in dispute; 1855 would not be wrong. "Guru" means spiritual teacher.

[31] Mahadev Haribhai Desai, *Epic of Travancore* (Ahmedabad: Navajivan Karyalaya, 1937), 11.

Yogam embodied the aspirations of countless Ezhavas who had been working to advance themselves as the nineteenth century ended. Besides, to paraphrase M. N. Srinivas, the ability of the SNDP Yogam to communicate gained certain emollients that came with Pax Britannica, including cheap paper, the building of roads, postage, and printing in the Malayalam language, thus enabling the Ezhavas to organize as never before. Postcards might announce meetings, travel to attend them was possible, low-cost newsprint helped circulation of reports and proceedings, all of which built solidarity and promoted the Ezhavas' interests. The accessibility of paper enabled the keeping of records, giving lasting form to precedents and debates that until then had been judged by the fallible memory of educated elders.[32]

Guru, an Ezhava born at Chempazhanthi, near Trivandrum, personified the aims of the Ezhavas and became the foremost religious and social reformer of modern Kerala.[33] Beginning life as a shepherd, in around 1877 he was admitted to a Sanskrit school run by a rich Ezhava family in Quilon, where he stayed for four years. Sanskrit is the ancient Indic tongue and language of Hinduism and the Vedas, the oldest Hindu scriptures, the learning of which traditionally was restricted to Brahmins.[34] Guru also learned Tamil and Malayalam, two of the major, old Dravidian languages of south India; he did not study English. Unique within his community, he was highly educated, resolutely religious, pursued a vow of celibacy,[35] and strongly advocated social reforms that were implicitly aimed at eradicating untouchability and unapproachability. By the 1890s, he had become renowned throughout south India. In the course of his travels, Guru met Kumaran Asan, who would become the first secretary of the SNDP Yogam and perhaps the greatest poet in the Malayalam language.

A meditative worshipper of Krishna and Vishnu, Guru wrote hymns to these gods. He also built and consecrated temples of Sanskritic

[32] M. N. Srinivas, "Caste in Modern India," *Journal of Asian Studies* 16, no. 4 (August 1957): 530. Mysore Narasimhachar Srinivas was a sociologist.

[33] Alappat Sreedhara Menon, *Kerala and Freedom Struggle* (Kottayam, Kerala: D C Books, 1997), 58.

[34] The classical literary language of India, Sanskrit is classified by linguistics experts as an Indo-European language, from which Hindi is derived and the family that includes English and many European languages.

[35] Obligated by customary tradition to marry, he never lived with his wife. Houtart and Lemercinier, "Socio-Religious Movements in Kerala," 12.

deities for use by the Ezhavas, and he officiated at consecration ceremonies, a rite customarily performed only by Brahmins of the highest
standing.[36] At the time Guru first consecrated a temple, Panikkar
observed, "he just picked up a stone from a nearby stream and installed
it as an idol; subsequently, he used a piece of mirror as an object of worship."[37] Yet he also urged that Ezhavas cease any discrimination against
other excluded castes and open their own temples to them.

In 1887 at Aruvipuram, Guru established the Temple Sivalingam, a
small temple to the god Siva (also Shiva), or the "Ezhava Siva," to use
his term. He would go on to consecrate sixty-four more. He was not
insensitive to the delicate cultural connotations of incorporating lower
castes into Brahminical forms of worship. A skeptic who doubted
Guru's authority to perform this role received his droll reply that he had
only installed an Ezhava deity, not a Brahmin deity. This led Justice A.
S. P. Iyer of the Madras High Court to refer to Guru's temple-building
campaign as a "parallel government" within Hinduism.[38] The Ezhavas
were more acceptable than Pulayas and were viewed as "mild untouchables," historian Suresh Jnaneswaran noted, shaving their heads so as
to cultivate an appearance similar to that of the Brahmins.[39] They were

[36] Sanskritization is a name given to attempts by lower castes and untouchables to a rise in status while staying within the traditional caste hierarchies,
through emulating high-caste norms, practices, and customs. In the process
called "Sanskritization," a low caste might, over a generation, lift itself in the
hierarchy by espousing practices such as vegetarianism, Sanskritizing its rituals
and deities, and adopting rites and thinking of the Brahmins, although theoretically prohibited. M. N. Srinivas advocates this view in "A Note on Sanskritization
and Westernization," *Far Eastern Quarterly* 15 (August 1956): 481–96, and other
works. Gandhi could be said to favor this approach, seeking changes while not
departing from Hinduism, and in that he showed little interest in Travancore's
many caste-reform endeavors. This explanation, however, minimizes the
degree of exertion, contestation, and resistance involved by those who extend
themselves to organize self-reform and self-uplift movements, and it underesti-
mates the costs of challenging the existing order.

[37] Panikkar, *Culture, Ideology and Hegemony*, 114.

[38] Aiyappan, *Social Revolution in a Kerala Village*, 135. Parallel, or alternative,
institutions are part of Gandhi's concept of the constructive program, about
which more will be said.

[39] Suresh Jnaneswaran, interview (Trivandrum, March 25, 2009).
Jnaneswaran is a professor of history, University of Kerala, Trivandrum.

not, however, permitted to worship the gods of the *savarna* Hindus in their temples (*chamundis*), and the only offerings they could proffer were toddy or sacrificial fowls.

By 1890 Guru's first temple and hermitage were attracting devotees, for whom he set up a kitchen to furnish meals. Guru had founded the *sanyasins*, an order of monks, to function as the spiritual, corresponding equivalent of the SNDP Yogam. These Ezhava monks were trained by Guru to manage the new temples, lead the rituals for temple worship, and spread philosophic Hinduism. As a caste reformer, Guru sought to create social and religious practices without looking to Brahminical tradition for legitimacy. In 1899 the Aruvipuram ashram was restructured as the Aruvipuram Temple Yogam, and Asan was elected secretary-treasurer.[40]

In December 1902, ten shareholders paid 100 rupees each for lifetime memberships and launched the SNDP Yogam, which was registered as a limited company in 1903. Its bylaws said its main objective was "to promote and encourage religious and secular education and industrious habits among the Elava community."[41] The Yogam would safeguard the temples established by Guru and disseminate his ideas.

Guru's reforms were creating an awakening that would be significant for the temper of the coming times. In 1904 to great acclaim, the Yogam held its second annual meeting in conjunction with a larger agricultural and industrial exhibition at Quilon, with only Ezhavas allowed to visit the displays. Some 3,000 Ezhavas toured dozens of exhibits, and the maharaja sent 300 rupees.[42] The respect shown to Guru and the success of the event foretold further growth of his following, recognition, and influence. The exhibition also provoked a serious backlash among upper castes, who feared the newfound assertiveness of the Ezhavas and wanted to destroy it.[43] An association called the Cochin Ezhava Sabha would be similarly established in the nearby kingdom of Cochin in 1916.

[40] An ashram is a secluded Hindu community gathered around a spiritual leader.

[41] Jeffrey, "Social Origins of a Caste Association," 51–2. Of the ten, six were from near Trivandrum and the others from Quilon, in central Travancore. Jeffrey, "Social Origins of a Caste Association," 52.

[42] Jeffrey, "Social Origins of a Caste Association," 54.

[43] See Jeffrey, "Social Origins of a Caste Association," 54–6, for details of incidents.

Asan, Narayana, and Palpu were fitting exemplars for the longing and dissatisfaction of the Ezhavas. In Robin Jeffrey's words:

> Dr Palpu, with his medical degree, turban and long black coat, exemplified "achieved" status. Narayana, respected even by *savarna* Hindus, was in a tradition of Kerala ascetics. . . . Kumaran Asan, the efficient organizer, was growing in fame as a Malayalam poet and builder of the modern Malayalam language. Narayana and Asan were virtually full-time workers for the Yogam. . . . [which], with its revered guru, successful doctor and promising poet and administrator, provided a focus for the widespread, but hitherto unconnected, ambitions of many Iravas.[44]

The Ezhavas' receptivity to these leaders' undertakings and leadership also fired social aspirations. Western education and the Travancore government's relatively more progressive views on learning had in its own way placed a priority on qualifications rather than origins. A subtle transition from assigned rank or standing to status based on one's preparation and accomplishment was underway.

By 1909, the SNDP Yogam had more than 900 members. With Guru's personal appeal and charisma, and Asan's intellectual prowess and poetic gifts, within two decades of the establishment of the SNDP Yogam, it had become a dynamic social force. By 1917, the Yogam began to shift its emphasis from the building of Ezhava temples to constructing schools. By 1918, with Ezhavas still prohibited from the outer precincts of Brahmin temples, Guru's founding of temples meant that Ezhavas had at their disposal funds that had previously flowed into upper-caste temple coffers. It also provided the Ezhavas new opportunities, including presiding over marriage and death rituals, and permitted them to prove to themselves and others their capacity to manage institutions. Such experiences generated solidarity among the Ezhavas. With his parallel religious institutions, Guru was raising the self-esteem of the Ezhavas, and others were noticing.

By 1927, one year before Guru died, the Yogam had been transformed into a mass movement. At the 1927 Palpathuruthy meeting of the SNDP Yogam, Ezhavas were advised to abandon the concept of converting to another religion and instead adopt the Guru's banner of "One Caste, One Religion, and One God."[45] This dictum expressed Guru's vision for an end of the caste system.

---

[44] Jeffrey, "Social Origins of a Caste Association," 58–9.

Local movements for self-improvement among the Ezhavas had come and gone since the 1890s. Guru, however, managed to weld from within the subdivided whole of what is now Kerala a resilient caste union that could collectively strive for progress in education, promote social reform, and take political action. Guru was able to promote incipiently revolutionary change, yet without arousing opposition from the authorities of Travancore, where much of his work originated. In Aiyappan's view, "Holiness is respected[,] and though in this case the holy man was born in a low caste, his personality and his spiritual accomplishment and scholarship commanded veneration. He took care to see that no one was criticised and no one's rights interfered with or questioned. Whatever he did was done quietly and within the broad religious framework of Hinduism."[46]

The SNDP Yogam, perhaps more than other caste associations in India, came into view as a result of the distinctive character of Travancore's local society and was to some extent able to take advantage of repressive governmental procedures. Guru's emphasis on religious reform gave it strength, allowing it to win wide support. This laid the groundwork for other leaders, who were just over the horizon, such as T. K. Madhavan and C. Kesavan, who would be able to use it as a precursor for more extensive political change. Furthermore, it had a perceptibly democratic character, which was important, because untouchable echelons throughout India lacked consensus on hierarchical order among themselves, with each claiming superior status in comparison with other untouchable groups.

The burgeoning emancipation movement became a two-pronged effort, fueled by the religious aspiration of lower castes and outcastes for gaining access to the status associated with worship of higher gods and the desire of rising middle classes to destroy a caste system that impeded their progress. The religious element could potentially influence the full Hindu constituency, because the entirety of the Hindu faithful was affected by the varying pollution rules and caste relations,

[45] *Madras Mail*, February 9, 1925, 4, as cited in P. Chandramohan, "Social and Political Protest in Travancore: A Study of the Sree Narayana Dharma Paripalana Yogam (1900–1938)," M.A. diss. (New Delhi: Jawaharlal Nehru University, 1981), 253n1.

[46] Aiyappan, *Social Revolution in a Kerala Village*, 148.

while interest in government employment would be an objective for a minority. The British colonial project had encroached, with its external derivation, abutting the caste hierarchical system, but the Ezhavas nonetheless had to arrive at their own social perceptions before they could galvanize a mass movement.

While the Ezhava movement grew under the sway of Palpu and Asan, at its core it was restricted to the urban lower and middle classes. Peasants and illiterate agricultural workers were not involved. The main nonviolent methods chosen by the SNDP Yogam and the Ezhava middle classes in their early struggles were fundamentally those of persuasion and protest, the mildest of a large historical repertoire of action measures. The nonviolent methods they chose included documentation, submission of materials and testimony, and representations based on resolutions passed at meetings, or deputations—essentially supplicating and politely petitionary. The memorial petitions were prime examples of these methods that are designed to convey a message. With momentum from a new secretary, T. K. Madhavan, the SNDP Yogam would take on a more secular character. Explicit, forthright, and targeted mobilization against the caste system would begin under the guidance of Madhavan and K. Ayyappan. At the start of the twentieth century the Ezhavas had not been granted the right to be heard on their own, but by 1920 their voice was intensifying and clear, such that the government expediently began to accommodate some of their interests in its schemes of administration. They would become, ultimately, a political force that no other single community could rival.

A Movement against Untouchability Attains Visibility

Earlier, in 1836 in what would become Kerala, Vaikunta Swami (1809–51) established the Samatwa Samajam, perhaps the earliest social organization opposed to the concept of untouchability. Even then, not one but several movements had begun to mobilize against this condition. Swami's emphasis on social equity was instrumental in setting the stage for the Shanar (Shanan) women of south Travancore to revolt as early as 1858 against a law that prohibited them from wearing jackets to cover their upper bodies.

Ayyankali (1863–1941) was a Pulaya leader who, among many, took encouragement from Sri Narayana Guru and would participate in several Dalit movements against the mercilessness of the caste system in the early twentieth century. Forbidden as a member of a formerly slave caste to enter the main street of a village or to ride a cart in front of upper castes, Ayyankali undertook direct action of his own and enacted an individualized witness of civil disobedience. He purchased two white bullocks and a cart and attached large brass bells to the necks of the animals. Disobeying the traditional requirement of keeping his upper body unclothed, on top of his dhoti—a customary rectangle of yards-long unstitched cloth, wrapped around the waist and legs, and knotted at the waist—he draped a piece of cloth normally worn by high-caste men at festivals and sported a turban, also forbidden. So costumed, he drove the cart from Venganoor, his village north of Trivandrum, to Vizhinjam, a fishing village that is now a port. The two hamlets were connected by a road forbidden to Dalits. His action created consternation. When confronted, Ayyankali unsheathed a long dagger and announced that anyone trying to stop him would taste his weapon.

Ayyankali's bullock cart and dagger are still celebrated today, because his action stands as an alternative approach of outright noncooperation that might have been used, in contrast to persuasive methods of protest and appeal such as declarations, petitioning, and denunciation. Although uneducated in his youth, as would have been true for all Pulayas, Ayyankali became a now-honored and pioneering iconoclast who succeeded in spearheading numerous reforms. In 1900 through his organizing, the Pulayas and other formerly serf castes won the right to walk on public roads near Venganoor. In 1907, Ayyankali founded the Sadhu Jana Paripalana Yogam, Association for the Welfare [or Protection] of the Poor, an untouchables union modeled on the SNDP Yogam, with branches across the state.[47]

Organized efforts for unapproachables to gain access to savarna temple roads began mounting in the nineteenth century, only to meet setbacks. Journalist A. J. Philip explained:

In 1865, the government of Travancore had allowed the public to walk on all roads. Twenty years later, in 1884, the same government had

---

[47] Sreedhara Menon, *Kerala and Freedom Struggle* (Kottayam: D C Books, 1997), 60; P. Sanal Mohan, "Imagining Equality: Modernity and Social Transformation of Lower Caste in Colonial Kerala," Ph.D. diss. (Kottayam: Mahatma Gandhi University, 2005), 40n38.

re-notified the public that they could walk on any road. The upper castes challenged this in court. The court was a traditionalist body and dominated by the upper castes, who won their challenge, so that by 1905 the temple roads had been closed to the unapproachables and untouchables.[48]

Coherent efforts to open the roads appear in historical records in 1905, and actual attempts to enter orthodox temples are documented for 1911, 1916, 1917, 1919, 1921, and 1922.[49] Most of these efforts were remonstrances, constitutional agitations, and legal initiatives, but they also included some creative methods. The Pulayas had coordinated a successful strike in the late nineteenth century for the right to use public roads in Travancore. Young Ezhava men in Travancore became involved in what Chandramohan describes as an "unprecedented awakening" and began organizing youth meetings across the state. As an example, in 1918, some 500 Ezhava youths convened at Eravavoor, vowed to use the public roads that had been closed to them, and set up a fund to raise money for a movement against untouchability. By 1919, Ezhava leaders were calling for their community to refuse to pay taxes, their purpose being to reduce the income raised by the temples until the ban on using temple roads was removed. Some began to advocate temple desertion and noncooperation with savarna temples.[50]

The advent of new leadership resulted in new, vigorous efforts to involve villages and stimulate broader mobilization on the issue of access to public roads. T. K. Madhavan and E. J. John also became involved in organizing with the League for Equal Civil Rights, formed in late 1918 by Syrian Christians. The local leaders were landlords, lawyers, merchants, newspaper owners, and others. Their work in Travancore was provoked by the denial of appointments of avarnas, who were not allowed to join with other Hindus, Christians, and Muslims working in the state's land revenue department. The stated reason for denying jobs to them was that the department was

---

[48] A. J. Philip, interview (New Delhi, March 12, 2009). Philip is publisher and journalist of the *Herald of India* newspaper and director of the Pratichi (India) Trust.

[49] Kawashima, *Missionaries and a Hindu State*, 175.

[50] Chandramohan, "Social and Political Protest in Travancore," 242–3.

responsible for administering temples to which their excluded castes were denied entry. At a public meeting in Kottapam, John argued that only twenty percent of Travancore's citizens "enjoyed true civil rights at the time, an injustice ascribable to purely social and religious considerations."[51] Its critics said the group represented solely the interests of Syrian Christians.

The league's efforts partially succeeded, as in 1922 the department would be split off from the temple management department, and avarnas could get government service jobs in the new division. The league soon atrophied, and let lapse the anti-untouchability feature of its original program when the main grievances of the educated Syrian Christians were met. For avarna Hindus, the divisions of departments were irrelevant to their continuing exclusion from various roads and public buildings, with only a scattering of positions available in the government service, and they were forbidden to enter or approach temples. Even so, the league stimulated a number of educated Ezhavas to become involved in Travancore's state-level politics.

The concept of temple entry may have first been advocated publicly by Shri C. Raman Thampi, a retired High Court judge, at a forum in Quilon in 1917.[52] In December of that year, an editorial in the weekly *Deshabhimani* (Patriot), edited by T. K. Madhavan, formally and possibly for the first time in print, raised the question of Ezhavas entering temples. It stated that the Ezhavas ought to be recognized as "respectable caste Hindus." The *Deshabhimani* editorial was by C. V. Kunjuraman and is viewed as the first of its kind written on the delicate issue of temple

---

[51] P. K. Karunakara Menon, *History of the Freedom Movement in Kerala*, vols. 1 and 2, 285. The *Malayalam Manorama* on December 14, 1922, reported that 3,817 jobs in the princely state's revenue department were held by caste Hindus, with 147 held by non-caste Hindus and non-Hindus. As cited in Menon, *History of the Freedom Movement in Kerala*, 289.

[52] Ravindran, *Vaikkam Satyagraha and Gandhi*, 47. Chandramohan, in "Social and Political Protest in Travancore," claims that Madhavan and his colleagues got their inspiration from Raman Thampi, 240. Mahadev Haribhai Desai uses a variation of this name and recalls being told that C. Raman Pillai, retired High Court justice, was the first in Travancore to call for "opening all State temples" to avarnas, in a public meeting at Quilon, in 1917. Desai, *Epic of Travancore*, 10.

entry by untouchables.[53] Reflecting the headway being made by the Ezhavas, a new slogan emerged: "the conversion of wealth into honour."[54]

From 1918 onward, Madhavan and other Ezhavas in the Sri Mulam Popular Assembly routinely advocated temple entry and acknowledgment of the standing of Ezhavas as respectable caste Hindus. In the 1919 assembly, Madhavan called for the abolition of untouchability and unapproachability and made a motion on the subject of entering temples for worship, but the dewan disallowed it for reasons of interfering with religion.[55] From 1919 onward, the issue of admitting all Hindus to temples of worship without distinction of caste came before the assembly, thus raising the issue before the government year after year.[56] In 1921, when Madhavan again tried to advance the question of temple entry, Dewan Bahadur T. Raghavaiah (also transliterated Raghava Aiya, or Ayya, 1920–5) disallowed the motion, declaring that the government could not intervene in such purely religious affairs.[57] In that same year, Madhavan and Chavarkkattu Marthandan Vaidhyan gave notice that a petition for equality of citizens' rights would be introduced, emphasizing entry for any Hindu into public temples. The chief secretary asked Madhavan to amend the petition so that it would not refer to temple entry.[58] Madhavan's conflation of the entry of lower castes into Brahmin temples with walking on temple roads created a strategic difficulty in Ravindran's eyes: "Perhaps [Madhavan] believed

---

[53] Ravindran, *Vaikkam Satyagraha and Gandhi*, 48. Chandramohan also cites the editorial by Kunjuraman as the start of the temple-entry movement in Travancore by the Ezhavas. It had been written much earlier, but K. P. Padmanabha Channar, owner of *Deshabhimani*, was "frightened" of the reaction from the government; thus it did not appear until December 1917. Chandramohan, "Social and Political Protest in Travancore," 241n2.

[54] Houtart and Lemercinier, "Socio-Religious Movements in Kerala," 13.

[55] *Proceedings of the Sri Mulam Popular Assembly of Travancore* (hereafter *SMPA*), 1919, 88–9, as cited in Ravindran, *Vaikkam Satyagraha and Gandhi*, 40.

[56] Ravindran, *Vaikkam Satyagraha and Gandhi*, 40.

[57] *Proceedings of the SMPA*, 1921, 148, as cited in Ravindran, *Vaikkam Satyagraha and Gandhi*, 40.

[58] Letter of February 20, 1921, from N. Rajarama Rao, Chief Secretary of the Travancore government to T. K. Madhavan as cited in P. S. Velayudhan, *S.N.D.P. Vharitram*, 215, as cited in Chandramohan, "Social and Political Protest in Travancore," 244n2.

that when temple entry was granted, it would automatically carry the right to walk along the temple roads. But the first thing he should have done was to concentrate on the civil right of using the road."[59]

In the seventeenth annual meeting of the SNDP Yogam, in 1919, a resolution passed unanimously to exert pressure on savarna temples until they were opened to the Ezhavas.[60] In December 1919, approximately 5,000 Ezhavas met at Kanichikulangara with the objective of gaining admission to state temples and making strides in equalizing differences in Hindu society.[61] The tactic of converting to other faiths was also being hotly debated during the period 1917–20, but Madhavan, Kumaran Asan, and especially Sri Narayana Guru were opposed to it. Within the orthodox sector of the savarna Hindus, the well-organized defiance of the Ezhavas was an abomination. Chandramohan asserts, "The vigour and enthusiasm of the Ezhavas to annihilate the humiliating casteism on the one hand and the interest of the *savarnas* to retain their caste hegemony over untouchables on the other caused a number of skirmishes. . . , in various parts of Travancore."[62] In this regard, the movement of the Ezhavas in the late nineteenth and early twentieth centuries is similar to a large number of caste and tribal assertion movements taking place elsewhere in India.[63]

The Ezhavas in Travancore were at the cusp of a major transition. The growing middle class wanted higher ranking in the social hierarchy, government jobs, and influence—all of which necessitated eliminating untouchability as it was practiced by the government and the upper castes. Offices in the army, palaces, and *devasam* (temple property) were closed to untouchables. Access to jobs in the array of government departments, plus the ending of untouchability, unapproachability, and unseeability was the only answer, and this would be achievable only by pressing for temple entry.

---

[59] Ravindran, *Vaikkam Satyagraha and Gandhi*, 41. Without giving details, Ravindran says that Madhavan came to realize the value of sequencing only through Gandhi's insistence. Ravindran, *Vaikkam Satyagraha and Gandhi*, 41.

[60] Chandramohan, "Social and Political Protest in Travancore," 243.

[61] Menon, *History of the Freedom Movement in Kerala*, 116.

[62] Chandramohan, "Social and Political Protest in Travancore," 245.

[63] For an example of another such movement that gave rise to sharp social conflict during these years, see David Hardiman, *The Coming of the Devi: Adivasi Assertion in Western India* (New Delhi: Oxford University Press, 1995).

T. K. Madhavan

Many in Travancore who were fighting for social justice for the untouchables were not satisfied with the incremental process, gradualism of
reforms, and often-broken official promises. T. K. Madhavan (1885–
1930) (Fig. 1), member of the Ezhava educated elites and prominent
leader of the Ezhava cause, is correctly viewed as the progenitor of the
Vykom struggle. Born into one of Travancore's wealthy matrilineal families, he was able to take advantage of the princely state's extensive
Western-style education and completed his secondary studies at a
Roman Catholic high school in Quilon. His education indelibly marked
him with an awareness of the disadvantages and prejudices experienced
by the Ezhavas. Madhavan was quoted later in life as saying:

> My companion on my daily trip to and from the school was a Nair boy
> . . . whose poor mother was a dependent of ours. He could go straight
> along all the roads, whereas I, in spite of being economically better off,
> had to leave the road now and then [so as not to "pollute" caste Hindus].
> This used to cut me to the quick.[64]

By age twenty, he had become involved in organizing Ezhavas in central
Travancore and served as English interpreter for Ezhava notables who
participated in a representative assembly in Trivandrum.

Madhavan was influenced by Sri Narayana Guru and the SNDP Yogam,
of which he became a member in 1914.[65] In the following year, he
founded and became editor of *Deshabhimani*, which publicized accounts

---

[64] T. K. Madhavan as quoted in Ayinipalli Aiyappan, "Iravas and Culture
Change," *Madras Government Museum Bulletin*, 1: 1943, 103–4, as cited in Jeffrey,
"Temple-Entry Movement," 12, 25n40.

[65] Although Madhavan was a well-known and respected figure, he was considered a maverick by some of his colleagues. In a letter to C. W. E. Cotton, the
British political agent to the governor-general of Travancore, Padmanabhan
Palpu refers to him as an "impatient reformer," who had managed to gain the
attention of observers outside Travancore regarding the local grievances being
faced, but without Palpu's knowledge or that of the most prominent leader of the
Ezhavas, Sri Narayana Guru. Palpu never mentions Madhavan by name, but the
reference is unquestionable. Political and Secret Annual Files IOR/L/PS/11/246
item P2117/1924, letter from P. Palpu to C. W. E. Cotton, August 4, 1924, and
memorandum from Cotton to Secretary of the government of India, Foreign and
Political Department, Simla, Madras States Agency, Camp Kunnamkulam, April
21, 1924, as cited in Ravindran, *Vaikam Satyagraha and Gandhi*.

Figure 1 T. K. Madhavan asserted critical leadership from the Ezhavas, the highest ranking of the excluded castes (Illustrated by Madanan Pv)

Note: T. K. Madhavan was as much as anyone the progenitor of the Vykom struggle. As an Ezhava, he was a member of the largest group within the ranks of Hindus with no caste, or the so-called untouchables, among whom many were highly educated elites. He is remembered as customarily wearing white homespun, and holding a walking stick in the handle of which a portrait of Gandhi was implanted.

of injustices encountered by Ezhavas as well as their accomplishments. He served as president of the All-Travancore Labour Conference and as an elected member of the Sri Mulam Popular Assembly. Early in his political career, Madhavan pushed for Ezhavas to unite their efforts with Christians, but he was unable to forget how Ezhavas in the League for Equal Civic Rights had been used to augment the Syrian Christians' pleas, which then took precedence over the concerns of the untouchables. As a result, the league had not functioned as a true alliance. His stance on working collaboratively with the Christians gave way to one of cooperation with caste Hindus, who were after all the rulers of Travancore. His strategy stressed the importance of seeking high-caste Hindu cooperation to combat untouchability and enlisting the cooperation of progressive, educated, Hindu upper castes. This, he believed, would bring the government to eradicate the customary disabilities. Gandhi's rise in prominence on the Indian stage would help Madhavan's strategy, as hundreds of upper-caste Hindus sought a way to involve themselves in Gandhi's campaigns.

Madhavan is remembered as usually dressing in white homespun, bearing a walking stick in the handle of which a portrait of Gandhi was embedded. In November 1920—purposely ignoring the teendal palakas on the roads near the Shiva temple in Vykom indicating the obligatory distances to be maintained from the upper castes—Madhavan trespassed and entered the prohibited area. He proclaimed to the district magistrate, "I am an Ezhava by caste. I came to Vaikom today and went to the temple here, past the notice board posted on the road."[66]

The Rising Voice of the Ezhavas

As the largest taxpayers in Travancore, the rising commercial and mercantile forces within the Ezhava community wanted any money collected from them in taxes to be spent to further their development. Attitudes were altering as a by-product of broader access to education, deepening nationalist thought, cooperation among the avarnas,

[66] T. K. Madhavan, quoted in the *Madras Mail*, May 18, 1920, 5; May 24, 1921, 6. K. R. Narayanan, "Ti Ke Madhavan," in *SNDP Yogam Golden Jubilee Souvenir* (Quilon: Vignanaposhini Press, 1953), 104. T. K. Madhavan to the District Magistrate, November 30, 1921, Kerala Secretariat, Travancore Confidential Section 554/1920, as cited in Jeffrey, "Temple-Entry Movement," 13, 25n43.

stimulus from the thinking being propounded by Gandhi, the impact from modern and Western thought, influence from missionary-educated rising groups, and competition with Christianity. The Ezhava community during this period was not depressed in a clinical sense, Narayanan insisted; "it had very highly educated groups of people, with English education, and also traditional education; they were even better educated than the Nairs."[67] The Ezhavas wanted the same rights and advantages they would have if they were to convert to Islam or Christianity. Chandramohan quotes Madhavan as saying, "communal justice ... was the proper basis for the spirit of nationalism."[68]

G. D. Nokes, once a public service commissioner of Travancore, stated that "the great national indoor sport of Travancore is the holding of public meetings."[69] Individuals vigorously partook of political commentary and activism, and lively media in the Malayalam and English languages developed throughout the region. The news media actively covered debates over government actions, so as the voice of the Ezhavas grew stronger, the government became less able to ignore their demands.

The Travancore government had issued a circular in 1884 (mentioned earlier by A. J. Philip) that removed exclusions to all public courts, government offices, markets, and public highways, with the wording "open alike to all classes,"[70] yet its implementation and enforcement had lagged. The roads around the Shiva temple in Vykom presented apparently unique circumstances. Despite numerous agitations[71] against unapproachability throughout Travancore, the local government

[67] Narayanan, interview (August 12, 2005).

[68] Chandramohan, "Social and Political Protest in Travancore," 240.

[69] As cited in Ouwerkerk, *No Elephants for the Maharaja*, 65.

[70] Kawashima, *Missionaries and a Hindu State*, 152.

[71] The word *agitation* has long been used in India by English speakers to convey a specific campaign or mobilization. The Travancore government wanted to preserve the status quo for two main reasons. Attempts by lower castes to gain temple entry assumed access to surrounding roads. Any concessions, however limited, might imply additional and wider reforms or demands, which the orthodox would vehemently resist. Also, the Travancore government may have feared a rebellion, such as had happened in early 1924 in the Salem district of Madras, where popular opinion had heaped blame on the opening to all castes of streets inhabited by the upper castes. Equally dreadful was the possibility of a recurrence of the Mappila rebellion, one of a succession of violent revolts in British Malabar, most recently in 1921 to 1922.

remained firm in its legalistic interpretation of the conservative Hindu custom. Despite its adamance in opposing temple entry for untouchables, it was nonetheless painfully aware of the simultaneously growing aspirations of several of the untouchable communities and their increasing economic prominence. From 1911 to 1921, crucial trends emerged in educational access and economic development, as literacy in Malayalam rose among males in Travancore from 29 percent to 38 percent. Ezhava males' literacy rose from 12 percent to 36 percent.[72]

The ideas and activities of Ezhava leaders like Madhavan, Guru, and Palpu must also be understood in the context of specific regional economic and technological changes in late nineteenth- and early twentieth-century Travancore. The Ezhava and Syrian Christian communities were the main beneficiaries of an intensified integration of the region into an expanding economy. Developments in the agriculture-based industries—opening of rubber plantations, large-scale backwater reclamations for rice fields, and technical developments in the coir industry—and improvements involving transport and communication infrastructure played a major role in the everyday life of the people. The economic life of the Ezhava community was discernibly shifting. Ezhavas from villages migrated to towns like Alleppey to work in the coir factories and coconut-oil mills, work settings that exposed them to varying customs and attitudes.[73]

Officials were also concerned about the rise in the number of lower-caste Hindus and untouchables converting to other religions, especially Christianity. Both Syrian and missionary Christians throughout Travancore were becoming politicized, along with the Muslims and Buddhists.[74] Although some Ezhava leaders advocated mass numbers

[72] Jeffrey, "Temple-Entry Movement," 9. In 1917, 364,000 students were studying in Travancore, some 10 percent of the total population. Jeffrey, "Temple-Entry Movement," 9.

[73] Justin Mathew, communication (October 14, 2010), Department of History, Hans Raj College, Delhi University, Delhi, India. Coir is fiber from the husk of the coconut, twisted for making brushes, mats, and ropes.

[74] Numerous groups were expanding their roles into political activities. Some were primarily charitable in nature; others promoted the interests of their members, acting as precursors to contemporary advocacy and lobbying. In 1913, the Christian Sadhu Jana Sangham was formed. In 1914, Nairs founded the Nair Service Society. Parayas created the Brahma Pratyaksha Sadhu Jana Paripalana Sangham.

converting to casteless religious faiths, according to Aiyappan, a large number remained faithful to Hinduism and "thought that conversion was equal to running away from the fight for social justice."[75] A "protector of the depressed classes" was designated in late February 1924, at the twentieth session of the Sri Mulam Popular Assembly.[76] At it, Dewan Bahadur T. Raghavaiah proclaimed, "The moral and material elevation of the depressed classes continues to engage the earnest attention of the Government. . . . providing them with house-sites and economic farms. . . . [I]n the opinion of the Government the time has now arrived for making the welfare of these classes the definite duty of a responsible officer."[77]

Conceptual Groundwork: Gandhi's Satyagraha and Persuasive Methods

Mohandas Karamchand Gandhi had "suffered terribly" in South Africa, along with the entire Indian community, many of them high-caste Indians, due to their treatment by Christians. So C. F. Andrews writes in 1929 explaining Gandhi's views on untouchability to the Western world.[78] Failing in his efforts to practice law in India, Gandhi would spend twenty years working there, a period that comprised his most accelerated political growth, while forming basic girders of his life and thought. Having begun to criticize untouchability publicly in South Africa, Gandhi permanently departed in July 1914, to return to India. In the Indian subcontinent the drive against untouchability had been building for approximately the two decades during which he had been abroad. Geographically dispersed, it was diverse and led by religious organizations, some national leaders, and caste associations such as those already encountered. Recognizing the implicit political

[75] Aiyappan, Social Revolution in a Kerala Village, 137.

[76] By this time, the assembly was known irreverently as "the monkey-house," referring to excessive chatter and inability to act, although it did bring popular needs to the government's attention. Ouwerkerk, No Elephants for the Maharaja, 67–8.

[77] Proceedings of the Twentieth Session of the SMPA (Trivandrum: Superintendent, Government Press, 1924), 17.

[78] C. F. [Charles Freer] Andrews, Mahatma Gandhi's Ideas, Including Selections from His Writings (London: George Allen and Unwin, 1929), 177.

significance of untouchability, Gandhi began working on its national implications, arguing that when Indians treated their own as being unworthy of contact, they could hardly criticize European and other foreign governments for regarding them as undeserving. As he began to rise in India's public awareness and lead the struggles for independence, he perceived that the divisions among Indians made them vulnerable to a British policy of divide and rule and that their appeals for more dignified treatment would be ignored. Preoccupied as Gandhi was with Hindu–Muslim unity as a major issue, the untouchables could not be ignored. Looked at from the standpoint of Hindu cohesion, cruelty was disclosed by Hindus who claimed purity toward those of their own faith, making untouchability, in Aiyappan's phrase, "disintegrative and suicidal to Hindu interests."[79]

Unapproachability was worse. Gandhi writes in 1924, as the Vykom struggle gained pace, "As if the sin of untouchability was not enough, we [Indian people] started another sinful practice, that of unapproachability, to add to the burden."[80] He makes clear that unapproachability, or *doorata* (remoteness) in Travancore state, will not be understood in Gujarat, where he was born and reared. When he would in due course visit Travancore in 1925, according to his secretary Mahadev Desai, Gandhi expressed dismay, "When I saw with my own eyes, what the State was, what a cultured ruler and what a cultured Dewan it had, this existence of untouchability staggered and puzzled me. How such an inhuman thing could exist in such a State, with such a sovereign, such a Dewan and such a people, baffled me, as it still baffles me."[81]

Gandhi first honed his methods for fighting injustice as a result of his experiences in South Africa, his observation of African struggles around him there, and from closely following cases in the news from China, Russia, Europe, and elsewhere. He also was cognizant of bygone traditional Indian nonviolent methods. For instance, an ancient exertion of pressure named *carita*, in which creditors sit at a debtor's door to create embarrassment over a debt; also, a twelfth-century variation

[79] Aiyappan, *Social Revolution in a Kerala Village*, 145–6.

[80] Gandhi, "Untouchability and Unapproachability," from Gujarati, *Navajivan*, April 6, 1924, in *Collected Works of Mahatma Gandhi* (hereafter *CWMG*), 100 vols., ed. K. Swaminathan (New Delhi: Ministry of Information and Broadcasting, Government of India , 1958–84), 27: 191.

[81] Gandhi, as cited in Desai, *Epic of Travancore*, 3.

on this practice called *kaya-vrata* and an adaptation known as *dharna*, similarly used by lenders.[82]

In Gandhi's renunciation of violence, his thinking was influenced by Jainism, the ancient faith of a reforming sect of Hinduism, which took form in the Ganges basin in the early centuries BCE and became prevalent in Gujarat. From boyhood, Gandhi was influenced by Jainism and assimilated a basic element of Jain philosophy, the Jain doctrine of ahimsa, meaning noninjury and non-killing of any living being. He found inspiration in a Jain lay savant named Rajchandra Raychandbhai (or Raychandrabhai) Mehta, about whom Gandhi writes in his autobiography, and admired his cleanliness of character and yearning for self-realization. Raychandrabhai became a spiritual adviser for Gandhi. Partially reflecting his influence, Gandhi was deeply affected by Gujarat's religious and cultural environment, suffused as it was with ahimsa. Gandhi applied ahimsa to the social and political realms of life, shaping the idea into a tool to bring about transformation, rather than a simple equation of victory or failure. Embodied in ahimsa's renunciation of any effort to injure is an idea of mutuality, in which shared change can result in collective benefits and responsibilities, realizing an end without injury to anyone. Modifying its quietism into dynamism, he harnessed ahimsa to the social and political realms of life as a kind of power or insistence, thus making it an instrument of nonviolent action to effect change. Jainism's code of morals emphasizes total renunciation of violence in word, thought, and deed. It also considers all knowledge to be relative. Gandhi found appealing Jainism's view of Truth as many-sided, as expressed by the well-known tale of six blind men who put their hands on an elephant, with one thinking it to be a fan, the other a rope, another a snake, and so on. Gandhi embraced the Jain concept of ahimsa as including a type of social power without reliance on violence.

---

[82] David Hardiman, *Gandhi in His Time and Ours: The Global Legacy of His Ideas* (London: Hurst and Company, 2003), 42–3. (Dharna, or *dhurna*, is an ancient customary action in India, in which a lender would sit in front of a debtor's door until repaid. Without necessarily being aware of its traditional Indian application, it is an antecedent for contemporary sit-in strikes, such as would be used on a grand scale in 1980, when Polish workers in the Gdansk Lenin Shipyard refused to work, but stayed in place, the genesis of the Solidarity Union.)

As other generations of Indian leaders had also pondered, Gandhi was perplexed by the question of how Britain had been able to conquer India. In ten days in 1909, on board a ship returning to South Africa from London, Gandhi wrote on the ship's stationery what would become a booklet, *Hind Swaraj*, or Indian Home Rule. The implausibility of the British controlling India without Indian cooperation and obedience was a major theme of this pivotal though short work. So important was it to him that he translated it himself from Gujarati to English, singularly bestowing an authority all of its own. Although published in South Africa, it discloses that then in his fortieth year, Gandhi was deeply contemplating Indian independence, and he presents his political philosophy in more intact form than he would in any other communication. Conveying his ideas about releasing India from British colonial domination, the booklet was partly aimed at those who were advocating violence to free India and their counterparts in South Africa. He specifically hoped to invalidate the arguments for armed insurrection being promoted as an answer by zealous anarchists and terrorists, many of whom he had met with in London, because he was persuaded that "violence was no remedy for India's ills"; "her civilization required the use of a different and higher weapon for self-protection."[83] Artfully arranged as a question-and-answer dialogue between an editor (Gandhi) and a reader, the handout's ninety-two pages of debate on self-rule, nationalism, and British suzerainty is aimed at expatriate Indians who, allured by prospects for terrorism and guerrilla warfare, were unready to put into practice the ideals and principles that he was championing. Also significant is that Gandhi's strategy and life's vision were laid out in this small work, revealing that nearly all the elements of his noncooperation policy and program were initially tried and developed by him in South Africa. He had gone there a well-prepared barrister of British tutelage and on January 9, 1915, would return to India with a well-formed philosophy and technique that

---

[83] M. K. Gandhi, *Hind Swaraj or Indian Home Rule* (Ahmedabad, India: Navajivan Publishing House, [1909] 1938), 15. Also see Gandhi, *Hind Swaraj or Indian Home Rule*, ed. Mahadev Haribhai Desai (South Africa, n.p., 1909; English ed. repr., 1938; Ahmedabad: Jitendra T. Desai, Navajivan Mudranalaya, 1995); and *Mohandas K. Gandhi, Hind Swaraj and Other Writings*, ed. Anthony J. Parel (Cambridge: Cambridge University Press, 1997).

would provide the scaffolding for his work that lay ahead. "The English have not taken India; we have given it to them," he asserts. "They are not in India because of their strength, but because we keep them."[84]

Gandhi knew full well that most colonial officers in India who staffed the civil service, law courts, police, and army were Indians, not British, and that the funds for operating the colonial apparatus were raised by taxing Indians. *Swaraj* (*swa* derived from Sanskrit for self; *raj* for rule) was the term that he preferred to democracy, which for him often conjured centralization of power, corruptible elected officials, and bureaucracies. He wanted to express a polity in which with double meaning the individual rules himself or herself, and at the same time, national self-rule in which the people were in charge and not at the mercy of government. Not only could it not be bestowed or granted by colonial rulers, it was not a matter of constitutionalism, court rulings, parliamentary capacity, Westernization, industrialization, or the skills of civil servants. Although he did explicitly define the nature of the democracy he sought, he wanted to decentralize both political and economic power as it would maximize popular sovereignty and minimize state control. Indeed, Gandhi's swaraj inadequately translates into English as self-rule, Bhikhu Parekh says, because its moral connotation alluding to the character and civilization of the community is more significant than the matter of law or politics. Swaraj is a positive state that can only be achieved; it is more important than independence in which rule by an "arrogant indigenous minority" could replace the "colonial predecessors."[85]

Back in his homeland, Gandhi traveled widely for one year, thinking deeply about the predicaments of India as he observed them. As had other forerunners in Hindu traditions, he grappled with the alienation that had resulted from extensive and pernicious foreign rule and concluded that India had become sundered, morally degenerate, caste-ridden, and "diseased." He judged that the political servility of the Indian people had resulted from a deep moral crisis that would have to be addressed before other social abasements could be altered. Gandhi's

[84] Gandhi, *Indian Home Rule*, 35, 36, 90. The Gujarati version of the booklet was banned in India by British officials upon publication.

[85] Bhikhu C. Parekh, "Gandhi's Theory of Nonviolence: His Reply to the Terrorists," in *Terrorism, Ideology and Revolution*, ed. Noel O'Sullivan (London: Wheatsheaf Books Press, 1986), 187.

swaraj would, he hoped, engender unity among Indians of all faiths, but chiefly between Hindus and Muslims; the eradication of untouchability; and a practice known as *swadeshi* (or generally self-reliance in a sense of simplification of material needs). Brooding over the consequences of imperial rule for India's ancient civilizations and the society to which he had returned, he came to believe that unless India could be rejuvenated, it could neither achieve independence nor sustain it. He came up with a farsighted national program of Indian regeneration, a composite of three interrelated components: the spirit of swadeshi, satyagraha, and the constructive program.

The first essential element, swadeshi, has a long and complex Hindu significance, which Gandhi redefined in an effort to put forward an expressly Indian alternative to European doctrines of nationalism. He spoke of the swadeshi spirit, with *swa* meaning one's own and *desh* the full environment to which one belonged.[86] Indeed, swaraj would manifest the swadeshi spirit, connoting autonomy and genuine self-rule. Gandhi saw the depth of Indian poverty as partly attributable to disastrous departure from swadeshi in the country's economic and industrial life. When the swadeshi movement stressed using goods "belonging to one's own country," it indicated reliance on Indian rather than foreign-made wares, sometimes manifested in boycotting British products. Furthermore, Gandhi felt that Indians had been alienated from their own hereditary derivations and were weighed down "under a terrible handicap" by an "almost fatal departure from the swadeshi spirit," which included the educated classes being educated in the English language rather than their own tongues, causing them to lose connections with their own genesis.[87]

The second vital and integral part of national regeneration was satyagraha, which is fundamental to the enduring impact of Gandhi's example. It derived from Gandhi's response to disquieting experiences and immersion in political experiments in South Africa. As an attorney representing largely Indian merchants and traders there, he began to work full-time to organize them in opposition to racist Transvaal legislation, in the course of which he developed a method for social

[86] Bhikhu C. Parekh, *Gandhi's Political Philosophy: A Critical Examination* (Houndsmill, Basingstoke, Hampshire, and London: Macmillan Press, 1989; repr. 1991), 56.

[87] Gandhi, Speech on Swadeshi at Missionary Conference, February 14, 1916, *Young India*, June 21, 1919, in *CWMG*, 15: 161.

and political action, to be more fully addressed in Chapter 6. Returning to India in 1915, he believed that it would work there, including in Vykom, but he would end up revising it repeatedly during his maturity. Finding the right word for the technique he had developed in South Africa for bringing about social and political change without violence proved to be a task for Gandhi. The term *passive resistance*, which he had originally used to describe his process of nonviolent action for English speakers, had negative aspects. He believed that the term was not only imperfect, but reinforced a misperception: that nonviolent civil resistance was passive, when in reality it was an active force. As he explained:

> When in a meeting with Europeans I found that the term "passive resistance" was too narrowly construed, that it was supposed to be a weapon of the weak, that it could be characterized by hatred, and that it could manifest itself as violence, I had to demur to all these statements and explain the real nature of the Indian movement. It was clear that a new word must be coined by the Indians to designate their struggle.[88]

In 1906, Gandhi offered a small prize through *Indian Opinion*, his journal in South Africa, for the best suggestion of a single Gujarati word to describe the principles of Truth and Love as forces of power and change. Also welcoming a word in Sanskrit or Urdu, Gandhi altered the winning entry, *sadagraha* (firmness in good conduct), to satyagraha (literally, holding on to Truth, firmness in Truth, a relentless insistence on Truth).[89] Satyagraha can be interpreted as converting the power in nonviolence, or

[88] Mohandas K. Gandhi, *An Autobiography: The Story of My Experiments with Truth*, trans. from Gujarati by Mahadev [Haribhai] Desai (Ahmedabad: Navajivan Publishing House, 1940; repr., Boston: Beacon Press, 1993), 318.

[89] While in South Africa, Gandhi published weekly dispatches in *Indian Opinion* as "From Our Johannesburg Representative." In one he writes,

> The editor had invited [suggestions from readers for] a Gujarati equivalent for "passive resistance." I have received one which is not bad, though it does not render the original in its full connotation. I shall, however, use it for the present. The word is *sadagraha*. I think *satyagraha* is better than *sadagraha*. "Resistance" means determined opposition to anything. The correspondent has rendered it as *agraha* [firmness, insistence]. *Agraha* in a right cause is *sat* or *satya* [Truth] *agraha*. The correspondent therefore has rendered "passive resistance" as firmness in a good cause ... we shall use *satyagraha* till a word is available which deserves the prize.

M. K. Gandhi, "Johannesburg Letter," before January 10, 1908, *CWMG*, 8: 80.

ahimsa (literally, do no harm), into political action; *himsa*, violence, a brute fact of life, was to be shunned. Subsequent to Gandhi's lifetime, satyagraha has sometimes been translated as "truth force," although the term *force* could be construed to imply violence, which he did not intend to suggest. For the contemporary reader, satyagraha may best be grasped as connoting the power of Truth—a concept equivalent in modern meaning to nonviolent direct action or civil resistance.

Regarding the expression "civil resistance," which is assuming broader use among contemporary English speakers, Gandhi clarified:

> Civil disobedience is not necessarily an accurate expression of the attitude indicated in "civil resistance." ... Looking for a new phrase, I fixed upon "civil resistance." The current phrase was "passive resistance." But my way of resistance or the force which I had in mind was not passive. It was active, but "active" might also mean violent. The word "civil" suggests nothing but non-violence. I, therefore, joined it with "resistance."[90]

India in the years prior to 1949 would become the site of substantial mobilizations built on Gandhi's conception of satyagraha, embarked upon half a dozen times under diverse justifications.[91] It manifested the swadeshi spirit in the sense that Gandhi met people where they were, accepting that as a result of political action they could learn new ways of being and develop moral courage that they did not know they had. R. R. Diwaker explains:

> Satyagraha comes as the last and yet as the most potent of peaceful weapons. After all the remedies, such as constitutional agitation and others have been exhausted, Satyagraha steps in. It takes the place of violent direct action. It comes in where violence would have been resorted to in

---

[90] Gandhi, letter to Mathuradas Trikumji, "Civil Resistance and Disobedience," June 4, 1934, in *The Moral and Political Writings of Mahatma Gandhi, Nonviolent Resistance and Social Transformation*, ed. Raghavan Iyer (Oxford: Clarendon Press, 1987), 112.

[91] Depending on definition, these would include indigo planters in Champaran (Bihar), 1917; peasants of Kheda, or Khaira (Gujarat), 1918; Ahmedabad (Gujarat), 1918; against Rowlett Acts, 1919; 1920–2 noncooperation movement; Vykom, 1924–5; Bardoli (Gujarat), 1928; 1930–4 civil disobedience movement; 1940 individual civil disobedience; 1942 Quit India Movement.

the ordinary course, and those in command followed the usual methods of resistance and fighting. The dissatisfaction, the tempo of resentment, the degree of desperation, and the inevitability of using the last remedy are the same in Satyagraha as in the case of violent resistance.[92]

The term is today used in India for Gandhi's method, with which he experimented in the use of nonviolent action over the course of his adult life, and also to describe distinct struggles using the vocabulary and nonviolent methods that he had formulated.

Gandhi wanted to be true to his own intricately elaborated belief system and in constancy with his personal sense of integrity. Yet he also yearned for India to adopt his full set of convictions and his comprehensive belief system, in an all-encompassing set of principles, which he called the "nonviolence of the brave." He often commented on the inner requirements for satyagraha: "Experience has taught me that civility is the most difficult part of Satyagraha. Civility does not here mean the mere outward gentleness of speech cultivated for the occasion, but an inborn gentleness and desire to do the opponent good. These should show themselves in every act of a Satyagrahi."[93] A *satygrahi* was a person who had acknowledged Gandhi's precepts and believed in satyagraha as a matter of stern principle. The motivation of each *satyagrahi* was important to the success of nonviolent struggle; thus Gandhi saw the quest for Truth in satyagraha as bringing together the mind, body, and soul for the attainment of personal and, ultimately, social transformation. He sought a radical, intense divestment from violence within one's person and environment: "For me non-violence is a creed. I must act up to it whether I am alone or have companions. Since propaganda of nonviolence is the mission of my life, I must pursue it in all weathers."[94]

India's middle classes and educated intellectuals were ideologically inclined toward a national independence movement and could act on

[92] Ranganath Ramachandra Diwaker, *Satyagraha in Action: A Brief Outline of Gandhiji's Satyagraha Campaigns* (Calcutta: Signet Press, 1949), 23.

[93] Gandhi, *Autobiography*, 437.

[94] Gandhi, "Both Happy and Unhappy" (*Harijan*, June 29, 1940), in *Non-Violence in Peace and War*, ed. Mahadev Haribhai Desai, vol. 1, 3rd ed. (Ahmedabad: Navajivan Publishing House, [1942] 1948), 275. Hereafter, *Non-Violence in Peace and War*, vol. 1, appears as *NPW* (1).

these inclinations. The indigent classes, however, had been exploited to an extent that the middle classes had not. Indian resistance to colonial rule had occurred throughout the nineteenth century, in what scholars conservatively estimate to be 110 peasant revolts.[95] Any hopes and aspirations of the poor were thus more likely to be expressed in politically shallow and easily suppressed uprisings, although several nonviolent movements cohered in the nineteenth century.[96] Gandhi saw equality as a prerequisite to a new social order, feared that violence was sown by economic inequality, and thought that unless eliminated through nonviolent means, violent revolution could erupt. How, then, to involve the poor—who were often unemployed and in misery—to see themselves as persons who were not helpless and who, by rejecting passivity, might alter their own circumstances?

This would be addressed in the third element of the national program of renewal and regeneration that Gandhi conceived and developed, called "constructive work" or the "constructive program." Wanting levers for involving the whole of India, including the poorest of the poor, his quandary was how to achieve major alterations in the existing social and political order without depending on customary approaches, each of which had its own shortcoming. Personal reclusiveness was privatistic, charity needed generosity from others, and individualized good works would not make an imprint on national needs. Entitlements were unavailable and would be mistrusted if proposed, and measures implemented by a cumbersome or unjust state apparatus were not likely to result in the desired institutional change. Swaraj could not be conferred by India's rulers; it would be a manifestation of the swadeshi spirit and a state of being to be created by a renaissance of individuals and the society. What's more, Gandhi feared that centralization of power and thought could become an impediment to realization of swaraj. His ideal was direct democracy, which he believed could diminish the potential for political violence, while enhancing voluntary assumption of responsibility and freedom, and he was persuaded that democracy had its best guarantor in decentralization. If adopted by the entire nation of India, Gandhi believed, constructive

[95] Ravi Dayal, introduction to *We Fought Together for Freedom*, xii.

[96] David Hardiman, "Towards a History of Non-Violent Resistance," *Economic and Political Weekly* (June 8, 2013): 41–8.

work could lead to the achievement of *poorna swaraj*, narrowly defined as self-rule but more broadly meaning "complete independence."

As one of the earliest, pivotal non-Western thinkers of the modern period and a nationalist leader who had not cut himself off by assimilation, having worked out a political theory originating within the Indian history and character, expressed in the endogenous philosophical nomenclature of his nation, he most certainly was not seeking a Westernized and industrialized state with swaraj defined as freedom from British colonialism. In 1941, Gandhi wrote a pamphlet about the constructive program, evocatively stating that such social reconstruction had "to be built up brick by brick by corporate self-effort."[97] Originally addressed to members of the Indian National Congress, among the eighteen large and small measures through which Gandhi's political philosophy could be implemented in the constructive program was the making and wearing of khadi (or khaddar, meaning cotton, to be hand loomed). The promotion of handspun khadi represented a campaign within a much larger struggle that should be interpreted against the backdrop of the powerlessness of the destitute. In khadi, Gandhi found a way for the poorest of the poor to participate in their country's regeneration. Other elements included cottage industries, including making soap, paper, and pressing oil; village sanitation; adult education; advancement of women; and the growth of labor unions committed to nonviolent action. To Gandhi, the constructive program was a way of actualizing a new social reality in the midst of the old order, through the construction of alternative, or parallel, institutions. What's more, strategies of noncooperation benefit from detaching oneself from reliance on one's antagonist, thus his avowed national stratagem of noncooperation would also be under construction. This program also included civil disobedience, which, similarly, requires objectivity.

Making use of the traditional handloom and spinning wheel, or *charka*, for producing khadi—with which Gandhi would become emblematically associated—could not represent a concrete comprehensive economic solution for the condition of poverty of peasants and low-wage workers, nor could or would it free India from colonial

---

[97] Mohandas K. Gandhi, *Constructive Programme: Its Meaning and Place* (Ahmedabad: Navajivan Publishing House, [1941] 1948), 21–2; also in *CWMG*, 81: 354–74.

extortion. Gandhi called the spinning wheel "the symbol and central sun" of the eighteen-fold constructive program and "the best way of achieving social solidarity and non-violent organization."[98] Audacious in conception, its aspirational effect derived from the uplift and self-respect gained by the poor for themselves by its actual and symbolic use. In the humble spinning wheel, Gandhi chose an icon that was bursting with multiple meanings, starting with the paying of tribute to manual labor and those who carried it out—whom he had seen scorned during his time in London studying for the law, painfully experienced personally in South Africa, and scrutinized in India. Conveying independence from the importation of cotton processed in British mills, khadi was a motif of self-reliance that could unify rural and urban areas, even as it provided a way for the most impoverished to participate in the national striving. Subtly repudiating an undifferentiated and assumed superiority of modern technologies, it reasserted the value of a rural way of life. People who did not need the cloth they loomed were encouraged to donate it to others, representing a programmatical bid for more generosity of spirit in India. Hand looming had a meditative element, because one needed to concentrate and thus was alone with one's thoughts in silence for part of the day.

The flavor of Indian news reportage on Gandhi's understated but intrepid constructive work can be sampled in a few sentences. According to a 1925 account, Gandhi thought:

> [E]veryone should wear hand woven cloth [khadi], spin yarn using the "charka" and encourage the handloom industry. He believes that spinning yarn and weaving cloth will to some extent alleviate the problem of unemployment. . . . In a speech which resulted in his arrest and incarceration he said that the weaving industry which was spread all over the country was destroyed by the policies of the British who encouraged imported textiles. The collapse of the native handloom industry was speeded up by the practices of the city dwelling Indians who preferred imported clothes.[99]

---

[98] Gandhi, "Non-violent Technique and Parallel Government" (*Harijan*, February 17, 1946), in *Non-Violence in Peace and War*, ed. Bharatan Kumarappa, vol. 2, 1st ed. (Ahmedabad: Navajivan Publishing House, 1949), 8, 9. Hereafter, *Non-Violence in Peace and War*, vol. 2, appears as *NPW* (2).

[99] "Mahatmaji's Message," *Malayala Manorama Daily*, March 25, 1925, in *Mahatma Gandhi's Visits to Kerala: 1924, 1925, 1927, 1934, 1937*, English trans. (Kottayam: Malayala Manorama Daily, 2009), 21.

Moreover, constructive work, with its making of khadi, could help prepare for participation in a bigger and more complex agenda involving nonviolent resistance. Spinning could become a form of organizing and would build self-respect. Such an approach, Gandhi surmised, could minimize outbreaks of violence in a noncooperation campaign. He thought constructive work could be effective in a village or an entire country, and that any district that adopted the organized spinning of yarn to make homespun would be potentially preparing for satyagraha. With self-respect indispensable for self-governance, hand looming in his eyes was thus linked to home rule. By, in effect, creating a set of decentralized institutions to serve as the infrastructure for a just society, eliminating dependency on the adversary, it would be possible to proceed toward a new order in the midst of the old. Many, including Indian Marxists, ridiculed Gandhi's views as reactionary, but Gandhi's khadi drive could touch the inertia of the poor, negating some feelings of impotence. The making of homespun on the unassuming spinning wheel meant not only hand-loomed fabric for garments, but symbolically signified that all strata could be full participants in the national struggle. Participation by India's poor in the khadi movement and other aspects of the constructive program could make them part and parcel of the national independence movements and encourage self-respect and dignity, in some ways a prerequisite of civil resistance, and often a by-product.

What T. K. Madhavan called "Gandhi's methods" resonated with him, and by 1920, Madhavan was enthralled by Gandhi. Frustrated with the gradualism of the incremental approaches emphasizing petitions, supplications, and appeals that had previously been utilized in Travancore for combating untouchability, Madhavan saw Gandhi's seemingly unlimited permutations of nonviolent sanctions as providing strategies that the Ezhavas could employ. He also felt that efforts to eliminate untouchability in Travancore meshed well with Indian nationalism, and would help to create the all-caste Hindu movement that he and others were seeking.

A Struggle Congeals

The question of untouchables entering temples percolated during the first nine months of 1921 in Travancore, while a massive noncooperation movement blazed in much of British-controlled India. Madhavan and his colleagues took the issue of temple entry directly into the villages of central and northern Travancore, holding meetings and distributing materials on the subject. They would draw 2,000 to 3,000 participants to their gatherings. Orthodox Hindus responded with counterdemonstrations and literature. Armed police were put on alert to prevent riots.

With sixty-four-year-old Maharaja Sri Mulam Thirunal regarded as a staunchly conservative arbiter of Hindu dogma and orthodoxy, under his reign, there was little hope of temples being thrown open to all castes. A letter from leading Ezhava Padmanabhan Palpu to the British resident in 1924 reflects a doubtless widespread view that "supreme power here [in Travancore] actually vests, . . . in old-fashioned, blindly selfish priests. . . . [T]he Governments are only subordinate Institutions."[100] The British may have been covertly sympathetic to the demand for free entry to temples, but they were not ready to intervene in favor of underprivileged Hindus. As M. N. Srinivas states, "No alien government would have dared to declare the practice of Untouchability in any form an offense, or to enforce the right of Harijans to enter Hindu temples and draw water from upper-caste wells in villages."[101] They might otherwise have seized the opportunity to urge progressive social reforms, but were bogged down in British India in responding to the escalating Indian noncooperation movements and, thus, were ready to consider any mobilizing in a princely state as subversive.

The notice boards that the Travancore government had posted demarcating restricted areas on temple roads had been erected at varying distances from the temple walls. Choosing to focus on these discrepancies instead of the actual issues of untouchability, unseeability, and unapproachability, officials insisted that the signs be placed at a uniform distance from the temples. In doing so, the authorities stated that their decision was based strictly on Hinduism. A legal battle ensued when discussions turned to whether the temple roads were private or public, with the latter theoretically open to all Travancore subjects. The government essentially upheld the status quo ante by enforcing breaches of unapproachability.

[100] Palpu to C. W. E. Cotton, letter, August 4, 1924, 2, Political and Secret Annual Files: IOR/L/PS/11/246, item P2117/1924.

[101] M. N. Srinivas, *Social Change in Modern India* (Berkeley: University of California Press, 1966), 49.

Those Ezhavas who had gained employment in the government service of Travancore state were concerned about retaining the maharaja's goodwill and wanted no part in talk about disobeying the notice boards and forcibly entering temples. Regardless, Madhavan decided to widen the base of his ongoing initiative against untouchability. With his previous campaigns, he had already taken the first step in reshaping the Ezhava community into the group most favoring fundamental and groundbreaking political action in the princely state.

In 1921, Gandhi visited south India. Within the preceding two years he had become an all-India leader, and newspapers and media shared information about him in all corners of the country. His attention to untouchability had been mounting. Just five years earlier he had termed it "an ineffaceable blot," a "curse," and a "great and indelible crime."[102] Not only did Gandhi identify untouchability as a spiritual impurity within Hinduism, he was also aware that untouchables comprised a significant segment of the Indian people on the subcontinent. The population of the "depressed classes" in British and princely India in 1921 was 52.1 million, or 16.34 percent of the total population.[103] Thus, in addition to the moral crisis that Gandhi perceived as facing the nation, he viewed untouchability as a hindrance to Indian home rule. The lower rungs of Hindu society, corresponding with today's OBCs (Other Backward Classes), were in some areas a majority, particularly in south India, and would prove essential to any successful countrywide struggle for swaraj. Yet throughout India, they had often turned to the British to protect their interests, thereby potentially causing rifts in the base of the nationalist movement. Gandhi personally determined to combat untouchability by concentrating his efforts within the Indian National Congress, although the organization sometimes resisted.

Madhavan met with him in Tinnevelly on September 30 to ask for guidance. It is worth taking note of their dialogue. Having taken particular interest in Travancore's severe form of unapproachability, Gandhi told Madhavan, "I do hold that India cannot have complete

[102] Gandhi, February 16, 1916, "Speech on 'Ashram Vows' at YMCA," Madras (*Indian Review*, February 1916), in *CWMG*, 15: 172–3.

[103] S. K. Chatterjee, "Emergence of the Scheduled Castes in the Indian Polity," *Dimensions of Human Society and Culture: Essays in Honour of Professor Prabodh Kumar Bhowmick*, ed. M. K. Raha (New Delhi: Gyan Books, 1996), 393.

swaraj so long as untouchability is not blotted out from India. Hence it is that I have put it down as the very first item in my programme."

Madhavan told Gandhi, "We Ezhavas in Travancore are trying to remove the stigma of untouchability by getting all public temples thrown open to all classes of Hindus. . . . We take it as a matter of reforming Hinduism. . . . The removal of untouchability is an abstract idea. Temple-entry is a concrete representation of the abstract idea."

Gandhi responded, "Removal of untouchability assumes a concrete shape when you demand temple-entry. On strategical grounds, I would ask you to drop temple-entry now and begin with public wells. Then you may go to public schools."

To this, Madhavan countered, "Except half a dozen schools including the one in Trivandrum situated just on the southern side of His Highness the Maharaja's Palace, all public schools in this state are open to us."

Gandhi replied, "You are ripe for temple-entry then."

Madhavan put in plain words that many temples in Travancore were maintained from public funds. He described how the Travancore High Court had "convicted some members of our community for entering and offering worship in a temple on the ground that our presence in the temple was 'defiling'. . . . (but retain closing quotation mark) We have protested against that in the Popular Assembly and requested the Government to publish Proclamation [sic] abolishing untouchability. . . . What will Mahatmaji [affectionate rendering of mahatma, meaning great soul] advise us?"

Gandhi replied, "I would certainly advise you to offer civil disobedience. You must enter temples and court imprisonment if law interferes. It is wrong to prevent you from entering temples on grounds of religion. You must keep strict non-violence. You must not go and enter temples in masses. Go only singly. You must act with perfect self-restraint."[104]

Madhavan was later quoted as saying that Gandhi had said that "as to the right of entry into public temples for Ezhavas and others, they had a perfect right to enter there and offer worship precisely on the

[104] Gandhi, interview to *Deshabhimani* [T. K. Madhavan] (Tinnevelly, September 23, 1921), in *CWMG*, 24: 308. Ambedkar in Mahad first focused on access to public water facilities; yet Madhavan did not respond to this suggestion, focusing only on schools.

same footing as other non-Brahmin Hindus."[105] Madhavan thus received Gandhi's blessing, after some hesitation, for starting to galvanize for Ezhavas to enter the temples in Travancore. Still, Gandhi remained wary, cautious, and conservative. He was concerned with protecting the relative political autonomy of the princely states under circumstances of foreign rule in India, and did not want to jeopardize the Indian states' relative sovereignty.

Gandhi urged that the matter of temple entry be taken to the Kerala Provincial Congress Committee (KPCC), which had come into existence as a result of a decision by the Indian National Congress party at its annual meeting at Nagpur in December 1920 to reorganize provincial committees on a linguistic basis. The KPCC could thus now function in the Malayalam language. This same session represented a milestone for the nation and the Congress: a strategy of nonviolent noncooperation with the British had in September been accepted in a special session in Calcutta, it was now confirmed in Nagpur a few months later, and a resolution was passed on the removal of untouchability among the Hindus. Also, on April 23, 1921, the first All Kerala Provincial Conference drew adherents of the Congress party from across the area. Gandhi's support was exhilarating public opinion; even some reform-minded caste Hindus were intrigued.

The Travancore government took the view that anything associated with the Indian National Congress party was as much a foreign influence as the British. Gandhi's involvement complicated the picture. Historian Balram R. Nanda observes:

> Gandhi got no credit from the British for the restraints he imposed on his followers. The British rulers of India tended to see in Gandhi only a Machiavellian politician, with the Congress as his pliant tool, who was exploiting men and situations for his own ends. . . . They could hardly see the intellectual and ethical roots of the movement for political liberation. . . .
> To Gandhi the non-violent basis of the movement was its most significant feature; to the British the conscious moral superiority of Gandhi and his followers was simply an additional irritation.[106]

---

[105] P. K. Madhavan, *Life of T. K. Madhavan* (Mal.), 1: 169, as cited in Ravindran, *Vaikkam Satyagraha and Gandhi*, 49.

[106] B. R. Nanda, *Gandhi and His Critics* (Bombay, Calcutta, Madras: Oxford University Press, 1985), 67.

Notwithstanding the immutability of his strong concerns about ending untouchability, Gandhi had at this stage seemed equivocal about the caste system and even defended it. He considered that some kind of division of labor was unavoidable and that members of a community offered mutuality and reciprocity toward each other. This ambiguity, expressed after returning from South Africa, is often cited against him. In his early years he was not against caste in an absolute sense, perhaps because the Hindu epics had given him an optimistic interpretation of the *varnashrama* of ancient India, the basic fourfold social division that characterized traditional Hindu society, in which castes were like trade guilds, and birth alone did not define standing and privilege. If this system had cushioned individuals during tumultuous circumstances, there might be merit to knowing that an occupation or profession awaited someone because, in his view, the person would then be able to concentrate on inner growth and social rehabilitation. He envisioned that caste could act as a trade union of sorts, protecting individuals and encouraging them to follow certain livelihoods, yet he believed that it should not limit people's possibilities or bind them into economic exploitation. If individuals had a sense of community, it could diminish the role of the state. Caste had helped to protect some cultural traditions, and its social organization helped to manage human relationships, offering webs of support when needed.[107] Still, considered against his entire life's journey, any complimentary references probably rested on his youthful interpretations of the caste system from past times. Although he called himself an "Honorary Harijan," but never applied the name in unmodified designation to himself, within his personal domain he welcomed an untouchable family into the Sabarmati Ashram that he had established at Ahmedabad in 1915, and he adopted an untouchable girl as his daughter. At Gandhi's ashrams,

---

[107] Political scientist Rajni Kothari expresses a viewpoint akin to Gandhi's perspective after returning from South Africa: "The caste system not only determines the individual's social station on the basis of the group to which he is born but also differentiates and assigns occupational and economic roles. It thus gives a place to every individual from the highest to the lowest and makes for a high degree of identification and integration." Rajni Kothari, introduction to *Caste in Indian Politics*, ed. Rajni Kothari (Hyderabad: Orient Longman Limited, 1995), 10.

he insisted that every resident help with sanitation work and clean latrines, to show that no work was demeaning. Later, in 1946, he announced that no marriage would be celebrated at Sevagram unless one of the partners was "untouchable by birth." He wanted to reclaim Hinduism by eliminating odious traditions that sullied it. Gandhi was, in the words of Eleanor Zelliot, "the first prominent caste Hindu to proclaim that [untouchability] was harmful to Hinduism, to make its removal a personal responsibility of the caste Hindus, [and] to keep it before the public eye. . . . Perhaps as important as his ideology and his pronouncements was his personal example, from the beginning, of touching the Untouchable."[108]

Still, it was his exposure to the untouchability, unapproachability, and unseeabilty of Travancore that culminated in a decision that the caste system's ingrained inequities, social dislocations, and causation of pain put it beyond repair. Might Gandhi's equivocalness have been calculated? Jawaharlal Nehru, subsequently and while prime minister, in 1956 told Hungarian journalist Tibor Mende that he had asked Gandhi repeatedly why he did not "hit out at the caste system directly." Gandhi replied that the current caste system was "thoroughly bad and must go. I am undermining it completely, . . . by my tackling untouchability. . . . If untouchability goes, he said, the caste system goes. . . . He made untouchability the one thing on which he concentrated, which affected ultimately the whole caste system."[109]

Having a right to certain types of work might allow a sense of security to, for example, a scavenger, who might work for a group of families, and who could bequeath the claim to this job, even if he was only paid in kind and had to sell the leftovers and scraps. In one contested viewpoint, a certain stability came with knowing that astrologers could be found in the Panikkar community, carpenters in the Asari, blacksmiths in Karuvan, goldsmiths in Tattan, washing and laundry workers in Vannan, musicians in Pana, fishermen in Mukkuva, boatmen in Kanakka, laborers in Vettuva, and basket-makers in Paraya.[110] Untouchables had a monopoly over village orchestras and were

---

[108] Zelliot, *Untouchable to Dalit*, 155.

[109] Tibor Mende, *Conversations with Mr. Nehru* (London: Secker and Warburg, 1956), 27–8.

[110] Derived from Aiyappan, *Social Revolution in a Kerala Village*, 93.

allocated any dealings with dead animals (contact with dead animals rendered the handler impure); drums were made of skins of dead animals, so only untouchables could be musicians.[111] This questioned outlook held that the chandler or tanner could each feel certain of a place in society. Teachers were often in the Kaniyan caste.[112] Agriculture and trade had been occupations of Gandhi's subcaste—the Baniya, belonging to the Vaishya, or commercial, caste, usually classified as third in the hierarchy.[113] His family name implies that originally the Gandhis were grocers or vendors of drugs derived from vegetables, although his family members later rose to high position in state service. Gandhi himself had been expelled from his family's subcaste because he had traveled abroad, considered polluting, and he never sought readmission.

When Madhavan met with Gandhi in 1921, in the mind of any observer would have been the violent rebellion that was moving with intensity across the southern half of the Malabar district in British India.[114] Known also as the Mappila Uprising, revolts by Muslim peasants of Malabar had occurred almost regularly from 1836 to 1919, and in 28 separate occasions their grievances were such that they sought their own deaths.[115] In 1921, for a time they won control over large

---

[111] Dumont, *Homo Hierarchicus*, 78.

[112] Aiyappan, *Social Revolution in a Kerala Village*, 92.

[113] Hardly any Baniyas were farmers, although many became non-cultivating landlords by foreclosing on debts incurred by peasants, changing the erstwhile landowners into tenants. Peasants were normally considered to be Sudras, in contrast to the Vaishya status of the Baniyas. See David Hardiman, *Feeding the Baniya: Peasants and Usurers in Western India* (Delhi: Oxford University Press, 2000).

[114] "Owing to the continuance of an oppressive land tenure which created conditions of mass poverty and socio-economic stagnation, and the distrust and hatred with which the rulers continued to treat the poor tenants, particularly in the name of religion, the entire period of British rule in Malabar was punctuated by violent peasant uprisings of the most virulent type." Gopinathan Nair, "Education and Socio-Economic Change," 33. Malabar had been formed into a single administrative unit by the 1820s and was administered directly by the British as part of the Madras presidency, comprising today's Tamil Nadu, Malabar in northern Kerala, areas of Andhra Pradesh, and districts of Karnataka.

[115] Conrad Wood, "Peasant Revolt: An Interpretation of Moplah Violence in the Nineteenth and Twentieth Centuries," in *Peasant Resistance in India 1858–1914*, ed. David Hardiman (Delhi: Oxford University Press, 1993), 127–8.

parts of southern Malabar, until the British, who favored the landed proprietors, harshly suppressed the outbreak late that year. Elsewhere, they imposed martial law. Countering the widespread view that British rule in India was relatively benevolent, in one encounter, 200 Mappila rebels were killed. In another, 90 Mappila rebels were put in a closed railway car at Tirur on the way to jail; 64 were asphyxiated.[116] In some places, the British were forced to withdraw. Regardless, the Hindu middle classes attributed to the Indian National Congress the brunt of responsibility for the violence and blamed it for inciting a furor among uneducated Muslim peasants, even though murder, arson, and looting of Hindu property had occurred at Muslim hands. Some local leaders worked hard to restore communal harmony, but it would require two years for subsidence of the resentments against members of the Congress party from Malabar. Thus, in the background, as another mobilization began to materialize, was the notion that the reputation and credibility of the Congress could be thrown into doubt, if matters became reckless and chaotic. In 1929, occupancy rights would be granted to the tenants of Malabar by law, after which no more Mappila revolts occurred.[117]

The Indian National Congress: A Local and National Decision

The Indian National Congress had come into being in 1885 in Bombay, and was in some circles regarded as an association of effete middle-class gentlemen, from all parts of India.[118] Its members were upper-caste, often Brahmins, and generally connected with ownership of land. The ideas that it created, however, would not remain the monopoly of

---

[116] Sreedhara Menon, *Kerala and Freedom Struggle*, 67–72. Some 10,000 people may have lost their lives in the uprising, and thousands were left homeless. Menon, *Kerala and Freedom Struggle*, 70.

[117] Hardiman, introduction to *Peasant Resistance in India*, 25.

[118] This was true until the swadeshi movement in Bengal from 1905 onward. With the advent of Gandhi, the Congress became a vehicle for the assertion of many disparate communities, including peasants and untouch-ables. In Tamil Nadu, however, the leadership remained largely Brahmin, and was challenged by the Non-Brahmin movement.

a thin crust. The Congress party activated itself swiftly in Malabar, which was directly administered by the British and the target of its militancy. It would be 1919 in Travancore, however, before a committee affiliated with it would be formed, in Trivandrum, when it organized a boycott of foreign products. The party was not so much responding to popular clamor from the princely state's peoples as it was trying to counteract British policy, which sought to play off the princes against the steadily emerging nationalists. A foothold in the princely states would help the Congress to contend with the British.

At Gandhi's behest, after A. K. Pillai returned from reading the law in London, he became involved in political action in Travancore. He joined with V. Achuta Menon to begin the Congress's activities there. Within two years, Pillai (also Pillay) would organize sixty-four Congress committees and serve as the secretary of the Travancore Congress Committee.[119] Provincial Congress committees promoted the spinning of khadi, swadeshi (relying on one's own origins and environment), noncooperation, inter-dining, and opposing untouchability. Hence, the rapidly increasing social reform issues became linked to the freedom movement.

With most social mobilizations it is all but impossible to pinpoint a single event or moment for its origin, but evidence from various sources points to the aforementioned Congress meeting at Nagpur in 1920.[120] Even with multiple derivations probable, the 1920 resolution against untouchability offers a sense of historical scope. People in and around Vykom today, however, are more likely to point to the struggle's likely gestation as the late nineteenth-century efforts of outcastes to open the Vykom temple roads.

The annual session of the Congress at Nagpur in December 1920 was climactic. In addition to passage of a resolution on removal of untouchability among Hindus, it formally adopted Gandhi's program of nonviolent noncooperation with the British, based on boycotting foreign products, educational institutions, courts of law, and legislatures. (The significance of this determination should not be underestimated: discipline and preparation are necessary groundwork for using the methods

---

[119] Ramachandran Nair, *History of the Trade Union Movement in Kerala*, 12.

[120] "If you want to identify the beginning of the Vykom satyagraha, the Congress party's resolution against untouchability at the Nagpur session, in 1920, was the start." N. N. Pillai, interview (March 12, 2009). Pillai knew individual participants in the 1924–5 Vykom struggle.

of noncooperation; the withdrawal of obedience or cooperation to the target group or adversary are at the core of civil resistance.) The Congress also accepted Gandhi's constructive program, including eradication of untouchability and uplift of the Harijans; promotion of hand looming, with wearing of khadi; and popularization of Hindustani as a national language. Prohibition was also included, as the Congress sought to popularize the reduction of the number of liquor stores and the consumption of alcoholic beverages as part of the constructive program. Madhavan had been an early leader in spreading the concept of temperance in Travancore, particularly among the Ezhavas, with some success.

By 1920, with Gandhi's leadership, "the Congress was transformed from a middle class organization into a revolutionary one representing the masses," Sreedhara Menon asserts; it had become a well-organized political party for carrying out the fight for self-rule.[121] Notwithstanding the fact that major noncooperation movements were coalescing in British-controlled India, Gandhi and the Congress remained sensitive to the predicament of the maharajas, as he discloses in writing in July 1920: "Our princes are in a sorry plight. They are in the position of subjects themselves, their power and their wealth depend entirely on the British Empire and are safeguarded by it. The people living in dependencies being subjects of subjects are doubly dependents."[122]

The Congress's national mobilization aimed to change India's governance on a grand scale. In Gandhi's phrasing, "[W]e are bent on mending or ending the whole system of Government." In comparison, he is appreciably more guarded and tactical concerning the means for working to eradicate untouchability, stating, "In Travancore, the satyagrahis are not attacking a whole system. They are not attacking it at any point at all. They are fighting sacerdotal prejudice."[123] And again, "The leaders of the [Vykom] movement with a view to remedying the evil have taken up only a fragment of the evil, hoping no doubt that if they

[121] Sreedhara Menon, *Kerala and Freedom Struggle*, 65. This session also gave support to the Khilafat cause that had perturbed India's Muslims, arising from what was perceived as the dishonorable treatment by the British at the end of World War I of the sultan of Turkey, considered the caliph of Islam, thus reinforcing the vitality of the 1920 Congress gathering, and Gandhi's leadership role.

[122] Gandhi, *Madness in Junagadh*, from Gujarati, in *Navajivan*, July 11, 1920, in *CWMG*, 21: 36–7.

[123] Gandhi, "Notes: Vykom Satyagraha," April 24, 1924, in *CWMG*, 27: 284.

deal with it successfully, they will have dealt a death-blow at least in that part of India in which direct action is now going on."[124] He wanted the issue of untouchability in Travancore segmented from the larger political mobilization underway in British India:

> I do not regard this campaign as a part of the [noncooperation] movement, as such. It is certainly a part of satyagraha. But it has no direct connection with the [larger noncooperation] movement. . . . I am personally averse to Congressmen creating directly or indirectly any complications in Indian States, who are themselves no better circumstanced than British Indian subjects. A mere Resident or Political Agent is enough to frighten Rajas and Maharajas out of their wits. . . . This Vaikom movement is a socio-religious movement. It has no immediate or ulterior political motive behind it.[125]

Given Gandhi's concern that the emerging struggle should not antagonize the maharaja of Travancore, the local Congress leaders were to keep the mobilization about upper-caste temples within agreed parameters and avoid targeting the state's royal house and government.

The Congress's involvement in Travancore was to be experimental and personally supervised by Gandhi. Given the difficulty of unifying the leaders and personalities from various provinces and regions into a defined, coherent mobilization, Gandhi did not believe that a single local struggle would have sweeping effects: "Victory in Vaikom, if nonviolent, will no doubt shake the citadel of sacerdotal superstition in general, but the problem will have to be everywhere locally tackled wherever it arises."[126] His wariness about mobilizing in a princely state was also derived from a concern that if and when the Congress took part in a local matter, a precedent could be established implying that the Congress would take on district and regional grievances in 562 other states.[127]

The Congress was promoting at the national level a one-man, one-vote system, which could further reduce the influence of the upper castes. Its Working Committee on January 1, 1921, gave to the people of the princely states the right to send delegates to the annual meetings and assigned these states to contiguous provincial congresses based on

---

[124]   Gandhi, *Young India*, April 17, 1924, in *CWMG*, 27: 263.

[125]   Gandhi, interview, *Hindu*, April 17, 1924, in *CWMG*, 27: 247.

[126]   Gandhi, *Young India*, May 8, 1924, in *CWMG*, 27: 363.

[127]   Vanaja Rangaswami, *The Story of Integration: A New Interpretation in the Context of the Democratic Movements in the Princely States of Mysore, Travancore and Cochin 1900–1947* (New Delhi: Manohar, 1981), 83.

linguistic homogeneity. Travancore and Cochin were assigned to the Kerala Pradesh Congress Committee; Mysore was apportioned to the Karnataka Pradesh Congress Committee. The entry of the Congress into the princely states with a program of integration raised the priority of unity in India at the moment that British policy was trying to delink them.

The Congress party's newfound affiliation with the native states was ambiguous as to exact policy and effect. For the coming struggle in Vykom, this vagueness would be beneficial, as it would allow leaders associated with the Congress to draw upon it for strength, yet the party would not be directly involved in the princely state's politics. Gandhi said that abstention by the party did not mean nonparticipation by Congress members, who were free to work to influence a state's government. Local committees could help to guide the efforts of oppressed people but not in a clash with the maharaja's government; when they acted, they would do so as individuals.

The Congress party would reserve for itself a role as intermediary between the people of the princely state and its government, with this involvement of the Congress in Travancore its first experiment with this delimited function. This circumscribed configuration may also help to explain what has seemed to many observers in the years since to be Gandhi's comparatively forgiving and even soft outlook on south India's practices of untouchability. The efforts to persuade the maharaja's government and the upper-caste Hindus to act against untouchability and unapproachability were taking place without assistance from some of the larger political waves cresting across India.

In 1921, fees had gone up at the Maharaja's College in Trivandrum, leading to a student strike and ensuing involvement of the Congress on the side of the scholars. The government reacted with "an iron hand" in putting down the rebellion, because it reflected sympathy for the non-cooperation movement in British India.[128] This episode sparked calls for a responsible government in Travancore. It created an opening in which Madhavan began setting aside supplications, appeals, and methods designed to persuade. Instead, he began to advocate nonviolent direct action as the way of tackling untouchability, to make focused

---

[128] Sreedhara Menon, *Survey of Kerala History*, 357. The student strike was repressed with *force majeure*, as it was "the first manifestation of the Gandhian technique." Ravindran, *Vaikkam Satyagraha and Gandhi*, 147–8. Also see Menon, *History of the Freedom Movement in Kerala*, 105–12.

interventions to challenge road and temple-entry policies.[129] He claimed that left unaddressed, the Ezhavas would begin to violate laws and use the roads encircling temples, even entering temples for worship. Madhavan and his allies undertook to organize a campaign for not only walking the temple roads but also contesting the proscribed entry of outcastes into Brahmin temples. In just months, the Ezhava movement took on a different complexion.

At the forefront of this incipience stood the SNDP Yogam, led by Palpu, Asan, and Madhavan, who would give the growing social movement a sharpened political and civic context. Actions by these and others included the passing of resolutions within respective organizations, protest meetings, submitting petitions, distributing literature, and additional methods of protest and persuasion. Meetings were being held at an assortment of places. At one session in Changanacherry (also Changanassery), A. K. Parameswaran Pillai, a former high court judge, articulated "feelings of concern and sympathy" for avarnas, expressed on behalf of savarnas. Groups such as the Kerala Hindu Sabha, the Nair Service Society (of which Pillai had been a long-term president), Yogakshema Sabha (the leading organization of Nambudiri Brahmins), and the Kshatriya Mahasaba had spoken of their support.[130] The Nambudiri Yogakshema Sabha, started in 1910–11 with a goal of ending obsolete social conventions, had at its annual sessions passed resolutions in support of opening temples to avarnas.[131] The government did not exhibit enthusiasm for maintaining the exclusions, but neither was it promoting any alterations.

---

[129] Nonviolent direct action may refer to acts of omission and commission that are purposefully conducted without physical violence, in which the nonviolent contenders embark on (1) acts of omission, in which they refuse to undertake acts that they normally perform, are customarily expected to do, or are obligated by law or regulations to fulfil; or (2) acts of commission, in which people may insist on performing acts that they do not usually perform, are not customarily expected to make, or are prohibited by law or regulation from performing; or (3) both. Gene Sharp, "A Study of the Meanings of Nonviolence," in *Gandhi: His Relevance for Our Times*, eds. G. Ramachandran and T. K. Mahadevan, 2nd ed. (New Delhi: Bharatiya Vidya Bhavan; Bombay: Gandhi Peace Foundation, 1967), 27–8.

[130] Ravindran, *Vaikkam Satyagraha and Gandhi*, 50; Desai, *Epic of Travancore*, 11.

[131] Desai, *Epic of Travancore*, 11.

3 The Satyagraha

The stage was set for the Vykom satyagraha by south India's broad activation of campaigns against unapproachability, untouchability, and the various prohibitions placed on the excluded classes of the social hierarchy, plus their antecedents in the late nineteenth and early twentieth centuries. Numerous organizations and leaders had been making significant contributions leading up to the Vykom endeavor. Caste associations and their predecessors were hard at work. Sri Narayana Dharma Paripalana Yogam (SNDP Yogam) at its meetings had diligently been passing resolutions demanding temple entry. The poet Kumaran Asan's efforts in the Travancore Legislative Council forced the issue of temple roads onto the council's deliberations in 1922. Still, the princely state's government dithered. When a few Ezhavas walked through the roads on the northern and western sides of the Vykom temple's outer walls on May 5, 1922, no purification ceremony was conducted afterward to cleanse the supposed pollution, and the trespassers were not prosecuted.[1] Gandhi had since 1920 been unrelenting in his opposition to untouchability. Missionaries continued to promote its end.

---

[1] T. K. Ravindran, *Vaikkam Satyagraha and Gandhi* (Trichur, India: Sri Narayana Institute of Social and Cultural Development, 1975), 42–4, 45, 50.

The 1923 Kakinada Congress

The Indian National Congress customarily held its annual conference in different cities. Seeking to re-establish its credibility after the bloody Mappila rebellion of 1921–2, the Congress had Madhavan, through the SNDP Yogam, arrange a meeting of the party in south India not far from the areas of the Mappila upheaval, to neutralize the taint of revolt spilling onto it from the unrest. On December 23, 1923, the yearly session was held in Kakinada (Cocanada), in Karnataka state, the adjacent state to what is now Kerala, close to its present border. It was the thirty-eighth session of the Indian National Congress, presided over by Maulana Muhamed Ali.

At the gathering, attended by Sardar K. M. Panikkar, K. P. Kesava Menon, and T. K. Madhavan, Panikkar introduced Madhavan, describing the situation in Travancore and indicating that the government, more so than Hindu orthodoxy, was impeding the hopes of untouchables to enter the temples there.[2] Madhavan had not initially been active in the Congress, but had concluded that Gandhi and the Congress could benefit his cause, especially after his negative experience with the League for Equal Civil Rights. In addition, fear of reprisals had led many Ezhavas to retreat, so Madhavan had little choice but to turn to the Congress for support in galvanizing the movement.

Ali had invited Madhavan to attend the Working Committee as a special guest, as he had not yet formally enrolled in the Congress. Madhavan circulated a letter calling for "creative action"—invoking Gandhi's concept of the constructive program—for the eradication of untouchability in India. Seizing upon opportunity, he moved a resolution to establish the Kerala Aithochodana, or Anti-Untouchability, Committee and asked that the Congress formulate programs to combat untouchability.

Despite the promotion of efforts by the Congress against untouchability, divisions existed about how the organization should pursue its political and social goals, with steep differences of opinion between Congress leaders, and divergence of opinion in the Anti-Untouchability

[2] Sardar Kavalam Madhava Panikkar served the colonial Indian princely states, including as foreign minister of Patiala princely state and chief minister of Bikaner princely state. Chancellor of the Chamber of Princes, which convened the rulers of the princely states, he was known as "Sardar" K. M. Panikkar, in this context indicating his position as a respectable ruler.

Committee. Early national Congress leaders had believed that social concerns, such as untouchability, should rank below national independence, which ought to be the main point. Others did not want their energies squandered on social reform, thinking it would weaken their quest for political freedom. Gandhi had assigned a central place to the removal of untouchability in the constructive program, but the Congress had not immediately embarked on actions to achieve it, though it would pass several resolutions over the years.

In 1917, a broader vision of the national struggle had crystallized in the Congress and included overtly fighting caste divisions; that year the party at its annual session in Calcutta passed a resolution concerning "the necessity, justice and righteousness of removing all disabilities by custom on the oppressed classes." As noted, in Nagpur in 1920, the Congress passed a resolution urging access for untouchables to temples. In the December 1921 Congress session in Ahmedabad, and again in 1922 at Bardoli, resolutions were similarly passed to ban untouchability. The Bardoli meeting also resulted in the Congress adopting the constructive program. This represented an about-face, partially attributable to Gandhi but also reflective of a computation of how the Congress could build a mass movement. Some now saw temple entry as one of the Congress's significant concerns. As a result of the Kakinada Congress, the fight against untouchability moved onto the main agenda of provincial Congress committees.

The measures taken by the Kakinada Congress had more resonance in what is today Kerala than in other places, not just because the problem of untouchability was worse there, but because there were already local movements that had gained critical public awareness. Indeed, the mounting efforts of people like Madhavan had considerably predisposed the delegates of the Kakinada Congress and were a factor in the party's embrace of the anti-untouchability program. The committee against untouchability created at Kakinada was scheduled to hold its first meeting in 1924.

The Anti-Untouchability Committee Takes Action: Preparations for the Satyagraha

The Kerala Provincial Congress Committee (KPCC) met on January 24, 1924, in Ernakulam and selected Koyapalli Kelappan as the convener for the first meeting of the Anti-Untouchability Committee, as planned.

K. Kelappan Nair was a Malabar Nair who had worked in Travancore in the past and was the founding president of the Nair Service Society, a pressure group for reform among Nairs of central and northern T. He helped to start the *Mathrubhumi* (Motherland) newspaper in nearby Calicut and was its editor for some years. He came to believe it better to drop permanently his caste name "Nair."[3] In addition to Kelappan, the committee comprised T. K. Madhavan, Kurur Nilakantan Nambudiripad (also transliterated as Kurur Neelakantan Namboodiripad), T. K. Krishna Swamy Iyyer (also Krishnaswamy/Krishnaswami Aiyar), and Kannathodathu Velayudha Menon.[4] Another Malabar Nair, Kizhakke Potta (K. P.) Kesava Menon, was instrumental in founding the *Mathrubhumi*, became its chief editor, and was president of the KPCC.

On February 6, 1924, the Anti-Untouchability Committee met at Quilon and adopted a resolution to attempt "to eradicate untouchability through all just and peaceful means."[5] The members developed a plan for "intensive propaganda"[6]—that is, extensive work to spread information among the public. The plan included the submission of a "monster petition" to the maharajas of Travancore and its neighboring state of Cochin, observation of a Hindu festival to promote anti-untouchability activities,

[3] P. K. Karunakara Menon, *The History of the Freedom Movement in Kerala*, 2 vols. (1600–1885; 1885–1938) (Trivandrum: Regional Records Survey Committee, Government of Kerala, 1970), 116n2. K. Kelappan Nair will hereafter be referred to as K. Kelappan.

[4] P. Chandramohan, "Social and Political Protest in Travancore: A Study of the Sree Narayana Dharma Paripalana Yogam (1900–1938)" (M.A. diss., Centre for Historical Studies, School of Social Sciences, Jawaharlal Nehru University, 1981), 251n3.

[5] K. N. Panikkar, "Vaikkam Satyagraha: The Struggle against Untouchability," in *We Fought Together for Freedom: Chapters from the Indian National Movement*, ed. Ravi Dayal (Delhi: Oxford University Press and Indian Council of Historical Research, 1995), 130.

[6] In India in the 1920s, English speakers used the word "propaganda" in close alignment with its original sense, meaning to reproduce and disseminate. This was accomplished through publicity and getting out the news. At a most fundamental level, intensive public communication strategies are important in any nonviolent struggle, because public information can be essential to help the target group to comprehend the nature of the claimants' criticism, whether related to policy, changing practices, or addressing grievances. Equally, it can be critical for the challengers' recruitment, messaging, and ability to reach a wider public.

mixed meetings of *avarnas* and *savarnas*, and processions into public thoroughfares and prohibited roads. The idea was to appeal to as wide a cross-section of caste Hindus as feasible. The primary demand would be for the right of access for avarna Hindus to the Nambudiri Brahmin temple roads in the village of Vykom. The upper castes accurately perceived this as the opening bid for a list of demands that could only expand.

Shortly after the Quilon meeting, K. Kelappan, K. P. Kesava Menon, Kurur Nilakantan Namboodiripad, and A. K. Pillai set off on the propaganda tour in Travancore, going from village to village to urge the formation of an anti-untouchability committee in every village. Throughout the region, the four proponents recruited volunteers and collected funds. By February 28, the committee members had reached Vykom, the place chosen for their inaugural campaign. According to P. K. Karunakara Menon, "The news of the impending Satyagraha greatly stirred the people as it was a novel method of action so far not resorted to in South India."[7]

Why Vykom?

Vykom was selected for beginning the work against untouchability, in Ravindran's words, "because it was the worst spot where the evils of untouchability and unapproachability were preserved in their pristine purity."[8] Of Travancore's twenty small towns, Vykom, in the northern part of the princely state, was easily accessible by water and roads from the neighboring princely state of Cochin. Four roads, one from each cardinal direction, led directly to the temple dedicated to Lord Shiva at the town center.

The temple is enclosed within four walls; the entire temple area consists of about ten acres. The main gate stands on the western side of the compound. The connecting roads encircling the outer walls of the temple compound were used for processions and ceremonies, but did not lead directly to the temple. Access to these roads by Ezhavas, Pulayas, and other non-caste Hindus was restricted to specific points specified by *teendal palakas*. Apart from the inherent social injustice, the

---

[7] Menon, *History of the Freedom Movement in Kerala*, 117. The group visited Alleppy, Balaramapuram, Chengannur, Changanachery, Quilon, Kayamkulam, Kottayam, Mavelikara, Nagercoil, Padmanabhapuram, Tiruvalla, and Trivandrum. Menon, *History of the Freedom Movement in Kerala*, 116n2.

[8] Ravindran, *Vaikkam Satyagraha and Gandhi*, 53.

distance restrictions meant that untouchables had to take longer routes to reach their quarters, where their abodes were segregated. Others—Christians, Jews, and Muslims—encountered no such restrictions.

In the mid-nineteenth century, an incident whose memory lives on occurred at the temple. As historian Vasu Thillari recounts the event, four or five members of the "backward castes" had tried to enter the temple, whereupon, "[u]pper-caste men killed them and threw their corpses in the pond adjacent to the temple." Although no written records substantiate this oral history, this attempted entry may have been the first assertion of the rights of untouchables and thus an antecedent to the Vykom satyagraha.[9] A local folk historian, N. K. Jose, disputes the number and reports that the local residents of Vykom consider that approximately 100 lower-caste men were killed. According to Jose, "Everyone in the vicinity of Vykom knows about this incident, even though there is no memorial."[10] The pond still stands at the northern gate.

In the twentieth century, wealthy, educated, and able Ezhavas, such as Padmanabhan Palpu, were still unable to use roads in their areas,

---

[9] Vasu Thilleri, interview (Kozhikode [Calicut], Kerala, August 11, 2005).

[10] N. K. Jose, interview (Vykom, August 14, 2005).

It was only in Vykom that even a hundred years before the Vykom satyagraha started, the backward castes not only used the public roads and prepared to enter the temple and worship, but also lost their lives for it. The pond in which the bodies of those who gave up their lives were buried is even now known as Dalavakkulam (translated as Dalava pond). Though the next generations of the then untouchables who were mostly living in Vykom municipality transformed the burial place of their forefathers into a private municipal bus stand, they still gave it the name of Dalavakkulam bus stand.

N. K. Jose, *Vaikom Sathyagraham Oru Prahelika* [*Vykom Satyagraha: A Question that Bothers Us*], trans. Dinoo Anna Mathew, from Malayalam (Kottayam: Hobby Publishers, 2005), 9.

Further: "A hundred years back, during the time of Veluthampi, when the Ezhavars had embarked on a similar activity (Pulayamahayogam, a big meeting of the Pulayars) in Vykom, Vykom Pathmanabha Pilla and the co-workers of Veluthampi including Kuthirapakki, murdered them and buried them in a pond. This is the Dalavakkulam (Dalava pond) that is still seen there today." Jose, *Vaikom Sathyagraham*, 45. Jose's information has not been substantiated in the published literature.

despite enjoying respect from the savarnas. Palpu would later write to Gandhi in 1925 that the right to "walk through the public road is one that even dogs and pigs enjoy everywhere without having to resort to any satyagraha at all."[11] As noted, the Ezhavas, while often agricultural workers, were also active in commerce and trading, with some becoming prosperous. The proscription of roads was an impediment to conducting business; the humiliation of distance pollution also affected self-respect.

On February 29, in Vykom, the Anti-Untouchability Committee held a public meeting attended by a large number of Ezhavas and Pulayas in addition to the high-caste Hindus. The principal speakers were Kesava Menon, Pillai, and Madhavan.[12] Apart from denunciations of untouchability, the meeting's leaders announced at its conclusion that a large group of persons of all castes or those of no caste would on March 1 proceed from the boat jetty to the western gate of the Shiva temple and march on the roads around the temple, pausing for a few minutes at various stops to worship.

Some wanted the march deferred until March 30, to improve preparations, allow time for publicity and soliciting of opinions, and secure participation from national figures. George Joseph and others believed that "insufficient effort had been expended in educating all and particularly high-caste Hindus about the enormity of the evils of untouchability and the urgent need for reforms." Joseph, a barrister, believed that the struggle should be waged as a "civic rights" issue so that all inhabitants could have free access to public roads, instead of making it a question of temple entry. He considered that this distinction had not been amply aired.[13]

The Anti-Untouchability Committee appealed to the Travancore government to no avail to throw open the temple roads, while the temple

---

[11] Chandramohan, "Social and Political Protest in Travancore," as cited on 234, 234n4, letter of April 21, 1925, to Mohandas K. Gandhi, Dr. Padmanabhan Palpu Papers, Nehru Memorial Library, New Delhi, file no. 1, 4.

[12] Ravindran, *Vaikkam Satyagraha and Gandhi*, 53. George Joseph was invited to address the session but could not attend. George Gheverghese Joseph, *George Joseph: The Life and Times of a Kerala Christian Nationalist* (Hyderabad: Orient Longman), 163.

[13] Joseph, *George Joseph*, 164. "Civic rights" is the biographer's wording.

authorities maintained that any infringement of custom would bring bloodshed. Whether due to insufficient debate, callousness, or the rigidity of their ideology, the temple officials and savarna leaders were implacable in their opposition. The government appeared to be complicit in disagreeing with any accommodation of the mobilization. Conservative Hindus made plans to defend the road. Sensing this reaction, local officials persuaded the committee to postpone the planned procession to March 30.

Kesava Menon wrote to Gandhi on March 12, advising him of a planned procession of Ezhavas and Pulayas on a temple road. "Contrary to popular belief," George Gheverghese Joseph asserts, expressing a widely held view, "the Vaikkom Satyagraha was not initiated by Gandhi. It was practically forced on him by actions taken by people of different castes and creeds within Travancore."[14] Gandhi had, in early 1924, been released from prison and was recovering in Juhu near Bombay (Mumbai) from illness and an operation for appendicitis. He declined to assume an active leadership position in the movement, but agreed to offer guidance. From Bombay on March 19, Gandhi sent Kesava Menon a letter of approval, offering advice:

> I know that the condition of the suppressed classes in your part of India is quite pitiable. As you say, they are not merely untouchable, but they may not walk through certain streets. Their condition is truly deplorable. I do not wonder that we have not yet attained swaraj. . . . a species of satyagraha. . . . There should be no show of force if any of our people oppose their progress. You should meekly submit and take all the beating, if any. Everyone taking part in the procession should be acquainted with the conditions and be prepared to fulfill them. There should be only a limited number. There should be no defiance, and if you find that the processionists are not likely to comply with the conditions, there should be no hesitation in postponing the procession. I fear that we have not canvassed enough the opponents of the reform.[15]

Gandhi's message heeds caution and nonviolent action. It does not approve a full-fledged civil disobedience campaign in Travancore. "The success of the struggle depends not on any vain spirit of bravado," Gandhi said in the *Hindu* newspaper, "but upon the silent preparation

[14] Joseph, *George Joseph*, 159.
[15] Gandhi, Letter to K. P. Kesava Menon, in *Collected Works of Mahatma Gandhi* (hereafter *CWMG*), 27: 82–3.

and solid organization behind the campaign ensuring non-violence and the enlistment of the sympathy of the disinterested public."[16]

Meanwhile, at a session of the Sri Mulam Popular Assembly, several members raised the issue of untouchables using temple roads. During the debates, the legal positions of the reformers and the orthodox took clear form. The advocates for change argued that the roadways in question were in effect public, given that they were maintained with funds from the state treasury. The orthodox opposition held that the temple roads were private, falling within the jurisdiction of the *devaswom* (temple authorities), which managed all caste-Hindu temples, facilities, infrastructure, and property. Karuva S. Krishnan Asan, a nominated (government-appointed) member of the assembly referred to the "mischievous activity" of some Ezhavas and spoke at length about their "questionable" activities, as they sought to "poison the mind of the Government." Asan articulated an unsurprising concern for upholding public order:

> [S]ome people were having recourse to methods of non-co-operation, passive resistance, etc., for securing privileges not hitherto enjoyed. As such conduct on their part was likely to lead to a breach of the peace in the country, he [Asan] hoped that the Government would take the necessary precautionary measures and suggested that all those who were in receipt of any recognition from the Government should be warned not to join or countenance any such action on pain of forfeiture of the privileges enjoyed by them.[17]

Whatever publicity had been generated did not produce the expected support for reform. Orthodox opposition, led primarily by the Savarna Mahajana Sabha, the upper-caste people's assembly, was intense. It presented several representations and petitions to authorities on behalf of the Nambudiris, reiterating the prohibition of the avarnas from temple roads. Responding to such pressure, the district magistrate issued a prohibitory order against opening the temple roads based on section 127 of the Criminal Procedure Code of Travancore.

---

[16] Gandhi, *Hindu*, March 24, 1924, as cited in Ravindran, *Vaikkam Satyagraha and Gandhi*, 54.

[17] *Proceedings of the Twentieth Session of the Sri Mulam Popular Assembly of Travancore* (hereafter *SMPA*) (Trivandrum: Superintendent, Government Press, 1924), 211–12.

Meetings were conducted for and against the anti-untouchability movement, as two deputations from the assembly departed for the capital Trivandrum, reflecting these contrasting positions. "From all accounts," Ravdindran states, "it is clear that the party in favour of the reform was much larger and stronger than the conservative group who wanted to perpetuate the injustice done to the avarnas for centuries."[18]

As the date for the satyagraha approached, the maharaja instructed the *dewan* and police commissioner to take precautions to prevent violent clashes. In accordance, on March 26, four days prior to the rescheduled date of the demonstration, the district magistrate ordered the police to set up pickets and barricades of bamboo poles and to stand guard at the notice boards of the restricted temple roads. The magistrate called these actions preventive measures to avert outbreaks of conflict between the *satyagrahis* and enraged orthodox Hindus.[19] Kesava Menon and other leaders arrived in Vykom on March 27. They included Changanacherry K. Parameswaran Pillai (who had been a president of the Nair Service Society), M. N. Nair, C. V. Kunjuraman, Alummootil Channar, and Mannath Padmanabha Pillai (whose father, a Nambudiri, had founded the Nair Service Society in 1914).

The Kottayam newspaper *Malayala Manorama* shows that it regarded both Pillais as preeminent leaders in the Nair community. Decades later N. N. Pillai remembered Mannath Padmanabha Pillai as general secretary for a half century and leader of the Nair Service Society, as "a very powerful speaker of a large organization of colleges and scholars. He took the initiative for the untouchability program and was the first among the caste Hindus of the Vykom area to take a lower caste, a Pulaya, to his home, where his mother washed the plate on which the Pulayas ate."[20]

As Madhavan, Kesava Menon, and the other leaders arrived, they were each served with the prohibitory order. Issuance of this

---

[18] Ravindran, *Vaikkam Satyagraha and Gandhi*, 56.

[19] Robin Jeffrey, "Travancore: Status, Class and the Growth of Radical Politics, 1860–1940, the Temple-Entry Movement," in *People, Princes and Paramount Power: Society and Politics in the Indian Princely States*, ed. Robin Jeffrey (New Delhi: Oxford University Press), 152, 167n48, citing "Official Note Regarding the Vycome Satyagraha with the Remarks of the Officer in Charge of the Administration Thereon," April 17, 1924, Travancore Records, Vaikom Bundle, no. 1.

[20] N. N. Pillai, interview (March 12, 2009).

notification had the effect of altering the planned march from an action of protest and persuasion—for some it was a form of personal witness—into an implicit if unplanned act of civil disobedience, because any action would now involve breaching the governmental edict. Ironically, if the prohibitory order had not been issued, the march might have proceeded calmly through the roads, keenly watched by journalists and bystanders, yet the Congress may have lost part of its justification for supporting a major struggle in Vykom.

The Congress committee had set up an initial camp for the volunteers arriving at Vykom, to which large numbers of young men thronged. Volunteers initially registered at a temporary office, coming as they often did through a connection to the Indian National Congress. It was in a modest shed, most likely with a thatched roof of coconut leaves. With the Vykom satyagraha meant to start on March 30 and in order to appeal to as many caste Hindus as possible, Kesava Menon announced publicly that he would break the law by drawing near the temple in the company of Hindus who were not allowed to do so.

The Satyagraha Begins

On March 30, a conch shell bugled the volunteers to wake at 7:30 A.M. The message that Gandhi had sent was read aloud, instructing the volunteers to refrain from resorting to force, even if attacked, and including his admonition that the procession be postponed if deviation from such discipline appeared probable. From the first day, Gandhi sought to control the direction of the struggle strictly in accordance with his rudimentary standards for satyagraha. Having adopted the umbrella of the Indian National Congress and with leadership from T. K. Madhavan, K. P. Kesava Menon, Kannathodathu Velayudha Menon, K. Kelappan, Kurur Nilakantan Namboodiripad, and George Joseph, the Vykom satyagraha began, its defined purpose to open the roads surrounding the place of worship, which had been closed to the excluded groups.

A large crowd gathered as the participants in the procession assembled. People from across southern India were arriving, assembling themselves in rows, two abreast, to walk toward the prohibited roads surrounding the Shiva Temple. In the lead were T. K. Madhavan, A. K. Pillai, Krishna Swamy Iyyer (also Krishnaswami Iyer), K. Kelappan, and Velayudha Menon. Following the leaders were the ebullient volunteers, led by K. P. Kesava

Menon. Estimates of the crowd size vary, and a relatively accurate estimate may forever remain elusive; some accounts say that those attempting to use the roads numbered in the thousands. Ravindran describes the atmosphere as redolent of "the burning odour of nationalist sentiment."[21]

The demonstrators stopped approximately twenty yards from the prohibited demarcation and notice boards. From their number, three khadi-wearing volunteers—Kunjapy (a Pulaya), Banuleyan (an Ezhava), and Govinda Panicker (a Nair)—were sent forward, wearing garlands around their necks (Fig. 2). Volunteers who enlisted were either loosely or directly involved with the Congress's untouchability program and would have been aware of the larger connotations of wearing homespun khadi, including the identification with self-respect flowing from constructive work and solidarity with the poor. They had been preparing themselves for the campaign, taking classes, and learning Gandhi's discipline of not reciprocating any violence inflicted upon them.

"The calm and solemn appearance of the volunteers added luster to the brightness of the morning hour," Ravindran exudes. "When this batch of three proceeded alone towards the prohibited lines, the human walls on the road-sides vibrated with suppressed excitement. As the batch reached the line where the prohibited line began, the volunteers were stopped by the police." The large contingent of police would permit only Panicker, the sole savarna, to continue.

When he refused to detach himself from his fellow demonstrators, the three men quietly sat down before the pickets. After an hour of what Ravindran calls a "stately struggle of opposite wills," police arrested the three men.[22] The *Mathrubhumi* gave the episode a full page.[23] On March 31, another threesome, a Nair and two Ezhavas, walked to the disallowed demarcation and were arrested.[24] On that date, according to P. K. K.

[21] Ravindran, *Vaikkam Satyagraha and Gandhi*, 58.

[22] Ravindran, *Vaikkam Satyagraha and Gandhi*, 58.

[23] "The Beginning of the Vykom Satyagraha: The Awakening among the Polluted Castes—A Pulaya, an Ezhava, and a Nair Were Arrested," *Mathrubhumi* (trans. from Malayalam by Vasu Thilleri), April 1, 1924, p. 3. Thilleri, associate professor of history, Pocker Sahib Memorial Orphanage College, Tirurangadi, Malappuram (DT) near Calicut, transliterates the names of the three arrestees as Kunhappa, Bahuleyan, and Gobinda Panikkar. Thilleri, interview (Kozhikode [Calicut], March 17, 2009). Kunhappa is also transliterated as Kunhappy.

[24] Ravindran, *Vaikkam Satyagraha and Gandhi*, 58–9.

Figure 2   On March 30, 1924, first day of the Vykom satyagraha, three volunteers of mixed-caste status approached the bamboo pole barriers erected by police in order to halt passage of so-called untouchables onto the forbidden temple roads (Illustrated by Madanan Pv)

Note: Wearing garlands and the homespun cotton of the nationalist movement, three volunteers garbed according to their status in the caste system—a Pulaya (formerly a slave echelon), an Ezhava, and a Nair from the upper castes—were sent forward but barred from proceeding.

Menon, K. P. Kesava Menon moved forward in the company of Madhavan and a volunteer, whereupon they were arrested, sentenced to six months imprisonment, and dispatched to the central jail in Trivandrum.[25]

On April 1, Gandhi received a telegram from K. P. Kesava Menon:

VAIKOM SATYAGRAHA STARTED YESTERDAY. THREE VOLUNTEERS PEACEFULLY ENTER-
ING PROHIBITED AREA WERE ARRESTED. THEIR DIGNIFIED BEHAVIOUR GREATLY
IMPRESSED PUBLIC. CONDUCT OF POLICE PRAISEWORTHY. ANOTHER BATCH THREE
PROCEEDED TODAY ALSO ARRESTED. ORDERLY CROWDS WITNESSING SATYAGRAHA
EVERY DAY. FIRST BATCH SENTENCED SIX MONTHS.[26]

[25] Menon, *History of the Freedom Movement in Kerala*, 118. Ravindran gives no names in *Vaikkam Satyagraha and Gandhi*, 58–9. Menon's date for Kesava Menon and Madhavan's arrest conflicts with other accounts.

[26] K. P. Kesava Menon to Gandhi, telegram, received April 1, 1924, in *CWMG*, 27: 146, note 2, S.N. 10265.

The police were informed that the same procedure would be duplicated each morning by the action takers until those with no caste were permitted to use the temple roads.[27]

The *Mathrubhumi*

The *Mathrubhumi* (Motherland) had been founded in 1923 in nearby Calicut with the mission of advancing the position of the Indian National Congress and serving the nationalist purpose.[28] It became a standard-bearer of the Vykom satyagraha, closely covering it for the duration of the struggle. According to K. Gopalankutty:

> One of the reasons why *Mathrubhumi* was started was the 1921 Mappila revolt. This Mappila revolt took the Indian National Congress by surprise, because they had been propagating nonviolent struggle, and this rebellion was very violent. They felt that the riot had gone out of their control and they couldn't do anything about it. One reason why it became violent, according to the Congress leaders at that time, is that they were unable to propagate Gandhian ideals of nonviolence. They thought, let's start a newspaper to promote Gandhi's views on nonviolence.[29]

For twenty months, the *Mathrubhumi* published news accounts from Vykom three times a week and carried at least one editorial on the events at Vykom in each edition; it also published editorials from other newspapers. A year later in Malabar, Muhammed Abdur Rahiman began publishing *al-Amin* with the purpose of raising the spirit of nationalism, especially among Muslims. A group of individuals who were nationalists was behind *Mathrubhumi*, Gopalankutty emphasized. "They were not for profit, and made this clear in their first editorial in 1923, in which the *Mathrubhumi* quotes Gandhi as saying that there is not to be motivation by profit, that the newspaper is not to be run in a commercial way, and that its motivation should be service—in the cause of the nation."[30] Additionally, the *Malayala Manorama* in

[27]   Robin Jeffrey, "Temple-Entry Movement, 1860–1940," *Social Scientist* 4, no. 8 (March): 15, citing the *Hindu*, March 31, 1924.

[28]   A. Sreedhara Menon, *Kerala and Freedom Struggle* (Kottayam: D C Books, 1997), 147.

[29]   K. Gopalankutty, interview (Calicut, Kerala, August 11, 2005). Gopalankutty is reader in history, Department of History, University of Calicut, Kerala.

[30]   Gopalankutty, interview (August 11, 2005).

Kottayam had a policy of fighting for acknowledgment of the political claims of forgotten communities.

Newspapers were ardently read. By 1905, Travancore had more than twenty Malayalam and English papers. Their reach was far greater than the circulation. Gopalankutty explained:

A landlord or wealthy person would buy a paper, and it would be read out to a group. Another would sponsor a copy of the paper for a library or reading room, where it would be read out loud. . . . *Mathrubhumi* had an advantage: Kerala is the most literate state in India; literacy rates were very high, compared to other districts in the Madras presidency. A literate public went back to the late nineteenth century.[31]

The *Mathrubhumi* executives exploited their unique asset to work on the state's liability as they saw it, making it one of a moderate number of small newspapers that were pro-nationalist, pro-reform, and able to play a constructive role in the Vykom engagement. Others, published by the landowning class, were in opposition.

The authorities sought unsuccessfully to silence the *Malayala Manorama* and *Mathrubhumi*. "During the dark days of the [freedom] struggle the *Mathrubhumi* shone as the guiding star of inspiration," P. K. K. Menon notes, "carrying out its task as an instrument of social will and national dedication, without fear or favour and without personal or communal considerations."[32] During the 1920s the *Mathrubhumi's* editors and managers considered Vykom as their own struggle, because theirs was a newspaper of the Congress, and figures prominent in running the paper were influential in the party and also leaders of the struggle.[33] The daily is still run by a collective, and boasts of a progressive nationalist outlook.

---

[31] Gopalankutty, interview (August 11, 2005).

[32] Menon, *History of the Freedom Movement in Kerala*, 519.

[33] Thilleri, interview (August 11, 2005). *Mathrubhumi* could openly support the movement, partly because of its location in the Malabar district. A newspaper published from the British Indian territory had more freedom to take positions and support movements than in the princely states. *Malayala Manorama* newspaper was published from Kottayam, a territory under the direct control of the Travancore government, and it supported the struggle for responsible government in Travancore. In revenge, Sir C. P. Ramaswamy Iyer, the dewan of Travancore, banned the *Malayala Manorama*, and K. C. Mamman Mappilai, its chief editor, was thrown into prison. Justin Mathew, communication, October 14, 2010.

The *Mathrubhumi* offers a contemporaneous historical record of the satyagraha. Its first article on the Vykom campaign, datelined April 1, 1924, takes up the entire third page and reports that volunteers from across the country are proceeding to Vykom to take part in the movement. It also editorializes that the first day's struggle was free of incidents and that although it was expected that the volunteers would violate the government's prohibitory order, they did not. Observing that the police were friendly, it says the first day passed peacefully.[34]

Gandhi Advises from Afar

Not surprisingly, the attention garnered by the satyagraha and the police involvement exacerbated the frustrations of orthodox upper-caste Hindus. In response, on the advice of a few notables from Vykom, the Anti-Untouchability Committee leaders decided to suspend activities for a few days. Seizing an opportunity, the orthodox opposition sent two representatives to meet with Gandhi to persuade him that the roads in question were private and that continuing the satyagraha would cause the Indian National Congress to become an enemy of the orthodox community. The *Mathrubhumi* published a letter that Gandhi wrote to Kesava Menon on April 1, 1924, after meeting with two Nambudiri brothers from Vykom who had traveled to see Gandhi at his ashram in Andheri, a suburb of Mumbai:

> Messrs Shivram Iyer and Vancheswara Iyer have come here in connection with your satyagraha. They tell me that the roads in dispute are private property belonging to the temple which they lead and that it is in exclusive possession of Brahmin trustees who, these gentlemen claim, have perfect right to regulate entry. I then asked them if these roads were private property, exclusively belonging to the Brahmins, whether any non-Brahmins had the use of them, and they admitted that they had. I then told them that, so long as a single non-Brahmin was allowed the use of the roads, the so-called untouchables and unapproachable[s] must have the same right as other non-Brahmins. They agree, but they say that it will take some time before they can bring round to their view of thinking

[34] Editorial, "The Beginning of Satyagraha," *Mathrubhumi* (trans. Thilleri), April 1, 1924, 4.

the trustees and other Brahmins who are interested in temple and roads.[35]

The paper reported that Gandhi advised his supporters in Travancore to seek a compromise. Gandhi did not, however, accept the Iyer siblings' arguments; rather, he was more concerned that the Anti-Untouchabily Committee had not done enough preparatory work to sway the opinions of the higher castes in Vykom, a "serious defect" of which, Ravindran says, "Gandhi was well aware."[36] Gandhi suggested that it might be prudent for the organizers of the endeavor to suspend the satyagraha for a period and perhaps wait until Pandit Madan Mohan Malaviya could visit to mediate within two months.[37] Gandhi would several times in the course of the events of 1924–5 express his hopes for the intercession of Malaviya, a renowned educator, Hindu nationalist, Brahmin from Uttar Pradesh, and proponent of unfettered temple entry, who would serve as president of the Indian National Congress for three different terms.

Gandhi's advice to postpone activities and wait for mediation came from his desire to bring about change through persuasion, preserving social harmony. He was seeking what he called "conversion" of the targeted group by acting upon their thoughts and emotions—today termed attitudinal change. Gandhi had written about conversion in *Young India* on April 2:

> For the opening of the roads is not the final but the first step in the ladder of reform. Temples in general, public wells, public schools, must be open to the "untouchables" equally with the caste Hindus. But that is not the present goal of the Satyagrahis. We may not force the pace. The schools are almost all open to the "untouchables." The temples and the public wells or tanks are not. Public opinion should be converted before the reform can be successfully carried out. . . . I have no doubt that the

[35] Gandhi, Letter to K. P. Kesava Menon, April 1, 1924, in *CWMG*, 27: 145.

[36] Ravindran, *Vaikkam Satyagraha and Gandhi*, 59.

[37] "The Vykom Satyagraha: Mahatmaji's Letter," *Mathrubhumi* (trans. Thilleri), April 8, 1924, 5. The delay in publishing Gandhi's April 1 letter on April 8 was due to the limited postal system, dating to the nineteenth century. Thilleri, interview (August 11, 2005). A *pandit* is a scholar or master, traditionally a scholar or teacher of Sanskrit and the Veda scriptures, almost always a Hindu Brahmin. The word has been absorbed into English as *pundit*.

movement for the removal of untouchability has made tremendous
headway. Let us not retard it by indiscretion or over-zeal. Once the idea
of pollution by the touch of a person by reason of his birth is gone the
rest is easy and bound to follow.[38]

Meanwhile, when the satyagrahis actively engaged in Gandhi's
"experiment" were away from the temple roads, they passed the time in
their ashram, a temporary shed in poor condition said to have been
donated by Sri Narayana Guru and formerly used by the SNDP Yogam
as a meeting house. A Trivandrum newspaper reported otherwise: "The
asram at Vycome is built on the S.N.D.P. Yogam land. But it was done
without the Guru's knowledge and sanction, although after the act, he
was informed of it. If the movement was begun with his permission, if
the initiative came from him, he could have been associated with the
movement."[39] Eventually, Guru gave formal blessings to the Vykom
mobilization, and it was even said that he was seeking donations to
support the satyagraha.

Deadlock

The dewan visited the ashram on April 18 and offered to provide more
convenient roads for the public, including for untouchables. A local
newspaper correspondent said that the leaders had as their only objective "to establish a right of way over the prohibited roads."[40] The satyagraha leaders believed that their moment had come and continued to
inform Gandhi of the situation in Vykom, according to their individual
perspectives; in turn, Gandhi episodically provided guidance.

Expectations that opposition from the higher castes would evapo-
rate in the face of a march were unrealistic, as Kesava Menon divulges:
"We were under the impression that they [the Brahmins] could be won

---

[38] Gandhi, "The Vaikom Struggle: The Duty of the Satyagrahis;
Mahatmaji's Advice," *Hindu*, April 6, 1925 (*Young India*, April 2, 1925). Among
his publications were three weekly newspapers, *Young India*, in English (1919–
32), *Navajivan*, in Gujarati (1919–31), and later *Harijan*, in English (1933–48),
through which Gandhi conversed with supporters.

[39] "Sri Narayana Guru," *Western Star*, July 29, 1924. The *Western Star* was a
regional newspaper published from British-ruled Cochin and the oldest English-
language newspaper on the state's west coast.

[40] *Pioneer Mail*, April 23, 1924.

over by Satyagraha. On the contrary they turned more bitter and ireful than before."[41] As rumors spread of a confrontation between Nairs and Ezhavas, and with Gandhi recommending waiting to mediate a settlement, the organizers in Vykom opted to take a six-day break, after which they would resume their efforts. They decided to use the intervening time to intensify their efforts at communications and publicity.

Volunteers were enlisting in such numbers that the organizers announced that prior approval to join should be obtained along with a certificate of good character from a worthy citizen. Travancore's political life had awakened, as the satyagraha represented not only a newsworthy struggle against untouchability and the oppressions associated with caste, but local people of varying strata began to feel themselves allied with a broader nationalist pursuit of emancipation and freedom from social and political bondage. Notwithstanding the limits applied by Gandhi, many felt that they were part of a struggle that encompassed all of India.

In the initial period, the number of committed volunteers hovered at thirty, occasionally with a low of ten, but later reportedly reached a high of 120. In the beginning the group included a few Christians and Muslims.[42] They were "educated and illiterate, old and young people with widely differing social, economic intellectual and religious backgrounds," some of whom, Ravindran notes, "were apt to be led away from the ideal set by Gandhi by momentary impulses."[43] They kept meticulous details of their time: eight hours for sleep, six for satyagraha, two for spinning, one for learning Hindi, two for ashram work (cleaning, laundering), two for meals and bathing, one for reading, and two for prayers and meetings.[44] Some volunteers went door to door to collect rice and vegetables.

[41] K. P. Kesava Menon, as cited in Ravindran, *Vaikkam Satyagraha and Gandhi*, 59.

[42] Panikkar, "Vaikkam Satyagraha," in *We Fought Together for Freedom*, 131. No firm reports of the number of volunteers have surfaced; hence, it is not possible here to resolve the discrepancies in numbers cited in various accounts.

[43] Ravindran, *Vaikkam Satyagraha and Gandhi*, 117.

[44] See Gandhi, Notes, "From Vykom," February 5, 1925, *Young India*, in *CWMG*, 30: 182. Gandhi encouraged satyagrahis to account for every minute of their day.

The Anti-Untouchability Committee, initially helped by followers of Narayana Guru but now under the auspices of the Congress, managed as best as possible to clothe and feed the volunteers. Their efforts to collect public donations and in-kind contributions sustained them at a minimal, subsistence level. Various forms of support were also lent by district and regional organizations from several castes, including the Kerala Hindu Sabha, the Nair Service Society, the Yogakshema Sabha (the Nambudiri organization), and the Kshatriya Mahasabha.[45] The All-India Congress Committee was donating 1,000 rupees per month to support the satyagraha,[46] and other assistance came from elsewhere in the country.

Vykom's orthodox became even more enflamed during the campaign's suspension. The satyagrahis began to receive anonymous death threats via letter. The Travancore government escalated its response and had the district magistrate issue a search warrant for the confiscation of satyagraha campaign literature and correspondence. Affidavits from approximately fifty individuals who had volunteered to work for the Anti-Untouchability Committee were hauled away. The government justified this action as necessary to prepare a case against the leadership on the ground of endangering security.[47]

As the campaign's temporary suspension approached its end and more leaders arrived on the scene, the district magistrate sought to skim off the senior figures and bade Madhavan, Kesava Menon, Kelappan, A. K. Pillai, and two other leaders of the movement to appear in Kottayam, some 25 miles from Vykom, on April 7, the day that the satyagraha was scheduled to resume. All six of those summoned disobeyed the order. Madhavan and Kesava Menon instead approached the notice boards to provoke arrest.[48] The suspension effectively ended as they defiantly walked to the forbidden area, where they were arrested and transported

[45] Mahadev Haribhai Desai, *The Epic of Travancore* (Ahmedabad: Navajivan Karyalaya, 1937), 11. To everyone's surprise, the Yogakshema Sabha at its annual meetings passed resolutions calling for opening temples to the lower castes. Desai, *Epic of Travancore*, 11.

[46] Menon, *History of the Freedom Movement in Kerala*, 119.

[47] File no. 665/1924, vol. 4, English records, Government Secretariat, Trivandrum, as cited in Ravindran, *Vaikkam Satyagraha and Gandhi*, 60.

[48] Ravindran, *Vaikkam Satyagraha and Gandhi*, 60.

to the Trivandrum central jail by automobile. With each sentenced to six months in prison, their detention raised the morale of the participants and increased support for the movement, especially from many who had been previously indifferent. More leaders arrived on the scene to fill the gaps created by the arrests. Satyagrahis continued to go daily to the offending roads to court arrest.

On April 10, the *Mathrubhumi* reports, Gandhi offered congratulations for the arrest and imprisonment of Kesava Menon and Madhavan, and termed the courting of arrest and getting locked up acts of patriotism, for which one should be congratulated.[49] That day's editorial focuses on the *Mathrubhumi*'s role, especially because of Kesava Menon's position at the paper as managing editor. The paper editorializes and claims credit for his and Madhavan's arrest; it states that the detentions represent a loss, but boasts that the paper is "proud of sacrificing our stalwarts and we will strive for high standards—even though we may not be able to reach them." It mentions a request from K. Kelappan, active in the Nair Service Society and also a manager of the *Mathrubhumi*, asking that other leaders take the struggle forward. "What is going on in the Vykom temple premises is not merely an attempt to get the freedom of the oppressed classes in Kerala, but a struggle to decide whether untouchability or freedom should reign in India."[50]

The police at this stage were still politely proper in their deportment. On April 24, Gandhi wrote in *Young India* that he had congratulated the government for "their considerate treatment of the satyagrahi prisoners." He praises the Travancore authorities, who remained "unbending" concerning the prohibition order, for courteously carrying out their duties. He reinforces the beneficial role played by officials in checking violence against satyagrahis and applauds the treatment they received in the jails. Gandhi cites Kesava Menon, in captivity:

> I am now within the walls of the Trivandrum Central Jail along with my friend Mr. Madhavan. We are treated as State prisoners. A separate block is set apart for our use. We are allowed our own clothes. A convict cooks for us. I am having the same food as I take at home. So is my friend Mr.

---

[49] "Kesava Menon and Madhavan Were Given 6 Months Imprisonment," *Mathrubhumi* (trans. Thilleri), April 10, 1924, 5.

[50] Editorial: "The Great Struggle at Vykom," *Mathrubhumi* (trans. Thilleri), April 10, 1924, 4.

Madhavan. Books and newspapers are also allowed. Of course, in writing letters we are not allowed to say anything about the Vykom affair. Friends can see us between 8 A.M. and 4 P.M. every day except Sunday. I am sure that you would be glad to hear that the Superintendent and other authorities of the Jail are doing everything to make us comfortable. We receive from them the same polite treatment as we received from the Police officers at Vykom.[51]

In the initial phases, the government acted with "the rules of civilized politics as befitted a model state," particularly in its treatment of arrested leaders.[52] Nonetheless, as time went on and the satyagraha gained momentum, both sides would become openly contentious toward each other.

Meanwhile, vigorous efforts were being made to spread the ideals of satyagraha, encourage the making and wearing of khadi, and popularize the eradication of untouchability and unapproachability. A fluttering Congress flag preceded demonstrators in recurring processions accompanied by cries of "Vande materam" (Mother [India] I bow to thee) and "Mahatma Gandhi ki jai" (Hail victory).[53] Petitions were submitted to the maharaja of Travancore. Meetings large and small were organized in which Hindus, Christians, and Muslims spoke and participated. Minutes from these sessions show resolutions being passionately passed, pleading for the wearing of khadi, bidding brewers and distillers to hold back their alcoholic beverages in the interest of the struggle, applauding the satyagrahis for their vigilance, deploring the barbarity of Travancore's government and asking that the roads be opened, and setting up committees to work on various aspects of the fight against untouchability, unapproachability, and unseeability.

Congress leader George Joseph was arrested on April 11, along with K. G. Nyar and P. W. Sebastian.[54] According to V. Balambal, the leadership group in prison concluded that the one individual who could compensate for their being under lock and key was Periyar E. V.

[51] Gandhi, *Notes: Vykom Satyagraha* (orig. *Young India*, April 24, 1924), in *CWMG*, 27: 283.

[52] Vanaja Rangaswami, *The Story of Integration: A New Interpretation in the Context of the Democratic Movements in the Princely States of Mysore, Travancore and Cochin 1900–1947* (New Delhi: Manohar, 1981), 81.

[53] Rangaswami, *The Story of Integration*, 82.

[54] Ravindran, *Vaikkam Satyagraha and Gandhi*, 63; Joseph, *George Joseph*, 168.

Ramasamy Naicker of Erode, in Tamil Nadu. Considered one of the most indispensable lower-strata leaders in south India, he was their unanimous choice. Kurur Nilakantan Namboodiripad and George Joseph sent him a secret letter by messenger from the prison requesting that he assume the leadership:

> We had already started a mission that is too great. As the consequence, governmental opposition too have been let loose. We had never imagined that we would be behind bars so soon. Only if you come here to Vaikom and assume the leadership of the satyagraha and prolong the struggle, our honour and the honour of our Kerala will be left unscathed. There is no time to think over deeply and delay.[55]

Upon receiving the message, Ramasamy Naicker canceled his tour on behalf of the Congress in Tamil Nadu and proceeded to Vykom.

This was an important development. With virtually all of the prominent Brahmin figures incarcerated by the government of the princely state, the struggle would soon benefit from one of the great social reformers of the time, from Tamil Nadu, Periyar E. V. Ramasamy Naicker. The movement was bereft of prepared leadership, but, Kusuman observed, "the second rank of the leaders invited Naicker, who was also spearheading similar movements in Tamil Nadu. When invited, he came to Vykom and took the leadership for some time."[56] Indeed, in April 1924, Gandhi references a call across India for leaders to journey to Vykom: "As most of the leaders have been imprisoned, an appeal has been made to the leaders all over India to come to the rescue."[57]

[55] *Modern Revolutionist* 4, no. 8: 9, E. V. Ramasamy, "Who Abolished Untouchability" [in Tamil] (Erode, Tamil Nadu: 1968), 22, as cited in Balambal, "E. V. R. and Vaikom Satyagraha," *Journal of Kerala Studies* 7 (March, June, September, December 1980): 248n8. Periyar means "the great one." Ramaswamy is how his name appears in some records and literature, but he preferred Ramasamy as it conveyed a stance against Brahminism.

[56] Kusuman, interview (August 15, 2005). The word *agitation* among India's English speakers retains its nineteenth-century British meaning of keeping a political or other matter continually before public attention, through appeals, discussion, and generating public excitement. Still in usage concerning India's nonviolent struggles past or present, its meaning is similar to mobilizing or galvanizing.

[57] Gandhi, Notes, *Young India*, April 17, 1924, on Vykom satyagraha, in *CWMG*, 27: 263.

Figure 3   Periyar E. V. Ramasamy Naicker of Erode, Tamil Nadu, among the great social reformers of south India and an ardent orator, was called to join the Vykom struggle (Illustrated by Madanan Pv)

Note: With the main leadership group of the struggle imprisoned, from jail they sent for Periyar E. V. Ramasamy Naicker of Erode, from Tamil Nadu. He is recalled as a fiery orator.

While Ramasamy Naicker was en route to Vykom, the maharaja Mulam Thirunal sent the police commissioner and the dewan, Peishkar Subramania Iyer, to bring him to the palace, in V. Balambal's account, reciprocating an occasion when the raja had enjoyed Ramasamy Naicker's hospitality at Erode. Notwithstanding caste demarcations, he had dared to enter a career in trade and politics, and joined the Congress in 1920 "in order to strengthen its constructive programmes which included the amelioration of the underprivileged communities."[58] Ramasamy Naicker describes his personal motivation: "My ardent desire is to make the people rationalists. Caste must go and Brahmanism should not exist in the world. I joined the Congress only for this."[59] Famed for his powerful speeches in colloquial Tamil, he was in 1920 elected president of the Tamil Nadu Congress. Not long after arriving in Vykom, Ramasamy Naicker would be under arrest, but, Balambal notes, "The Maharaja was very lenient and ordered ... one month's imprisonment in Aruvikkuthu prison."[60]

Ramasamy Naicker enjoyed popular acclaim, because when due to be released from prison, notices appeared saying, "Mr. E. V. Ramaswami Naicker will be released from Arukkutti station this month. . . . [H]e will be received and taken in a special boat with a local musical band and accompanying boats to the Thaliya Parambu Grounds, where there will be a public meeting."[61] After being freed, he continued speaking out against untouchability and unapproachability. He would soon be back behind bars, sentenced this time to six months and treated like a common criminal in Trivandrum's central jail—forced to wear prison garb and an ankle iron in addition to being confined in solitary detention.[62]

[58] Balambal, "E. V. R. and Vaikom Satyagraha," 248. Note Ramasamy Naicker's interest in the "constructive program," with its inclusion of work on untouchability.

[59] "The Reasons for My Policy Change" (in Tamil), *E. V. Ramasamy's 90th British Commemoration Souvenir* (1968), 23, as cited in Balambal, "E. V. R. and Vaikom Satyagraha," 248, 248n9.

[60] Balambal, "E. V. R. and Vaikom Satyagraha," 249.

[61] Notice from Panavalli, in Malayalam, trans. Dinoo Anna Mathew, June 18, 1924, Kerala State Archives, vol. 3, Vaikkom Satyagraha Bundle. Hereafter, the Kerala State Archives are cited as KSA, and this collection as VSB. The VSB comprised ten volumes at the author's last viewing.

[62] Menon considers his conviction illegal because he had made no incitement to violence. Menon, *History of the Freedom Movement in Kerala*, 121, 122n16.

Less than one month from its start, the satyagraha had reached a deadlock with leadership and in sustenance. When Gandhi was interviewed by the *Hindu* he was asked how to resolve the predicament of deficiency in leaders, who were behind bars. He responded that he had received a letter showing that "the movement has gone so far that volunteers will continue to offer satyagraha, even when all the leaders are arrested. I would ... advise that at least one leader keeps himself in reserve and directs the movement without courting arrest."[63] No tangible evidence has come to light that a leader was minimally held in reserve. Of the key leadership group, nineteen were in prison, far removed from the deliberations in Vykom. The step of proceeding solely with volunteers would prove to be a serious defect for the struggle.

Change in Police Policy

The initial police policy had been to arrest the nonviolent challengers and lock them up for months. On April 10, however, the British police commissioner, W. H. Pitt, issued orders to cease the detentions of satyagrahis and leaders of the movement.[64] The new police tactic was aimed at making the activists stand for long hours under the heat of the sun, thereby intensifying their misery.[65] In this way, the now-concerned British authorities hoped to break the resolve of the movement.

Normally, the British had "looked with sympathy and consideration at the socially backward and underprivileged classes," Ravindran observes, but in this instance they had espoused another mind-set, seeing

the nationalist struggle of British India spreading its tentacles to Travancore. They were on tenterhooks with regard to the success of the

[63] Gandhi, interview, *Hindu*, April 17, 1924, in *CWMG*, 27: 247.

[64] Of the nineteen men who were arrested and convicted in this period, only seven were from Travancore, and Madhavan was the only avarna Hindu. The maharaja's government viewed the satyagraha as a political mobilization, rather than a social movement. Correspondence between officials in British Malabar and Travancore shows that the British shared this perspective.

[65] "The Satyagraha Struggle at Vykom: The New Policy of the Travancore Government, Not Arresting Satyagrahis: 'Shadow for the Police, and Sunshine for Volunteers,'" *Mathrubhumi* (trans. Thilleri), April 16, 1924.

campaign; its defeat at any cost was what they wanted. Instead of trying to measure the tensile strength of Satyagraha and to prove its merits in a princely state, they liked to put heavier odds on it and break it in such a way that its efficacy would be doubted by people elsewhere.[66]

Ravindran says that the record is clear that the British were prepared to go so far as to let Christian and Muslim pedestrians be excluded from the prohibited roads and had contemplated advising the Travancore government to curtail the civil rights of non-Hindus—if that was what it would take to break the back of the mobilization so that people across India would doubt the effectiveness of satyagraha.[67] Concrete verification of fear of spreading sedition is disclosed in an archival document in which Pitt lists twelve individuals from British-controlled India who were involved in the Vykom satyagraha, were convicted, and held behind bars. Listed separately are seven others, also convicted, regarded as able to disseminate the contagion of civil resistance as waged in Travancore. The "leading agitators," in most cases refusing to post bond, were George Joseph (date of conviction, April 12, 1924), K. G. Nair (April 9), A. K. Pillai (April 12), K. Velayudha Menon (April 12), T. K. Madhavan (April 7), K. Kumar (April 7), and K. Sankaran Nair (aka Chittadathu Sanku Pillai, May 15).[68]

As the Travancore government's policy of ceasing the arrests was implemented after April 10, the police reinforced barricades at the notice boards to prevent the volunteers from trying to enter the proscribed roads. If arrested, the volunteers would at least be sheltered and fed in jail. That the satyagrahis made a conscious decision to shift to a

---

[66] Ravindran, *Vaikkam Satyagraha and Gandhi*, 63.

[67] Ravindran, *Vaikkam Satyagraha and Gandhi*, 63. Ravindran draws his conclusion from correspondence between C. W. E. Cotton, agent to the governor general in Travancore, in writing to the chief secretary of the government of Madras (Chennai), April 21, 1924, Political Department files, Ordinary Series, G.O. no. 151, as cited in Ravindran, *Vaikkam Satyagraha and Gandhi*, 63.

[68] W. H. Pitt, commissioner of police, October 18, 1924, "List (A) of British Indians Who Were Convicted in Connection with Satyagraha Movement at Vaikom, and (b) of the Leading Agitators of Travancore Who Have Been So Convicted and Who Are Likely to Visit British India to Attend Political Conferences and to Assist in Agitation," KSA: VSB, file no. 615. Joseph, Nair, Pillai, Velayudha Menon, Madhavan, and Kumar refused to "furnish sureties," meaning to post bonds.

new policy of not passing beyond the posted lines is shown repeatedly in archival documents after this date in which police often refer to the volunteers' adherence to the demarcations as showing that the satyagrahis were adhering to the "reformed model" or the "revised plan."

The policy of arresting the leadership on charges of conspiracy to disobey the orders from the district magistrate had most likely been done on the advice of the resident. Indeed, C. W. E. Cotton, the aforementioned British political agent to the governor-general in Madras, writes in a letter, "I expressed the opinion to Pitt and the District Magistrate that with Mr. Joseph out of the way, the movement might collapse altogether, for none of the other leaders seems to have any ideas or drive. I have since heard that he was arrested in the same afternoon."[69] The resident would not have been worried about the survival of the movement. If anything, the resident took umbrage because of the heavy involvement of the Congress party, with its members serving as volunteers and avidly participating in frequent processions flying the Congress flags. Yet the satyagraha's presentation as an avowedly "socioreligious" mobilization, as Gandhi insisted, meant that the resident could not justify becoming involved.

A Kottayam newspaper questioned the credibility of the opposition. Citing leaders of a "conclave of upper caste Hindus" to the effect that a "powerful force" was at work opposing the Congress party and hinting at the likelihood of rioting, the reporter says that a petition had been put forward asking the government to banish the Congress workers. The correspondent, however, comments: "Actually the truth is that the situation is not unfavorable to Congress" and "a vast majority of Ezhavas, Nairs, and Muslims were preparing to help the party." In a revealing excerpt, he challenges as "not very real" the validity of a so-called powerful force hostile to the satyagraha.

Some workers and dependents of the temple, throwing decency and decorum to the wind, were putting out false statements and abusing and hooting at the workers supporting the satyagraha. They were the people known as the

---

[69] C. W. E. Cotton, political agent to the governor-general of Travancore, to Majoribanks, April 14, 1924, Political Department files, Ordinary Series, G.O. no. 151, as cited in Ravindran, *Vaikkam Satyagraha and Gandhi*, 64. Cotton alleged that the British authorities did not want the princely states offering platforms for blustering political personalities from British India. Ravindran, *Vaikkam Satyagraha and Gandhi*, 64.

"powerful force." Except for three or four Nairs, the vast majority belonging to this community were vociferously stating that the low caste people who were striving for their civil rights should not be hindered or prosecuted.[70]

What might appear to be insignificant objectives were highly symbolic for the Vykom struggle; any success would represent a wedge—both for organizers and opponents—that could be further expanded to gain recognition of rights for southern India's outcastes. The struggle in a precise sense would last for slightly more than 600 days. Its course would be neither smooth nor incremental. The first phase of the struggle lasted from the initial arrest of three demonstrators on March 30 until April 10, when the government decided not to make further arrests.[71] The struggle then entered a quiescent stage, as the volunteers restrained themselves from crossing the boundary into the prohibited area and the police made no arrests.

"An Essentially Hindu Question"

The unfolding campaign appealed to a broad cross-section of Indian interests and attracted the attention of others elsewhere in Asia and beyond. A number of personages visited Vykom in their efforts to support the struggle, including C. F. Andrews, a British priest in the Anglican Church of England and an educator who had become a close friend and associate of Gandhi, and C. R. Das, a famous Bengali lawyer and leader in the Indian independence movement. Chakravarti Rajagopalachari was among this group. A Brahmin from Madras, he was a preeminent lawyer and statesman, general secretary of the Indian National Congress for a year in the early 1920s, was jailed five times by the British, became a government minister, and would be the last (and only Indian) governor-general of India.[72]

[70] "Satyagraha Movement in Vaikom: Mr. Gandhi's Request," *Malayala Manorama Daily*, April 5, 1924, in *Malayala Manorama, Mahatma Gandhi's Visits to Kerala: 1924, 1925, 1927, 1934, 1937* (Kottayam: *Malayala Manorama*), 5.

[71] Jeffrey, "Travancore: Status, Class and the Growth of Radical Politics," 152. The author concurs with Jeffrey's assessment of the struggle's five phases, subsequently to be noted without further attribution.

[72] Rajagopalachari is described in the *New York Times* as a "titan" of India's independence struggles, "a trenchant journalist, a subtle philosopher, and a gifted political leader."Alden Whitman, "Chakravarti Rajagopalachari of India Is Dead: Proclaimed the Republic," *New York Times*, December 26, 1972.

Christians and Muslims also became engrossed in the campaign. In one example, the *Mathrubhumi* reports an April visit to Travancore by T. K. Paul, a member and leader of a Christian youth organization. Paul notes, "I have no doubt that in this struggle at Vykom, which is being waged to establish the birthright of man, the Indian Christians will have great sympathy."[73] In the United States, African American leaders were from afar following various struggles in India, as covered by black-owned newspapers. The U.S. black community, subjected as it was to legalized segregation, according to historian Sudarshan Kapur, was generally "sensitive to the issue of untouchability as an internal contradiction of the Indian struggle. Certain sections of the African American press highlighted the similarities between the two situations—that of segregation in the United States and that of untouchability in the Indian subcontinent."[74] Some would travel to India to learn for themselves.

As the fascination with the mobilization in Vykom drew supporters from a variety of backgrounds and diverse faiths, thereby broadening the lens through which the struggle was viewed on the subcontinent, Gandhi stepped forward and repudiated this widening scope. He based his refutation on the grounds that the issue at hand concerned Hindus and must therefore be resolved by them alone. In 1924, at the Belgam session of the Congress Party, Gandhi accentuated his position: "Untouchability is another hindrance to Swaraj [self-rule]. Its removal is just as essential for Swaraj as the attainment of Hindu Muslim unity. This is an essentially Hindu question and Hindus cannot claim or take Swaraj till they have resorted to liberty of the suppressed classes."[75]

[73] "Letter from T. K. Paul: The Vykom Satyagraha and Indian Christians," *Mathrubhumi* (trans. Thilleri), April 29, 1924, 2.

[74] Sudarshan Kapur, *Raising Up a Prophet: The African-American Encounter with Gandhi* (Boston: Beacon Press, 1992), 60. Based on research in U.S. newspapers and journals that were privately owned by African Americans, Kapur documents that black leaders began traveling to India from the United States during the 1920s, and even more so in the 1930s, until the outbreak of World War II, deriving inspiration and wisdom for their own impending confrontation with what they considered a caste system. More will be said in Chapter 7.

[75] Congress Presidential Address, Silver to Golden Jubilee, 2nd series, Madras, 747, as cited in Chandramohan, "Social and Political Protest in Travancore," 237n2.

Gandhi's encouragement of the campaign's management had continued until George Joseph assumed the leadership of the satyagraha and was arrested on April 11 (convicted on April 12), along with Nyar and Sebastian, the three of them sentenced to six months in prison by the magistrate and sent to the central jail in Trivandrum.[76] Joseph, educated at Edinburgh and called to the bar in London, had by April become a leader in the Congress party, having earlier been a student leader in the growing nationalist cause when Gandhi's noncooperation and civil disobedience mass movements in 1920–1 brought pupils into the national mobilization. He was among a number of student leaders, who included Muhammed Abdur Rahiman and E. M. S. Namboodiripad, who would go on to play other leadership roles. Joseph became involved in student conferences that had begun to be held to mobilize a younger generation, which flanked the regular Congress political meetings. In 1921 he had been imprisoned in Agra, where his cellmate was Jawaharlal Nehru, who would become independent India's first prime minister in 1947. That same year, he had presided over a student conference held in Ottappalam in April. In 1923, Joseph became editor of *Young India* at Gandhi's behest. He was a rising star of the Congress party, but the fact that he was a Syrian Christian would produce an encounter during the satyagraha that still vexes some.

From Bombay, Gandhi had had been corresponding with Joseph in Chengannur, Travancore. On March 27, after Joseph had become part of the core leadership group working on Vykom, and Gandhi had heard that civil disobedience was being discussed, he wrote to ask: "Will you kindly let me know what the facts are, and if it is a fact that you have threatened civil disobedience, the grounds for it."[77] In another missive written at the same time, Gandhi says guardedly, "Generally speaking, it is quite true that I have been averse to civil disobedience being started in the Indian States."[78] On April 6, Gandhi sent Joseph a letter that still echoes:

> As to Vykom, I think that you should let the Hindus do the work. It is they who have to purify themselves. You can help by your sympathy and

[76] "Arrest of Mr K. Mathew," May 11, 1924, *Malayala Manorama Daily*, in *Mahatma Gandhi's Visits to Kerala*, 7; Ravindran, *Vaikkam Satyagraha and Gandhi*, 63.

[77] Gandhi, letter to George Joseph, in *CWMG*, 27: 125.

[78] Gandhi, letter to E. R. Menon, March 27, 1924, in *CWMG*, 27: 126.

by your pen, but not by organizing the movement and certainly not by offering satyagraha. If you refer to the Congress resolution of Nagpur, it calls upon the Hindu members to remove the curse of untouchability. I was surprised to learn from Mr. [Charles Freer] Andrews that the disease has infected even the Syrian Christians.[79]

The last sentence of Gandhi's message hints that if Joseph wished to work against untouchability, he should do so among Syrian Christians. Before Joseph received Gandhi's advice, however, he had joined the Vykom satyagraha and taken the place of Keshava Menon, who had been incarcerated. When Joseph was himself arrested on April 11, he sent a telegram to Gandhi informing him of his situation. Their communications crossed. P. K. K. Menon notes that K. M. Panikkar claimed responsibility for advocating an all-Hindu campaign, which later received Gandhi's approval.[80] George Joseph's great grandson, George Gheverghese Joseph, believes that Panikkar "was behind the campaign to remove George Joseph from the leadership."[81] Ironically, Gandhi had during this time called Joseph "my predecessor."[82]

Part of Gandhi's insistence that Hindus conduct the removal of untouchability and that the Vykom satyagraha should be solely a Hindu affair rested on his view that a Hindu's silent suffering would be more effective than legions of non-Hindus. Gandhi often spoke of "silent suffering," which was related to his conviction that change could be brought about through persuasion and appeals, or conversion of the upper castes. He began requesting that Christians, Muslims, and Sikhs alike retire from the struggle.

Retroactively, it was not so much that Gandhi did not want to have others involved; he thought that the demands at Vykom could be

[79] Gandhi, letter to George Joseph, April 6, 1924, *CWMG*, 27: 196. Andrews became an interpreter of Gandhi's ideas, writing periodically in the Manchester *Guardian*.

[80] P. K. K. Menon says Panikkar's position that solely Hindus should take part in the satyagraha was approved by Gandhi, despite the Kerala Congress Committee being highly critical of this suggestion. A delegation composed of Kurur Nilakantan Nambudiripad and K. Madhavan Nair met with Gandhi at Ahmedabad, where Panikkar was present. Gandhi "continued to support Panikkar's view-point." Menon, *History of the Freedom Movement in Kerala*, 120n12.

[81] Joseph, *George Joseph*, 166.

[82] Gandhi, *Young India*, April 17, 1924, in *CWMG*, 27: 263.

misinterpreted by the orthodox Hindus, who would construe it as Christians disrupting harmony within the Hindu order. To avoid misinterpretation, Gandhi said that it was Hindus who should make the fight. Otherwise, he feared it might be counter productive to the larger purpose.

Joseph had grown up in a unique cultural setting rich with Hindu, Jewish, Christian, Muslim, and Buddhist loyalties, and all the multifarious identities of caste in Travancore's exceptional milieu of communal politics coexisting with diverse fidelities. This amalgam made it difficult for him to comprehend what was essentially a dictum by Gandhi that the Vykom struggle should be led by high-caste Hindus. He also knew that Hinduism was not monopolistic and that a variety of traditions could be found within its broad folds. In George Gheverghese Joseph's view, Gandhi actually believed that the Vykom struggle "should be waged only by the Hindus its being a matter of temple entry." Yet as George Joseph perceived it in the 1920s, "the struggle was primarily about the civic rights of all inhabitants to use public roads."[83]

The interchange with George Joseph caused E. V. Ramasamy Naicker to lose confidence in Gandhi. Religion was at the heart of the social predicament in Ramasamy Naicker's eyes, but not in Gandhi's sense. As he saw it, "Roots of evil in a society are to be found in religion. Religion or superstition has prevented development in society. Religion must be abolished by rationalism. Caste system and domination of Brahmins must be destroyed."[84] Ramasamy Naicker believed that religion would have to be eradicated before progress and justice could prevail. He would in 1925 leave the Congress because he believed that the party had given benefits to the Brahmins, while discrediting those who were not of their caste. According to Balambal, he was not satisfied with how Gandhi had handled the Vykom satyagraha.[85] Ramasamy Naicker's disagreement with Gandhi went beyond the Brahmin question. He also substantially disagreed with upper-caste leaders concerning the limited participation of the Dalits and former slave castes in the Vykom struggle.

[83] Joseph, *George Joseph*, 23–4. It will be recalled that George Gheverghese Joseph is the great grandson of the barrister and leader.

[84] Balambal, "E. V. R. and Vaikom Satyagraha," 250.

[85] Balambal, "E. V. R. and Vaikom Satyagraha," 249.

Vykom manifests "the contradiction between the state as the traditional protector of the *jati* order and the modernizing role of the state
(within the limits of colonialism)," as J. Devika put it.

> George Joseph had planned to press this point. But Gandhi thought it a
> bad strategy. . . . Gandhi wanted to bring his critique to the situation and
> force the state to modernize. Joseph wanted to exploit the discrepancy
> between the two roles. Gandhi was very conservative. In his view, agency
> lay with the upper castes, therefore Gandhi wanted to make the upper
> castes feel guilty.[86]

In other words, Joseph had intended to take the greatest possible advantage of the conflicting roles of the state government as guardian of the
caste system on the one hand, while on the other hand being responsible for bringing about social change for the benefit of the people.
Gandhi was too cautious to take advantage of this split self-perception
and to play them against each other. Rather, because he viewed the
upper castes as already possessing the power to bring about alterations,
he wanted to drive them toward reform by making them feel remorse.

Gandhi was looking at the Vykom satyagraha as a Hindu, from
within the Hindu religious community, which is the ground on which
he stood regarding untouchability. In his view, the practice and justification for untouchability cast degradation on caste Hindus and outcastes alike. In his discussions with the Dalit leader Babasaheb R.
Ambedkar, he adhered to a position that they were part of Hinduism,
K. N. Panikkar argued. Panikkar said:

> In actual fact, the untouchables were hardly part of Hinduism. A large sec-
> tion was outside all the tenets of the Hindu religion. Gandhi was very keen
> on reclaiming them as part of Hinduism. Not for the reason of increased
> numbers supporting the nationalist struggle, but for solidarity as far as the
> nationalist struggle was concerned with poor people, and because he saw
> untouchables, Dalits, as an important category. But by the same logic, he
> should have widened the struggle to include non-Hindus.[87]

The role of Gandhi was complex, contradictory, and even perplexing
at this stage. At the very least it seems likely that Gandhi did not want

[86] J. Devika, interview (Trivandrum, March 23, 2009). Devika is an associate professor at the Centre for Development Studies in Trivandrum.
[87] Panikkar, interview (August 15, 2005).

the higher castes to have any opening to claim that people of other faiths wanted to weaken Hinduism. He also wanted to reclaim the untouchables not solely for Hinduism, but for the larger project of rejuvenating Hindu cultural nationalism. Caste and nationalism were closely connected in India, particularly in the context of Travancore, but the question remains: could untouchables be nationalists in the form ushered by the Congress party and simultaneously earn dignity and equality, while Gandhi was oblivious to their various endeavors of self-transformation?

Increasing numbers of people wanted to become involved in the satyagraha. The *Malayala Manorama*, published in Kottayam, reported that respected Nairs were among those seeking to make a contribution. Teachers who had participated in a meeting about the Congress party at Ettumanoor were beaten violently, which is when Kurivilla Mathew, at the forefront of organizing the teachers' session, stepped forward and unabashedly embraced the Congress movement. Reporting on May 11, 1924, *Malayala Manorama* notes that upon Mathew's arrival in Vykom, he told police officials that he knew there was a warrant for his arrest, but even so he would "be making a speech condemning the government policy of ruthless suppression of the movement by force." Mathew was arrested and taken to the Kottayam police station, where "he was thrown into the lock up along with . . . hardened murderous criminals. . . . The stench from inside the cell made it difficult for a person to stand even in front of it. . . . [H]e was not permitted to take a bath for . . . 25 days."[88] Prominent individuals visited him in jail.

Brochures were widely posted to advocate involvement in the satyagraha. One flyer appeared, published by Alumoottil A. K. Govindan, in Kuttanad, Alleppey district, explaining the satyagraha in Vykom as "an attempt to purify the Hindu community." It stated:

> Untouchability is a great sin that has been practiced by Hindus in the name of religion. To save people from this sinful practice would be a blessing to the nation. There is no sacrifice greater than this, no duty greater. . . . The more people and money we have, the quicker we'll reach our goal. Victory depends on this. We have been receiving help from all over India, but now Gandhiji has advised that it is not correct to accept

[88] "Arrest of Mr K. Mathew," May 11, 1924, *Malayala Manorama*, in *Gandhi's Visits to Kerala*, 7, 8.

help from outside Kerala. So we need to come forward and contribute greatly in terms of personnel and funds.[89]

The upper-caste Hindu notables whose leadership had been aroused individually tended to have "a strong personal conviction that the practices of untouchability and unperceivability were a travesty of the Hindu social and religious system and that temples should be thrown open to all Hindu believers," Shreekumaran Nair argues. "They were, in fact, doing something in the form of 'atonement' for the sins of their forebears."[90] This sentiment resonates with Gandhi's repeated assertion during the 1920s and 1930s that "[t]o remove the curse of untouchability is to do penance for the sin committed by the Hindus of degrading a fifth of their own religionists."[91]

The satyagrahis and their opponents both sought to influence public opinion. The district magistrate penned a note to the government's chief secretary on June 4: "[T]he Satyagraha Committee propose to call a public meeting today to know the strength of public opinion in favour of allowing entry in the prohibited roads. . . . The caste Hindus too, it is stated, are to hold another meeting to express their protest against such entry."[92] Telegrams poured in to the dewan from across Travancore. As an example: "Dewan Trivandrum. Public meeting Nedunganda requests Vykom temple and similar roads thrown open to all. [signed] President."[93] One is particularly indicative: "Dewan Trivandrum. Public begs politicals release public roads for all. President begs public roads for all. [signed] President."[94]

---

[89] Alumoottil A. K. Govindan, 1924, n.d., flyer, "Vykom Satyagraha: A Special Notice," KSA: vol. 2, VSB.

[90] Shreekumaran Nair, review, Ravindran, *Vaikkam Satyagraha and Gandhi*, 765.

[91] Gandhi, Letter to Mrs. Maddock, March 14, 1924, in *CWMG*, 27: 53, 55.

[92] District Magistrate, Kottayam, to Chief Secretary of the Government, Trivandrum, June 4, 1924, letter, KSA: vol. 3, VSB, file 569 (handwritten 50).

[93] Telegram, to Dewan, Trivandrum, June 4, 1924, KSA: vol. 3, VSB, file 6 (handwritten). Such telegrams surged in early June 1924 to Dewan Bahadur T. Raghavaiah, Trivandrum. They were sent by presidents of citizen groups, conveying decisions taken at public meetings in Travancore, from Arathupuzha, Changanacherry, Chirayinkil, Jammu, Kayangulan, Muvathupuzha, Oachira, Quilon, Shertallay, Thrikundapuzha, and elsewhere. Some asked the release of imprisoned satyagrahis. At least one came from Lahore. Expressions of opposition from savarna Hindus are also filed. KSA: vol. 3, June 1924, VSB, *varia*.

[94] Telegram from Mavelikara, Alleppey, to Dewan, Trivandrum, June 4, 1924, KSA: vol. 3, VSB, file 3 (handwritten).

The maharaja, though considered an educated and enlightened leader, was orthodox in his private and personal views and remained opposed to opening the roads to the excluded castes in his domain. Furthermore, he resented the interference of the Congress party. Consequently, according to Ravindran, his "government thought it necessary to curb the activities of the outsiders in Travancore as well as the agitational reformism of local radicals."[95] A letter to the dewan in Trivandrum, on the distinctive palace stationery with its engraved logo of two elephants, discloses this policy clearly: "His Highness the [maharaja] has been pleased to approve the draft [government order] forwarded therewith, which you propose to issue sanctioning the continuance until further orders of the prohibitory order issued by the District Magistrate, Quilon, against Mr. Chengarathu Kunjan Pillai of Chengannur from delivering public speeches of any kind within the District of Quilon."[96]

The participation of outsiders was an issue and not only for the government. As the local news media continued to follow events with great interest, some observers were dismayed about the lack of involvement by the lower ranks themselves. The perception, and it appears the reality, was that the great majority of the volunteers were middle-class Hindus from Malabar; very few untouchables were participating in the Vykom satyagraha. "If the outsiders had left, the movement would have failed," Suresh Jnaneswaran maintained. "There was no chance of success without them. . . . The Travancore authorities saw the struggle as important precisely because of the Congress involvement. They refused to acknowledge the local sentiments."[97]

Support from the Ezhavas, including those who had managed to get jobs in government service, was not readily forthcoming for a social struggle against untouchability. Although Madhavan was prominently active in the SNDP Yogam, neither the SNDP Yogam nor the Ezhava community had produced the Vykom satyagraha. Although the struggle included participants from all strata, leadership was primarily from the savarnas. The Ezhava community was largely indifferent.[98] Many

[95] Ravindran, *Vaikkam Satyagraha and Gandhi*, 56.

[96] Palace, Trivandrum, letter to T. Raghaviah, June 7, 1924, KSA: vol. 3, VSB, 575 (handwritten 1599). Signature illegible.

[97] Jnaneswaran, interview (March 25, 2009).

[98] M. P. Sreekumaran Nair, review of Ravindran, *Vaikkom Satyagraha and Gandhi, Journal of Indian History* 54, part 3 (December): 763.

Ezhavas were too afraid of their caste-Hindu landlords and bosses to participate openly in such activities. Support from the Ezhava middle class came warily and clandestinely. Some of the large Ezhava landed families in central Travancore, among them Madhavan's kin, offered support.[99] Although meetings were held during this period by various caste and religious organizations, some of which passed resolutions against untouchability and protested against the government, the SNDP Yogam was the only avarna organization that actively backed the satyagraha, but even it did not adopt a straightforward policy regarding temple entry when the Vykom struggle was launched. Indeed, Ayyamuthu Gounder, one of the satyagraha leaders, sent a message to the Ezhava community stating that their number in the Vykom struggle could be "counted on fingers."[100]

In addition to warning against non-Hindu participation in the saty-agraha, Gandhi asserted that the movement should neither seek nor receive assistance from outside Travancore, even from Hindus. Forgotten was the April appeal for leaders from across India to come to the rescue. His rejection of help from outside and altering the form of the struggle generated a number of practical difficulties. A group of Akalis had been inspired by what was taking place in Vykom, and ten had traveled hun-dreds of miles from the Punjab to Vykom to set up a canteen for the satyagrahis, as reported by the *Mathrubhumi* after their arrival.[101] The Akalis were a Sikh reformist organization that had been engaged in their own long struggle against the British government's control of Sikh religious shrines.

Led by Lala Lal Singh and Kripal Singh, the canteen the Akalis set up in the vicinity and their acts of charity helped to feed thousands of vol-unteers each day.[102] Gandhi called for its closure. He argued that rely-ing on outside assistance would have the effect of lessening the sacrifice of the volunteers and could thereby reduce the possibility of melting

---

[99] Jeffrey, "Travancore: Status, Class and the Growth of Radical Politics," 153.

[100] Ravindran, *Vaikkam Satyagraha and Gandhi*, 73. Ravindran transliterates his name Ayyamuttu Gaundar.

[101] "Satyagraha Struggle at Vykom: Akali Group Has Started from Amritsar—Kerala State Congress Committee Welcomes Them," *Mathrubhumi* (trans. Thilleri), April 29, 1924, 3.

[102] Ravindran, *Vaikkam Satyagraha and Gandhi*, 68.

the hearts of the opponents—his perception of the aim of satyagraha.[103] The well-informed dewan penned a note, "Information just received Akalis leave Vykom tomorrow for return to their homes ... presumably they will entrain from Ernakulam."[104] They departed on June 25.[105] The Akali kitchen was soon replaced by one run by the local satyagraha committee.

Discipline and Perseverance

After the new April 10 police policy was implemented, volunteers responded by fasting at the barricades. By the end of that day, six volunteers had fainted, having refused food or water while exposed under the scorching sun. T. V. Chathukutty Nayar led a group of volunteers and remained there, refusing to return to the camp at night. He stayed at the road without eating for two days and two nights, and on the third day collapsed, unconscious, and had to be taken for medical treatment.[106] Perturbed by the government's shift in tactics, George Joseph wrote to the *durbar* accusing the police commissioner and district magistrate with "inhumanity for leaving them [the satyagraha volunteers] to die of starvation and exposure [to the sun]" and complaining that the new policy was not "playing the game."[107]

[103] "'The Stayagraha Struggle at Vykom: The Statement of Mahatma Gandhi," *Mathrubhumi* (trans. Thilleri), May 22, 1924, 3. In a statement published in the *Bombay Chronicle*, picked up by *Mathrubhumi*, Gandhi speaks against non-Hindu participation in the Vykom satyagraha and says that accepting help from non-Hindus would be a sign of weakness of the satyagrahis. He stipulates that the canteen run by the Akalis is unnecessary and says that participation by non-Hindus would provoke the savarnas. Thilleri, interview (March 17, 2009).

[104] Dewan, June 6, 1924, handwritten note by the Dewan to Rapiebam, Kottayam, KSA: vol. 3, VSB, file 539.

[105] K. Rama Varier, Police Inspector, Vaikom, letter to District Superintendent of Police, Kottayam, June 6, 1924, KSA: vol. 3, VSB, file 635.

[106] Menon, *History of the Freedom Movement in Kerala*, 122.

[107] Memorandum from C. W. E. Cotton to Secretary of the Government of India, Foreign and Political Department, Simla: Madras States Agency, Camp Kunnamkulam, April 21, 1924. Also see the *Times*, June 3, 1924 (article title unavailable from file). Both available in Political and Secret Annual Files: IOR/L/PS/11/246 item P2117/1924.

This period of fasting at the boundary of the forbidden areas resulted in the police and satyagrahis sitting and standing opposite each other in six-hour intervals, in varying patterns. Instead of sending three volunteers to the main road on the northern side of the temple, a vigil was undertaken; in Gandhian terminology satyagraha was "offered" on all four sides of the temple. On April 13, however, under the leadership of E. V. Ramasamy Naicker, twelve volunteers participated solely on the western side of the temple.

The satyagrahis' morale fluctuated. The end of the arrests had the effect of lessening the movement's thrust. Hunger strikes were suggested along with the scaling of the barricades. Although the fasting brought attention and enthusiasm to the movement, Gandhi telegraphed the satyagrahis advising them to omit it and instead to stand calmly until arrested.[108] He recommended to the volunteers through George Joseph that they could stand or squat in relays with quiet submission until arrested.[109]

Avoidance of fasting became part of Gandhi's principles for the Vykom struggle. These precepts were periodically laid out for the satyagrahis and "scrupulously observed," according to Mahadev Desai, four of which follow:

1. The goal of the satyagraha was limited, although "the ultimate goal was for [the] throwing open, not only in Travancore, but throughout the whole of India, to the Harijans, of all public roads, all public schools, all public wells and all public temples which were open to the other Hindus."

2. "[T]he movement was entirely Hindu, and ... non-Hindus may not participate in it either by organizing, leading or by financing it." "Hindus alone must bleed for the movement and pay for it." No assistance of nonviolent direct action from Hindus beyond Travancore should be asked, because "it would betray unreadiness on the part of the local Hindus for reform."

3. Breaking through barricades, scaling fences, or piercing the police lines "would be a species of violence."

4. Fasting is out of the question because fasting against authorities, too, "was a species of violence."[110]

---

[108] This message was not received until April 14.

[109] Gandhi, *Young India*, May 1, 1924, as cited in Menon, *History of the Freedom Movement in Kerala*, 147.

[110] Desai, *Epic of Travancore*, 12–13.

Fasting had been part of Hindu practice for centuries if not millennia, based on a belief that through sacrifice, the pious could realize their desired goals when faced with calamity, and that self-denial could become a way to pursue one's ends. Gandhi drew from the Bhagavad Gita an inspiration for his lifelong practice of fasting.[111] Having been reared in Gujarat, where Jains in their pursuit of non-attachment, renunciation of worldly matters, and an extreme variation of a doctrine of nonviolence would embrace *sallekhana*, dying voluntarily by a protracted process of fasting unto death, Gandhi was familiar with the practice of fasting from a tender age. In adulthood, he fasted for a variety of reasons, but first and foremost as a process of self-purification, although he staunchly believed that such sacrifice should be used only under particular circumstances. His genius was in understanding that in the totality of Indian cultural circumstances, fasting could be used as a tool for social action. Most noteworthy were his fasts for Hindu–Muslim unity, against the use of violence, and on three occasions against untouchability. Parekh notes, "He never fasted against the colonial government to extract political concessions or to exert political pressure."[112] Gandhi contended that fasting should not be used to coerce, but to reform or convert. Over time, he came to believe that such a potent method of emotional compulsion should only be used as a last resort, when other means for redress had been shuttered. In Vykom, he believed that it should not be used merely because the opposition had switched tactics and was no longer arresting volunteers. If the Vykom satyagrahis were to fast for the reason that officials would not arrest them, in P. K. K. Menon's words, "it would be a beggar's fast rather than anything else."[113]

[111] Mohandas K. Gandhi, *An Autobiography: The Story of My Experiments with Truth*, trans. from Gujarati by Mahadev [Haribhai] Desai (Ahmedabad: Navajivan Publishing House, 1940; repr., Boston: Beacon Press, 1993), 332.

[112] Bhikhu C. Parekh, *Gandhi's Political Philosophy: A Critical Examination* (Houndsmill, Basingstoke, Hampshire, and London: Macmillan Press, 1989), 159–60. More will be said about fasting in Chapter 6, but a definitive tally would be difficult, because Gandhi fasted annually in commemoration of certain events, such as the Jallianwalah Bagh massacre at Amritsar of April 13, 1919. For a listing of separate fasts undertaken in nineteen different years of his life by Gandhi, provided by historian B. R. Nanda, see Mary King, *Mahatma Gandhi and Martin Luther King Jr*, 514–16.

[113] Menon, *History of the Freedom Movement in Kerala*, 121n14.

"Rabid Speeches"

Government records reveal that Ramasamy Naicker and others were
being targeted for their fervent public speaking. One police officer's
perusal of public speeches given around this time by K. Aiyappan indicates that such orations were thought likely to enflame religious hostil-
ity, incite offenses, disturb public peace, and to be a "great danger to the
safety and public tranquility of Vaikom and other parts of the State."[114]
On May 20, the maharaja had been asked to approve the prosecution
of Ramasamy Naicker, K. Aiyappan of Vykom, and Dr. Emperumal
Naidu of Nagercoil.[115] Their speeches were found to be "objectionable."[116] Some lectures were imputed to offend provisions of the
Criminal Law relating to sedition.[117] The offending speeches are cited
as evidence for prosecution.[118]

The volume of court orders against individuals speaking on behalf
of the struggle appears to have been sufficiently large to demand

[114] Pitchoo Iyengur, Assistant Superintendent of Police, Vycome [Vykom],
District Magistrate, Kottayam, handwritten letter, December 17, 1923, KSA:
vol. 8, VSB. The letter was written in December 1923, when the Congress party
was seeking to restore itself after the Mapilla rebellion of 1921–2 and planning
its annual meeting in Kakinada.

[115] N. Krishnan Oonithan, Palace, Trivandrum, Letter, May 20, 1924, KSA:
vol. 8, VSB [no addressee, no file number].

[116] A letter asks W. H. Pitt to arrange the prosecution of Mssrs. Ramasamy
Naicker, Emperumal Naidu, and Aiyappan, indicating that copies of their "objec-
tionable speeches" will be forwarded. Letter to W. H. Pitt, Police Commissioner,
Travancore, May 20, 1924, KSA: vol. 8, VSB [no signatory, no file number].

[117] R. Anandadao, Government of Travancore, to R. Krishna Pillai, Chief
Secretary to Government, Travancore, "Urgent and Confidential Letter," May
13, 1924, KSA: vol. 8, VSB, file 982. Anandadao's letter says that he has studied
reports of speeches given at public meetings in Nagercoil, Trivandrum, and
Vaikom [by Ramaswami Naicker, Emperumal Naidu, and Aiyappan]. A handwritten note asks which speeches "offend the law of India?"

[118] A tabular statement charts details of E. V. Ramaswami Naicker,
Emperumal Naidu, and K. Aiyappan, dates, place, section of the Travancore
Penal Code under which each is to be prosecuted, name of the complainant
(police), court before which each is to appear, and which speeches may be con-
sidered as evidence. Chart: List of persons to be prosecuted, May (n.d.), 1924,
KSA: vol. 8, VSB [no file number].

creation of a pro forma magistrate's arrest order, in which a name could be inserted for purposes of issuing a detention order in 1924. The prototype justifies the taking into custody if the accused "uttered words calculated to bring into hatred and contempt and excite disaffection towards, the Sovereign of this Kingdom and his Government and also to promote feelings of enmity and hatred between the several classes of people in His Highness's territory."[119]

Government reports from April to June speak of the Vykom challengers as making violent speeches, vehement attacks, and virulent attacks. At a public meeting on April 15, 1924, in Shertallai, Aiyappan was reported by the police inspector of that town to have spoken to an audience of two thousand. The inspector recounted:

> K. Aiyappan, editor of the *Sahodaran* [Brother], spoke in strong terms that just as the Russians managed to obtain freedom by putting an end to their Royal family, so the Ezhavas also must fight to the end without carrying the guns of the Sepoys, batons of the Police, or even [of] the Maharaja. They all must with indomitable courage and bravery sacrifice of their lives and money for the sake of their freedom, that they all must be prepared to sacrifice their lives when time comes.[120]

Points accentuated in impassioned speeches by the leadership of the satyagraha in April, some by individuals from outside Travancore, are noted in a government report on a Trivandrum meeting, for which no date is given. In the first chronological mention in archival records of the notion of a discrete road, K. G. Kunjukrishna Pillai, presiding over the session, said that he had heard that the government was contemplating the construction of a separate road for the lower-caste Hindus in Vykom. He mentions that the satyagraha had not started because of a lack of roads, but to establish the rights of all Hindus to walk upon those in place. He went on to say regarding the dewan, "His Highness is the only one who is really against the Sathyagraha [sic]." In the meeting, Ramasamy Naicker stated that stayagraha "is not a fight against [the] Government. It is not a religious fight and it is not a communal fight. It

---

[119] Form: Order from court of First Class Magistrate of.....................
Case no...... (n.d.) 1924, KSA: vol. 8, VSB [no file].

[120] Ananta Shenai, Police Inspector, Shertallai, to Kottayam District Superintendent of Police, Shertallai, April 24, 1924, report, KSA: vol. 5, VSB, files 108–10.

is an act of a public good. It is intended to establish equality." He argued that any violence would bring down the harshest of reprisals: "We must be nonviolent. The slightest violence will set at naught all our efforts." The police officers' response to the slightest violence, Ramasamy Naicker explained, would be to employ guns and other weapons, and if the Travancore government does not put down the situation, British forces will arrive with airplanes and machine guns. He described a comparable struggle in the village of Edapadam, where "there was complete nonviolence"; as a result, "[t]he authorities found it difficult to meet the situation." Mannath Padmanabha Pillai, in his turn, remarked that "the government that ordered the arrest of the leaders is an uncharitable Government. It is the government who did the injustice."[121]

M. E. Naidu soon fell under the magistrate's gavel, after saying, "The Hindu Religion acknowledges no unapproachability. . . . Travancore is ruled by a Hindu [maharaja] and he is deadly against the depressed classes." The police report claims Naidu said that the maharaja was a *Hindumathadrohi* (traitor to the Hindu tradition). A note was attached to the police report saying that Dr. Naidu, medical practitioner, should be served with a prohibitory order "so as to prevent him from making such rabid speeches."[122] Ramasamy Naicker was banned from Kottayam district by the district magistrate's court, "to prevent probable riot."[123]

---

[121] C. S. Ramachandra Iyer, Cantonment, Trivandrum, to Trivandrum District Superintendent of Police, Report of speech extracts, April 28, 1924, KSA: vol. 5, VSB, handwritten files 127–32 (6 pp.), 1, 2, 4, 5. Last sentence trans. Dinoo Anna Mathew, 5.

[122] Subrahmanya Pillai, Police Inspector, Kottar, to Kottayam Assistant Superintendent of Police, Nagercoil, report, April 24, 1924, KSA: vol. 5, VSB, handwritten files 121–2. Appended note, April 24, 1924, signed by V. Chandamiah, District Superintendent of Police, Trivandrum.

[123] The District Magistrate's Court order was as follows:

[W]hereas it is necessary that you should be prohibited from making any public speech in any place in this District, in view to prevent probable riot, I do hereby prohibit you under section 127, Criminal Procedure Code, from making any public speech in any place in this District, and strictly warn and enjoin you not to take any part in any public meeting in any place in this District.

K. Narayanan Pandalai, to E. V. Ramasamy Naicker, "Order under Section 127, Criminal Procedure Code, District Magistrate's Court, Quilon," May 26, 1924, KSA: vol. 3, VSB, file 724 (handwritten 192).

Songs of the Volunteers

Some volunteers sat and carded cotton, or handloomed khadi. As mentioned, the handlooming of khadi on a national basis was not only a way for the poorest to participate equally in the independence struggles, it could also free India of dependence on foreign manufacturing, specifically from importing from the cotton mills of England. During their long days of vigil, satyagrahis would sing about the removal of untouchability, nonviolent action, spinning khadi, and Gandhi-led freedom for India. A sheet of song verses in the Kerala State Archives conveys the pain of the outcastes' conviction in the worthiness of their struggle. A few excerpted lines suggest their yearning:

I: . . . . Are the untouchables, who till the land and raise the crop and consequently secure prosperity, meaner and more depraved than the unrighteous who are the perpetrators of evil deeds? . . .

Converts from Hinduism, who despise the Hindu religion, are freely admitted into the villages. . . .

How can Pachan[124] pass through the temple road in a motor car and cause no pollution, while a poor untouchable will cause pollution by coming near? . . .

[I]f the various castes should shun each other, will the communities prosper? Will this not be hurtful to the country? . . .

II: . . . . There are a thousand castes here. What right have the foreigners to enter the land? . . .

III: Is there a fight like Satyagraha which involves no loss of human lives? It is a fight fit for the good, and none other can rival it in this respect. It is the art of war taught by Gandhi . . . with a view to rescue his mother country. It is the vigour-giving element for rehoisting the flag of independence in the country. . . .

VI: Oh! Charka [spinning wheel for hand-looming khadi] rotate—whirl and rotate Charka.

Whirl that Swaraj [self-rule] is attained. . . .

---

[124] Pachan is a common name among lower-caste men. Upper-caste men never use this name. The name alone reveals the caste hierarchy. Justin Mathew, communication, October 14, 2010.

Whirl Charka that following the rules of the Congress with Gandhi, we will cast off the foreign goods, vessels, and drinks. . . .

Whirl Charka that we shall burn all the silk goods, garments, and other rich foreign clothes, in big fire[s] and shall wear Khadar [the homespun of the constructive program]. . . .

VII: Seeing the condition of the Indians, our great leader Mahatma Gandhi—who is the fountain of humaneness and sympathy and who is well versed in vedic [pertaining to the Vedas, Hindu sacred literature] love—started the non-cooperation movement and caused it to be spread everywhere with a view to better our lot. In his laudable work he was greatly assisted and admired by the people. . . .

VIII: Give salvation to us who are born as human beings in Kerala the hell where unapproachablity prevails.

The prohibition boards are more dreadful than death and we pray to God for the disgrace to the earth being wiped out by the removal of the boards. . . .

[We] are come to Vaikom to pray in a lawful manner, and endowed with the power of endurance, . . . are not afraid of death. . . .

IX: . . . . We received blows and suffered punishment for having ventured to tread on the road through which cats, cows and dogs are allowed to pass.

Some people say that it would be wiser to accept Christianity instead of waiting for beneficial results. . . .

XI: . . . . The talk everywhere is about liberty. It is settled that all are equal. . . . Let us proclaim it to all the world. . . .

In our land we have come to know what ours is, and what our rights are. We will not be slaves to any one on earth. We will live as the servants of God.

XII: . . . . Freedom of passage to all is the aim of [nonviolent] resistance.

We carry no arms and we entertain no enmity towards any one; but we rely on truth, justice and Dharma. . . .[125]

Music and the singing of songs is a universal feature of nonviolent struggles, binding participants together, enlivening, unburdening, helping to find a collective response to apprehension or fear, and sometimes contributing to the making of decisions.

[125] National Songs, typed translation of songs initialed by Commissioner of Police W. H. Pitt on August 26, 1924, KSA: vol. 1, VSB, files 1190–6 (7 pp.).

Sloughs and Peaks

Gandhi's congratulations on the arrest of Madhavan and Kesava Menon did not go without notice, and his growing involvement in directing the Vykom encounter was keenly watched by people of all walks of life, including the intelligentsia among the upper castes. "Every word uttered by him ... added weight to the cause of the campaign and instilled confidence in the Satyagrahis," in Ravindran's words.[126] Desai says, "The movement was carefully watched and nursed by Gandhiji at every stage."[127] Professor N. N. Pillai commented, "Gandhi directed the Vykom satyagraha, but he did not participate in it."[128] Regardless, Gandhi's "conditions" also created quandaries, and new debates arose among supporters and critics alike.

After the government stopped making arrests, the satyagraha lost some of its allure and appeared to be adrift. The fasting that followed the cessation of arrests had attracted the interest of onlookers, but their support and attentiveness atrophied when Gandhi advised against fasting. The injunctions against non-Hindu help, external assistance, and fasting were hard to accept, although the approximately 120 volunteers tried to follow Gandhi's advice. The ashram had financial problems. "[T]he meager financial help the Keralites gave was sufficient only to keep the volunteers above starvation."[129] Though Gandhi on principle opposed the camp at Vykom receiving help from Hindus outside, local sources of funding dried up quickly, and the Congress as an entity barely existed in Travancore.

The *Mathrubhumi* published appeals for money and food. In its April 17 edition, the upper center of one page had a black-bordered box with a solicitation. It asked merchants, car owners, lawyers, landowners, and others, for contributions.[130] Two days later, the paper carried an appeal from T. K. Madhavan's wife, Narayan Amma, for personnel and funds. Referring to the arrest of her husband, along with K. P. Kesava Menon, she spoke of the need to protect justice and

---

[126] Ravindran, *Vaikkam Satyagraha and Gandhi*, 62.

[127] Desai, *Epic of Travancore*, 12.

[128] N. N. Pillai, interview (New Delhi, March 12, 2009).

[129] Ravindran, *Vaikkam Satyagraha and Gandhi*, 67.

[130] "Brothers and Sisters of Kerala," *Mathrubhumi* (trans. Thilleri), April 17, 1924, 5.

truth.[131] In reality, the restrictions drawn by Gandhi had alienated a large number of supporters. His stipulations left the Vykom campaign movement bewildered and hesitant about its future plan of action—if any such conscious preparation had been undertaken. The struggle was in a slump.

With the original leaders for the movement behind bars, the lack of immediate, well-informed counsel was acute. Firsthand wisdom, locally fluent with Travancore's singular background, was missing. The Vykom satyagraha had become, in Ravdindran words, "a cautionless jump into a crevice of unknown and unknowable possibilities."[132] The volunteers who "jumped" had to prepare themselves for the possibility of ostracism.[133] According to Desai, "The Satyagrahis not only went through much silent suffering, but also through social boycott at the hands of the orthodox and considerable unkindness on the part of their family members, and some of them were even threatened with the deprivation of their share in the family property."[134] Volunteers also encountered objective obstacles and personal difficulties as well. The areas surrounding the temple were unsanitary with filth and debris, including food waste from temple feasts.[135] At one point, an outbreak of smallpox infected the ashram shelter.[136]

[131] "Help the Moral Strength at Vykom: The Request of the Wife of Shri Madhavan," *Mathrubhumi* (trans. Thilleri), April 19, 1924, 5.

[132] Ravindran, *Vaikkam Satyagraha and Gandhi*, 118.

[133] Joan V. Bondurant, *Conquest of Violence: The Gandhian Philosophy of Conflict* (Berkeley: University of California Press, 1965), 50. Other sources also mention such censure, but with few or no details given.

[134] Desai, *Epic of Travancore*, 14. Gandhi writes of volunteers being denied their share of family property, being ex-communicated, and losing family privileges. Gandhi, Notes (Vykom Satyagraha), *Young India*, September 18, 1924, in *CWMG*, 29: 172.

[135] The sanitation problem must have been extensive, given that in 1924 K. N. Govinda Pillai, member of the Municipal Council from Vykom, spoke in the Sri Mulam Popular Assembly of the surroundings of the temple being kept in "a most unsanitary condition." The "remnants of daily feasts, which are a feature of the temple. . . . decayed and stinked" and during the rainy season were carried to the canal on the eastern side. He raised the issue of drainage due to the "bad stench" on the western side, and also asked that "proper drainage arrangements might be made" along the main, eastern side. *Proceedings of the SMPA*, 1924, 116.

[136] Desai, *Epic of Travancore*, 15.

As a result of these predicaments, the Anti-Untouchability Committee appointed a delegation to meet with Gandhi in mid-May 1924 to discuss future plans for Vykom. It was composed of Kurur Nilakantan Namboodiripad and K. Madhavan Nair, who joined him at Ahmedabad. Gandhi offered two major pieces of advice: First, he suggested forming a deputation to propagate the satyagraha throughout Travancore, while also collecting money and recruiting suitable volunteers. Second, Gandhi suggested arranging an organized procession, or *jatha*, from Vykom to Trivandrum and back, to issue a "monster petition" to the maharaja.[137]

The volunteers who were the backbone of the satyagraha accepted Gandhi's first idea but decided to postpone the second endeavor. The deputation they formed consisted of appointed members of the Congress; its influence generated considerable support among orthodox Hindus.[138] Although demurring on the concept of a large procession, they hoped that opposition to the movement would be quelled through focusing on public information efforts.

Despite some despondency in the satyagraha camp, and the avarnas as a whole remaining on the fringes of the campaign, some of the waves created by the movement's propulsions were producing momentum and bearing results. A joint meeting on May 16 of the SNDP Yogam and the Kerala Nayar Samaj was held near Vykom, in a high-water mark of unity between caste-Hindu middle classes and avarnas. Attendance was notable. The *Trivandrum Daily News* called the gathering "the most inspired spectacle ever witnessed in Travancore ... attended by about 15,000 people ... the hugest gathering ... ever assembled in

---

[137] In an indicative quotation, Gandhi writes to George Joseph suggesting a supportive role, "You must be patient. You are in an Indian State. Therefore, you may wait in deputation on the Dewan and the Maharaja. Get up a monster petition by the orthodox Hindus who may be well-disposed towards the movement. See also those who are opposing. You can support the gentle, direct action in a variety of ways." Gandhi, "Letter to George Joseph," April 12, 1924, in *CWMG*, 27: 225–6.

[138] Higher-caste Hindu support usually came from families from north and central Travancore. The climate in these areas made reliance on agricultural labor more significant than in the south. Therefore, the former felt more susceptible to the demands, economic or social, of non-caste Hindus and even Christian and Muslim laborers.

Travancore."[139] The session resulted in the formation of a deputation of ten people, five from each of these two groups, to present a memorial to the maharaja that would request the opening of temple roads to all untouchables.

The rest of India was observing keenly. Letters in large numbers were arriving in the capital. The communications of resolutions that had been passed by Arya Samaj were particularly numerous. Arya Samaj, an organization of upper-caste Hindus (calling themselves nobles), was formally founded in Kathiawar in 1875 by Swami Dayanand Sarawati (1824–83). The swami was a Sanskrit scholar who sought reform based on a return to the Vedas, sacred Hindu scriptures, and "pruning" the shoots that had been grafted onto them. He was monotheistic and opposed image worship, caste restrictions, and child marriages; he supported education of women and remarriage of widows. The Aryasamajists had no caste bar; their ranks included people whose backgrounds ranged from no caste to upper caste.[140]

The Arya Samaj at Dholpur, Rajasthan, passed a resolution on April 18 that was translated into English and sent to the dewan asking the government to "do justice":

> From the newspapers published in India it is well known that under the Travancore government ... the depressed classes who have been deprived of their social rights are doing Satyagraha to obtain their birth-rights, but the government there totally refuses to give their rights and disallows them to walk on the public roads [obliging them to pass] through special streets, and by sending Satyagrahis to jail the government is doing injustice and inhumanity.[141]

[139] *Trivandrum Daily News*, May 26, 1924, as cited in Jeffrey, "Travancore: Status, Class and the Growth of Radical Politics, the Temple-Entry Movement," in *People, Princes and Paramount Power*, 154, 167n60.

[140] Kali Kinkar Datta, *A Social History of Modern India* (Delhi: Macmillan Company of India, 1975), 371–2, 376. The Aryasamajists still exist, run educational institutions, and support philanthropic work, including the establishment of orphanages and widows' homes, famine relief, help for lower castes, and medical relief.

[141] Arya Samaj Secretary, Dholpur, Rajasthan, Letter to Travancore state Chief Minister (Dewan), June 13, 1924, KSA: vol. 3, VSB, file 643 (110 handwritten).

A resolution from Arya Samaj at Hoshiarpur in the Punjab, also sent to the dewan, reads:

> The Arya Samaj, Hoshiarpur, in its general meeting held on 25th May, 1924, strongly protests against the conduct of the High caste Hindus at Vykom, for denying the untouchables the ordinary human rights. It lends its support to the non-violent Satyagrahis who are doing their utmost to win the rights. The Arya Samaj, Hoshiarpur, requests the Travancore Government to be either neutral or settle the dispute, by throwing open the temple roads to all Hindus irrespective of invidious distinctions.[142]

On June 4, C. V. Kunjukidan Vaidyan, a member of the Sri Mulam Popular Assembly in Chavarakodu, Pengodu, wrote to the dewan of Travancore to say that he had chaired a public meeting at the Ayurveda Dispensary, which took several decisions:

> 1. We request the government to assure that all subjects irrespective of religion and caste should have the freedom of movement in public roads.
> 2. This meeting strongly protests the violence inflicted by the government on the satyagrahis.
> 3. This meeting requests the government to release the satyagrahis who are imprisoned without charges.
>   This meeting entrusts the chairman to inform the Honorable Dewan of the above three decisions.[143]

Telegrams pulsed across India:

> To Dewan Sahib Travancore. Snalandharan pratindhi Sabha Punjab. Resolved about Vaikom that (1) untouchables as such have a right to tread on roads on which Muslims and Christians are allowed it makes no difference if they become Christians, Muslimans or Aryasamjists that is they should be regarded . . . the same . . . . [signed] Parsinghlal, Secretary Snalandharan Publicity Bureau.[144]

Meanwhile, the satyagrahis remained steadfast and adaptive as the situation evolved. Overall, the volunteers followed Gandhi's

---

[142] Devi Chaud, Secretary, Arya Smaj, Hoshiarpur, to Dewan Bahadur T. Raghavaiah, Trivandrum, May 25, 1924, KSA: vol. 3, VSB, file 530.

[143] C. V. Kunjukidan Vaidyan, letter in Malayalam to the Dewan of Travancore, June 4, 1924, trans. Dinoo Anna Mathew, KSA: vol. 3, VSB, file 531.

[144] Telegram from Punjab, to Dewan, Trivandrum, June 11, 1924, KSA: vol. 3, VSB, file 81.

instructions. This could be seen with some directions developed with help from the esteemed lawyer, Chakravarti Rajagopalachari, as shown in a letter from the district magistrate to the government's chief secretary of June 1: "The recent instructions of Mr. Gandhi and the advice of Mr. Rajagopalachariar [or Rajagopalachari], the offer of Satyagraha by volunteers at night, has already stopped. Further, the number of volunteers is arranged to be reduced to 50 or below, and they are given special instructions not to cause the least violence."[145]

On May 31, 1924, a dispute between the spiritual head of the SNDP Yogam and Gandhi emerged. The *Deshabhimani*, a Malayalam weekly, published an interview with Sri Narayana Guru, conducted by K. M. Kesavan, at Quilon. In it Guru asks how the satyagraha is doing. Kesavan replies that it was being "vigorously conducted" and the satyagrahis "are probably drenching themselves in the rains." Guru asks why they could not use umbrellas. Kesavan explains Gandhi's thinking: "By forebearance the satyagrahis should enlist the sympathy of the opponents and of the government and should thereby achieve their goal." Guru acknowledges "the power of endurance," but notes that it is not required to expose oneself to rain, nor to starve oneself:

One should enter where he is prohibited from entering; and he should endure the consequent troubles. If belabored, that could be calmly put up with, and it should not be retaliated. But if any barricade is put up, one should not remain on this side of it. It should be scaled. It is not sufficient to walk along the roads; but one should enter the temple itself. Temple entry is not to be conducted in one place only. One should enter all temples, at all times; and all people should enter the temples.[146]

Were Guru's statements an attempt to openly incite his disciples to rebellion? By early June 1924, the difference of opinion between Guru and Gandhi was the talk of Travancore, eagerly ventilated in the local newspapers. Guru is quoted in the *Hindu* observing that

the volunteers standing outside the barricades in rains will serve no useful purpose. . . . [V]olunteers . . . should scale over the barricades, and not only walk along the prohibited roads but enter all temples including the Vaikom

[145] Office of the District Magistrate, Kottayam, letter to Chief Secretary of Government, Trivandrum, June 1, 1924, KSA: vol. 3, VSB, file 521.

[146] May 31, 1924, interview of Sri Narayana Guru, by K. M. Kesavan, Quilon, in *Deshabhimani*, English trans., KSA: VSB, vol. 1, file 1254.

temple. They should inform the government of their actions from time to time and should be prepared to give up their lives if needed. It should be made practically impossible for anyone to observe untouchability.[147]

Late in June, Guru wrote to tell Gandhi that his interview in *Deshabhimani* had gone into print without a correct understanding of his meaning: "I have no objection whatsoever to the satyagraha movement started by Mahatma Gandhi to fight this evil nor to the cooperation of people in the movement. Any method of work that may be adopted for eradicating the evil of untouchability must be strictly nonviolent."[148] The conflict was smoothed over in the press, but Guru dissociated himself from satyagrahis and the SNDP Yogam.[149] (He and Gandhi would meet in March of the following year.) Despite Guru's protestation, the evidence suggests that he was not fully persuaded of the effectiveness of satyagraha, and was ambivalent about it, viewing it as an effort to hold back the untouchables. "Narayan Guru was disgusted with Gandhi and the movement," Gilbert Sebastian asserted.[150] K. N. Panikkar's perspective merits attention:

Why have a satyagraha for entering the temple, which Gandhi blessed, and which became a major movement in India? Implicit in it is an assumption of Brahmanic superiority. In other words, the form of worship of the untouchables—the Ezhavas had their form of worship and they had their own gods—was considered inferior to the Brahmanical gods and the Brahmanic forms of worship, which is a very elitist view. The whole temple-entry movement therefore in a way could be seen as a strategy of containment of the untouchables, who were coming into politics in India at that time, becoming conscious of their place, thus the movement had a restraining effect.

This is one of the reasons why Narayana Guru did not take much of an interest in this temple-entry movement. Not that he did not go there [to Vykom], he did. So did Ramasamy Naicker, the other major low-caste movement leader. But as far as Narayana Guru is concerned, his whole involvement was lukewarm. He would possibly not have given great

[147] Associated Press of India, "Sri Narayana Guru's Views," *Hindu*, June 6, 1924.
[148] Guru to Gandhi, June 27, 1924, *Young India*, July 10, 1924, in *CWMG*, 28: 278.
[149] Menon, *History of the Freedom Movement in Kerala*, 124–5.
[150] Sebastian, interview (March 12, 2009). Sebastian's 1996 doctoral dissertation at New Delhi's Jamnalal Nehru University is "The Role of Narayana Guru in Kerala Society: A Contextual Analysis."

importance to the Brahmanical mode of worship, because he had been developing alternate forms of worship. This Brahmanic superiority is something that many of the Dalit activists and leaders would not have accepted. There was no reason why they should go to an upper-caste temple at all.[151]

By June, confusion had crept in among the satyagrahis. The district magistrate penned a note to the government's chief secretary on June 5 stating, "It is … reported that the volunteers are now instructed to enter the prohibited area unless there is physical restraint. This appears a recent innovation to court trouble and arrest."[152] The inspector of police noted, "The bamboo poles on the eastern side of the temple were … removed today so that to the volunteers all the four sides are open now. The work of the police officers has become extremely difficult; for the volunteers are ever ready looking for an unguarded point through which they may set foot on the prohibited ground."[153] The implementation of such policy for the satyagrahis is confirmed in a document from the Vykom police inspector of June 14: "The Satyagraha Committee have intimated that the volunteers have been instructed to enter the prohibited areas unless there is actual physical restraint preventing them from entering."[154] In other words, if barred, comply. The police inspector explained that objections had been strongly raised in different quarters to bamboo poles being sunk at the entrance to the barricades; as an experiment, they were removed from the western and northern sides on June 14.

The volunteers were trying to restrain themselves in accord with Gandhi's directives, but any gap in the barricades tested their resolve.

The Floods: "Worst in Human Memory"

The method of standing silently before the barricades, a stand-in, akin to a vigil, continued during the monsoon season, locally called the Edavappathy rains. In 1924, Travancore experienced heavy downpours

[151] Panikkar, interview (August 15, 2005).

[152] Office of the District Magistrate, Kottayam, handwritten letter to Chief Secretary of Government, Trivandrum, June 5, 1924, KSA: vol. 3, VSB, file 577 (handwritten 58).

[153] Letter from K. Rama Varier, Inspector of Police, Vaikom, to District Superintendent of Police, Kottayam, June 4, 1924, KSA: vol. 3, VSB, file 634.

[154] Varier, Vaikom, to District Superintendent of Police, Kottayam, June 14, 1924: vol. 3, VSB (letter), file 638 (handwritten 105).

beginning in April. A devastating hailstorm occurred on May 9. The volunteers were not always entirely without protection against rain, as a police report notes: "The third batch of volunteers who appeared after 12 o'clock today had puttils, the well-known rain-proofs of the Pulayas of middle Travancore which serve many useful purposes over and above being used as rain-coats. Some of these puttils show evident signs of long usage while others were brand new."[155] These coverings, however, would be futile as the rains continued.

By June, the deluge had become serious. It would come to be known as the Great Flood of 1924.[156] The flooding resulting from the heavy rains was the "worst in human memory," according to the *Mathrubhumi*, whose reports describe in detail how the volunteers stood neck deep in water, for three-hour shifts, with boats ferrying them to and from their positions. The police, in contrast, were provided boats, tethered to nearby houses, to allow them to remain in the vessels at their posts protecting the barricades. Some of the boats from the temple administration struck the volunteers with the prows. One volunteer, who is not named, died by drowning as he attempted to rescue someone.[157]

Archival records disclose riveting details. K. Rama Varier, inspector of police and acting commissioner of Vykom, on July 21 reported the following to his superior in the state capital:

> The lake has swelled and has nearly approached the door of the Police Station. Near the eastern barricade the flood has risen to the level of the

[155] Varier, Vaikom, to District Superintendent of Police, Kottayam, June 6, 1924, KSA: vol. 3, VSB (letter), files 634–5.

[156] The great flood of 1924 (the year 1099 in the Kollavarsham, the Malayalam calender) would play a considerable role in the caste-based modernity movements of the early twentieth century in this part of south India. The deluge created a condition in which all the caste groups were obliged to work together to manage the disaster. For a while, the orthodox upper castes had to compromise on their notions of untouchability. For example, to transport people and goods from flood-affected areas required cooperation between various castes. Much of the time anyone traveling had to journey together in *wallams*, wooden boats, which would otherwise have been unimaginable in the early twentieth century. Justin Mathew, communication (October 14, 2010).

[157] "The Satyagraha Struggle at Vykom: The Tireless Steadfastness of the Satyagrahis," *Mathrubhumi* (trans. Thilleri), August 2, 1924, 5. The newspaper's correspondent notes that no outside communications were possible, because of broken lines; no telegraph or post was in operation. Thilleri, interview (March 19, 2009).

Figure 4   Despite rising waters during the Great Flood of August 1924, the Vykom volunteers earnestly maintained their vigils (Illustrated by Madanan Pv)

Note: With heavy rains, the "worst in human memory," water rose to the level of the platform of the police shed and the Brahmin shops on the eastern side of the temple. The volunteers on the eastern side maintained their vigils in flood-waters that were waist-deep in the morning and would later each day swell to shoulder height.

platform of the Police shed and it extends to the centre of the Brahmin shops on the eastern side of the temple. The volunteers on the eastern side had to stand in water which was waist-deep in the morning and has since risen breast-high. In the morning the volunteers were relieved every one and a half hours; but after 9 A.M. sturdy volunteers were chosen and they have been offering Satyagraha for three hours at a time unaffected.[158]

[158] Varier, Vaikom, to Trivandrum Commissioner of Police, Travancore, July 21, 1924, KSA (letter): vol. 1, VSB, file 1084.

Varier also graphically describes the circumstances a few days prior:

The Satyagraha campaign continues in spite of the heavy rain and unprecedented flood. The western street is under water which has risen to the
level of the shop verandahs. The western road leading to the boat-jetty is
covered with water for most of its length. . . . The volunteers who offer
Satyagraha near the eastern barricade are standing in water neck-high.
The police sentry has to stand in water waist-deep. The police platform
on the eastern side is under water which has risen to a height of one and
a half feet above the platform. In the morning the Satyagrahis on the
eastern side were relieved after three hours; but in the afternoon they
were relieved every one and [a] half hours. The flood does not allow any
sign of abatement now.

The Reserve men are complaining of starvation and I spent one hundred
and seven rupees from my pocket. . . . Unless the men are properly fed
they could not stand the exposure to very cold blasts of wind and remain
waist-deep in ice-cold water. So I pray that the pay of the men on duty
here as well as the advance paid to them be sent here without delay.[159]

In July, as flooding continued from the rains, the district magistrate
of Kottayam notified the chief secretary to the government:

I have the honour to inform you that it is seen from Vykom reports that
the satyagraha situation remains unchanged. The volunteers at the
Eastern barricade are standing in water and they are relieved every three
hours in the forenoon and one and a half hours in the afternoon by fresh
volunteers. It is reported that about 600 flood refugees from the affected
areas near about Vykom were fed with *kanji* [rice porridge] on July 21,
1924, in the satyagraha camp.[160]

Again, Varier's reports provide specifics:

At the instance of the Satyagraha Committee there was a feeding of the
poor in the Satyagraha camp today. About 400 poor people including
Valans (a fishermen community), Ezhavas, Pulayas and a few Christians
were fed with kanji and tapioca curry. One full sack of rice was spent

[159] Varier, Police Inspector and Acting Commissioner of Police, Vaikom, to
Trivandrum Commissioner of Police, Travancore, July 19, 1924, KSA (letter): vol.
1, VSB, files 1090, 1091. (Police reserves got their advance, so says a letter from
Varier to the Acting Police Commissioner R. K. Krishna Pillai, July 28, 1924.)

[160] Kottayam District Magistrate, to Travancore Chief Secretary to the
Government, July 29, 1924 KSA (typed note): vol. 1, VSB, no. 1135.

today for the feeding of the above 400 who came from various corners of Vaikom. These are the persons who have been rendered helpless and houseless by the unprecedented flood. . . . The Satyagraha Committee have decided to feed the people affected by the flood till it subsides completely.[161]

Tremors of sympathy occasionally filter through the formality of the police reports.

Failings and Tribulations

The ongoing incarceration of the key local leaders who had conceptualized the Vykom struggle created a vacuum, resulting in a lack of direction and discernible lull within the movement. To the doubtful extent that a plan existed, those with a grasp of it were locked up early in the campaign. Certainly there was no grand strategy, in the sense of having various approaches envisaged for contributory campaigns that were to be part of a whole. The Vykom satyagraha proceeded in the initial stages more or less from individual initiatives, without much deliberate oversight or sense of sequencing. Any learning proceeded awkwardly.

In the beginning, the volunteers had been represented by identified spokespersons, who consistently informed the government of their positions on the basic grievance to be resolved, their intentions, and their principles. With the main leadership locked up—based on the supposition that "courting arrest" and being imprisoned would appeal to the sensibilities of the upper-caste temple authorities—no new course was being charted. The satyagraha became reactive. Gandhi, based in central India, was also responding to events rather than sketching a comprehensive plan of action. Although making the most wide-ranging use of Gandhi's empirically developed principles of satyagraha to date, the Vykom campaign was unrefined. Vykom became a hatchery for ideas on satyagraha—it had been less than a decade since Gandhi's permanent return from South Africa in January 1915—rather than implementation of calculated thinking that had been laid out with planning, as its mistakes showed.

[161] Varier, Vaikom, to Trivandrum Commissioner of Police, July 24, 1924, KSA (letter): vol. 1, VSB files 1097–8.

The indiscriminate recruitment of volunteers had generated problems. K. N. Govinda Pillai claimed that the majority of the Vykom satyagrahis were runaways and failures, who lacked productive work and merely wanted free meals. Other accounts of the time referred to volunteers as ne'er-do-wells, and even thieves in some cases, who had little if any dedication to the movement.

The stated attempt to "convert" the opponents was undermined, when volunteers became undisciplined and their frustrations led to verbal insults of orthodox Hindus and even the maharaja.[162] Madhavan was forced to make a public statement disapproving of such actions taken by the satyagrahis, while Gandhi informed Commissioner Pitt about the advice that they had been given. A vivid flyer appeared in the satyagraha camp:

> To the Satyagraha Warriors and Heroes: It's shameful that certain sections of the populace in Kerala are denied their basic rights. It is to remove this injustice that we started the satyagraha, and are still working toward it. You were jailed and released, and at this point we have only one thing to say to you: For whatever goal we started this struggle it still has not reached its victory. The tenets that you were following have been followed by these people even when you got jailed. There might have been some shortcomings in our following closely the tenets and that may be the reason why we still have not achieved our goal.[163]

Despite the satyagrahis' efforts at persuasion of the orthodox and the temple custodians as Gandhi emphasized, some of them lacked the discipline required for the struggle, while their adversaries were pushing toward extreme and violent opposition.

Caste-Hindu Opposition Intensifies

Upper-caste Hindus began to hold anti-satyagraha meetings in a number of places. Government reports from this period state that satyagrahis were trying to provoke police to lose their tempers. Moreover,

---

[162] Lakshmi Raghunandan, *At the Turn of the Tide: The Life and Times of Maharani Setu Lakshmi Bayi, the Last Queen of Travancore* (Bangalore: Maharani Setu Lakshmi Bayi Memorial Charitable Trust, 1995), 125.

[163] "To the Satyagraha Warriors and Heroes," flyer in Malayalam, 1924 (trans. Dinoo Anna Mathew), KSA: vol. 1, VSB, file 1266.

official correspondence speaks of the satyagraha camp as containing "discontented, unruly and boisterous young men, without any proper leader."[164] When physical attacks began to be made against some of the satyagrahis, the government disingenuously responded that the aggression had been carried out by parents of volunteers who were unhappy with their children's actions.

On June 19, an incident occurred between police and volunteers, suggesting the struggle's irresolution. The assistant superintendent of police, Pitchoo Ayyangar, saw "a new development and a change of attitude on the part of the Satyagrahis." He claims that the satyagrahis were purposely singing out of tune and badly, at the top of their voices in the faces of police, "howling almost in the ears of the sentry constables most defiantly and deliberately to annoy them," until ordered by police to stop. He disparages the volunteers as discontents, rowdies, runaways, and "disappointed students." At the ashram shelter, Ayyangar "found no leader worthy of the name." He authorizes his officers, in response to volunteers' yowling, to push them, seize their spinning wheel, and says he will prosecute them for obstruction and annoyance. Avowedly concerned about "world-wide publicity" of the struggle, he accuses the Congress party of "deliberate suppression of the facts" and the party's publicity bureau of making a bid for the sympathy of humanity outside the local parameters "by depicting the Police action in the darkest colour possible and giving to the whole situation a tyrannical outlook." Granting that the orthodox Hindus have "begun a counter move," a small group of them obstructing the satyagrahis near the western barricade, he admits that the authorities are "between the devil and the deep sea."[165]

Ayyangar contends that he had "conferred with the leaders of the anti-movement and severely warned them against the recurrence" of lawlessness. In his lengthy report, he concedes, "I have not come across any case in which a Satyagrahi returned blow [sic] and in this particular attitude of theirs, they are non-violent. In other respects their attitude is

[164] Letter from District Magistrate, Kottayam, to Chief Secretary of the Government, Trivandrum, June 21, 1924, KSA: vol. 3, VSB, file 634.

[165] Pitchoo Ayyangar, "A Police Officer's Report on Vaikkam Satyagraha, July 5, 1924," in Ravindran, *Vaikkam Satyagraha and Gandhi*, 311, 313–14, 316. A full text of the police report on the events of June 19 appears in 311–19.

violent, defiant, provocative and offensive."[166] Another police report is similarly derisive, noting the singing of

> annoying songs ... to annoy both the policemen ..., passersby and the neighbouring shopkeepers" and adding that "a charka [spinning wheel] is placed on the public street, half a dozen ... sit around it and sing in like manner ... a public nuisance causing great obstruction and annoyance to the general public.[167]

The entrance of the impassioned E. V. Ramasamy Naicker was reported to officials of the princely state with scorn:

> There was a meeting in the [June] evening in which Naicker spoke in Tamil, ... [H]is speech was a very violent one. Subramonya Chettyar also spoke and said that any amount of money and any number of volunteers can be sent from Tamil country and that all that the local people need is to be patient and cause no violence.
>
> As a matter of fact the volunteers are doing just the reverse—by their boisterous singing and spinning in the middle of the road they are ... [arousing] the feelings of the local people. [I'm] afraid that if things are [allowed] to go on in this manner, some opposition is bound to come from the people. . . .
>
> Yesterday 12 of these volunteers came singing in front of the [magistrate's] court and refused to stop it even after the magistrate sent word to them. The magistrate took up proceedings against them for contempt of court ... and fined them one rupee each or imprisonment to the rising of the court. After some time, all of them put in a written apology. . . . These persons are being prosecuted for obstructing the roads under the public regulation.
>
> In today's meeting Naicker has advised them to continue the spinning in spite of the police taking away the charkas. The District Magistrate having request [sic] to accord sanction for persecuting Mr. Naicker again for continuing to remain here in spite of the ... order.[168]

---

[166] Ayyangar, "Police Officer's Report, July 5, 1924," in Ravindran, *Vaikkam Satyagraha and Gandhi*, 311.

[167] Assistant Superintendent of Police, to Commissioner of Police, June 22, 1924, KSA: vol. 3, VSB, file 157.

[168] Confidential three-page handwritten letter, from Camp Vycome, to R. Krishna Pillai, Chief Secretary, Travancore, June 22, 1924, KSA: vol. 3, VSB, file 692–3.

Ravindran says cases of police squeezing the testicles of some volunteers and causing injuries in the genital area were reported.[169] Shortly after these confrontations, groups of young, often drunk, men dressed themselves as caste Hindus and instigated fights with satyagrahis and anyone nearby wearing the handloomed khadi. The organization of such groups, possibly agents provocateurs, remained unclear, but it is apparent that the police allowed such actions to continue unabated.[170] Certainly, police were not unaware of the attacks on the satyagrahis, as shown by an inspector's report on July 10, to the effect that Thathvananda Sivasari, a goldsmith by caste and a former overseer in the British service, was lecturing about the movement at Vykom: "He was giving out to the audience that the Satyagrahis at Vaikom are bodily injured by the High Caste Hindus."[171]

As aggression against the volunteers continued, new barricades were erected approximately one hundred yards before the original barriers. Orthodox Hindu brutes, who came to be known as *goondas*,[172] conducted still more organized violence and were suspected by some to be policemen as well. As the satyagrahis tried to pass in front of the newly installed barriers, they were halted, beaten, insulted, had their spinning wheels destroyed, and their khadi ripped off and burned.

"War on the *Charka*": Arrest of the Spinning Wheel

Provision for spinning wheels had been made, a police inspector's report shows:

> Thirty charkas have been arranged for, for the use of the volunteers both
> in the Asrama [ashram] and near the four barricades. As soon as the char-
> kas are received it is proposed to give a charka each to each of the batches
> of volunteers on the three sides and two charkas to the two batches of

---

[169] Ravindran, *Vaikkam Satyagraha and Gandhi*, 107.

[170] The attacks occurred under the auspices of the acting police commissioner, R. K. Krishna Pillai.

[171] T. R. Venkitachari, Police Inspector, Kottayam, to District Superintendent of Police, Kottayam, Report, July 10, 1924, KSA: vol. 2, VSB, file (handwritten), 213.

[172] Likely the origin of the English word *goon*, meaning rascal, rowdy, or brute; most examples given in the *Oxford English Dictionary* are from India.

volunteers on the western side. One of the volunteers of each batch must always spin on the charka supplied to each batch.[173]

Police were keeping tabs, on one day recording that thirty charkas were received from Palghat.[174]

While spinning on June 21, the volunteers had been singing patriotic songs about the Congress. In a dispatch hilariously headlined "The Police Arrest the Spinning Wheel," the *Mathrubhumi*'s correspondent says the singing infuriated the police, who asked cessation of the songs as they were highly patriotic in nature and could therefore be construed as critical of the government, the British, and of colonialism. As the volunteers continued to sing, the police took away their charka and "tortured" the volunteers, beating them with *lathi*, wooden batons. As the police removed one spinning wheel, volunteers brought another. It, too, was confiscated by police.[175]

When the police seized a third spinning wheel, the *Hindu* reported on it, subtitling the story "War on the Charka." The countrywide newspaper was not persuaded by police complaints:

Asked why they should object to the Volunteers spinning and singing, the Police authorities state that the public are disturbed by the Volunteers singing and turning their wheels. Anyone who visits the [pickets] will be convinced, all the same, that no disturbance of any kind whatsoever is caused either to the public or the passers-by as the spinners remain in the centre of the road plying their wheel.

The correspondent wrote that "most of the songs are devotional hymns invoking the blessings of the presiding deity of the Vaikom Temple to rid the land of the curse of untouchability and unapproachability." Accordingly, "[t]he Volunteers who have so far been mercilessly beaten

[173] Varier, Police Inspector, Vaikom, to District Superintendent of Police, Kottayam, June 6, 1924, KSA: vol. 3, VSB, file 635.

[174] Police Inspector, Arukutty (on special duty at Vykom), to Commissioner of Police, Travancore, June 25, 1924, KSA: vol. 3, VSB, file 699.

[175] "The Satyagraha Struggle at Vykom: The Advent of the Police Superintendent and Its Effect—The Police Arrest the Spinning Wheel" [reporting on events of June 21], *Mathrubhumi* (trans. Thilleri), June 24, 1924, 5. Thilleri described the sequence as follows: volunteers sang songs; police removed charka; police beat volunteers; police took second spinning wheel; police again beat volunteers.

have remained at their posts absolutely nonviolent even under extreme provocations. The Police sentries are also abusing the volunteers all the time using the worst epithets."[176] News accounts describe the routine:

> The Volunteers on duty are at their post singing religious and national songs and the Police first ask them to stop singing. They continue singing and the Policemen immediately start fisting them and kicking them. This process is kept on as long as it pleases the Police to do so. It is only at the Western gate that spinning is carried on and as soon as the spinners commence their work a Head constable issues a mandate to his men who advance and forcibly snatch away the [spinning] wheels, knocking the Volunteers as they seize the Charkas.[177]

About this period, when the goondas of the temple authorities were beating volunteers, N. N. Pillai years later recalled the following:

> A Nair named Chithdatka Sanka Odea was beaten so badly that he died. He was the first martyr of Vykom. There were atrocities, beatings, and limestone was thrown into the eyes of the satyagrahis, causing burns. Elayathu, one of many Brahmins among the satyagrahis, lost his eyesight as a result. One of my headmasters, Mandapathil Narayanan Nair, headmaster of the NSS Middle School, Vechoor, Vykom, coughed for the rest of his life. This he attributed to the beatings administered against the satyagrahis.[178]

Gandhi, in Ahmedabad, told a wire service:

> If the reports are to be relied upon, the Travancore State authorities have abandoned the innocent satyagrahis to the goondas said to have been employed by the orthodox opponents [of] reform for which the satyagrahis have been fighting. . . . Limes are thrown into their eyes and their khaddar shirts torn from them and burnt. Why the authorities can possibly take away inoffensive charkhas from the volunteers passes my understanding. . . . I hope, too, that the satyagrahis will remain calm, unperturbed and withal particularly non-violent. It is a time of great trial for them.[179]

---

[176] Correspondent, "The Struggle at Vykom: War on the Charka," *Hindu*, June 23, 1924.

[177] Correspondent, "The Struggle at Vykom," June 23, 1924.

[178] Pillai, interview (March 12, 2009).

[179] Gandhi, interview, Associated Press of India (July 1, 1924), *Hindu*, July 2, 1924, in *CWMG*, 28: 246–7.

Although police were obviously aware of such incidents, the Travancore government would not denounce the attacks until late July.

Nevertheless, the police were not of one mind; divisions existed within their ranks. Correspondence between S. Kumara Pillai, acting commissioner of police for Kottayam, and R. K. Krishna Pillai, acting commissioner of police for Trivandrum, discloses ruptures, which may have been instigated by Krishna Pillai, who was appointed acting commissioner while Pitt was away. Ravindran describes Pitt as "outwardly very considerate towards the Satyagahis."[180] Kumara Pillai writes to Krishna Pillai as follows:

> As instructed by you I visited Vaikom today and accidentally met the C.I.D. [Crime Investigation Department] Inspector there. He told me that he was specially sent by you with instructions to put a stop to the new barricade created by the oppositionists and also to put down the illegal activities of the Savarnas of Vaikom. He also told me that you have no objection to allow a single charka being quietly worked in a corner of the road by the side of the barricade and that you would like to stop the seizure of charkas by the Police. I called on the leaders of the Satyagraha campaign at their Asrama [ashram] and spoke to Mr. Narayana Ayyar M.A., B.A.[,] in charge of the Satyagrahis and others. The leaders have agreed to send a single charka in future and use it without creating any kind of obstruction or annoyance.[181]

In the same "strictly confidential" handwritten letter, Kumara Pillai says that he had heard at Vykom that savarna Hindu agents had been posted at the barricade to prevent anyone clad in khadi from passing. He indicates that the C.I.D. inspector had told him that he, too, had heard of such confrontations. Pillai says that he warned the agents in the presence of the local inspector of police.

Krishna Pillai, in response to Kumara Pillai, contests the Kottayam acting police commissioner's implication that he favored halting a new barricade and letting the volunteers spin quietly on a single spinning wheel: "Occupation of any part of the road ... is an obstruction and an

---

[180] Ravindran, *Vaikkam Satyagraha and Gandhi*, 106.

[181] S. Kumara Pillai, Acting Commissioner of Police, Kottayam, to Acting Commissioner of Police R. K. Krishna Pillai, Trivandrum, July 8, 1924, KSA ("strictly confidential" letter): vol. 1, VSB, file 1184 (handwritten 96).

offence. No distinction can be made lest others also claim such privileges." Krishna Pillai instead faults the satyagrahis:

> [A] warning is necessary. If they offer insults to Savarnas and are ill-treated
> as a consequence, they alone are to blame. It cannot be said that the con-
> duct of the volunteers have been such as to move the heart of the Savarnas
> in sympathy. They are arrogant and insulting in their conduct and conse-
> quently produce the opposite impression in the minds of the Savarnas.[182]

The *Hindu* corroborates Ravindran's portrayal of Krishna Pillai as the
"clandestine father" of the anti-satyagraha campaign.[183] It reports that
when police tactics changed, "sensational developments" occurred, and a
"resumption of assaults" on the volunteers occurred after Krishna Pillai
visited Vykom in June. Indeed, two volunteers who sustained injuries had
to be treated at a dispensary.[184] That Krishna Pillai was unalterably opposed
to the satyagraha, and conceivably the covert opposition leader within the
police force, can be confidently argued based on a number of police documents. He may have been an agent provocateur.[185] Ravindran reports an
episode in which Krishna Pillai leaves no doubt as to his complicity in
stimulating the anti-satyagraha movement. In a statement to the Travancore
Legislative Council, Pillai claims that the opposition movement had begun
on June 10, but that he had played no part in its formation:

> While I admit that some replies that I gave Savarna Hindus who came to
> represent their grievance might have induced them to start the movement,

[182] R. K. Krishna Pillai, Acting Commissioner of Police, Trivandrum, to
Acting Commissioner of Police S. Kumara Pillai, Kottayam, July 10, 1924, KSA
(letter): vol. 1, VSB, file 1185.

[183] Ravindran, *Vaikkam Satyagraha and Gandhi*, 110–11. "There is clear evidence to prove that the anti-satyagraha movement by a section of the orthodox
was mooted out by the Acting Commissioner of Police himself." Ravindran,
Vaikkam Satyagraha and Gandhi, 110.

[184] "Struggle at Vykom: War on the Charka," *Hindu*, June 23, 1924.

[185] In R. K. Krishna Pillai, Acting Commissioner of Police, Trivandrum, to
Chief Secretary of the Government, July 22, 1924, KSA (letter): vol. 1, VSB, file
1182, he submits to the chief secretary

> a petition from the people of Vaikom, complaining against the permission
> given to the Satyagrahis to use the road for spinning the Charka there. . . .
> The petitioners now say that, it is an obstruction caused to them in using
> the road and that if this is allowed, others also are likely to bring in Charkas
> and other implements and use the road for working with them.

I must disclaim all knowledge of their intention to start it. Had I known
it then, I would have requested them to at least postpone starting it by a
day, so that I might get away from the place.[186]

Local news media severely criticized the Travancore government for
its failure to maintain peace, with some surmising official involvement
in the attacks and the anti-satyagraha movement. So far as archival documents permit reconstruction, the police never reprimanded the orthodox opposition for their known actions against the satyagrahis. On July
14, a nationalist newspaper, *Swarajya* (Independence), slammed a government report on police actions at Vykom:

> The report is coloured by animus against satyagrahis, and leniency, at
> points ludicrous, towards the Police. While the Police assaults wear the
> harmless garb of "some pushing back or so," the conduct of the
> Satyagrahis is made to loom terrible indeed by comparison. We are told
> that the latter sang songs "hoarsely" so-called national songs which were
> offensive to Police dignity; that they blocked up the traffic of the roads
> with their charkas; and that they rendered themselves generally an intol-
> erable nuisance to their neighbours. Police intervention, we are told, was
> a last concession, which could not be helped, to the clamour of a tor-
> tured and outraged public which had been driven to the end of its
> patience. . . . [T]hese allegations . . . stand condemned by their own exag-
> geration and lack of balance. . . . We refuse to accept a report . . . hatched
> in bureaucratic comaraderie [sic].[187]

In the case of a legislative or parliamentary body, bloc voting, delay
tactics, and abuse of procedure is normal. *Swarajya*'s correspondent
reports an interview with the barrister Chakravarti Rajagopalachari,
who was questioned about the view of the Legislative Council. "As far
as I could gather," Rajagopalachari responds, the council was "almost
unanimously in favor of throwing open the roads and removing the
present restrictions against the depressed classes. A large number of the
Councillors are active sympathizers of the Satyagraha movement."
Mentioning conservative members of the council, he says that their
interventions in the deliberations "show the unanimity of all sides of

---

[186] *Proceedings of the Travancore Legislative Council*, August 4, 1924, vol. 5,
227, as cited in Ravindran, *Vaikkom Satyagraha and Gandhi*, 111n14.

[187] "Notes and Comments: Official Apologia for Vykom," *Swarajya*, July
14, 1924.

opinion in this matter beyond doubt." (A resolution had been formulated and balloted to the effect of throwing open the Vykom temple roads to all castes, but the council failed to adopt it because, Rajagopalachari says, it could not be taken up in time due to the pre-eminence of other legislation.) He indicates that councilors were preparing a memorial for the maharaja, in effect a recommendation. Rajagopalachari asserts that if the state could make bold innovations in the law regarding inheritance, marriage, and divorce, which previously had religious sanction, "it can interfere to protect its subjects against exclusion from public roads on the grounds of caste." Concluding, he says that he "cannot imagine that His Highness the Maharaja can long withstand the oral pressure of the whole cultured society in India. He is bound to yield if we are patient but determined."[188]

Upper-Caste Hindu Meetings

Meanwhile, Nambudiris and Nairs were conducting and participating in meetings both for and against the satyagraha. A letter of July 16 from the office of the district magistrate of Kottayam to the chief secretary of the Travancore government describes a meeting of high-caste Hindus in Vykom opposed to the satyagraha. About 300 attended a gathering that passed resolutions and expressed their regret at the "apathy" of the police. They also decided to start their own newspaper to convey their views.[189] P. K. K. Menon describes the July 16 gathering as having eighteen conveners and wanting to redress the "disadvantages" resulting from the satyagraha. O. Narayana Pillai brought forward a resolution that caste Hindus should boycott members of the Congress associated with the struggle, neither voting for them nor engaging them as lawyers or teachers. The resolution passed. The question of access to the temple roads was considered the opening to broader demands for entering the temples themselves, by those who were opposed to the demands of the satyagraha. Boycott and shunning

---

[188] Correspondent, "C. Rajagopalachar Interviewed," *Swarajya*, June 14, 1924. As noted, Rajagopalachari is also transliterated as Rajagopalachar.

[189] Office of the District Magistrate, Kottayam, letter to Chief Secretary of Government, Trivandrum, July 16, 1924, KSA: vol. 1, VSB, file 1085.

were thus being added to the methods being used at Vykom, albeit by the adversaries to the satyagraha.

Menon also describes a July 7 meeting of caste Hindus in central Travancore, at Chengannur, presided over by M. R. Madhava Warrier, member of the Legislative Council, which resolved, with no opposition according to Menon, that the non-caste Hindus be given entry into the Vykom temple roads. Based on the *Trivandrum Daily News*, M. N. Nair, an orator of note, protested against abuses by the police and some caste Hindus against the satyagraha; Mannath Padmanabha Pillai supported Nair's resolution. The resolutions were sent to the maharaja.[190]

Another July 16 letter, from the district magistrate to the chief secretary, describes a meeting at the former SNDP Yogam quarters, "attended by persons of all castes [including] Nairs, Nambudiris, Ezhavas &c." There, "they also passed resolutions to throw open the roads around the Vaikom temple to all classes of His Highness' subjects and expressing regret for the violence committed against the volunteers." The session appointed a committee of seven to get out the "real facts of the assault on the Volunteers." The missive says the group resolved to ask the Legislative Council "to bring in a resolution … to declare these roads open to all classes."[191]

As long as orthodox opposition was well articulated, decisive upper-caste support would not be forthcoming. Violence against the satyagrahis was, however, beginning to cause divisions within savarna communities. Among the properties of nonviolent action is its ability to split the ranks of the target group. Conversely, within the Ezhava community, the attacks were now generating even greater support, both in numbers of volunteers and funds. As contributions were collected by sending volunteers door to door throughout the locality and neighboring areas, the message of the satyagraha and fight against untouchability was able to spread. The

[190] *Trivandrum Daily News*, July 7, 1924, as cited in Menon, *History of the Freedom Movement in Kerala*, 123, 123n19. The newspaper details two July savarna Hindu meetings, one supporting and the other denouncing the Vykom struggle. Menon, *History of the Freedom Movement in Kerala*, 123, 123n20. Menon notes that access to temple roads had been effected at Chengannur, Tiruvalla, Aranmula, and Korattiyil. Menon, *History of the Freedom Movement in Kerala*, 123n20.

[191] Office of the District Magistrate, Kottayam, to Chief Secretary of Government, Trivandrum, July 16, 1924, KSA (letter): vol. 1, VSB, file 1085.

anti-satyagraha efforts paled in contrast to the popular surge of the satyagraha and its nationalistic calls for civil rights.

Without doubt, the Vykom struggle had been galvanized by local and regional upper-caste figures. This energizing of the higher-caste Hindus was deliberate, recalling Gandhi's admonishments for appealing to orthodoxy, although in many cases the high-caste leaders that became involved were from next-door Tamil Nadu. For understandable reasons, less support for the satyagraha came from the poor, lower castes, and untouchable Hindus, the great majority of whom were too apprehensive about their high-caste Hindu landlords and employers to be seen publicly taking any action.

Small gains suggested that internal divisions were occurring among the orthodox. On June 24, the district magistrate advised the government's chief secretary that caste Hindus under the leadership of P. C. Krishna Pillai and G. Venkitrama Iyer had organized volunteers at the temple's four gates, where "they intend to send ... one savarna volunteer for each of the satyagraha volunteers and that they are to be relieved every three hours by fresh batches. It is said that the Satyagrahis contemplate sending a number of lady volunteers to match the savarna volunteers." The district magistrate referred to these developments as a "new movement."[192]

Women in the Struggle

A ferment of ideas and entitlements was brewing in Travancore, related to caste reforms and other modernizing social issues. As the Ezhavas' social reform efforts were fueling struggles against the privileges of the savarnas, established social structures and traditional value systems were colliding with new, emerging classes and forces. Meera Velayudhan writes of the Vykom satyagraha as coalescing with these social reform and nationalist movements to usher in a "new phase in women's participation in struggles."[193] She describes Ramasamy Naicker at a

[192] Letter from District Magistrate, Kottayam, to Chief Secretary of the Government, Trivandrum, June 24, 1924, KSA: vol. 3, VSB, file 697.

[193] Meera Velayudhan, "The Growth of Political Consciousness among Women in Modern Kerala," in Kerala State Gazetteer, ed. P. J. Cherian, vol. 2, pt. 1, Perspectives on Kerala History: The Second Millennium (Trivandrum: Kerala Gazetteers, Government of Kerala, 1999), 492.

meeting in Chertallai as particularly requesting women volunteers to join the struggle, with 100 enlisting "on the spot," and notes that at Mavelikkara, Sarada Ammal, daughter of jailed T. K.Madhavan, spoke publicly to denounce the practices of unapproachability and untouchability.[194] On a modest basis, women were stepping out, beyond the defined path.

In 1896, the Malabar Marriage Act had been passed, legalizing Nair marriages, which had not been formalized before, and extending some property rights for women. It ushered in a variety of social alterations that would bring normative changes, including notions of individual rights, eventually affecting conceptions of women's rights. A reform movement among Nambudiris, for example, emphasized access to English education and the right of Nambudiri men to marry within their own caste, because marriage customs had been at the crux of maintaining the Nambudiris position as a landed aristocracy. This trend also elevated choice in marriage, property ownership, and inheritance, opposition to old men marrying young girls and child marriage, and polyandry and polygamy issues. Abolition of *purdah*—the system of sequestering women, keeping them unseen—became a focus of attention among Nambudiri women.[195]

Figures such as Sri Narayana Guru, Padmanabhan Palpu, Kumaran Asan, and T. K. Madhavan could gain adherents in this concoction of contesting ideas in Travancore. In April 1924, "Two thousand men and a few Ezhava women" were present at a meeting in Karuvatta, where, according to a police report, "One Parvathi Amma an Ezhava young woman of Muthukulam . . . said that women of Savarna Hindu community should take a prominent part in such meetings and try their level best to uplift women in the Avarna communities. She advocated interdining, intermarriages and said that 'pollution' should be rooted out."[196]

By May, women had begun to take a larger part in the Vykom satyagraha. The *Mathrubhumi* reports that for the first time, on May 24, the

[194] Velayudhan, "The Growth of Political Consciousness," 494. No dates are given.

[195] Louise Ouwerkerk, *No Elephants for the Maharaja: Social and Political Change in the Princely State of Travancore, 1921–1947* (New Delhi: Manohar, 1994), 59.

[196] J.J.Janiel, Asst. Supt. Police, Chengannoor, to Trivandrum Commissioner of Police April 23, 1924, KSA (report): vol. 5, VSB, handwritten files 113–15, 1.

volunteers' group included five women, among them the wife of E. V. Ramasamy Naicker. Of these five, one was from the excluded castes. The women were halted at the entrance of the prohibited road by the police, who told four of them that they could enter, but informed the lower-rank woman that she could not. The other four replied, "We are going together and we won't leave her alone at the entrance." As a result, they were made to stand for hours at the entry point.[197] Local women living in the environs of Vykom were not substantially active in the satya-graha, although this picture started to change several months into the struggle in 1924. Files in the Kerala State Archives show that the chief secretary of the government was being advised of increases in the number of women volunteers taking part.[198]

Archival and newspaper records reveal the episodic involvement of women in the satyagraha, sometimes noteworthy.[199] The *Mathrubhumi* reports, approximately three weeks later, on roughly June 14, 1924, that Mrs. Naicker and six or seven of her Brahmin friends were not allowed to enter the Vykom temple. They proceeded to purify them-selves, called *poojah*, in the open air. (Normally poojah is carried out inside; given that they were not allowed entry, they did the purification rites themselves outside the temple without a priest.) They asked the priest who prevented them from entering the house of worship why

[197] "Torture Policy of the Government at Vykom: Mr. Charavarthy Ayyankar Gets One Month Imprisonment; Mr. Naicker Violates Prohibitory Order; Satyagraha by Women Volunteers," *Mathrubhumi* (trans. Thilleri), May 24, 1924, 3.

[198] May–June 1924, several reports to the Chief Secretary from District Magistrate, on women volunteers becoming actively involved during May and even more so in June 1924, KSA: vol. 3, VSB.

[199] In October 1924, Poonen Lukose, a surgeon appointed to head the Women's and Children's Hospital in Trivandrum, would become the first woman appointed to the Legislative Council. The following year, in January 1925, in Gujarat, Gandhi would address a women's conference and speak about women as vital for *swaraj*: "I ask you to participate in public life," and to "work for India's salvation," in part by wearing khadi. Gandhi, Speech at Women's Conference, Sojitra (January 16, 1925), in *CWMG*, 30: 108, 110. Upon visiting Travancore in the following March, detailed below, Gandhi will regularly note the presence of girls and women in audiences for his speeches. He will observe that women bring prowess to the handlooming of khadi, which in the national context was not related to gender.

they were prohibited. The staff reporter writes that he responded that they had polluted themselves by passing near the avarna camp.[200] On June 24, K. Rama Varier, police inspector for Vykom, reported that three Ezhava women from [coastal] Mavelikara—Lakshmi, Karthoo Kunju, and Kalyani—had arrived to become satyagrahis.[201] In one of the few extant firsthand texts from an Ezhava woman participant in Vykom, Kalyani calls the satyagraha "a struggle for one of the fundamental rights of human beings, the freedom of movement." She mentions their hope for fifteen volunteers at every shift for each of the four gates to the temple, which "must include both *avarnas* and *savarnas*." At that point no savarna woman had stepped forward to support the satyagraha, which Kalyani calls "ignominious," because it would affect their effectiveness. She optimistically states that women are "capable of bearing the entire financial burden" of the struggle, and that the Ezhava community had opened a canteen through the cumulative actions of women collecting "handfuls-of-rice."[202] Two days later, Varier notes, "The second batch of volunteers for the western side today consisted of six lady volunteers two of whom were Tamilian ladies and the rest Ezhava ones."[203]

"The women who were involved were generally from Tamil Nadu," development studies professor J. Devika observed. According to her:

They were not from Vykom. In 1924, the local men and women were not involved very much. Travancore is not like Malabar. In Malabar, women were very active. The *savarna jatha* [a grand procession that

[200] "The Satyagraha Struggle at Vykom: Mrs. Naicker Was Not Given Entry to the Temple [event in the June 14 report]," *Mathrubhumi* (trans. Thilleri), June 19, 1924, 3. This was the wife of Periyar E. V. Ramasamy Naicker.

[201] Rama Varier, to District Superintendent of Police, Kottayam, letter with three notes of different dates, this report dated Malayalam calendar 24-10-1099 (June 24), KSA: vol. 3, VSB, file 635.

[202] Vatakkecharuvil P. K. Kalyani, "An Appeal to the Hindu Women of Kerala," in *Her-self: Early Writings on Gender by Malayalee Women, 1898–1938*, ed. J. Devika (Calcutta: Stree, 2005), 83, as cited by Devika from "Keraleeya Hindu Streekalodu Oru Abhyarthana," *Malayala Manorama*, July 24, 1924. The handfuls of rice, or *pidiyari*, were held apart by women so they could respond to appeals. Kalyani, "An Appeal to the Hindu Women of Kerala," 86n5.

[203] Rama Varier, Police Inspector, Vaikom, to District Superintendent of Police, Kottayam, letter, June 16, 1924, KSA: vol. 3, VSB, file 640 (handwritten 107).

would take place in autumn 1924] was the first of its kind. *Mathrubhumi* newspaper was more familiar with women's activism, being based in Malabar, but in Travancore, women's activism was almost nonexistent then.[204]

During the Vykom satyagraha, the authorities incarcerated ten to fifteen who were from the outside, from British India, not from Travancore.[205]

For his part, Gandhi was imbued with a deeply patriarchal world-view that persists even today in India and elsewhere throughout the world, although his experiments during twenty years of working in South Africa had led him to appreciate as a pivotal concept the central involvement of women in political action. By 1921, he was calling for women to become involved in the national political deliberations, to secure the vote, and to benefit from legal status equal to that of men. The handlooming of khadi alone animated millions of women in pursuing India's independence and placed the nationalist cause before the hearth. By the late 1920s, Indian women were in some places leading local struggles. As Gandhi construed the capacity of nonviolent civil resistance, even a frail woman or child can pit herself on equal terms against an onerous opponent, including one armed with military weaponry, because it aims at the power of the opponent, not the lives or limbs of the adversary or its supporters. In his three major movements, where the Congress formally took up the strategy of satyagraha (1920–2, 1930–4, 1942), large numbers of women in different areas of India participated. Nonetheless, as David Hardiman aptly points out, "Fellow nationalists and women activists never subjected Gandhi to any strong criticism for his patriarchal attitudes. In this, we find a contrast to his other major fields of work, in which sharp differences were expressed in a way that forced him to often qualify or modify his position."[206]

---

[204] Devika, interview (March 23, 2009).

[205] Jnaneswaran, interview (March 25, 2009). Regarding women's participation in 1924, 15 years later, by the early 1940s, women were still not active in the public space. "An effort to get Dalit women to wear Ezhava women's garments failed. The Dalit women were reluctant to participate. In the domestic sphere also they enjoyed little freedom." Jnaneswaran, interview (March 25, 2009).

[206] David Hardiman, *Gandhi in His Time and Ours: The Global Legacy of His Ideas* (London: Hurst and Company, 2003), 116.

Interest Gathers

On July 1, 1924, an article in the *Hindu* reports that June 28 marked the departure on foot from Nagpur in central India of M. Kumaran, a local worker for the Congress and a supporter of the satyagraha, who was setting off to walk to Vykom.[207] Across India, interest was gathering. In Travancore, more upper-caste Hindus were stepping forward, made clear by a confidential police report from a gathering at Umayattukara School, attended by some of the foremost citizens and figures mentioned thus far. A gathering in Chengannur (also transliterated as Chengannoor) on July 6 passed a resolution: "This meeting is of the opinion that the non-caste Hindus should be given freedom to walk along all the roads round the walls of the great temple at Vaikom and other places, which are now open to non-Hindus even, and requests Government to immediately issue a Proclamation permitting the non-caste Hindus to pass along such roads." Neelacanta Pillai asserted that "the public roads were constructed with the money of all classes of subjects, they should be open to all classes; there is no principle either in the Vedas or the Tantras on which to argue that the roads round the outer-walls of a temple should be closed to any caste."[208] Yet some of the orthodox attending the meeting walked out.

For the most part, the individuals who were participating in the events, and would join in the large processions to come, were from Tamil Nadu. E. V. Ramaswamy Naicker, Ayyamuthu Gounder (also Ayya Muthu Goundan, or Ayyamuttu Gaundar), and Emperumal Naidu were Tamil leaders who courted arrest. Of the nineteen men locked up in the early phase of the struggle, just seven hailed from Travancore, and only one—T. K. Madhavan—was an Ezhava. Backing for the struggle was coming from middle-class caste Hindus who were adherents of the programs of the Indian National Congress. Key figures, such as K. Kelappan and K. P. Kesava Menon, both managers of the *Mathrubhumi*, came from Malabar district. Muslim sentiments of sympathy were being aroused by the tidal wave from the Vykom earthquake, Ravindran notes.[209]

---

[207] Correspondent, "Caste Hindu Procession," *Hindu*, July 1, 1924, dateline Cannanore.

[208] Proceedings of Meeting Held in the Umayattukara School, Chengannoor, 3:30 P.M., July 6, 1924, KSA: vol. 2, VSB, 7 pp.

[209] Ravindran, *Vaikkam Satyagraha and Gandhi*, 67.

Christian involvement had been lost earlier, in April, when Gandhi had asked the Syrian Christian leader of the Congress, George Joseph, to let the Hindus run the satyagraha.

By July the government was well aware that plans were under way for a major demonstration. The acting commissioner of police advised the chief secretary of the Travancore government that the date of the caste-Hindu procession was as yet unsettled and unlikely for the near future.[210] As July turned to August, with the rains unreduced, the daily vigils of volunteers continued as in previous months. Writing as inspector of police and acting commissioner of police in Vykom on August 1, K. Rama Varier reports to his superior that the satyagraha campaign was continuing with no change of program: "The flood has abated a little and the volunteers on the eastern side are standing in water a little above two and a half feet in depth. One bamboo charka was brought at 12 o'clock to the western side and the volunteers spun on it in turn."[211] On that day, curry was served to 750 poor refugees in the Vykom municipality.

The second phase of the struggle would come to an end in August, although the highest period of enthusiasm had lasted intermittently from April to September. Vykom was commanding the attention of all of India. The satyagraha had come through its stage of greatest ineptitude and was about to enter a third period.

[210] R. K. Krishna Pillai, Acting Commissioner of Police, Travancore, to Travancore Chief Secretary to the Government, August 1, 1924, Satyagraha at Vykom—Caste Hindu Procession (refers to a document dated July 7, 1924), KSA: vol. 1, VSB.

[211] K. Rama Varier, Vaikom, to Trivandrum Commissioner of Police, Travancore, August 1, 1924, KSA (letter): vol. 1, VSB, file 1139.

4 The Maharani Regent and Travancore Governmental Change

Indicative of where things stood five months into the Vykom struggle, on August 5, the district magistrate of Kottayam invoked the Criminal Procedure Code and banned the Tamil leader, Ayyamuthu Gounder, from visiting Vykom or elsewhere in the district. The magistrate attributed his action to reports of speeches and activities by Gounder, who is quoted earlier complaining about the lack of effort from people in the vicinity of Vykom. The magistrate claims his additional entry into or staying at Vykom is "likely to lead to riot and affray."[1]

Two days later, on August 7, Maharaja Sri Mulam Thirunal died, and the Vykom satyagraha was suspended for three days of mourning. On September 1, Sethu Lakshmi Bayi was installed as the maharani regent. She would act in lieu of the young heir, Chitra Thirunal Balarama Varma, her nephew, who was seven years shy of being able to assume the throne. The royal house of Travancore followed the long-prevalent Nair *Marumakkathayam* system of matrilineal inheritance.[2] The head of

---

[1] M. V. Subrahmanya Ayyar, August 5, 1924, Proceedings of the District Magistrate, Kottayam. under Section 127, Criminal Procedure Code, letter transmitting order, July 28, 1924, Kerala State Archives (hereafter KSA): vol. 1, Vaikkom Satyagraha Bundle (hereafter VSB), file 1167.

[2] The matrilineal system of inheritance and matrilocal residence based on a joint family was followed by Nairs (and Ezhavas) until recently. Divorce was uncomplicated, as noted earlier: "a woman had only to place the sandals of her former husband ... outside the door and the husband knew that he had to retire." Louise Ouwerkerk, *No Elephants for the Maharaja: Social and Political Change in the Princely State of Travancore, 1921–1947* (New Delhi: Manohar, 1994), 41.

the royal family was the senior *rani*, called *maharani* in the same way that the king, or *raja*, with its appendage *maha* to amplify the title, meant "great king."[3] The senior rani, whoever she was, usually acted as regent while the new raja was still a minor.

Travancore's new maharani regent, who would rule over approximately four million persons, was installed by the British agent C. W. E. Cotton.[4] In actuality, she held the title of maharaja, because she ruled in her own capacity, not as a spouse of the maharaja as in the other princely states, but the appellation she would use for the next few years would be maharani.[5] Following her temple consecration and formal investiture, a *durbar* (grand reception) was held at which she spoke. With her husband, Valia (meaning Senior) Koil Thampuran, in the audience, she said that she found it "gratifying to know that in the discharge of my arduous duties I can always look for help and advice to His Imperial Majesty's Representative at my court, Mr. C. W. E. Cotton." She assured him:

> I shall honestly strive to live up to the high ideals he has set before me. It
> shall be my earnest endeavour to maintain unimpaired the hereditary

[3] The ranis had an estate at Attingal, 25 miles north of Travancore. Royal princes were sons of princesses in the Attingal family. The oldest male in the family would become the raja and rule Travancore, while the senior rani administered the estate. The raja's choice for marriage or a liaison was unimportant, because their sons could not claim the *gaddi* (throne). The rajas habitually married Nair women from Trivandrum's established families. Their sons were called *thampi* (younger brother), and they were members of their mother's caste. Palace officials were nearly always Nairs and relatives of the raja's consort (who was not a wife).

[4] Although not well educated, during her reign, the maharani would institute a number of reforms to abolish customs that "undermined the position of women in society" and take constructive steps to promote women's welfare, including midwifery training and raising salaries for schoolteachers. Lakshmi Raghunandan, *At the Turn of the Tide: The Life and Times of Maharani Setu Lakshmi Bayi, the Last Queen of Travancore* (Bangalore: Maharani Setu Lakshmi Bayi Memorial Charitable Trust, 1995), 135. She would also raise the caliber and status of the women's college in Trivandrum and establish village *panchayats* (councils) to reform and develop self-governance in rural areas of the state. Under her rule, animal sacrifice in south Travancore temples was abolished. A. Sreedhara Menon, *A Survey of Kerala History* (Kottayam: Sahitya Pravarthaka Co-operative Society, 1967), 334.

[5] Raghunandan, *At the Turn of the Tide*, 116. Raghunandan gives details of the maharani's investiture, 109–20.

friendship that has always subsisted between the British Nation and my house from the days when the … East India Company obtained a plot of ground in Anjengo from my progenitor, the Attingal Rani.[6]

The police commissioner at the time of her coronation was R. K. Krishna Pillai, considered by T. K. Ravindran to be the "clandestine father" of the hostile campaign against the satyagraha.

One of the first acts of the maharani regent was to free fifty-six prisoners, among them twenty participants in the Vykom satyagraha, including T. K. Madhavan and K. P. Kesava Menon. Although Gandhi's secretary Mahadev Desai is often worshipful toward Gandhi, his evaluations have elements of truth, that the maharani's deed was "as much due to the Maharani's generosity as to the scrupulously non-violent way in which the Satyagraha was being conducted."[7] Ramasamy Naicker worked behind the scenes to help bring about their release and approached Bahadur T. Raghavaiah (also called Rajaji), a close friend of the *dewan*, according to Balambal. Although he gives no details, Balambal says that Rajaji explained to the maharani the "intricacies of the problem" and "insisted" that the dewan expedite the opening of temple roads.[8]

Approximately a hundred persons set off for the prison to receive A. K. Pillai and others upon their release, but only one was allowed at the main gate, while the others waited, including a tailor, Perumal, who was carrying flags.[9] By August 28, at least six other leaders had been freed from prison: C. A. Aiyanmuthu Goutan (Ayyamuthu Gounder), T. R. Krishnawamy Aiyer (also Krishna Swamy Iyyer), A. K. Pillay (also Piallai), Narayana Menon Velayudha Menon, K. Kelappan [Nayar], and Kuruvila Mathew.[10] The rest would follow. The maharani's action was heralded and drew approbation.

[6] Raghunandan, *At the Turn of the Tide*, 118.

[7] Mahadev Haribhai Desai, *The Epic of Travancore* (Ahmedabad: Navajivan Karyalaya, 1937),13.

[8] V. Balambal, "E. V. R. and Vaikom Satyagraha," *Journal of Kerala Studies* 7 (March, June, September, December, 1980): 252.

[9] V. Chandamiah, August 9, 1924, to R. K. Krishna Pillai, Acting Commissioner of Police, Travancore, reporting release of A. K. Pillai and others from jail, KSA (letter): vol. 1, VSB, file 1180.

[10] Superintendent of the Central Prison, Trivandrum, August 28, 1924, list of satyagraha prisoners released from central prison, KSA: vol. 1, VSB, file 1217 (handwritten 110). Names are listed here as in document.

Gandhi had expressed concerns that the previously ruling maharaja possessed rigidly orthodox views on untouchability, but he now saw an opportunity to urge the maharani in a different direction:

> Let me hope that Her Highness the Maharani Regent will recognize that untouchability is no credit to Hinduism but it is a serious blot on it. The best service that a Hindu State can render to Hinduism is to rid it of the curse and set an example in liberalism to Hindus of British India. The Satyagrahis ... do not want anything more than a recognition of the most elementary human right for the unapproachables and untouchables.[11]

On September 11, an article in the *Hindu* reports that in *Young India*, Gandhi, writing from Ahmedabad, had congratulated the maharani for releasing all of the *satyagrahi* prisoners and praised the satyagrahis for temporarily suspending their struggle for mourning: "It paves the way for understanding and enables the state authorities to review their attitude towards satyagrahis without embarrassment."[12]

With recently released satyagraha leaders having returned from prison to the ashram, interest was rekindled in Gandhi's earlier suggestion for a procession, or *jatha*, and the issuance of a "monster petition" to the maharani. George Joseph and T. K. Madhavan traveled to meet with Gandhi and issued a statement to the news media. Their encounter with Gandhi occurred on September 18, during a time when Gandhi had undertaken a twenty-one-day fast, from September 17 to October 7, for Hindu–Muslim unity. Madhavan suggested that there was "some doubt amongst the public in general and the Ezhavas in particular whether Mahatmaji fully approved of the movement." Gandhi expressed his regret that there should be "any such doubt or ambiguity." He outlined a work program of tasks that he asked Joseph and Madhavan to carry out, among which was for them to go to Simla carrying a letter from him to Pandit Madan

---

[11] Gandhi, as cited in P. K. Karunakara Menon, *The History of the Freedom Movement in Kerala*, vols. 1 and 2 (1600–1938), compiled by the Regional Records Survey Committee, Kerala State (Trivandrum: Government Press, 1970), 126. No source given.

[12] "Vykom Campaign: Mahatma Congratulates Regent—Satyagrahis' Duty," *Hindu*, September 12, 1924.

Mohan Malaviya, asking him to "proceed to Travancore and undertake a settlement with the authorities." Gandhi still hoped for the intervention of Malaviya.

A newspaper says that Madhavan felt ill, and hence Joseph went on to Simla alone. Malaviya "was anxious to accept the invitation at once," but due to some delays it was decided that he would be at Vykom on November 10 and at Trivandram later.[13] Madhavan made up for sickness in subsequently telling 800 people meeting in the Vykom ashram of the visit with Gandhi, in which he "emphasised about Mr. Gandhi's taking the leadership of the Satyagraha at Vaikom." The report notes that Gandhi had specially deputized Malaviya to open negotiations with the Travancore government to reach a settlement on the question of Vykom. The same meeting learned that a telegram indicated that the All-India Congress Committee had resolved to give financial help for the satyagraha.[14]

Meanwhile the Anti-Untouchability Committee worked to gather signatures for the monster petition and recruit participants for the jatha. Word spread as efforts were made to recruit upper-caste Hindus. A telegram to the maharani regent states:

> We saverna Hindu citizens of Tiruvalla Taluq in meeting assembled numbering over 3,000 pray that your exalted highness will be graciously pleased to grant liberty of passage to all classes of your highness [sic] subjects along Vaikom roads and all other similar in the state.[15]

[13] Associated Press of India, "Vykom Campaign: Gandhiji's Advice; Pandit Malaviya to Visit in November," *Hindu*, September 26, 1924 (dateline Delhi, September 25).

[14] S. Venkitachala Sarma, Police Inspector, Arukutty, to Commissioner of Police, Travancore, October 10, 1924, KSA (memorandum): vol. 4, VSB, file 1307 (handwritten 205). Corroborated by "Detailed Report of the Meeting Held at the Satyagraha Ashram on October 7, 1924," to District Superintendent of Police, Kottayam, October 7, 1924, KSA: vol. 4, VSB, file 1298 (handwritten 190), Madhavan told the gathering, according to the October 7 report, that "his own jail experience was happy."

[15] Neelakanta Kaimal, to Her Highness the Maharani Regent, Trivandrum, November 4, 1924, KSA (telegram): vol. 4, VSB, file 4073.

Petitions were being circulated, so that the signatures collected could be combined into one.[16]

Also in early October, Sri Narayana Guru visited the satyagraha ashram in Vykom. The *Mathrubhumi* reports that he conducted a meeting in which "he prayed for the health and mental peace" of Gandhi, because of his fast. While at Vykom, Guru decided to spin khadi. Although special arrangements had been made for his morning meal, he chose to eat instead with the satyagrahi volunteers.[17] The police inspector reported, "Sri Narayana Guru has made a donation of Rs. 1000/- for Satyagraha as well as all the offerings made by him during his stay here. The first khadder cloth woven in the Asramam [ashram] was sent to Mr. Gandhi, the second was presented to Sri Narayana Guru who accepted it with great pleasure."[18] The district magistrate of Kottayam duly informed the chief secretary of the government in Trivandrum of the gift and that the Guru had promised to offer satyagraha himself.[19]

Grand Processions and 25,000 Signatures

On October 13, *Mathrubhumi*'s correspondent reports that a *savarna jatha*, an upper-caste procession, is planned from Vykom to the capital, Trivandrum, to present a memorial petition to the maharani regent to which thousands of high-caste signatures were being affixed. The appeal would request that she open temple roads to the lower castes.[20] On October 28, centered in the middle of a full page of related articles

[16] Petition of approximately 110 Saverna Hindus to the Maharani Regent opposing discrimination toward lower-caste Hindus, 1924 (trans. Dinoo Anna Mathew), KSA: vol. 4, VSB, file 1424.

[17] "The Satyagraha Struggle at Vykom: The Visit of Sri N. G. Swamikal Ascetic," *Mathrubhumi* (trans. Vasu Thilleri), October 4, 1924, 3.

[18] K. Rama Varier, Police Inspector, Vaikom, to Commissioner of Police, Travancore, October 4, 1924, KSA (letter): vol. 4, VSB, file 1295 (handwritten 195).

[19] "Reference to Sri Narayana Guru Swamy's Donation of Rs. 1000/- to Satyagraha Fund," in *Selected Documents on Vaikom Satyagraha*, ed. Sundarannadar Raimon (Trivandrum: Kerala State Archives Department, Government of Kerala, 2006), 35. Raimon, former director of the Kerala State Archives, has the author's gratitude for his ample assistance in 2005.

[20] "The Satyagraha Struggle at Vykom: The Saverna Hindu Jatha [Procession] Will Start Shortly," *Mathrubhumi* (trans. Thilleri), October 16, 1924, 3.

covering five columns is a boxed chart on the preparation for the savarna jatha, listing departure dates from towns along the route from Vykom to Trivandrum and times of arrival. The procession, the paper notes, is to start on November 1 and culminate on November 10 and be led by Mannath Padmanabha Pillai.[21]

Government reports show the increasing involvement of outsiders and supporters from beyond Travancore. The district magistrate informed the chief secretary in Trivandrum on October 17:

Mssrs. George Joseph, K. P. Kesava Menon, T. K. Madhavan, T. R. Krishnaswamy Iyer, Raman Menon, Velayudha Menon, Kuroor Nambooripad and others have arrived at Vaikom and commenced their activities. . . . It appears that the All-India Congress Committee has wired to the Ashamom promising to give Rs. 2000 per month. . . . [T]he Satyagrahis have circulated 100 books to get the signatures of a 100 thousand Savarnas, to the monster petition.[22]

W. H. Pitt, the British commissioner of police, wrote to the chief secretary of the government on October 19: "The organizers say that only those persons who have the correct mentality will be allowed to march. There was a talk of limiting the numbers to 500 but I understand now that there will be no limit."[23] Apparently reassured, on October 21, Pitt reduced the strength of the armed detachment at Vykom from four head constables and forty constables to two head constables and twenty constables.[24] Yet other government reports during October reflect nervousness, as district magistrates and subordinate magistrates were advised to keep a close eye on the processions and not to hesitate to apply the Criminal Procedure Code if necessary, although they should do so tactfully and discreetly. With the

[21] "Program of Saverna Jatha," *Mathrubhumi* (trans. Thilleri), October 28, 1924, 3.

[22] District Magistrate, Office of the District Magistrate, Kottayam, to Chief Secretary, Trivandrum, October 17, 1924, KSA: vol. 4, VSB, file 1309 (handwritten 3529).

[23] W. H. Pitt, Commissioner of Police, Camp Vaikom, to Chief Secretary of Government, Trivandrum, October 19, 1924, KSA: vol. 4, VSB, file 1319 (handwritten 212).

[24] Pitt, Commissioner of Police, Camp Vaikom, to Chief Secretary of Government, Trivandrum, "Vaikom Satyagraha—Reduction of Strength," October 21, 1924, KSA (letter): vol. 4, VSB, file 1333 (handwritten 3808).

serendipity afforded by archival records, it is possible to chance upon
remarkable particulars. The police inspector's report to the district magistrate is a sign that extensive, detailed planning was now being made
by the satyagrahis:

> The unit of the Jatha is a Captain and 10 men under him. Ten such units
> will form a Company under a Lieutenant. The whole Jatha will be under a
> Commissioner and the whole administration of the business of the Jatha
> will rest with a Commissioner in Chief. Captains will be chosen by the
> Unit. Lieutenants and Commissioners are to be appointed. . . . Mannath
> Padmanabha Pillai will be the Commissioner in Chief and Mssrs
> Edavarat Padmanabha Menon, K. Kelappan Nair, A. K. Pillai, Parakulam
> Parameswaran Pillai and K. P. Kesava Menon will be the Commissioners.
> Each Commissioner to lead the Jatha through a specified area. His duty
> ends there and he is free to remain or to go as he pleases. . . .
>
> The Commissioner in Chief will have a coat, shirt, yellow head-dress,
> double cross-belt and yellow badge with green centre. The Commissioners
> will have the same suit but the cross-belt will be single. The Lieutenants
> will have no cross-belt but the other items of dress will be the same. The
> Captain will have only a shirt, but the same badge and yellow head-dress.
> The members of the Jatha will have each a shirt, second cloth, . . . and
> yellow badge.[25]

  "[T]here was no likelihood of the public peace being disturbed,"
the stationary magistrate notes in his report from Quilon, advising the
district magistrate that police were posted along the way. "At Prakkulam
I found arrangements were in full swing for the reception of the Jatha
in the premises of the Nair Service Society English High School. . . .
Preparations were being made to feed about one thousand persons."[26]
A leaflet detailed the anticipated itinerary, with hours of arrival and
departure from each station:

> The jatha will leave the respective stations at 6 A.M. every day so as to
> reach the next station at 10:00 A.M. After a rest of 4 hours for bath and
> meals, the jatha will leave and reach the next station by 6 P.M., and will
> halt there for the night. Arrangements have been made for two meals a

---

[25] K. Rama Varier, Police Inspector, Vaikom, to District Magistrate,
Kottayam, memorandum, October 9, 1924, KSA: vol. 4, VSB, file 1328 (handwritten 219).

[26] Stationary Magistrate, Quilon, to District Magistrate, Quilon, 3 Thulam,
1924, KSA: vol. 4, VSB, file 1443 (handwritten 327).

day. . . . Arrangements have been made to receive the jatha in each station and for holding meetings.[27]

Approximately one hundred persons, including Nambudiris and Nairs, began the journey on the morning of November 1, at 6:00 A.M., under Congress party auspices.[28] Flags were flying and music accompanied pipes and drums for the departure.[29]

Yellow could be seen everywhere. The *Mathrubhumi* correspondent was on hand, verifying that Mannath Padmanabhan Pillai was commander in chief and accompanied by other commanders wearing special headwraps and regalia to identify themselves. Pillai wore his yellow headdress, double cross-belt, and yellow badge with green center. A flag of khadi cloth painted yellow cited the place names of origin of the leaders. Another big, brightly painted banner stated the objectives of the jatha. Participants came from all castes to watch the spectacle, but in the procession itself only upper-caste Hindus took part. Their slogans included "Mahatma Gandhi, Be Victorious," "Hail Mahatma Gandhi," and "Hail Maharani Regent." Clapping, the marchers were singing "patriotic Congress songs." The *Mathrubhumi* reports that members of the procession were given food along the way by people of the localities through which the jatha passed.[30] Proceeding in military formation from Vykom to Trivandrum, 200 kilometers (124 miles), their numbers swelled to a thousand, despite pouring rains. The *Mathrubhumi*'s correspondent notes that the jatha went to the Shivagiri Mutt ashram, where Sri Narayana Guru resided, and Guru blessed the procession. En route, a group of Pulayas gave a rice dish to the savarnas in the procession.[31] Map 2 depicts the route of the savarna jathas.

[27] Leaflet no. 2 (one page), "Savarna Hindu Jatha (Revised Programme)," n.d. (before November 1, 1924), KSA: vol. 4, VSB, file 1367 (handwritten 107).

[28] The Vykom satyagraha was suspended both on the day the jathas began and the day that the walkers reached Trivandrum.

[29] K. Rama Varier, Police Inspector, Vaikom, to Trivandrum Commissioner of Police, November 1, 1924, KSA: vol. 4, VSB, file 1375 (handwritten 255).

[30] "The Satyagraha Struggle at Vykom: The Procession Started Its Journey: The Enthusiasm of the Savarna Hindus," *Mathrubhumi* (trans. Thilleri), November 4, 1924, 3.

[31] "The Victorious Journey of the Jatha: Welcome by Ezehava Women of Mayyanad—Giving of Food by Pulayas," *Mathrubhumi* (trans. Thilleri), November 11, 1924, 5. "It is significant that the Pulayas, among the persecuted castes, offered food, which was accepted by the upper castes." Thilleri, interview (March 19, 2009).

Figure 5   Mannath Padmanabha Pillai was commander in chief of the *savarna jatha*, a grand procession of hundreds of high-caste Brahmins, who walked 200 kilometers (124 miles) to Trivandrum, to present a memorial petition to the Maharani Regent (Illustrated by Madanan Pv)

Note: Led by Mannath Padmanabha Pillai, an active upper-caste leader for more than half a century against untouchability, the procession set off from Vykom on November 1, 1924. Walking in military precision to the princely state's capital, the marchers in the hundreds would present a petition to the maharani regent, with thousands of high-caste signatures affixed. With yellow headpieces and regalia in profusion, banners billowing, pipes and drums, signs displayed the purposes of the jatha. Participants from all caste levels watched the procession—the first of its kind. A second jatha of 500 upper-caste marchers left from Vykom and Kottar, south Travancore. En route to the capital, which they reached on November 11, their numbers swelled, despite pouring rains.

Meanwhile, a separate jatha set out from Kottar in south Travancore, where M. Emperumal Naidu led 500 savarnas on the march. The two processions sought to spread word of the satyagraha and the underlying grievances throughout the state of Travancore, including in remote villages and hamlets. Still marching in disciplined military order, the two jathas came together in Trivandrum eleven days later on November 11.

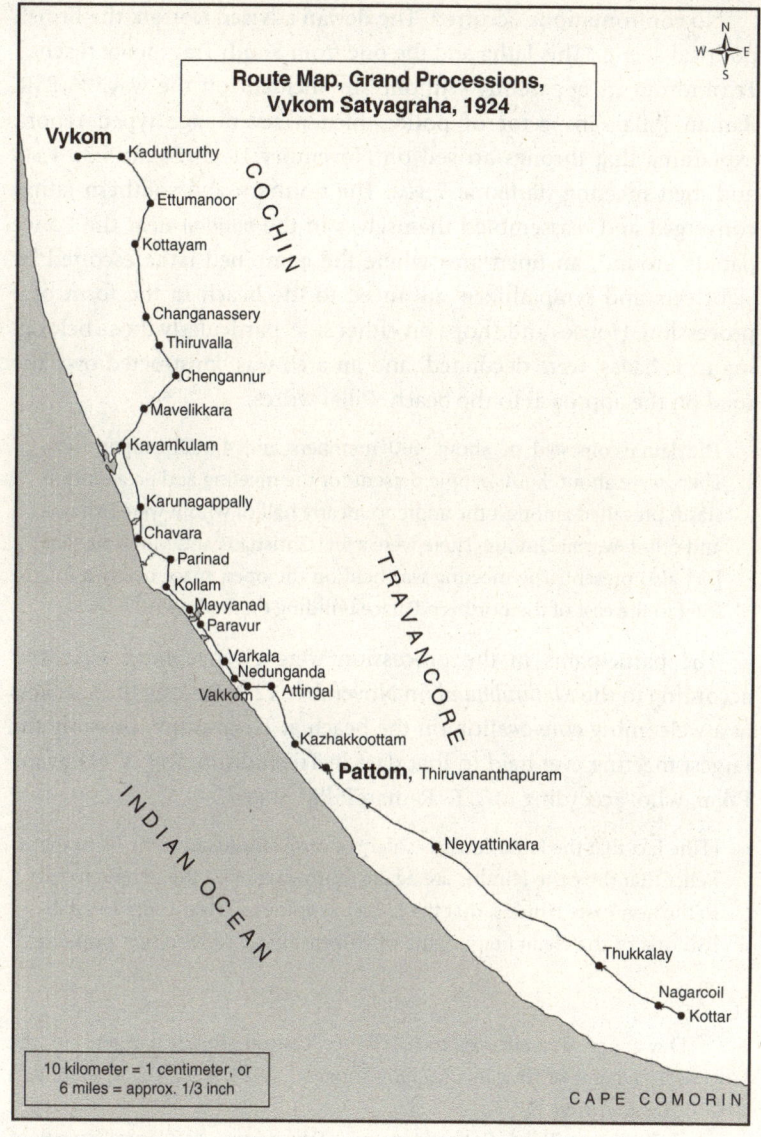

Map 2 Route Map of Vykom *Savarna Jathas*, November 1–11, 1924
Source: Vasu Thilleri and Madanan Pv

No confrontations occurred. The dewan advised Cotton, the British political agent, "This Jatha and the one from South Travancore reached Trivandrum ... apparently without any incident on the way."[32] T. R. Raman Pillai, inspector of police, filed a seven-page typed report, explaining that throngs arrived on November 11, 1924, at 5:30 P.M., and their meeting started at 7 P.M. The northern and southern Jathas converged and reassembled themselves in the *maidan* near the Police parade ground, an open area where the combined jatha escorted by sightseers and sympathizers advanced to the beach in the form of a procession. Houses and shops on either side, particularly those belonging to Ezhavas, were decorated, and an arch was constructed over the road on the approach to the beach. Pillai writes:

> The Jatha consisted of about 400 members and 4,000 sympathisers. There were about 5,000 people present for the meeting and great enthusiasm prevailed amongst the audience nearly half of whom were Ezhavas and other Avarna Hindus. There were a few Christians and Mohomedans [*sic*] also present. The meeting was held on the open space nearly a furlong to the east of the northern Palace building on the beach.[33]

The participants in the procession were given a huge welcome, according to the *Mathrubhumi* on November 12.[34] Among the speakers at a welcoming convocation on the beach at Trivandrum, possibly the largest meeting ever held to that date in Trivandrum, was A. Narayana Pillai, who, according to T. R. Raman Pillai, stated:

> [T]he fact that the Jatha consists solely of caste Hindus gave the lie to the belief that the caste Hindus are against throwing open the temple roads to the non-caste Hindus, that the Jatha has come to Trivandrum to establish one of the elementary rights of citizenship ... to represent popular

[32] Dewan of Travancore, to C. W. E. Cotton, Political Agent to the Governor-General of Travancore, November 13, 1924, KSA: vol. 4, VSB, files 1454–5 (handwritten 305–6).

[33] T. R. Raman Pillai, Police Inspector, Trivandrum, to Commissioner of Police, Trivandrum, November 15, 1924 (7 pp.), KSA: vol. 4, VSB, files 1470–76 (handwritten 345).

[34] "The Savarna Hindu Procession: Great Reception at Trivandrum," *Mathrubhumi* (trans. Thilleri), November 12, 1924, 3.

grievances to the sovereign, ... similar deputations and demonstrations were in vogue in good old days also.[35]

Another speaker, P. K. Govinda Pillai, proposed a resolution to be submitted without delay to the maharani that the Vykom temple roads should be opened to all Hindus. He "deplored" the absence of unity among Travancoreans and said, "They should not be disappointed if they do not get a favourable reply from H. H. the regent [Her Highness the maharani regent], that such social reforms can be effected only by continuous and strenuous agitations which may sometimes have to be carried through more than one generation."[36] Y. Ramaswami Ayyar, a judge, declared that "unapproachability and untouchability are against the principles of True Hinduism which ... is slowly dying out owing to the observance of such meaningless customs"; he "appealed to the audience to remove this curse and save Hinduism from utter annihilation," also affirming that "temples and temple properties are gifts of pious Hindus and that Government are only the trustees of these endowers."[37]

Audience with the Maharani Regent

The next morning, November 12, a twelve-member deputation comprising leaders from both jathas presented a memorial petition to the maharani regent at Satelmond Palace, at 8 A.M.[38] Fewer had signed than previously anticipated; even so it bore signatures from more than 25,000 caste Hindus. The petition, addressed "To Her Most Gracious Highness the Maharani Regent" and bound in silk and inscribed in

[35] Raman Pillai, to Commissioner of Police, November 15, 1924: vol. 4, file 1471, 2.

[36] Pillai, November 15, 1924: file 1472, 3.

[37] Pillai, November 15, 1924: file 1472, 3.

[38] The palace's chief secretary notes that "permission has been granted to a deputation of not more than twelve representative members of the Jatha ... to pay their respects ... and submit their memorial at 8 A.M. on the 12th." R. Krishna Pillai, Chief Secretary, Palace, Trivandrum, November 4, 1924, KSA (confidential note): vol. 4, VSB, file 1835, handwritten 265.

gold, was presented by the deputation leader, Changanacherry K. Parameswaran Pillai. It reads in part:

> This Jatha has . . . been organized for the purpose of submitting . . . this humble memorial to prove . . . that there is no . . . opposition on the part of the Savarna Hindus and that they are ready and willing to co-operate with the Government in removing the disabilities of their Avarna Hindu brethren.
>
> We feel sorry that Travancore which . . . stands today in the forefront of the Indian States in education, enlightenment and all-round progress should in any way impair its reputation by the exclusion of the large majority of its Hindu population from the elementary right of citizenship which all other people of whatever nationality and religion are permitted to enjoy in this State.
>
> We therefore . . . pray that Your Gracious Highness may be pleased to command that all roads and public institutions without reservation be thrown open to all classes of . . . subjects without distinction of caste or creed.[39]

The maharani received the petition in person. She could have directed that the deputation meet instead with the dewan, whose role made him the accepted conduit for public issues to be brought before the sovereign. Indeed, the delegation met with him following the audience with the maharani. Menon considers that she gave a "frank reply" and the only one possible under the circumstances: "It is not possible to

---

[39] Printed petition to the maharani regent, English version, prepared for deputation meeting the Maharani, hand dated November 19, 1924, KSA: vol. 4, 4 pp., files 1486–7 (handwritten 361–4). The four-page English version was carried by the deputation for the meeting, as a handwritten note on the original specifies. The document opens by citing an 1865 government notification that "all public roads in the state are open to all classes of people alike and in July, 1884, the Government by a fresh notification re-affirmed the policy laid down in the previous order and enjoined that any violation of these orders will be visited with the severest displeasure of Government." Deliberately assuming an authoritative voice in speaking for upper-caste Hindus, it says, "Though sixty years have elapsed since these orders were issued it is painful to find that even today certain public roads are closed to Avarna Hindus and that officers of Government far from protecting the rights of these people in regard to this matter, are taking steps to support those who infringe the notifications of Government." It closes with the sentiments in the indented quotation. Also see Menon, *History of the Freedom Movement in Kerala*, 130.

Figure 6   Presentation to the Maharani Regent of the 25,000-signature "monster petition," November 12, 1924 (Illustrated by Madanan Pv)

Note: At Satelmond Palace, the Maharani Regent Sethu Lakshmi Bayi received the "monster petition" suggested by Gandhi, with 25,000 signatures of caste Hindus. Bound in silk and inscribed in gold, it asked that she command all roadways and public institutions to be "thrown open" to all subjects without regard to caste or creed.

give a reply at once in this all important matter. A resolution has come up for discussion in the Legislative Council and will be taken up in the next meeting of the Council. When final orders are passed the representation contained in the memorial will receive due consideration."[40]

All of the resolutions from the public meeting were submitted to the palace, while additional missives were still arriving. A telegram from Hindus in Sind, in what is now Pakistan, conveyed "respectful appeal prayers of Hindus of Sind to set noble example of removing blot of

[40] As cited in Menon, *History of the Freedom Movement in Kerala*, 129. See also "The Great Procession Has Ended: The Reply of the Queen to the Memorandum: Decision Only after Knowing the Opinion of the Legislature," *Mathrubhumi* (trans. Thilleri), November 12, 1924, 5. The maharani and the government were generally preoccupied with managing the crisis caused by the massive flooding of the previous months.

unapproachability from Hindu religion by granting petition of caste
jatha and opening all public roads to untouchables and thus win
enduring gratitude veneration of enlightened Hindu world of present
day and coming centuries."[41]

The following day, with the satyagraha still suspended for the jathas,
Pitt continued at work. The police inspector recorded on November 13
that owing to "great objection from various quarters to the bamboo
poles being kept at the entrance of the barricades, as an experimental
measure, they were removed from the western and northern sides
today."[42]

Shortly after the jathas, apprehension rose over a forthcoming fete,
a major yearly event on the religious calendar drawing large numbers.
The Ashtami Hindu temple festival on November 21, 1924, would be
celebrated at the Shiva temple in Vykom. There, after dusk, the deity
would be taken out in procession and joined at midnight by deities
from other temples, to be followed by offerings of gifts. Gandhi had
through Madhavan asked the leaders of the satyagraha "not to discon-
tinue [the campaign] on any account."[43] The matter had been debated
within the Vykom campaign and government alike, but with different
concerns. The maharani regent approved an additional thirty-eight
men at arms in addition to the twelve normally sent to Vykom in connection with the festival.[44] Nearly 50,000 caste-Hindu pilgrims would
gather for the celebration.

Meanwhile, quietly, at Vykom, as Gandhi hoped, the satyagraha per-
severed during daylight hours, between 6:00 A.M. and 6:00 P.M., as volunteers sustained their picketing of the four barricades. Only
"experienced volunteers" were involved, the police inspector reported
to Pitt, because of the large crowds of upper-caste Hindus expected for
the fete. Police removed the barricades in order for several processions

[41] To Her Highness the Maharani Regent, Trivandrum, November 11,
1924, KSA (telegram): vol. 4, VSB, see files 1457–9.

[42] K. Rama Varier, Police Inspector, Vaikom, to District Superintendent of
Police, Kottayam, November 13, 1924, KSA: vol. 4, VSB, file 1469 (handwritten 344).

[43] S. Venkitachala Sarma, Police Inspector, Arukutty, to Commissioner of
Police, Travancore, October 10, 1924, KSA (memorandum): vol. 4, VSB, file
1307 (handwritten 205).

[44] To T. Raghaviah, Dewan of Travancore, Palace, Trivandrum November
15, 1924, KSA (letter): vol. 4, VSB, 1483 (handwritten 358).

to have access to the temple grounds, as purification ceremonies were conducted inside the temple. The next day, the procession was rescheduled for night-time, so as to avoid the satyagrahis (and their pollution). All parties displayed strict discipline and ingenuity in avoiding a confrontation.[45]

Defeat of the Legislative Council Resolution

On October 2, N. Kumaran, an Ezhava leader, general secretary of the SNDP Yogam, and a nominated member of the Travancore Legislative Council had introduced a resolution calling for the opening of every Vykom temple road to all castes. He supported this motion eloquently with a brief history of activities from early social movements through the current satyagraha, including a review of government and orthodox opposition responses. Kumaran's resolution reads in part, "This Council recommends to the Government that all roads round the Vaikkam temple and all other roads similarly situated in Travancore be thrown open to all classes."[46] In offering it, he mentioned that "41 per cent of the citizens of the total population . . . comprise the untouchable country—loyal, hardworking, peace-loving subjects . . . [and] are prevented from enjoying some of the elementary rights of citizenship for the purpose of satisfying the supersensitiveness of a small portion of the caste Hindu population."[47] Ravindran devotes nearly nineteen pages of his book to Kumaran's speech, calling his remarks eloquent and "one of the best ever delivered" before the legislature.[48] Several other caste and non-caste members spoke on behalf of the resolution. A government spokesperson, Subba Aiyar, attempted to defend the status quo by offering a strictly legal interpretation of the situation: the

[45] Such was the atmosphere in which C. F. Andrews arrived in early January 1925. His personal accounts of visiting Vykom highlight the satyagrahis' discipline. By that time, the satyagraha was well organized, with a local leadership secured and with volunteers and funding fairly secure. Andrews had missed the chaotic, erratic, and rudderless months of the previous spring and summer.

[46] *Proceedings of the Travancore Legislative Council*, October 2, 1924, 6: 318, as cited in T. K. Ravindran, *Vaikkam Satyagraha and Gandhi* (Trichur, India: Sri Narayana Institute of Social and Cultural Development), 120.

[47] N. Kumaran as cited in Ravindran, *Vaikkam Satyagraha and Gandhi*, 121.

[48] Ravindran, *Vaikkam Satyagraha and Gandhi*, 120.

temple roads were private, thus the right to walk along them was not free to all peoples of Travancore.

In the debate that followed, the dewan's formal recitation shows how little the satyagrahis' efforts at conversion had stirred sympathy and understanding. A brief excerpt is justified in disclosure of his adamantine opposition:

> The roads immediately surrounding the temple are the private property of the temple and are not public roads. Those that converge towards the temple are, on the contrary, public roads. But, according to admitted and immemorial custom, they are up to within a certain distance of the temple public in a qualified sense only, viz., that they are open to certain classes of the public alone and are not king's highways open to all communities. There is no public institution necessitating the entry into them of the entire public. The only real material inconvenience occasioned by the prohibition of entry into this area is the necessity to take devious and more lengthy routes from one point of the town of Vykom to another. This inconvenience the Government promised to remove by opening new roads for the use of the entire public on the outskirts of the prohibited area. This offer was not accepted, so that the sole justification for the demand for the removal of the prohibition is a feeling of self respect or, in other words, sentiment.[49]

Discussions on the resolution continued for several months in the council. Among the legislators in the Travancore Legislative Council at that time two prevailing views could be discerned. The first was that the satyagraha challenged the existing stability, hence any consent to its demands would generate bigger claims, thereby undermining the social structures, for which caste distinctions were obligatory. The second major stance was a blend of pragmatism and awareness of national perceptions, affected by India's national freedom movement. This position held that such discrimination was intrinsically wrong and needed to be rectified. Inherent in this viewpoint was a perception that a way could be found that was, as K. N. Panikkar put it, "within the social understanding of the various groups."[50]

[49] Dewan, "Appendix III: Extract from Dewan of Travancore's Speech on Vykom Satygraha," from *Young India*, March 19, 1925, in *Collected Works of Mahatma Gandhi* (hereafter *CWMG*), 30: 470.

[50] Panikkar, interview (August 15, 2005).

Kumaran's resolution came to a vote in the Legislative Council in early February 1925 at the initiative of the government. It was defeated in a 22:21 vote. Suspicion surrounded the outcome of the balloting, with most accounts suggesting that the government had surreptitiously influenced the outcome. P. Parameswaran, an official nominee and an Ezhava voted against the resolution.[51] Menon unambiguously says that "it was clear that the Government actively helped the defeat of the Vaikom Resolution, instead of remaining neutral."[52]

According to Desai, the winning side consisted of fifteen officials, three government-nominated council members (including Parameswaran), one Brahmin representative, and three elected council members. In Desai's words, "There was despair among the ranks of the Satyagrahis, impatience of the 'slow' method of Satyagraha, and even an inclination on the part of a few to cross the border-line."[53] Gandhi received a revealingly despondent note from one of the satyagrahis, prompted by the 22:21 defeat, to say that people in Vykom were agitated and aggrieved, as the voting resulted from "direct pressure brought by the Government on the voters":

> I am ashamed to say, one member of the depressed and prohibited classes himself voted against the entry and sided with the Government. The situation hereafter is fraught with all kinds of difficulties. There is very little enthusiasm now for the peaceful methods of satyagraha. Some have already begun to advocate "direct action" and even forcible entry into temples. Small-pox has broken out in the Satyagraha Camp itself and with the growing heat of the advancing summer it may attack more and more. We are carrying the struggle with faith in your leadership and

[51] Parameswaran was the elder brother of Dr. Padmanabhan Palpu, founder of the SNDP Yogam. *Travancore Lesgislative Council Proceedings*, February 7, 1925, 767–73, as cited in Chandramohan, "Social and Political Protest in Travancore," 261n1. Parameswaran was manager of Narayana Guru's temple properties. Robin Jeffrey, "The Social Origins of a Caste Association, 1875–1905: The Founding of the SNDP Yogam," *South Asia* 4 (October, 1974): 51; Jeffrey, *The Decline of Nayar Dominance: Society and Politics in Travancore, 1847–1908* (New Delhi: Manohar Publications), 190; Jeffrey, "Travancore: Status, Class and the Growth of Radical Politics, the Temple-Entry Movement," in *People, Princes and Paramount Power*, ed. Robin Jeffrey (New Delhi: Oxford University Press), 167n51.

[52] Menon, *History of the Freedom Movement in Kerala*, 133.

[53] Desai, *Epic of Travancore*, 15–16.

gospel of non-violence. But I am afraid the Provincial Congress Committee of Kerala is waning in its enthusiasm. They have collected very little money during the last many months by their own efforts. For everything we depend on your own esteemed help and advice. We are hard up for money.[54]

In response, Gandhi, writing in *Young India*, rises to link the Vykom campaign to the achievement of self-rule and urges perseverance in using direct action:

> The Vykom satyagrahis are fighting a battle of no less consequence than that of swaraj. They are fighting against an age long wrong and prejudice. It is supported by orthodoxy, superstition, custom and authority. Theirs is only one among the many battles that must be fought in the holy war against irreligion masquerading as religion, ignorance appearing in the guise of learning. If their battle is to be bloodless, they must be patient under the severest trials. They must not quail before a raging fire. Theirs is "direct action." . . . I am alarmed at the appearance of small-pox in the satyagraha camp. It is a disease born of filth and yields to hygienic treatment.[55]

Although he often maintained some vagueness, Gandhi's thinking was shifting slightly. The struggle had become as important as independence. What was to have been a circumscribed struggle in a princely state was beginning to bear down on politics and the national destiny of India. The demoralizing suffering and sacrifice of day-in-day-out vigils, with disciplined spinning of khadi in scorching sun before barricades might not be sufficient.

In fact, conservative savarnas were once again attacking the volunteers at Vykom. One of the satyagrahis, a Mr. Krishnapillai, was beaten.[56] Harassment continued. A Congress leader and director of the *Mathrubhumi* newspaper, Kuru Neelakanta [also Kurur Nilakantan Namboodiripad] Nambudiri, was arrested and sentenced to two years in prison for violating the order prohibiting him from entering the Kottayam administrative division, because he had made a speech critical of the government (*and* the satyagraha). The magistrate who

---

[54] Gandhi, "Vykom Satyagraha," *Young India*, February 2, 1925, in *CWMG*, 30: 266.

[55] Gandhi, "Vykom Satyagraha," 267.

[56] "The Present Condition at Vykom: The Savernas Attack," *Mathrubhumi* (trans. Thilleri), February 19, 1925, 3.

condemned Nambudiri claimed that his entering Kottayam would have resulted in rivalry between savarnas and *avarnas*.[57]

Gandhi had in the preceding April maintained that the Vykom campaign was a "socio-religious movement," one "directed purely against an age-long, intolerable sacerdotal prejudice." He wanted the struggle to be restricted, regimented, and controlled, and on April 17, 1924, had written that Vykom leaders had "taken up only a fragment of the evil" (without explaining his authorship of the policy of limitation). The evidence was plentiful that appealing to the high castes and their being confronted by the suffering of the satyagrahis was not showing results.

Although admitting that the movement was at a standstill, Gandhi's customary stance of unquestioning trust in satyagraha was unchanged. Yet, rather than repudiating and disavowing a role for supporters beyond the locale, Gandhi no longer insisted on isolating the struggle. He seemed to welcome the echoes from broader awareness and involvement across the country and even worldwide attention. As the stalemate continued, and knowing that the satyagrahis had suffered a terrible blow to their morale with the council defeat, Gandhi concluded that a personal visit to Travancore might alter the impasse. He also worried that the campaign might become violent and wanted to find a course acceptable to all parties.

At this point, the third stage of the satyagraha had ended. The volunteers were still quietly sustaining their presence in Vykom, but much of the engagement was occurring beyond the village as evidenced by the two grand processions of upper-caste Hindus and the vote in the Legislative Council. The fourth phase of the Vykom struggle was about to begin.

Gandhi Visits Travancore: "March with the Times"

In spring 1925, the *Mathrubhumi* eagerly promoted the planned visit by Gandhi.[58] His tour was aimed at supporting the satyagraha, but also sought to build the nationalist Congress movement. News of his forthcoming trip reached Travancore in advance of his arrival at the town of

[57] "The Satyagraha Struggle at Vykom: Gandhi's Advice," *Mathrubhumi* (trans. Thilleri), March 3, 1925, 5.

[58] "The Mahatma Will Visit Vykom in Two Weeks," *Mathrubhumi* (trans. Thilleri), March 5, 1925.

Ernakulam on March 8, 1925. On March 7, the *Mathrubhumi* devoted a full page to the treatment accorded to Gandhi en route in Madras (Chennai) and his preparations for journeying to Cochin (Kochi) and on to Vykom.[59] Gandhi boarded the train at Madras and was welcomed at receptions along the way. In each railway station through which he passed, he made a short speech to waiting throngs. The crowds were enormous, exuberant, and crying slogans in support.[60]

Local press attention emboldened the satyagrahis, but may have embittered the orthodox opposition. The upper-caste leadership had been urging the government to deny Gandhi entry into Travancore. The dewan, explicitly following the advice of the British political agent in Madras, decided instead to treat Gandhi as a state guest and arrange for all of his travel and associated needs during his visit. The dewan's telegram to the resident said, "As prohibiting Gandhi coming to Travancore seems unwise it is considered expedient to treat him as a state guest at time and place he interviews Her Highness, if you have no objection such courtesy being shown. Awaiting reply by wire."[61] C. W. E. Cotton replied, "Experience has proved I believe, that he [Gandhi] gives less trouble when treated in this way, than a free lance."[62]

Journeying with his secretary, Mahadev Desai, and his son, Ramdas, Gandhi arrived by motorboat from Ernakulam on March 9 at 6:00 P.M. Local recreational boats escorted his craft to the jetty, with people

[59] "Mahatma Gandhi's Visit: The Apt Action of the Madras Corporation," *Mathrubhumi* (trans. Thilleri), March 7, 1925, 5. The article praises the Madras Corporation for welcoming Gandhi. Municipal corporations were dominated by government officials and government supporters; they generally opposed the nationalists. *Mathrubhumi* considered this newsworthy. Thilleri, interview (March 17, 2009).

[60] "The Coming of Gandiji: The Journey from Madras to Vykom—Hearty Welcome from Keralites," *Mathrubhumi* (trans. Thilleri), March 10, 1925, 5.

[61] Telegram dated March 7, 1925, file no. R. Dis 783, English records, Secretariat, Trivandrum, as cited in Ravindran, *Vaikkam Satyagraha and Gandhi*, 146, 146n15.

[62] C. W. E. Cotton to Watts, letter, April 5, 1925, as cited in Ravindran, *Vaikkam Satyagraha and Gandhi*, 146, 146n16. The new dewan, announced in May 1925, was Maurice E. Watts, an Anglo-Indian Roman Catholic, whose father had formerly been chief secretary of the Travancore government. He held office from 1925 to 1929.

singing songs and beating drums as they accompanied Gandhi's vessel.[63] A large assemblage waited, as he was officially welcomed with a garland made of khadi. According to a reporter, Gandhi stood on a high platform before a disciplined crowd that stretched out for 3 kilometers. During the reading of an address in his honor in both English and Malayalam, Gandhi received a registered letter of protest from a group of prominent local orthodox Hindus, stating that although pronounced to be on behalf of the public, the speech did not represent the whole of public opinion in Travancore, as many disagreed with Gandhi's views on untouchability and unapproachability. Gandhi said nothing because on that day he was observing a vow of silence. He would be speaking publicly the following day.

As Gandhi was driven slowly to the ashram, volunteers from the satyagraha encircled his car with hands held, while government civil servants and the public greeted him with folded hands. Gandhi returned their salutation. T. K. Madhavan waited at the ashram's entrance to receive him. A journalist reported from inside the shelter that welcome messages were displayed and "bunches of tender coconuts were tied to the poles to make the place look attractive."[64] That evening the district magistrate brought a letter from the maharani, inviting Gandhi to meet with her.

Commissioner Pitt accompanied Gandhi throughout the visit and prepared written reports for the government's chief secretary on his meetings and activities. On March 10, Gandhi went to the satyagraha ashram to meet the volunteers, who then numbered approximately fifty. Pitt writes that Gandhi "asked me to satisfy him that the Satyagrahis had always been non-violent and well-disciplined. I replied that for the past six months their behaviour had been exemplary but earlier was unsatisfactory." According to Pitt, Gandhi replied that satyagraha "was based on truth and non-violence and the moment the Satyagrahis deviated from these virtues, he would separate himself from them."[65]

---

[63] "H. H. the Regent Maharani Extends Invitation," March 10, 1925, *Malayala Manorama* in *Gandhi's Visits to Kerala*, 10.

[64] "H. H. the Regent Maharani Extends Invitation," 11.

[65] Pitt, "Report on the Tour of Mr. M. K. Gandhi in Travancore" (March 9–18, 1925), in Raimon, *Selected Documents on Vaikom Satyagraha*, 133.

Offers to the Orthodox Hindus

On March 10, Gandhi experienced possibly his first face-to-face encounter in his life with the intransigence and presumed privileges of Namburidi Brahmins.[66] At 2:30 P.M., accompanied by Desai, Brahmin lawyer and independence leader Chakravarti Rajagopalachari, and other close colleagues, Gandhi went at the request of local orthodox Hindus to the residence of Indanturuttil Nambiathiri, near the temple compound, for a private discussion with the upper echelons of the orthodox opposition. The meeting lasted three hours.[67] The transcript, prepared from shorthand and in the Kerala State Archives, cites 17 participants and others.[68] Discussions focused generally on untouchability and unapproachability, particularly on matters related to the issue of the access to roads surrounding orthodox temples. The upper-caste stance remained unyielding, despite Gandhi's exertions. In concluding the session, Gandhi extended three alternatives—which he called "sportsman-like offers"—to the Nambudiri caste-Hindus for settling the conflict:

1. a one-day referendum of all upper-caste orthodox Hindus on opening the temple roads, either within the Vykom district or in the entire state of Travancore;

---

[66] Bhikhu C. Parekh, *Colonialism, Tradition and Reform: An Analysis of Gandhi's Political Discourse* (New Delhi, Thousand Oaks, and London: SAGE Publications, [1989] 1999), 246.

[67] This author visited the temple compound, village, and environs, including the house in Vykom where Gandhi's meeting with the Nambudiri temple custodians and leaders is said by local oral tradition to have taken place. In a remarkable historical irony, the house is today the headquarters of the Ezhava toddy tappers union. Accompanied by Sanal Mohan, associate professor, School of Social Sciences, Mahatma Gandhi University, Kottayam, the author talked with individuals there on August 14, 2005, who acted out how, according to oral histories, Nambiathiri sat at the farthest distance from the entrance during the session, while Gandhi was kept standing just inside the doorway for much of the meeting. Sanal Mohan (interview, Vykom, August 14, 2005).

[68] Proceedings of the [March 10] conference held at Indanturuttil Devan Neelakantan Nambiatiri's house, Vaikom (transcript from shorthand), March 28, 1925, KSA: vol. 9, VSB. Desai took notes. Desai, *Epic of Travancore*, 17–21.

2. arbitration of the issue of unapproachability, with each party nomi-
    nating a pandit (a learned Hindu, instructed and conversant with
    Sanskrit and philosophy, religion, and jurisprudence); the dewan
    would make the final decision, to be accepted by all segments of
    society; or

3. a decision to be made by acknowledged pandits; Gandhi said, "Let
    there be a board of three arbitrators with the Dewan as the umpire,"
    and suggested that he would choose Pandit Madan Mohan Malaviya
    as one of the three.[69]

Neither side persuaded the other, yet Gandhi committed himself
"to accept any or all of the decisions but left it open to the orthodox
Hindus to do so, or not, as they liked."[70] One of the Nambudiris at
the meeting summed up the orthodox position when he said,
"Mahatmaji, we beseech you to prevent the *avarnas* from depriving us
of our age-old privileges."[71] Ravindran calls this meeting with "caste
fanatics" a "farce," in which "their villainy was let free"; he includes
in his book the transcript of the "melodrama" as a concession to
precision.[72]

That evening, Gandhi attended an open-air meeting in the Vykom
village attended by approximately 10,000 people, of which "non-caste
Hindus and women were present in large numbers," Sundarannadar
Raimon notes.[73] Ezhavas from Ambalapuzha presented remarks.
Gandhi replied. He stated that untouchability and unapproachability
"have no place or sanction in the history of Hinduism," adding that
"untouchability is a blot upon humanity and therefore upon
Hinduism." He recounted for the crowd his long meeting with the
Nambudiri leaders: "I am sorry to confess to you that I was not able

---

[69] Proceedings [March 10], conference, Indanturuttil Nambiatiri's house,
transcript, 25–9. Gandhi continued hoping that Malaviya would step in, but he
did not become involved in offstage negotiations with the Travancore government at this time; he was in North India working to raise funds for his founding
of Benares Hindu University. He would visit Travancore in 1929.

[70] Pitt, "Report on the Tour of Mr. M. K. Gandhi," 133.

[71] Desai, *Epic of Travancore*, 18.

[72] Ravindran, *Vaikkam Satyagraha and Gandhi*, 164.

[73] Editor's note, in Raimon, *Selected Documents on Vaikom Satyagraha*, 142.

Figure 7 Gandhi meeting with high-caste officialdom from the Vykom
temple, March 10, 1925 (Illustrated by Madanan Pv)

Note: In a three-hour meeting on March 10, 1925, Gandhi confronted the
unbending obstinacy and prejudice of Vykom's orthodoxy. The upper-caste
stance remained unyielding, despite Gandhi's three concessionary offers.
Contemporary oral narratives, from local citizens, suggest that Gandhi was kept
waiting by the door.

to produce the impression that I had expected that I would be able
to." The crowd responded with laughter. Still seeking to induce alterations in the mind-sets of the upper castes, he gave credit to Dewan
Bahadur T. Raghavaiah, who "has told the orthodox people where his
opinion lies" and who "invites them to march with the times."[74]

[74] "Gandhi's Reply," in Raimon, *Selected Documents on Vaikom Satyagraha*,
144–5, 147.

Gandhi advocated as he did whenever he had the chance, the hand-looming of khadi, with its multiple economic, psychological, and emblematic purposes.

On March 11, Gandhi met privately with the satyagrahis at their camp in Vykom and departed in mid-afternoon for Alleppey by special boat. That evening he met with a large assembly, which, Pitt noted, included women. K. P. Panikkar presided and read an address. Remarks representing the local Ezhavas were also delivered before heavy rains sent the gathering home. On March 12, Gandhi arrived at 7:15 A.M. at Quilon, where he was taken to a public meeting at the cantonment maidan, an open space. The municipal president, N. Padmanabha Pillai, gave an address, following which Gandhi responded. At noon in the town of Warkalai, Gandhi had an audience with the maharani regent and the dewan. The *Mathrubhumi* would later report that the maharani regent told Gandhi that she had sympathy for the lower-caste people, but nonetheless could not open the roads. She hinted that a long tradition stood in the way, and as a ruler who cares about the sentiments of the people, she could not do away with the prohibitions on the use of the roads.[75]

Meeting with Sri Narayana Guru and Promoting the Nationalist Program

At 4:00 P.M., in the company of Chakravarti Rajagopalachari, V. V. S. Ayyar, and E. V. Ramaswami Naicker, who had joined the group at Warkalai, Gandhi met semi-privately with Sri Narayana Guru. "Only a few Ezhava leaders and sympathizers with the Satyagraha movement were allowed to be present," Pitt comments. He further writes that "it appears that the Guru declared that he was not a believer in non-violence in agitations for removing social disabilities and that though he excluded inter-dining and intermarriage he was anxious to secure for his community by any method, social equality in all other matters with

[75] "The Meeting between Mahatmaji and the Queen: The Maharani Regent Has Sympathy for the Efforts for the Freedom of the Depressed Classes," *Mathrubhumi* (trans. Thilleri), March 17, 1925, 5.

caste-Hindus including temple entry and admission to caste Hindu houses." Pitt concludes his report on the session with Narayana: "It is said that by means of argument Mr. Gandhi was able to convince the Guru of the efficacy and necessity of non-violence in all social movements and that the Guru agreed to follow Mr. Gandhi's advice."[76] In fact, Guru was not wholly persuaded of the "efficacy" of the method, despite his assertions otherwise.[77]

The most talked-about meeting on Gandhi's trip to Travancore was between Gandhi and Guru. Each appreciated the other's point of view, not solely on the Vykom satyagraha, but also on other topics. Gandhi later acknowledged that he was impressed and commented, "I met a great soul in Kerala."[78] On the other hand, Gandhi was not enamored of Narayana's slogan "one God, one religion, one caste," because, he said while in Travancore, "I feel that so long as the human race continues, differences of creeds and religions will indeed exist, since there are many minds and not one."[79] He appreciated that Truth was not monopolistic, and was himself eclectic in borrowing insights from different faiths, based on his own far-reaching reading and untutored analyses.

In a meeting held at Sivagiri Mutt, where Guru lived, and in response to an address presented by representatives of the SNDP Yogam, Gandhi recounted his meeting with the maharani:

> You are aware I was to have waited upon Her Highness the [maharani] Regent and similarly I was to have waited upon His Holiness [the Dewan] both of which I did yesterday. . . . Her Highness' sympathies, so far as she herself is personally concerned, are entirely with those who are trying to seek redress. I am free to tell you that she considers that these roads at Vykom should be open to all classes. [Applause.] But as the Head of the State she feels powerless unless there is public opinion behind her and

[76] Pitt, "Report on the Tour of Mr. M. K. Gandhi," 135. "Sri Narayana Guru remarked that he will enjoin every one of his disciples to come before him clothed in khaddar only." Gandhi, March 13, 1925, speech at Sivagiri Mutt, Vankalai (transcription from shorthand), KSA: vol. 9, VSB, 12.

[77] Guru, June 6, 1924, CWMG, 28: 278.

[78] Thilleri, interview (August 11, 2005).

[79] Gandhi, Speech at Advait Ashram, Alwaye, Travancore, March 18, 1925, replying to welcome address in Sanskrit presented by a Pulaya, CWMG, 30: 434.

unless therefore the public opinion of Travancore is organized in a perfectly legitimate, peaceful and constitutional manner, and unless that opinion is expressed in an equally constitutional, legitimate and peaceful manner, . . . she will feel powerless to grant the relief that is required.

I for my part entirely accept that position. It is for you and me to break the opposition of blind orthodoxy. You will not feel the glow of freedom and liberty unless you yourselves take a leading part in breaking down that opposition. . . .

[Y]ou cannot achieve durable reform by becoming impatient. Or if we must become impatient, we must be impatient with ourselves and not impatient with the wrong-doer.[80]

On March 13, Gandhi and his party left Warkalai and reached Trivandrum at 10:00 A.M. In early afternoon, he visited the science college and the women's college. He met with the dewan. At a 6:00 P.M. public meeting at the Trivandrum infantry parade grounds, a large assemblage awaited him. Speaking at the session, which lasted from 6:30 to 8:00 P.M., Gandhi replied to at least six speeches that night by representatives of various associations and made the following, selected points:

[T]he object of my visit is to express my deep sympathies to the Satyagrahis who are struggling against heavy odds at Vaikom. . . . I had also the privilege of waiting upon His Holiness Sri Narayana Guru and when I saw him I hung my head in shame and humiliation that even he could not pass the prohibited road in Vykom. (*Hear. Hear*) I heard some of the Pulaya boys reciting Sanskrit as very few Sanskrit students are capable of doing. (*Hear. Hear*) I had the honor of meeting there many distinguished Ezhava brethren. . . . [I]t hurt my sense of religion, my sense of humanity and my sense of nationalism that these men could not enter those prohibited roads in Vaikom. (*Hear. Hear*)[81]

Gandhi went on to explain the three offers that he had put before the Nambudiri leaders in Vykom on March 10. In response to the arguments made by the upper-caste representatives that savarna public opinion was opposed to the claim of the untouchables, he explained,

[80] Gandhi, March 13, 1925, speech, Sivagiri Mutt, Warkalai. In his remarks, Gandhi spoke of the Vykom satyagraha as "a test case," p. 6 transcript.

[81] Gandhi, March 13, 1925, speech text, Trivandrum cantonment parade grounds, KSA: vol. 9, VSB, 1–2 of 8.

"I straight-away offered them a referendum either in Vaikom or in the whole of Travancore. I restricted it only to Savarna Hindus. . . . I am sorry to tell you that the spokesman would not accept this proposal."[82] Gandhi then raised a challenge that goes to the purpose of this inquiry:

> I ask you, the Savarna Hindus of Trivandrum and through you the whole of the Hindu community of Travancore, to insist to break down the prejudice of orthodoxy in Vaikom and to compel, by pressure of public opinion, the acceptance of one of the three offers or, better still, to compel, by the same pressure of public opinion, the opening of these roads to the untouchables and the unapproachables.[83]

The necessity for compelling change, the exertion of compulsion, rather than persuasion, had entered the drama.

On March 14, responding to a municipal address in his honor at the Victoria Jubilee Town Hall, at 8:00 A.M., Gandhi remarked on the royal house of Travancore: "[T]he severe simplicity of the Royalty in Travancore has bewitched me. I know the position of so many Princes of India that I was, I must confess, totally unprepared for this simplicity of life that rules the Royalty in Travancore (cheers)." Pitt says that Gandhi "contrasted it with conditions obtaining elsewhere."[84]

In a long article on March 14, the *Mathrubhumi* reports on the "obstinacy of the conservatives" and notes that Gandhi had been making a point of meeting with opponents of the satyagraha. The newspaper compliments the participation of women in the campaign. Also of note is the paper's report that Gandhi and Pitt met together for half an hour on a day that was otherwise crammed.[85] That day, Gandhi also visited Aiyanimudu, Neyyattinkara, and Kuzhithurai.

On March 15, Gandhi and his party left Trivandrum for Vykom by car, making at least seven stops where Gandhi spoke or listened to

---

[82] Gandhi, March 13, 1925, speech text, Trivandrum, 3, 4.

[83] Gandhi, March 13, 1925, speech text, Trivandrum, 5.

[84] Gandhi, March 14, 1925, KSA (speech text): vol. 8 of 10, file 605, p. 1 of 7; Pitt, "Report on the Tour of Mr. M. K. Gandhi," 136.

[85] The newspaper described the encounter as their initial discussion and meeting, although this was probably inaccurate. "The Victorious Kerala Journey of Mahatmaji: Unprecedented Flow of the People to Vykom—Compliments to the Kerala Women," *Mathrubhumi* (trans. Thilleri), March 14, 1925, 5 (article covers two full pages).

addresses. They reached Chengannur at noon, where "[a] huge public meeting was held in the Perumkulam paddy fields"; approximately 15,000 people were present. Gandhi brought up the "painful heat" and said he was pleased to visit the town, because "this is Mr. George Joseph's place," which was greeted by applause. He mentioned that he had "extracted a promise from [Joseph's] father that inside of one hour he will discard all foreign clothing and dress himself in Khaddar. I wish I could obtain similar promises from every man and woman in this audience."[86] He listened to remarks at Thiruvella, and at Changanacherry he met with students at the Nair Service Society's English school, where he praised the pupils' colorful remarks.

Arriving at Kottayam at 5:30 P.M., 10,000 people awaited him at a meeting. Gandhi expressed pleasure when a student of Hindustani read his remarks in the main tongue of India; the learning of Hindustani was part of the Congress program. Gandhi said that he was unable to address the throng in Hindi himself.[87] He also expressed pleasure in visiting "a centre of Christian influence." He went on to say that he had many Christian friends and that there was nothing in the constructive program that he had placed before the nation in which a Christian could not unreservedly participate: "[A] Christian is the less a Christian if he does not wholeheartedly participate in this constructive pro-gramme." In speaking of the spinning wheel, he said that in it "lies the economic salvation of India." He spoke of the maharani regent: "Her Highness and the Dewan have assured me of their sympathy with the reformers. . . . [T]hey are only waiting for an emphatic, unequivocal, disciplined, articulate expression of public opinion on the part of Savarna Hindus in order to do away with this disgrace," referring to the temple roads forbidden to some Hindus.[88] When the group reached Vykom on March 16, Gandhi observed a day of silence. His secretary, Desai, "retired to bed exhausted"; Rajagopalachari was also ill.[89]

[86] Gandhi, March 15, 1925, KSA (speech texts): vol. 9, VSB, p. 1 of 6.

[87] Gandhi was able to communicate in Hindi and had addressed massive audiences in north Indian in Hindi. One possibility in the context of Gandhi's refusal to address the throng in the Kottayam meeting is that his command of Hindi may not have been such as to allow him to simplify it for those who did not speak Hindi. Justin Mathew, communication (October 14, 2010).

[88] Gandhi, March 15, 1925, speech texts, p. 5 of 6.

[89] Pitt, "Report on the Tour of Mr. M. K. Gandhi," 139.

On March 17 in Vykom, Gandhi met with Pitt again over breakfast to discuss civil disobedience. At the old palace, he met with Indanturuttil Nambiathiri, who handed him scriptural texts in Malayalam, purportedly in support of unapproachability. Gandhi promised to read them carefully after they were translated. At best, however, he questioned their authenticity and at worst challenged the upper-caste interpretation. That evening he presided over a conference of Pulayas and listened to addresses from a representative of the Vykom Pulayas and from the Ezhavas of Kumarakom. At a meeting of the Anti-Untouchability Committee, the decision was made not to initiate satyagraha at other temples for the moment.

On March 18 before 10:00 P.M., Gandhi departed Vykom in a motorboat, as he had arrived, and reached Parur at 4:30 A.M. He attended a public meeting at 6:00 A.M. and listened to an address by A. G. Menon, a member of the Legislative Council, and an address by a local Ezhava and others from Parur representatives. Gandhi responded by speaking about satyagraha and khadi. Going on to Alwaye, he spoke at Alwaye Union Christian College on similar themes and planted a mango tree. At the Sanskrit School, he counseled students to adhere to Sri Narayana Guru's guidance. Gandhi soon thereafter made his farewell to Travancore, walked to the rail station, and caught the 11:00 P.M. train for Trichur.

A *Mathrubhumi* report offers perspective, as it describes the reception given to him by the citizens of Trichur, because Gandhi's visit there unintentionally coincided with the largest annual festival in south India. During the Trichur Pooram fete, one hundred elephants paraded and fireworks were displayed. According to the *Mathrubhumi* reporter, "The people who had gathered to greet Gandhi outnumbered the festival-goers."[90] On Gandhi's return trip to central India, the *Mathrubhumi* correspondent wrote, based on an interview, that Gandhi had expressed his opinion that the lower-caste people should be admitted, not only to the adjacent temple roads in Vykom, but also into the temple itself. Gandhi's ambivalence on the temple-entry issue at the start of the struggle had obviously changed: "We would have no right to

---

[90] "Mahatma Gandhi's Journey to Vykom: Unprecedented Enthusiasm of the Citizens of Trichur—The Welcome of the People of Vykom," *Mathrubhumi* (trans. Thilleri), March 12, 1925, 5.

claim that untouchability has been eradicated without allowing these very primary rights to all in the God-given land." The article also notes that Gandhi considered it impossible to establish the *swaraj* of his dreams without the involvement of women. He called for women to take a more active part in the affairs of the nation.[91]

Pitt remarks that Gandhi said nothing "objectionable" during his sojourn and that any references to the British were friendly, although he judged that the news media had exaggerated the size of the crowds. He concludes by emphasizing that Gandhi had *advised*—characterized by Pitt as "the word with which he invariably describes his orders"—that the satyagrahis cease attacking the Travancore government in their program, but while Gandhi remained at Vykom "harangues to this effect were being delivered at the boat landing."[92]

Gandhi had wanted to meet with virtually every group that was involved in perpetuation of untouchability, an objective that he generally met. He also galvanized elements of public opinion in regard to the national struggle. On the other hand, Nambudiri leaders had summarily dismissed the three offers that Gandhi had extended on March 10. As Mahadev Desai puts it, "Blind unreason could go no further."[93]

A Bargain with Commissioner Pitt

Having been granted the status of a state guest, Gandhi had been accompanied throughout his visit to Travancore, as noted above, by W. H. Pitt, the British police commissioner, who supervised all of the administrative and security arrangements. During their joint travels, the two men informally, though frequently, discussed the situation in Vykom. "More than anyone else among the persons in authority in Travancore," Ravindran comments, "Pitt was freer, less prejudiced, with more initiative and in a better position to deal with Gandhi in order to bring about an honourable settlement of the issue."[94]

---

[91] "The Return Journey of Mahatmaji. . . . The Depressed Classes Should Be Allowed Not Only Freedom of Travel but Even Admission to Temples," *Mathrubhumi* (trans. Thilleri), March 26, 1925, 3.

[92] Pitt, "Report on the Tour of Mr. M. K. Gandhi," 141.

[93] Desai, *Epic of Travancore*, 21.

[94] Ravindran, *Vaikkam Satyagraha and Gandhi*, 198.

Upon leaving Alwaye, Gandhi had given Pitt a letter dated March 18 that disclosed Gandhi's search for a solution that all parties could accept. Gandhi's letter is worth including in some length because it reveals the contours of what would become a negotiated arrangement for settling the Vykom standoff:

> With reference to the conversations we have had as to the possibility and desirability of removing the barriers at Vykom and the picket [*sic*] which prevent satyagrahi volunteers from crossing the boundary-line on the roads leading to the temple, the position as I understand is this. It is common cause between Government and the reformers that the embargo upon the so-called untouchables making use of the roads around the temple should be removed. In your opinion the cause I have at heart will succeed earlier if I advise the satyagrahis to respect the boundary line [*sic*] pending final decision without the barricades and the picket. You tell me that the orthodox opinion gathers strength from the presence of the barricades and the picket, because the orthodox people wrongly infer that the intention in putting up the barricades and keeping the pickets is to help them to maintain their position. I have gathered from our conversations that it would be possible for you to have the existing orders withdrawn under which you are acting, if I undertake to respect the boundary-line in the manner suggested by you. Whilst I hesitate to believe that the action proposed by you, if taken by the satyagrahis, will soften the hearts of the orthodox people and weaken their position, I fully appreciate the motive that lies behind your suggestion. I am, therefore, prepared to advise, by way of trial, adoption of the suggestion made by you. After all, what the satyagrahis want is to create an active and overwhelming public opinion in their behalf. Their object is not to irritate orthodoxy but to win it over to their side. Their object moreover is in no way to embarrass the Government in the prosecution of the campaign but, so far as it is possible, to enlist its sympathy and support on their side. I am therefore prepared to act upon your suggestion immediately on learning from you that the prohibitory order referred to herein is withdrawn. The effect of this would be that a very small number, not larger than at present, will continue to march up to the boundary-line by way of pleading their cause and stand or spin as they are now doing in front of the lines. . . . I am hoping, with the assistance of the Travancore Government, to formulate public opinion so that it becomes irresistible and that without recourse to law on either side the common right of using public or semi-public roads is not denied to any class of people by reason of their birth.[95]

[95] Gandhi letter to W. H. Pitt, March 18, 1925, *CWMG*, 30: 431–2. According to *CWMG* editors, the "conversations" cited in the letter took place on March 10.

In other words, the government would revoke its prohibitory orders promulgated at the start of the campaign and remove the barricades, while the satyagrahis would in turn honor the *teendal palakas* and refrain from entering the forbidden roads. Pitt summarizes the letter's terms in a report:

1. The District Magistrate's order under Section 127 of the Criminal Procedure Code, subsequently made absolute by the state government, should be withdrawn.
2. Upon withdrawal, Gandhi would *advise* the satyagraha volunteers not to go into the temple area.
3. The number of volunteers who would spin or stand at the limits of the area shall not exceed the current number of fifteen, with five on the western side and three each on the other three sides.

Pitt's notes read:

The barricades and huts round the prohibited area are being pulled down, and the police pickets will all be withdrawn. . . . [T]he position will be the same as it was before the Satyagraha commenced with the single exception that 15 volunteers will be found spinning or standing on the roads. These volunteers have been there for a year past and even with more than half the width of each road permanently blocked by barricades and huts for the Police no inconvenience worth the name has been caused to other users of the road who are almost entirely pedestrians.[96]

Although not fully persuaded of Pitt's argument that the movement might fare better in melting the hearts of the orthodox high-caste Hindus if the barricades were removed and the satyagrahis remained in the restricted areas, Gandhi agreed nonetheless to try it and sent a telegram informing the secretary of the Vykom Satyagraha Committee on March 24. Pitt replied to Gandhi on March 25, stating that the local government had accepted the suggestion. Negotiations were well under way by March 1925 as shown by a handwritten draft of a letter to the British agent, C. W. E. Cotton, of April 6:

[M]y commissioner of police communicated to me an offer from Mr. Gandhi to eliminate civil disobedience for the satyagraha campaign at

---

[96] Pitt, "Report on the Tour of Mr. M. K. Gandhi," 141–2.

Vaikom on the understanding that should the order of the District Magistrate, Kottayam, under section 127 of the Travancore Criminal Procedure Code . . . prohibiting the entry of Ezhavas and other so-called pollution classes on the roads leading to and lying round the Vaikom temple be withdrawn, Mr. Gandhi would undertake to advise the satya-grahis to respect the notice boards at the entrance of the roads and refrain from entering the prohibited area. Mr. Pitt recommended the acceptance of the offer on the ground that the situation at Vaikom [is] under control and that there is no [likelihood of] a breach of the peace. . . . The District Magistrate, Kottayam, who was consulted in the matter, reported that the Satyagrahis would respect Mr. Gandhi's advice and recommended the withdrawal of the prohibitory notification on the strength of Mr. Gandhi's undertaking. An agreement was accordingly reached with Mr. Gandhi embodying the said terms . . . [and by] 7 April 1925, . . . the arrangement is to take effect. I consider that the cessation of civil disobedience would be a moral victory gained by Government and might ease the situation and facilitate negotiations with the orthodox party, and with this end in view, I have called upon the Dewan Pershkar, Kottayam, and the Devaswom Commissioner to explain to the orthodox section of the people the views of this government on the subject of Satyagraha . . . and endeavour to bring about a change in the outlook of that section which will accord with modern ideas.[97]

Thus, a solution of sorts evolved, though ultimately suffused with ambiguities. No formal accord or written agreement was produced that could be consulted for compliance or parsed by future generations. No one would be pleased with the compromise worked out between Gandhi and Pitt. In Pitt's words, Gandhi's March 18 missive offers "in effect to abandon 'civil disobedience' as an experiment."[98] Gandhi may have been against civil disobedience in a princely state, but neither Pitt nor the government saw it in this light.

On April 4, the government formally withdrew its March 1924 prohibitory order. That there was still nervousness is shown by a note on

---

[97] Judicial, Police Department, Trivandrum, to C. W. E. Cotton, Agent to the Governor-General, Madras States, handwritten draft letter, possibly drafted by Pitt for the Dewan to send, April 6, 1925, KSA: vol. 9, VSB, file handwritten 563/24 Judicial. The letter sheds light on the relationship between the Travancore government and the paramount power.

[98] Pitt, "Report on the Tour of Mr. M. K. Gandhi," 141.

the small stationery of the government of Travancore on which Pitt wrote to the dewan:

> Her highness the Maharani Regent in discussing Vaikom affairs asked me why I did not get Mr. Gandhi to put in writing his statement that for the present he would not allow satyagraha to be practiced in order to obtain temple entrance. I told Her Highness what I have understood from you that you were writing to Mr Gandhi on this point. Yours sincerely, W. H. Pitt.[99]

The agreement took effect on April 8 after it was clarified that both parties fully understood the conditions. It was a year and one week since the Vykom satyagraha had begun. The barricades on the four approaching temple roads were to be destroyed, with the police presence remaining in place until the task was completed. Pitt took further measures, attempting to ensure the safety of the satyagrahis from violent outbursts by orthodox Hindus after the removal of the barriers and agreed to assume responsibility if any untouchables used the prohibited temple roads.

The fourth phase of the Vykom satyagraha had come to its close. Gandhi had made himself accessible to all parties and viewpoints and had very nearly prostrated himself before the higher echelons of the temple custodians and upper castes. Yet the only reordering that he could produce was a reversion to the situation that existed before the mobilization had begun. The final stage of the struggle was about to start.

---

[99] Pitt, handwritten note to Bahadur T. Raghavaiah, April 8, 1925, KSA: vol. 5, VSB, file 3060.

5 The Settlement

The volunteers felt consternation. More problems lay ahead. At the end of May, the *Mathrubhumi* carried a statement by K. Kelappan, manager of the newspaper, about the condition of untouchability and the satyagraha: "The visit of Mahatma Gandhi had made a desirable change in the outlook of the Travancore government toward the Satyagraha," yet according to him, the government was not taking appreciable steps, as expected after Gandhi's visit. Kelappan and the *satyagrahi*s had expected a speeding up of a solution after Gandhi's March visit.[1] He was not the only one perplexed.

The Ezhava satyagrahis were displeased by the removal of the barricades. With progress appearing bleak, the SNDP Yogam leadership began advocating conversion to any faith. Some spoke of converting to Buddhism—another reforming sect of Hinduism regarded as a faith by its devotees. In 1924, Dalit leader Babasaheb Ambedkar spoke favorably about the Vykom satyagraha at the Depressed Classes Conference in Bombay, calling it "the most important event in the country today" for untouchables.[2] He also noted, correctly, that after a year of activities, nothing had resulted. This was also the time when he famously spoke out against the Hindu scriptures because they had been used to

[1] "The Satyagraha at Vykom," *Mathrubhumi* (trans. Vasu Thilleri), May 28, 1925, 5.

[2] Eleanor Zelliot, *From Untouchable to Dalit: Essays on the Ambedkar Movement* (New Delhi: Manohar, 2001), 162–3.

rationalize the opposition of the Nambudiris to the Vykom movement. He even called upon his adherents to burn the scriptures, and a public burning of the *Manusmriti*, in whose texts untouchability was justified, took place in 1927. Ambedkar had embarked on an extensive endeavor to shape an identity as the basis for promoting emancipation of the untouchables as the Broken Men, the first followers of Buddha, who remained adherents to Buddhism when others turned to Hinduism.[3] In 1935, Ambedkar announced that he had been born a Hindu, but would not die a Hindu, although he would not actually convert to Buddhism until 1956. (Both Jainism and Buddhism seek alternative views of the existential necessity for violence; both claim doctrines of nonviolence.) Nevertheless, T. K. Madhavan and Sri Narayana Guru had opposed mass conversion, and so the satyagraha plodded on?[4]

A Negotiated Solution

Subsequent to the removal of the barriers, the Vykom satyagraha continued with fifteen volunteers daily, soon reduced to ten, a consequence of the agreement with Commissioner W. H. Pitt. Early in June, the *Mathrubhumi* reported that Krishna Pillai, the acting *dewan* of Travancore, had expressed his views to the maharani regent that the roads around the Vykom temple should be opened to all.[5] Reacting to this piece of information, the newspaper's editor K. Kelappan issued a statement in his capacity as a leader of the satyagraha saying that this seemingly favorable development should not be cause for any slowing of the movement, despite expectations of a favorable decision on the part of the government.[6]

On June 20, the *Mathrubhumi* correspondent reports that the government was contemplating opening the roads on three sides of the

[3] Christophe Jaffrelot, *India's Silent Revolution: The Rise of the Lower Castes in North India* (London: Hurst and Company, 2003), 22.

[4] M. S. A. Rao, *Social Movements and Social Transformation: A Study of Two Backward Classes Movements in India* (New Delhi: Manohar Publications, 1987), 66.

[5] "The Favorable Opinion of the Acting Dewan," *Mathrubhumi* (trans. Thilleri), June 6, 1925.

[6] "The Request of Mr. Kelappan," *Mathrubhumi* (trans. Thilleri), June 13, 1925, 5.

Vykom temple. K. Kelappan, acting in his dual capacity as a member of the news media and a leader of the Vykom struggle, states that the Travancore government was ready to open the roads on three sides, except for the eastern side, the *shanthikar*, which was reserved for the priests and temple custodians as separate approaches to avoid ceremonial pollution from contact with the impure. Government authorities approached the Satyagraha Committee to ask whether they would stop their struggle if such a decision were taken. Kelappan, then managing the satyagraha ashram and also secretary of the Congress Anti-Untouchability Committee, spoke in his formal capacity and replied in the negative. He told officials that the satyagraha would end only if all the roads on all sides of the temple were opened to the public and issued a statement on the government's proposal in which he asserted, "This decision would not solve the issue of the lack of freedom of the depressed classes of this place or anywhere else."[7]

On June 21, according to a government report by the acting *devaswom* (temple authority) commissioner, three of the roads surrounding the temple were walked upon by lower castes:

> The prohibitory order in respect of the roads leading to the Vaikom temple having been withdrawn, there was nothing to prevent the avarnas using any or all of the roads. In deference to the wishes of the orthodox savarnas, however, the avarna leaders agreed not to use the eastern road where the Melshanthis (the priest of the highest order in a temple) live. As regards the remaining three roads, the avarnas began to walk through them with effect from June 21, 1925. There was no opposition from the savarnas.[8]

Two days later, a telegram arrived from Gandhi. The volunteers were told that they should take "no forward step" without his permission. In response, they pulled back from the positions they had newly taken on the previous day and returned to their original placements. The acting devaswom commissioner recorded, "Satyagraha is now offered at the four original posts in modified form. That is to say, instead of offering Satyagraha at all the posts simultaneously, they do it only for three

---

[7] "The Satyagraha Struggle at Vykom: Not Ended Yet," *Mathrubhumi* (trans. Thilleri), June 20, 1925, 3.

[8] R. Krishna Pillai, Acting Devaswom Commissioner, Trivandrum, "Report, Temple Entry: Entry by Avarnas into Ambalafourka Temple," June 29, 1925, Kerala State Archives (hereafter KSA): vol. 7, Vaikkom Satyagraha Bundle (hereafter VSB), file 772, p. 1 of 5. The word "confidential" is handwritten boldly.

hours at each post."[9] He then observed, "So far as I could see, the Melshanthis have no objection to carry on worship in the temple provided the eastern road is kept closed to Avarnas."[10]

The *Mathrubhumi* reports on July 4 that the *avarnas* had begun using all the roads around the temple, after withdrawal of the government order that had prohibited their use by the lower castes. Kelappan, speaking in his capacity as a leader, noted in the July 4 newspaper that the satyagrahis should not be using these roads for some time as part of the agreement between Pitt and Gandhi; he cautioned the avarnas not to make noisy celebrations while using the roads, so as not to provoke the conservatives among the upper castes.[11]

Pitt had met with a *Mathrubhumi* correspondent, who reported on June 27 that "after the agreement between himself and Mr. Gandhi the satyagraha volunteers have not violated the provisions of that agreement," referring to the police deployment in the area of the satyagraha and the volunteers' conduct. Gandhi had assured Pitt that there was no need of a police force, because the satyagraha volunteers would not use any violence, it being a cardinal principle of the campaign to use solely nonviolent means. Pitt expressed satisfaction that after the withdrawal of police from the satyagraha area, no violent incidents occurred; "the satygrahis had kept their word."[12] In a dispatch from the Satygraha Publicity Bureau on July 11, the *Mathrubhumi* reported that Ezhava youths had tried to walk the eastern road to the temple. Some in the leadership feared that such an attempt would create difficulties for the government in seeking a way to resolve the matter for all concerned.[13]

The *Mathrubhumi* also reported on attempts by lower classes elsewhere to assert their right to enter temples. A July 23 article about a procession at Ambalapuzha, near Alleppey, states that a group walked a forbidden road, pursuing their own rights and not as an expression of solidarity with Vykom. T. K. Madhavan addressed them and asked that

[9] Pillai, "Report, Temple Entry," 1–2.

[10] Pillai, "Report, Temple Entry," 3.

[11] "Satyagraha is Fruitful: All Are Using the Vykom Roads," *Mathrubhumi* (trans. Thilleri), July 4, 1925, 3.

[12] "Satyagrahis Have Not Violated the Agreement: The Opinion of the Police Commissioner," *Mathrubhumi* (trans. Thilleri), June 27, 1925, 5.

[13] Satygraha Publicity Bureau, "Vykom Satygraha," *Mathrubhumi* (trans. Thilleri), July 11, 1925, 3.

they not force the issue until after the successful completion of the Vykom satyagraha.[14] According to Vasu Thilleri, a few members of the Arya Samaj, the Hindu reform organization, had become involved. Its members, without caste, asserted that they could walk the prohibited roads. Conservative Hindus were taken aback by their audacity. On July 11, they had conducted a demonstration and had not been arrested: they could not be charged, as they had no caste.

The government weighed in against the Ambalapuzha confrontation and against the avarnas' right to walk the roads of various temples. In response, Kelappan alleged that the government was retreating from its pledge to address the issue of untouchability, which he substantiated by mention of the decision of the government to open only three roads around the Vykom temple to the avarnas. Kelappan challenged the government's contention that the eastern road could not be opened because the temple pond stands on the road, meaning that the high castes who bathed in it deemed any lower-caste passersby as polluting it. He also disagreed with a proposition that the pond be relocated, clearing the way for the eastern road to be opened. He reiterated that the fight was against untouchability, so repositioning the pond would not solve the issue—namely, to open all roads, temples, and ponds to everyone.[15]

The *Mathrubhumi* editorializes on August 20 about the roads around the Ambalapuzha temple being used by lower-caste people, with permission from the authorities. It notes that a favorable position had been taken by the majority of *savarnas* there to make this possible and attributes the advance to the impact of the Vykom satyagraha.[16] Confusion spread. The newspaper had previously reported that all the roads in Ambalapuzha were open. On August 27, it printed a correction: certain portions of the roads were for the Brahmins who resided there, and the temple pond was still not opened to the lower classes.[17]

[14] "The Freedom of Travel of the Avarnas: The Procession at Ambalapusha," *Mathrubhumi* (trans. Thilleri), July 23, 1925, 3.

[15] "The Satyagraha Struggle at Vykom: The Lack of Policy of the Travancore Government," press release by K. Kelappan, *Mathrubhumi* (trans. Thilleri), July 30, 1925, 3.

[16] Editorial Comment: "The Victory at Ambalapusha," *Mathrubhumi* (trans. Thilleri), August 20, 1925, 4.

[17] "The Incidents at Ambalapusha: Not All the Roads Are Open," *Mathrubhumi* (trans. Thilleri), August 27, 1925, 3.

In August, C. W. E. Cotton, the British resident, wrote that an effort in May and June to send a deputation to the palace for an audience with the maharani regent had failed for lack of funds.[18] The dewan had been sending regular reports to the British agent, and an August 9 confidential letter from a senior official in the Travancore government discloses that the makings of a settlement were in process:

> Since the starting of the Satyagraha movement at Vaikom, the Dewan has been sending confidential reports to the Agent to the Governor-General, Madras States, from time to time regarding its development. Now that the roads on the northern, western and southern sides of the temple have been made available to Avarnas, Satyagraha is now offered only on the eastern road and the situation is normal. This may be communicated to Mr. Cotton.[19]

Yet shifts were under way, as seen when in August, the maharani regent agreed to withdraw the prohibitory ban under which eight of the central characters in this saga were detained, including Dr. Emperumal Naidu of Nagercoil, K. Aiyyapan, Aiyamuthu Goundan of Coimbatore, and E. V. Ramaswamy Naicker of Erode, whose fiery speeches had led to their being locked up.[20]

Furthermore, in other parts of south India social movements were being inspired or stimulated at this time, although not all accepted Gandhi's premises. The *Mathrubhumi* reports on strong efforts by the lower strata in the town of Palghat, on Kalpathy Street, where the Travancore government supported their position. The government wrote an ordinance to clarify that public roads are maintained from public funds, and thus all citizens have equal rights. The Palghat struggle stemmed from a tributary of lower-caste movements that differed in approach from the Congress and Gandhi. The major point of difference

[18] Letter (signature illegible), from the Palace, Trivandrum, to C. W. E. Cotton, Agent to the Governor-General, Madras States, August 3, 1925, KSA: vol. 5, VSB, handwritten file 240, also 5774. Attachments refer to letters dated May 29 and June 9, 1925, with enclosures.

[19] Pillai (signature partially illegible), to M. E. Watts, Dewan of Travancore, Trivandrum, August 9, 1925, KSA (confidential letter): vol. 5, VSB, handwritten file 214, also no. 5875.

[20] Palace, Trivandrum, to M. E. Watts, Dewan of Travancore, Trivandrum, August 5/6, 1925, KSA (letter, signature illegible): vol. 5, VSB, handwritten file 213, also no. 5774.

was that the Gandhi had persuaded the Congress to address the issue of untouchability with the willing cooperation of the upper castes. The latter thought that the upper castes, who had oppressed those without caste for centuries, could not be trusted, and that only with the help of the government might the legal machinery be shifted into gear to fight this repression.[21] Others holding this perspective included Ambedkar; C. Krishnan, who published the *Mitavadi* (Moderate) newspaper in Calicut; and the SNDP Yogam.

In essence, on April 4 the government formally removed its prohibitory order of March 1924, and the barricades were dismantled. Various lower-caste individuals and visitors began quietly using the temple roads. Some satyagrahis continued a nominal protest. During the next few months, the government yielded somewhat. As a compromise, it came up with the idea of opening the roads on three sides of the temple, while creating a secondary pathway on the fourth side. In plain words, these roads were enclosed by a new connector road to create separation from the temple, a diversion at the eastern gate for the untouchables, to allow the temple authorities to retain their exclusive access without being polluted by unapproachables.[22] This was presented as a "solution," notwithstanding the fact that the struggle had consistently asked for the opening of all the roads to everyone. On the basis of this artful expedient, indeed legerdemain, the palace thought it could ask Gandhi to call off the satyagraha in November.

Gandhi learned the details through Chakravarti Rajagopalachari on October 8, 1925, whom he had empowered to act behind the scenes. Gandhi sent a message to the leader of the camp, K. Kelappan: "You may withdraw." Kelappan's response (as cited by Ravindran) was to issue a public statement, "We are satisfied that the purpose for which Satyagraha

[21] "The Serious Incidents at Palghat," *Mathrubhumi* (trans. Thilleri), November 7, 1925, 5. Thilleri, interview (March 19, 2009).

[22] In practice, the compromise meant that three of the four approaching roads leading directly to the temple were to be opened to everyone, while these roads were also cordoned off by a new lane set apart from the temple. The concept was that a small portion of the road on the eastern side of the temple would be designated as open solely to caste Hindus during hours of worship, while non-caste Hindus, Christians, and Muslims alike would be prohibited from this area. (It would be regressive if Christians, Muslims, and Jews were no longer able to walk roads surrounding the temple.)

was started has been achieved and we therefore under advice from our revered leader withdraw satyagraha from Vaikom roads."[23] It appears from various sources that Kelappan (and doubtless others) understood the government's provisions to mean that all four roads were opened. An unsigned draft in the Kerala State Archives describes the government's terms as follows: "All the roads round Vaikom Temple with the exception of two short lanes leading to the eastern approach road one from the south and the other from the north are open to all castes without distinction."[24] The unsigned draft seems to advise individuals who will be publicly interpreting what is called "the solution arrived at by the authorities."[25] No formal agreement has come to light for such government action. In the resulting ambiguity and confusion, Kelappan had evidently been misinformed or possibly had misinterpreted the settlement proffered by the government. All of the roads were not opened, nor were the roads opened to all persons of the state. (Some conditions were accepted after the new connecting road was completed.) The draft states that

> people will be admitted only for purposes of worship in the temple. All the approaches to the portion of the land which is now withdrawn from public use and which was hitherto being used as a thoroughfare by sufferance of the Devaswom Department are guarded by doors which will remain shut except during hours of service in the temple. We are informed by the Devaswom authorities that the enclosed portion will be open neither to Christians, Mohammedans nor to Hindus who have not got the right of worship in the temple nor even to caste-Hindus except during hours of service. A new road is constructed joining the eastern approach to the northern road for the convenience of the public. It is clearly to be borne in mind that all the roads lying round the temple at Vaikom are now alike open to all the members of the Hindu community be he [sic]a caste Hindu or a non-caste Hindu and that no invidious distinction is now made in the matter of the right of way.[26]

In preserving its ability to deny access to Christians, Muslims, and non-Hindus, the government could still exclude avarnas. It was, as K. K.

[23] T. K. Ravindran, *Vaikkam Satyagraha and Gandhi* (Trichur: Sri Narayana Institute of Social and Cultural Development, 1975), 203.

[24] Three-page, double-spaced unsigned draft, n. d. [after October 8, 1925], untitled, KSA: vol 10, VSB.

[25] Unsigned draft, n.d. [after October 8, 1925], KSA. The content would be "talking points" in today's media hype.

[26] Unsigned draft, n.d. [after October 8, 1925], KSA.

Kusuman tersely characterized it, "a compromise, and not a complete success."[27] The eastern road continued to be inaccessible to the lower classes.

At the end of October came news that the Social Conference of Nairs had passed a resolution: "[T]his conference is of the opinion that the roads maintained by the State be thrown open to all persons irrespective of caste or creed."[28] Word had spread that all the roads around the Vykom temple had been opened, but it would become clear that this was not true. The local police inspector sent to Commissioner Pitt resolutions passed by the Kerala Congress party's Anti-Untouchability Committee on November 17:

> I. In view of the information received from the authorities that all public roads round the Vaikom Temple will be thrown open before the beginning of the Ashtami festival to all classes of the people without distinction this Committee under advice from Mahatmaji resolves that the object of Satyagraha having been achieved Satyagraha may be withdrawn from the date of the actual opening of the roads. . . .

> III. Resolved that in view of the fact that the present Untouchability Committee ceases to exist on the termination of the Vaikom Satyagraha the Provincial Congress Committee be requested to constitute a new Committee.

> IV. Resolved that since the public opinion in Travancore has clearly expressed itself in favour of Temple entry for all Hindus, intense propaganda be started to strengthen public opinion and to conciliate and enlist the sympathy of orthodoxy.

The satyagraha will "cease within a few days and there will be a big public meeting after its termination," according to the police inspector.[29] Pitt transmitted his report to the chief secretary of the government in Travancore with the following letter:

> Sir, In forwarding herewith copy of report dated November 19, 1925, received from the Inspector of Police, Vaikom, I have the honor to report that the arrangements made by the Dewaswom [devaswom]

---

[27] Kusuman, interview (August 16, 2005).

[28] K. Narayana Menon, President, Nair Conference, letter transmitting resolution from the Social Conference of Nairs, October 31, 1925, KSA: vol. 10, VSB, file 8269.

[29] K. Rama Varier, Police Inspector, Vaikom, to W. H. Pitt, Commissioner of Police, Travancore, memorandum transmitting resolutions, November 19, 1925, KSA: VSB: vol. 10.

Commissioner for allowing the use by all classes of persons of the roads around Vaikom Temple with the exception of small portions that it has been found necessary to reserve, have long ago been accepted by the general public as fair and are now accepted by the Satyagrahis themselves who have at last found a suitable occasion for withdrawing. I have the honor to be, Sir, Your most obedient servant, s/Pitt.[30]

This bewildering period is punctuated by the *Mathrubhumi*'s abrupt account, in which articles in the satyagraha ashram at Vykom are being auctioned off, including cots, pots, pans, and lamps, because fewer volunteers were participating in the satyagraha.[31]

The End of the Vykom Satyagraha

The Vykom satyagraha ended on November 23, 1925—604 days after the first regimented walk to forbidden sections of the Vykom temple roads on March 30 of the preceding year. According to the compromise effected, a small portion of the eastern road was, indeed, reserved for the temple authorities' exclusive use in entering the temple compound, alongside of which was laid a separate pathway, upon which the lower castes could walk. On November 24, the police inspector in Vykom wrote to Pitt in Trivandrum to let him know that the variance was finished:

Sir, Satyagraha that was normally being offered at the eastern side of the Temple was also stopped yesterday as the new deviation road was complete by yesterday and the Avarnas have begun to pass through it. Avarnas are passing through that road today also. Mr. Kelappan Nayar has sent a long statement to the Press. . . . There will be a grand public meeting in the Satyagraha Asraman on the 29th instant [sic] when Mr. E. V. Ramaswami Naicker will preside.[32]

Exactly when the secondary road was completed may not be definitively discernible. Pitt's letter conveying the inspector's report to the chief secretary of the government went out ten days later.[33] Its attached

[30] W. H. Pitt, Trivandrum, to Trivandrum Chief Secretary of Government, letter on Satyagraha at Vaikom, withdrawal of, December 2, 1925, KSA: VSB vol. 10, file 9263.

[31] "Vykom Satygraha," *Mathrubhumi* (trans. Thilleri), October 15, 1925, 5.

[32] K. Rama Varier, Police Inspector, Vaikom, to Commissioner of Police, Trivandrum, letter regarding completion of new deviation road, November 24, 1925, KSA: vol. 10, VSB.

report countersigned by Pitt says that the deviation road was finished at Vykom on November 23.

On December 4, from elsewhere in the government in Trivandrum, the dewan was sent in a confidential letter resolutions passed on November 29, 1925, by a large public assembly led by E. V. Ramasamy Naicker. The declaration resolves:

> In view of the fact that the Government have thrown open all roads in Vaikom to all citizens irrespective of castes or creed and that they follow no invidious distinction in their use, the object of Satyagraha have been achieved, this meeting approves of the decision of the untouchability committees under instructions from Mahatmaji to dissolve the Satyagraha [ashram] and demobilize the volunteers thereof.[34]

The other resolutions pertain to starting struggles elsewhere for opening temples to all Hindus regardless of caste, "thankfulness to the Government of Her Highness the [Maharani] Regent for the liberal policy so far followed," and reiteration of the confidence in nonviolent struggle among those attending the meeting and request for adherence to nonviolent actions in all future reform activities.[35]

On December 7, K. Kelappan, steadfast in his leadership of the Anti-Untouchability Committee, sent the dewan a handwritten letter on the committee's stationery from Camp Vaikom:

> I have been instructed to convey to the Government of Her Highness the Maharani regent of Travancore the following resolutions passed at the public meeting held at Vaikom attended by over four thousand people and presided over by Mr. E. V. Ramaswami Naicker of Erode. I have the honor to be, Sir, your most obedient servant, s/K. Kelappan, Secretary.

His letter contains the same resolutions as those noted from the meeting led by Ramasamy Naicker, written by hand, referencing a fact that

---

[33] W. H. Pitt, Commissioner of Police, Trivandrum, to Chief Secretary of Government, Trivandrum, letter transmitting police inspector's report on deviation road, December 4, 1925, KSA: vol. 10, VSB, file 9385. Attached is K. Rama Varier, Police Inspector, Vaikom, to Trivandrum Commissioner of Police, "Letter on the New Deviation Road," November 24, 1925, KSA: vol. 10, VSB.

[34] R. Krishna Pillai, to M. E. Watts, Dewan of Travancore, confidential letter transmitting resolutions, December 4, 1925, KSA: vol. 10, VSB, file 9296, 1.

[35] Krishna Pillai, to M. E. Watts, Dewan, confidential letter, December 4, 1925, 2.

all roads in Vykom have been thrown open to all citizens. Four thousand assembled in Vykom had been told that all roads were open and "the present solution of the road question by the Government is satisfactory."[36]

By November 23, 1925, the last satyagrahi had departed.

Today in Vykom at the northern gate of the temple stand statues of T. K. Madhavan, Ramasamy Naicker, and Mannath Padmanabhan Pillai.

"A Compromise, and Not a Complete Success"

Warm acknowledgments flowed to the maharani, yet the specified "small portions that it has been found necessary to reserve" of the roads clearly showed that the settlement had not transformed the hearts and minds of upper-caste orthodoxy. Even when measured against its original circumscribed stated objective of opening the Vykom temple roads to all non-caste Hindus, the Vykom satyagraha had minimal success, since only three of the temple roads around the place of worship were fully opened. Whatever concessions occurred were not as a result of the persuasion, or conversion, of the orthodox Hindus, but, rather, capitulation by the local Travancore government. The final settlement is the most controversial aspect of the entire chronicle, the tentacles of which reach into contemporary debates worldwide on how to plan and aim for effective nonviolent civil resistance.

The maharani had moderate education and by all accounts tried to be a responsive monarch. From her other policies it can be seen that she held broadminded values, which may have facilitated the process. Yet, in retrospect, what was most influential with the government was public opinion, including that expressed by caste middle-class Hindus, for whom this denial was a civil libertarian issue rather than a matter of religion. A public road was ostensibly being opened to all inhabitants, yet the maharani was confronted with a kaleidoscopic situation in which the mobilization could continue to wield challenges. Not to be forgotten were impendng conversions to Christianity coming from the

[36] K. Kelappan, Secretary, Kerala Congress Untouchability Committee, Calicut, letter conveying resolutions, to His Excellency the Dewan of Travancore, Trivandrum, December 7, 1925, KSA: vol. 10, VSB, file 9287, 1, 2.

Figure 8 Statue of Mannath Padmanabhan Pillai at Vykom today
(Illustrated by Madanan Pv)

Note: Recalled as a potent speaker, Mannath Padmanabhan Pillai is thought by
many to have been the first upper-caste figure in Travancore to take a public stand
on ending untouchability in the Hindu caste system. For fifty years, as the general
secretary of the Nair Service Society, he was able to use the power of his rank in
taking initiative for confronting the oppression faced by the untouchables.

SNDP quarters and the Ezhavas. Additionally, the SNDP was consolidating and becoming mainstream, affecting all levels of the society. In
this light, the maharani's legitimacy was threatened, and she had to
throw open the Vykom temple roads, not from a point of view of granting rights or entitlements, but to bring about a subsidence of the continuing disruption in Travancore. From another perspective, the
construction of a new road linking the eastern approach to the northern road for the public would be prudent management of the conflict.

Ravindran, however, rants that the struggle resulted in "about eight
furlongs more ... added to these free roads."[37] His words rise steaming
off the page with ire: "After twenty months of relentless fight, Congress
withdrew from the scene with its finery torn, and its prestige tarnished,
leaving the cause of the depressed classes at the same spot whence they
picked it up in March 1924." For Ravindran, Gandhi's agreement with
Pitt led to a "deplorable situation," in which the satyagrahis had sustained their earnest best efforts, but the "Gandhi–Pitt pact concluded
over their heads nullified the effect of all their past actions."[38] Yet
Ravindran's is not the last word. The significance of the struggle's outcome was not as a specific breakthrough or tangible attainment, but
that a major penetration and upheaval in customary ideas about
untouchability had occurred.

"In struggles against social obscurantism based on religious beliefs,"
Panikkar observes, "the initial step is perhaps the most difficult one.
The Vaikkam satyagraha represented the difficult first step."[39] Gandhi's
communications in his all-India work referencing untouchability in the
1920s gained momentum from Vykom's tenuous settlement, despite its
elements of illusionism. In Gandhi's own wording, the settlement
worked out by the authorities was, "flimsy in one respect"—because the
government had reserved for itself the option of excluding the roads to

[37] Ravindran, *Vaikkam Satyagraha and Gandhi*, 205. A furlong is an eighth a
mile. Ravindran's book is in another edition titled, *Eight Furlongs to Freedom*.

[38] Ravindran, *Vaikkam Satyagraha and Gandhi*, 204, 206–7.

[39] K. N. Panikkar, "Vaikkam Satyagraha: The Struggle against
Untouchability," in *We Fought Together for Freedom: Chapters from the Indian
National Movement*, ed. Ravi Dayal (Delhi, Bombay, Calcutta, Madras: Oxford
University Press and Indian Council of Historical Research, 1995), 135.

non-Hindus, which could include the avarnas, so that the excluded castes would not be able to say that the roads opened to non-Hindus were not open to them.[40] Even so, Gandhi would call the solution "a bedrock of freedom," in a speech at Alleppey two years later, in 1927, referring to it as a contract of sorts between the people and the state "in the direction of liberty in one respect at least."[41]

After the Vykom struggle, piecemeal fights for access to temple roads continued. Roads around temples elsewhere, such as Thiruvarappu and Suchindram, were still being disputed. Gandhi had to re-enter negotiations with the dewan and police commissioner, to appeal to their executive powers to remove the standing prohibitory order that remained in force against Madhavan for delivering public speeches and a general order blocking meetings within a certain radius of Thiruvarappu. Satyagrahas over temple roads began at Suchindram in 1926 and again in 1930, but were unsuccessful. Numerous meetings in a variety of sites were held year-round to demand the opening of roads.

The effort in the state of Travancore expanded, aiming at temple entry elsewhere, as revealed in a police report. On April 1, 1926, at a public meeting in Trivandrum presided over by High Court justice T. K. Velu Pillai, the central issue discussed was "conducting propaganda work for effecting temple entry for the non-caste Hindus." What stand out are the lively and imaginative ideas debated, some presented through theatrical farces in hamlets. At this "500 strong" session, several demonstrations and processions preceded and followed. A signed and framed message from Gandhi was held aloft, along with a portrait of him, on a decorated elephant, ridden by an upper-caste member and a Pulaya side by side. In the program, T. K. Madhavan shared a signed message from Gandhi:

> The reforms in Travancore have done well in the matter of untouchability. The more I think of it in terms of religion, the more convinced I

[40] Mahadev Haribhai Desai, *The Epic of Travancore* (Ahmedabad: Navajivan Karyalaya, 1937), 21–2.

[41] Gandhi, as cited in Desai, *Epic of Travancore*, 22.

[42] T. R. Raman Pillai, Police Inspector, C.I.D., to Commissioner of Police, Trivandrum, memorandum on resolutions from public meeting on temple entry in Trivandrum, April 2, 1926, KSA: vol. 10, attached to file 2862E.

become that it is the greatest blot upon Hinduism. I therefore hope that the reformers will not rest content till every temple and every public school is open to the so called untouchables on a footing of equality with other Hindus.[42]

This animated gathering passed resolutions urging the immediate start of efforts "to create public opinion in favour of the movement," giving an intimation of the activities to follow. Each village was to hold meetings, generate pamphlets, produce newspaper articles, and conduct light dramas to popularize the movement. Public meetings should discuss "monster memorials" for submission. A general committee composed of many of the central characters in this saga would supervise the work on publicity and communications. A working committee headed by Changanacherry K. Parameswaran Pillai would collect funds, and Madhavan would act as secretary.[43]

Gradual reforms continued over subsequent years. Gandhi visited Travancore again, in 1927, in connection with the Thiruvarappu temple and held further conversations with Travancore dewan Maurice E. Watts.[44] When Madhavan became general secretary of the SNDP Yogam in 1927, he organized in several Travancore towns Vykom-style satyagrahas with caste-Hindu cooperation. (In 1927, Madhavan convened a meeting of the SNDP Yogam at Palpathuruthy, in Kuttana, where the decision was made to abandon the concept of mass conversion to another faith, at least temporarily.)[45]

[43] Raman Pillai, to Commissioner of Police, Trivandrum, April 2, 1926.

[44] Alappat Sreedhara Menon, *Kerala and Freedom Struggle* (Kottayam, Kerala: D C Books, 1997), 76.

[45] M. S. A. Rao, *Social Movements and Social Transformation: A Study of Two Backward Classes Movements in India* (New Delhi: Manohar, 1987), 67. The government continued to worry about avarnas converting to other religions, leading it to develop aggressive, anti-missionary policies while conceding to some demands of non-caste Hindus. See Koji Kawashima, *Missionaries and a Hindu State: Travancore, 1858–1936* (New Delhi: Oxford University Press, [1965] 1998), 178–9 and Louise Ouwerkerk, *No Elephants for the Maharaja: Social and Political Change in the Princely State of Travancore, 1921–1947* (New Delhi: Manohar, 1994), 96–9.

In 1928, the Travancore government ordered that the roads approaching temples across the state be opened to the avarnas.[46] Lamentably, for the magnanimity of his exertions, Madhavan would die in 1930 without being able to see all of Travancore's roads opened, to say nothing of the temples. Long-awaited constitutional reforms in 1932, instead of opening up the society to Christians, Ezhavas, and Muslims, had the effect of preserving caste-Hindu supremacy, especially the predominance of Nairs in the legislature.[47] By that year, however, the Travancore government had established the Temple Entry Enquiry Committee to look into specific temple-entry questions.[48] The committee's report did not advocate temple entry for the lower castes, but pleaded for uplift of the avarnas.[49]

Mahadev Desai notes the issuance of the following government communiqué in January 1934 on the eve of another visit by Gandhi to Travancore:

> Government share the view of the Committee [Temple Entry Enquiry Committee] that distance-pollution or *theendal* must cease and are of [the] opinion that no general public funds should be spent by Government in the maintenance of public tanks, public wells, *chatrams* (lodgings), etc., admission to which is denied to any person by reason of his belonging to *theendal* (polluting) caste. They have resolved, therefore, that all public roads, public tanks, public wells, *chatrams*, etc., maintained by them out of their general public funds, shall be thrown open to all classes of people, irrespective of the caste to which they belong. Measures to carry out these objects soon are being considered.[50]

[46] Menon, *Kerala and Freedom Struggle*, 76.

[47] P. Chandramohan, "Social and Political Protest in Travancore: A Study of the Sree Narayana Dharma Paripalana Yogam (1900–1938)" (M.A. diss., Centre for Historical Studies, School of Social Sciences, Jawaharlal Nehru University, 1981), 264.

[48] The new maharaja, Chithira Thirunal Balarama Varma (1931–41), who assumed full ruling power in 1931, appointed the committee. It was chaired by V. S. Subramanya Iyer, a retired dewan of Travancore, and included M. Govindan, an Ezhava, and Changanacherry Parameswaran Pillai, a retired High Court judge.

[49] Chandramohan, "Social and Political Protest in Travancore," 265, 265n2, n3, n4.

[50] Desai, *Epic of Travancore*, 23.

Gandhi's tour was specifically devoted to campaigning actively for the eradication of untouchability.[51] It would take until 1936 for these measures to be instituted.

What had transpired in Vykom had moral echoes and consequences, although if closely examined the government's response was only a managerial contrivance to alleviate a situation that was oppressive to a high percentage of the population and to mitigate the unrest resulting from the prolonged effort to correct the injustice. The modest concession of a compromise—masquerading as change, in fact sleight of hand—to ameliorate the pressures on lower-caste and untouchable people cannot be considered "resolution" of this conflict. Its ethical ramifications, however, laid the groundwork for future fights, struggles, developments, and advances.

Travancore society experienced a remarkable level of political action for reforms as the underprivileged castes sensed that deeper social currents, such as abolishment of slavery and opening up of education and business opportunities, along with influences from British and missionary values, were altering the status quo. Untouchability, unapproachability, and unseeability had been so exquisitely systematized that the resulting segregation of caste Hindus and avarnas from each other meant that any thrust for political and social alteration needed to come from within the ranks of the aggrieved. Travancore's singular social structure and the state's step-by-step decisions from the late nineteenth century onward to broaden education to expanding strata had worked beneficially for the development of caste associations, such as the SNDP Yogam, as its members obtained skills of self-representation and gained confidence in their own abilities. The spread of literacy among the lower ranks of those without caste brought with it modern ideas and concepts. Education stimulated excluded groups to seek greater rights and self-actualization. Bringing together comparable but isolated and scattered subcastes and untouchables into organizations with common purposes, the caste associations were inchoate alliances for democratic linkage, offering ways to communicate and voices for representation. In the course of time, Travancore's caste associations and similar groups that emerged became potent instruments and

[51] Sreedhara Menon, *Kerala and Freedom Struggle*, 141.

pressure groups, lobbying for the social acceptance that the palace and government could confer.

The SNDP and other modernity movements were altering perceptions. Then too, the privileged Nambudiris, even with their inferred loss of status, had aspects of their viewpoint refashioned by access to Western education. An infusion of liberal thinking was another element, as the liberalism of the West influenced newly educated, newspaper-reading elites, who were in the vanguard of the Vykom struggle, whether their origin was from the lower strata or the upper castes. The initiative of the dewan would become a factor. All of these influences gave cogency to social change.

Yet the fact remains that the government could have concluded the Vykom conflict earlier. Throughout the period being chronicled, it disregarded social shifts at play. The princely state's government did not want to antagonize the upper-caste Hindus, or weaken their status and privileges, especially as related to houses of worship, because the government identified itself with the caste Hindus. Instead, it exploited disorder among the volunteers, greatly worsened by the early voluntary incarceration of the key protagonists. The maharaja and his government remained pledged to protecting the status quo ante and contrived ways to diffuse the various inducements put forward to them by different groups. Dewan Bahadur T. Raghavaiah on March 9 responded to the resolution moved by N. Kumaran in the Legislative Council in 1925. His concern was about "wounding the religious susceptibilities of the caste Hindus" and the defying of orders that "had to be passed to preserve the public peace," both resulting from the actions of Hindus "outside the fold of caste." Dismissing the entire Vykom movement as having been started by "a band of Izhavas and their sympathisers," he said satyagraha in Vykom was "intended as an instrument for the coercion of the Government and through them the orthodox Hindus."[52] In previous situations of discord on issues of political, social, or even religious alterations in Travancore, the government had intervened to not only maintain social harmony but also enforce existing regulations and customs. When desired, the government had amended, adopted,

[52] *Proceedings of the Sri Mulam Popular Assembly of Travancore* (hereafter *SMPA*) (Trivandrum: Superintendent, Government Press, 1925), 26–7.

or enforced new practices. The prohibition of the temple roads to untouchables may have arisen from Nambudiri ideology and customs, but its enforcement rested in the hands of the government. The caste Hindus and the government did not comprise distinct groups, as the orthodoxy of the former maharaja had shown. In retrospect it can be seen that opinion among the more powerful savarnas, notwithstanding its obstinacy, had been jockeying, a slow but persistently building consequence of the mobilizing and organizing by *subha*s and caste associations that became increasingly visible near the end of the nineteenth century. With the Vykom struggle, the views of the educated middle classes were also altering, and they began to rally around this issue.

To the extent that there was a strategy in the satyagraha, the largely upper-caste leadership of the struggle believed that filling the jails with savarna leaders, most of them highly respected for their charitable or educational activities and their nationalist worldview, would appeal to the sensibilities of the orthodox Hindu opposition; it was not intended to challenge or overwhelm the capacity of the princely state. Many of these leaders were from Tamil Nadu or elsewhere, which offered a pretext for their dismissal. The deployment of a steady supply of police to Vykom must have taxed the capacity of Travancore, but archival documents allude to extra police officers being readily dispatched from adjacent and nearby districts.

Under historic patterns of caste exclusions, untouchables would have tended to approach the British rather than their caste superiors for help with social or religious grievances. Indeed, the British encouraged a princely state's subjects to turn to them for rectification of problems. It was known that the police commissioner, W. H. Pitt, was generally sympathetic to the satyagrahis and untouchables, and he may have averted violent episodes by tactfully managing the situation. To acknowledge Pitt's role in working with Gandhi, negotiating with him, and formulating the terms for a settlement is not to argue that social transformations in India depended on British innovation; nor is it to say that India's social mobilizations were catalyzed by British conceptions. Pitt's role was straightforward, Kusuman assessed: "Pitt was in support of the agitations, but being a Christian he did not want to identify himself with the movement. He was interested in the satyagraha and the points raised by the satyagrahis. . . . But he was just a spectator, a dispassionate observer of things."[53] When the maharaja accorded Gandhi the status of a state guest, it brought Pitt and Gandhi together on speaking terms from March 9 to March 18, during which their discussions led to a negotiated compromise to pull the struggle out of the trough into which it had sunk.

[53] Kusuman, interview (August 16, 2005). "Agitation" is equivalent to a campaign or mobilization.

6 The Vykom Compromise
Gandhi's Role and Broader Implications

Was it the case that the Congress needed something and Vykom came along as a blessing? Vykom was neither a creation of Gandhi's nor a conception of the Indian National Congress, but a situation arising from the mobilizing of the aggrieved, where they each had to respond. In the case of Vykom, Gandhi was face-to-face with severely vexing, vested issues. He knew that the maharajas had appointed themselves as defenders of the god Padmanabha and must be involved in implementing any alterations that would be deemed to threaten the deity. He was concerned about the dilemma of the princely states vis-à-vis the British, especially when ruled by influential upper-caste elites, who acted in the name of Padmanabha to govern it, and with the maharaja known as Padmanabhadasa (servant of Lord Padmanabha). Addressing the intricately complex caste system while aligning all the caste groups within his vision of inclusive nationalism was a formidable task. Caste and community were implicated in ideas of regional nationalism. Historian Justin Mathew observes that Gandhi's association with the Vykom satyagraha deepened the conception of Indian nationalism by including all caste groups.[1] Moreover, adhering to his position taken with regard to Vykom, Gandhi wanted the locus for action to be among Hindus: "the Hindu mass mind … has to be awakened."[2] As he saw it,

[1] Justin Mathew, communication (October 14, 2010).
[2] Gandhi, December 20, 1932, letter to C. F. Andrews, from Yeravda Central Prison, Poona, on file at Rhodes House, Oxford.

those who had inflicted the agony of untouchability, unapproachability, and unseeability should visibly make an atonement or penance; and conversion also remained an objective, for which the penal code should not be involved: "All that the reformers want is opportunity for progress, opportunity for converting public opinion, and when and where it is to be converted, opportunity for giving effect to that conversion."[3] All of these quandaries adjoined in Vykom.

A Significant Social Struggle: Challenging the Basis of Social Power

Viewed from a national perspective, Vykom was an important social struggle in modern India and was the first time that Gandhian satyagraha had been deployed specifically against the institution of untouchability. Consensus, mobilization, and public opinion developed in important ways during the campaign. Vykom marked the first public participation of broader segments of the population than in earlier periods, including the Ezhavas. Communications, means of transportation, and social mobility altered, despite the efforts of those who sought to control their pace and content. Freer political debate and action grew exponentially in Travancore, as the great flood of 1924 heightened the impact of caste-based modernity movements in this area of south India. The inundation, as a natural disaster, produced circumstances in which people of all castes were obliged to engage with each other to manage the catastrophe. The *savarnas* were forced to yield some of their strictures on untouchability for mutual survival, as individuals from all positions in society were obliged to travel together in flood-affected areas, something otherwise incomprehensible in the early twentieth century. Vykom was the first time that the Indian public came into action. "In the pre-modern period, we didn't have 'public opinion,'" M. G. S. Narayanan said; "the public as such was not constituted."[4] It may be an exaggeration to attribute the launch of democratization to the 1920s Vykom struggle, but an embryonic process of mobilization and vital surge of democratic impulses had begun.

Nevertheless, although Gandhi emphasized what he called propaganda and wrote often in *Young India* and the *Harijan*, the *satyagrahis*

[3] Gandhi, February 24, 1933, to Andrews.
[4] Narayanan, interview (August 12, 2005).

themselves either wrote very little to explain their rationale and argue their perspective, or such records have not survived. Therefore, the density and breadth of local upper-caste opposition to social change in Vykom is difficult to analyze from the archives available for research. Accounts of Vykom when the volunteers were still alive in succeeding years did not offer the participants' viewpoints—so important for historical analysis (and also crucial for improving the planning of nonviolent action). "India's history is the victor's history," commented Joseph Maliakan; "all of those who wrote about Vykom were upper caste."[5]

The Vykom satyagraha reflected a tradition of high-caste reform efforts that sought to cleanse Hinduism of its contaminants, although its effects were political, social, and cultural. The cooperation of the Indian National Congress and Gandhi offered a political platform for the struggle, while leadership from T. K. Madhavan, the social reformer Sri Narayana Guru, and the contribution of the SNDP Yogam contributed elements of political, social, and cultural significance. The result was an emerging sense of citizenship and democratic inclination. Prior to that time, the Indian national movement had not addressed issues that combined political and cultural substance. During the 1890s, the question of combining political reform with cultural social change had arisen in the national movement, with debates over sequencing. "The consensus was that political reform was more significant, and that once political changes had taken place, social change would follow," Panikkar reflected; "[t]herefore the national movement did not address itself on the question of cultural reform and change. In the 1920s, the Vykom satygraha sought to combine both."[6]

With proximity, an outcome from natural disaster, weakening some social restrictions and animating the broader public, came an implicit challenge to the customs and patterns through which power was protected. Hence, the second sociocultural meaning of the struggle is not solely the fight against untouchability, but the questioning of the basis of social power. It is unmistakable in the exchange between Gandhi and the Nambudiri leader of the Vykom Brahmins of March 10, 1925,

---

[5] Joseph Maliakan, interview (March 12, 2009), New Delhi. Maliakan is a retired journalist with the *Indian Express* newspaper. "The *Mathrubhumi* newspaper was upper-caste reporting." Maliakan, interview (March 12, 2009).

[6] Panikkar, interview (August 15, 2005).

in which the rationale for social power surfaced and resurfaced in the conversation. At the core of the conflict, manifested by the entrenched opposition to the Vykom satyagraha, was fear and anxiety that the mobilization would lead to the direct loss of the social privileges and power exercised by the Nambudiris. The upper castes were prepared to suppress it, including by violence if needed.

The satyagraha was important for Kerala's social and political evolution, because the untouchables were not at that time demanding temple entry. They sought the pedestrian rights enjoyed by Muslims or Christians and thought that such entitlements should be given to all sections of the Hindu population, including outcastes. As Kusuman observed, "It was the civil rights that they wanted, and it was against the denial of civil rights that they moved to agitation."[7] Kalyani, mentioned in Chapter 3, described the struggle as firstly about "freedom of movement."[8]

Notwithstanding Gandhi's blandishments about the narrowly socioreligious nature of the struggle, the *teendal palakas* excluding entry of the Ezhavas onto the temple roads were installed by the government, which also maintained the signs in good condition, necessarily with political implications. The question when submitted to the legislature was defeated solely because of the weight of the government bloc and its nominees, who voted against it. That politics could not be severed from the social context is what helped to bring the Indian National Congress to pursue the campaign for eradicating untouchability with vigor, in turn stirring large sectors of the disadvantaged portions of Hindu society to come within the compass of the national movement. Hence, Sreedhara Menon's conclusion: "But for the active participation of the backward sections of the Hindu society and the religious minorities in Kerala the freedom struggle would not have acquired the broad based and secular character which was its source of strength."[9]

Sympathy flowed from all of India toward the Vykom satyagraha, unifying local and national perspectives and priorities. Untouchability

[7] Kusuman, interview (August 16, 2005).

[8] Vatakkecharuvil P. K. Kalyani, "An Appeal to the Hindu Women of Kerala," in *Herself: Early Writings on Gender by Malayam Women, 1898–1938*, ed. J. Devika (Calcutta: Stree, 2005), 83–4.

[9] Alappat Sreedhara Menon, *Kerala and Freedom Struggle* (Kottayam, Kerala: D C Books, 1997), 125.

existed throughout various linguistic and cultural communities in India. Nearly everywhere a large untouchable class performed "polluted" functions and was exploited. Yet the severity of unseeability and unapproachability were elsewhere unknown. It was a revelation for the newspaper-reading public that outcastes walking on roads around or converging at sacred houses of worship would pollute the temples and their priests, and that temple-goers could be defiled by a shadow falling from an untouchable. This distant reality was revealed to continental India by the Vykom struggle. In Kerala, moreover, the Congress profited from the Vykom campaign by priming a broad base of support, hitherto lacking. The struggle had the effect of bringing the princely states into the Congress program, which wanted to integrate them in an all-embracing, future national government of India, with eventual formation of new states along linguistic and cultural lines. It wanted nothing less than a transfer of paramountcy, in which the supremacy of the British Crown, as acknowledged by various Indian princes during the British Raj, would be ended. Meanwhile the maharajas were trying to safeguard their autocratic rank by standing in opposition to the rising democratic forces for social mobility. Benefiting from the impact of the Vykom satyagraha, the princely states were helped onto the map of the national freedom struggle by the Congress. That all of these forces would collide was foreseeable.

In scale, the Vykom mobilization entailed large numbers, but few materials written by satyagrahis can be retrieved, as the volunteers were not for the main part actively involved in public advocacy, propaganda, or written communications. The two *savarna jatha*s converging on the capital exuding pageantry, pomp, and extravaganza—orthodox leaders marching with military precision, flamboyant yellow costumery, and banners billowing—make these processions an event worthy of a twentieth-century hall of fame for nonviolent enlistment. Gandhi's acuity in suggesting two grand processions of high-caste Hindus joining together for the final walk to present monster petitions to the maharani was perceptive, yet the impact was not immediate. It came circuitously. Only now is this singularly dramatic performance recovered from oblivion.

Even so, the campaign could have and should have been expanded. Social movements have long tended to create space for additional mobilization and new constituencies, yet in Vykom Gandhi obstructed the logical expansion of the movement. His role created predicaments because of his goal of securing agreement from upper castes. He did not understand that the organizing by untouchable communities was ultimately as important as the attitudes of the orthodox. In this way, he thwarted the movement rather than advancing it. "What you see in Vykom is an attempt by the Congress to make the anti-caste struggle meet it. But they were separate," A. K. Ramakrishnan contended. He said:

> There were many differences between the nationalist movement and the anti-caste movement. Agency was with the Dalits—the struggle was in the hands of the lower castes. The Vykom satyagraha was a Congress initiative, but the Kerala Congress Party had a patronizing attitude. The Congress had a lot to gain: Vykom could have made the nationalist movement more substantive; it was not anti-British.[10]

Had Vykom been expanded into mobilizing for democracy, caste could have been coherently addressed within a larger context. An alliance of *avarnas* and the middle classes of Hindu orthodoxy against untouchability never materialized as earnestly envisioned by T. K. Madhavan. Periyar E. V. Ramasamy Naicker, the Tamil Nadu leader, also sought such a broadly defined struggle, as did others. Ramakrishnan argued: "Naicker resigned from the Congress the day after Vykom ended! He wanted the movement to continue to democracy. He was unhappy that the movement was stopped. Naicker called Vykom a 'betrayal'."[11] Not only might the Congress have utilized Vykom for the development of India's self-rule and democracy, but the "solution" in Vykom thwarted the growth of a full democracy movement in Travancore, minimizing rather than maximizing the building of democratic institutions. The various Travancore anti-caste campaigns could have lent organizational heft to the Indian movements against colonialism, speeding the gaining of peoples' rights, had the struggles been based on rights and responsibilities. The cleavage between Ambedkar, and those like Naicker and Guru, on the one hand, and Gandhi, on the other, thus, had ethical and political implications.

---

[10] Ramakrishnan, interview (March 12, 2009). A. K. Ramakrishnan is professor with the Centre for West Asian and African Studies, School of International Studies, Jawaharlal Nehru University.

[11] Ramakrishnan, interview (March 12, 2009).

Even so, the Vykom struggle represented an early expression of burgeoning democratization processes. The entire nation could see that the revolutionary impact from the Ezhavas' mobilizing was not about distributing spoils. The temples would soon be opened to them, they would secure cabinet positions early in the future state of Kerala, and these and other changes would come in response to organized political action, not as favors conferred. Nevertheless, Gandhi's stipulations decreased the impact of the Vykom struggle, which might have been even more catalytically transformative for Travancore and India as a whole, because the exertion against untouchability, implicitly against caste, was at its deepest roots a democratic quest, which need not have been contained within any religious or faith community. Its mission was grander, more universal.

Indeed, Gandhi and the Congress may have contributed to a prolongation of the untouchability conflict in Travancore by concentrating on it as a single-issue campaign in Vykom. Gandhi persuaded Madhavan to narrow his focus solely to attaining access to temple roads, although Madhavan had envisioned a broader cooperative movement between local non-caste Hindus and caste Hindus. With its stellar cast of characters being largely drawn from Brahmin and Nair caste-Hindu families, often from outside Travancore and members of the Congress, the movement could be and was written off as a product of outside intervention. Initial lack of support from lower-caste Hindu communities in Travancore contributed to this liability, because the campaign was not at its outset well integrated with the growing local social movements of the time, such as that of the SNDP Yogam. Imported notables and regional figures might have played helpful roles, but they could not ultimately step into the shoes of the Travancore leaders with their distinctive wisdom and ideas. Gandhi's provisos and conditions "had an unfortunate dimension," Pannikar observed; "although people have not identified it as an unfortunate dimension."[12]

The early courting of arrest by leaders and their immediate detention, portrayed by Gandhi as an appeal to the high-caste leaders and the government acting at their behest, left a vacuum from which the movement never recovered. By April 1924, events were rambling without strategy, particularly as Gandhi had circumscribed both the movement's

[12] Panikkar, interview (August 15, 2005).

ends and means. Braced by the perception of drift, by June and July the orthodox Hindus had launched organized violence against the volunteers, with the police deeply suspected of collusion with the upper-caste establishment. Still resolutely adhering to Gandhi's mandate to pursue conversion of the upper castes, the volunteers sat unprotected in the sun and endured beatings. In the great flood of August 1924, as noted, they stood in drenching monsoons, sometimes neck-deep in water for long shifts, while the boats of temple officials struck them. Police tactics became violent. As months passed, the volunteers continued their appeals to the upper castes with disciplined persistence, but the movement had hollowed out and was in stalemate, mired by the lack of evidence that their efforts were affecting the sensibilities of the upper castes.

Vykom's untouchability struggle was narrowly portrayed as local, rather than acting as a springboard for larger mobilization on behalf of equitable rights and expanded democratic participation. It entered into the national debate, but on a diminished scale of magnitude from how it might have influenced the national perspective on the caste question, regardless of fears that such discussion might undermine the national solidarity and despite a tendency to subsume any topic into contention over nationalism versus colonialism. In Panikkar's view:

> Until then the caste issue was not taken up at all, and much of the earlier debate particularly was around the national versus the colonial. What was happening internally to Indian society, *within*, was not really part of the debate and discussion. Only after a very long time, particularly with the emergence of a new style of historiography, have these internal contradictions been taken up for analysis. Otherwise it was the mega-contradiction between nationalism and colonialism that was the main area of interest.[13]

To make a utilitarian argument for the sake of evaluation, notwithstanding its unsteady course and relatively high human cost in at least two lives lost and individualized suffering, the negotiated settlement could be said to have accommodated both sides, preserved face for the temple custodians and priests, created for the Nambudiri Brahmins a way out from their ideological rigidity, and shortened the walks home of those without caste. Furthermore, Vykom could have been a fiasco

---

[13] Panikkar, interview (August 15, 2005).

but for Gandhi's involvement and that of the Congress. Kusuman made this proviso:

> Remember that similar agitations were yet to occur in Kerala, in other places, after 1925, such as in 1928, four years later, the Suchindram satyagraha. Then there was the Ambalapuzha satyagraha near Alleppey, and the Tiruvarpu satyagraha. The Vykom compromise would not be immediately played out elsewhere. Moreover, subsequent satyagrahas did not succeed. Vykom would have failed too, but for Gandhi. The government refused to budge. Consider that these other three satyagrahas did not succeed and never assumed popularity and all-India attention, as did Vykom. The events were the same, but government and the caste Hindus were unmoved. Only after 1936, when the temple-entry proclamation was issued by the maharaja, would all these problems be settled.[14]

Chithira Thirunal Balarama Varma (1931–41) was the last of the ruling sovereigns of Travancore to sit on the pillowed *gaddi*. Even at that late hour, in 1935, 11 miles and 778 feet of road in Travancore still remained closed to non-caste Hindus.[15] Hence, it came as a shock in Travancore and elsewhere throughout India when the maharaja and his *dewan*, Chetpat Pattabhirama Ramaswami Iyer, issued the prince's official announcement of the temple-entry proclamation on November 2, 1936, also the maharaja's birthday, declaring:

> Profoundly convinced of the truth and validity of Our religion, believing that it is based on divine guidance and on an all-comprehending toleration, knowing that in its practice it has, throughout the centuries, adapted itself to the needs of changing times, solicitous that none of Our subjects should, by reason of birth or caste or community, be denied the consolations and solace of the Hindu faith, we have decided and hereby declare, ordain and command that, subject of such rules and conditions as may be laid down and imposed by us for preserving their proper atmosphere and maintaining their rituals and observances, there should be

[14] Kusuman, interview (August 16, 2005).

[15] Travancore Confidential Section (hereafter CS), Kerala Secretariat, 783/1925, Maramat Engineer to Chief Secretary, November 30, 1935; CS, 1365/1936; CS, 1622/1936, 772/1940, as cited in Robin Jeffrey, "Travancore: Status, Class and the Growth of Radical Politics, 1860–1940, the Temple-Entry Movement," in *People, Princes and Paramount Power: Society and Politics in the Indian Princely States*, ed. Robin Jeffrey (New Delhi: Oxford University Press, 1978), 139.

henceforth no restriction placed on any Hindu by birth or religion on entering or worshipping at the temples controlled by the Us and Our Government.[16]

The teendal palakas would remain on some temple roads in Travancore until as late as 1937, but the ideation of untouchability had been considerably depleted of meaning by the 1936 temple-entry proclamation.

The government's surprise concession came about for two main reasons. One explanation was the innovative social reform movement in Travancore led by Sri Narayana Guru and the SNDP Yogam. The other was an increasing trend of the lower castes abandoning Hinduism and converting to other faiths, generally preferring Christianity or Islam. This was an explicit threat to Hinduism. C. P. Ramaswami Iyer, dewan of Travancore, was a lawyer, who, in Kusuman's judgment, "persuaded the maharaja to grant temple entry, so that the lower-caste people would remain pacified. The initiative actually came from the dewan, and the maharaja, Chithira Thirunal Balarama Varma, confirmed it."[17] With the groundwork laid by Sri Narayana Guru, and at least one section of the caste Hindus already reconciled to the evolving situation, a large number of individual upper-caste Hindus had stepped forward energetically to participate in the satyagraha and offered leadership. To Kusuman, "They were in favor of change, a progressive change, dedicated to solving the injustice involved, and they were convinced. They thought we must have a new beginning."[18]

[16] Mahadev Haribhai Desai, *The Epic of Travancore* (Ahmedabad: Navajivan Karyalaya, 1937), frontispiece; Louise Ouwerkerk, *No Elephants for the Maharaja: Social and Political Change in the Princely State of Travancore, 1921–1947* (New Delhi: Manohar, 1994), 97–8. On November 3, 1936, an All-Kerala Temple Entry Conference met and submitted a memorial petition with signatures of 50,522 upper-caste Hindus from Travancore demanding temple entry for the Harijans. P. K. Karunakara Menon, *History of the Freedom Movement in Kerala*, vol. 2 (Trivandrum: Government of Kerala, 1970), 309.

[17] Kusuman, interview (August 16, 2005). The dewan during 1936–47, Iyer is remembered as constitutional adviser and éminence grise in Travancore. Yet according to Menon, Iyer alleged that the 1936 proclamation had not resulted from the efforts of Gandhi and had been granted only after he had failed. Menon, *History of the Freedom Movement in Kerala*, vol. 2, 309n40.

[18] Kusuman, interview (August 16, 2005).

The temple-entry proclamation was also an outcome of the 1924–5 Vykom satyagraha, with an enormity of effect, symbolism, and connotation. The seriousness of the Vykom struggle on India's national stage came from its reverberations for the Hindu elites beyond south India. Its lesson could be understood by all of orthodoxy outside Travancore. It assumed national importance, with Congress involvement and Gandhi's engagement, because the problem was pervasive, Kusuman recalled. According to him, "Vykom as well as the issue of temple entry had all-India significance. . . . Of course the orthodox attitude may still be present, but even the orthodox are not in a position to express it openly; they may hold it in their minds, but outwardly they behave properly."[19]

Gandhi's Role and the Meaning of Satyagraha

It is said that Gandhi wrote and spoke more on untouchability than on any other topic. He placed removal of untouchability and Hindu–Muslim unity as prerequisites for authentic Indian independence. Gandhi's involvement in Vykom had produced a compromise accepted by Travancore's princely state government in relation to Hindu orthodoxy; nonetheless, no concrete material gains were achieved for the untouchables.

By mail and telegram from Bombay in 1924, Gandhi had pressed the Vykom campaign to accept the suffering imposed. Observing the predicaments and dilemmas created by the refusal of the upper-caste Hindus in Vykom to accept loss of privileges and the intransigence of the government, he spoke with moral overtones upon arriving in Madras from Travancore in March 1925:

> Untouchability is a curse which every Hindu is bound to remove. . . . I have seen it in its worst form, not only as unapproachability but also as invisibility. Mere sight of a certain man is considered by blind orthodoxy as a sin. *Nayadis* are expected to remain invisible. I saw two men belonging to that caste in Trichur [Travancore]. Except for the human form I saw nothing of humanness about them. [I]t is a matter for shedding tears of blood. They had no eyes, but two openings in which eyes might have been if they had been treated as human beings. There was no lustre in

---

[19] Kusuman, interview (August 16, 2005).

their eyes that I see in yours. . . . If we had sufficient imagination and if we had sufficient love for our country or our religion, we would refuse to be satisfied until this curse was blotted out of this land.[20]

Perplexity over how untouchability could be fanatically practiced in a region where there were high levels of education, relatively good government, and where the people enjoyed many entitlements led Gandhi to conclude that with ancient customs "ignorance passes off as knowledge when it receives the sanction of tradition." His consternation toughened in the March 10 meeting with Indanturuttil Nambiathiri and high-caste notables in Vykom, as they disclosed intransigence over the acceptability of Christians using roads near temples but not avarna Hindus. "How well-protected are these temples! They are surrounded by six feet high walls. Around these are roads on which even bullock-carts move. And yet, no untouchable is allowed to pass that way." He had tried while in Vykom to win over the orthodox by downplaying his usual interest in reform, instead reassuring the high-caste leadership that he was equally at pains to preserve Hinduism as were they. Yet he revealed an error in reasoning, when he spoke of holding "undeviating faith" in positive results as long as the participants in the satyagraha "do not transgress the restrictions they have willingly accepted."[21] This last point reveals a serious defect in Gandhi's way of thinking: the erroneous belief that the suffering of the satyagrahis could sway the sentiments of those who for generations had immunities and benefits bestowed on them as high-caste landholders. If anything, Vykom proved that the satyagrahis' appeals and suffering were insufficient to produce immediately responsive social change. Much more pressure would be required. Gandhi may have wanted to authenticate reform in the footsteps of Hindu tradition and make his sought-after changes compatible with continuity, but most of all he needed to move to more coercive methods in the itinerary of political action.

The events chronicled here occurred at the peak of the British Empire, the most expansive in world history. For more than a century of its some 300-year existence, it held sway over nearly 500 million

[20] Gandhi, public speech (from the *Hindu*, March 23, 1925, Madras), in *Collected Works of Mahatma Gandhi* (hereafter *CWMG*), 31: 18–19.

[21] Gandhi, "Satyagraha at Vykom" (from *Navajivan*, March 29, 1925), in *CWMG*, 31: 79–80.

people, one-fifth of the global population at the time. For 30 years, Gandhi confronted the British based on a shrewd and canny application of an understanding that the British could not rule India without Indian cooperation, even if this meant breaking the law and accepting the penalty, including going to prison. The inability of the British to control India without Indian obedience was a major theme of his *Hind Swaraj* (Indian Home Rule), published in 1909, while still in South Africa. In Vykom, directly facing a theocracy of orthodox Hinduism, and perceiving the abolition of untouchability as a prerequisite to self-rule and independence, his "test" as he had called the Vykom satyagraha had severe limitations.

Gandhi sat astride a dilemma in Vykom. He wanted to abolish untouchability, as it was an impediment to national cohesion and independence, and he sought to bring all Hindus into a burgeoning nationalist movement. He also wanted to avoid flagrant political confrontation and civil disobedience against the traditional ruler of an Indian state. If being confronted with the sight of a lower-caste person could pollute an upper-caste individual, it meant that the freedom struggle was not solely against the British, but also against an evil inherent in the Hindu community. He was well aware that opening roads encircling temples was intrinsically linked to the larger question of untouchability, to which he gave prominence in the constructive program, although modestly defined.

Deriving from Gandhi's South African experiences, satyagraha was applied in a critical context in Vykom, although he would necessarily modify it in the years to come. Key participants in Vykom, such as K. P. Kesava Menon, and those who were on familiar terms with active contributors to its struggle, including N. N. Pillai, consider that Vykom was where the theory and practice of satyagraha received its experimental early refinement and development. Kesava Menon maintains that satyagraha was first tried in full form there as a program of action to achieve social justice.[22] Pillai, who was close to individual participants in the Vykom satyagraha, acknowledging Gandhi's desire for a change of heart

---

[22] K. P. Kesava Menon, *The Vaikkom Satyagraha* (Calicut: K. P. Kesava Menon 90th Birthday Celebration Committee, 1977), 74–91. Kizhakke Potta Kesava Menon, introduced earlier, was a founder of the *Mathrubhumi*, became its chief editor, and was president of the Kerala Provincial Congress Committee.

through the suffering of the satyagrahis, said, "The principles were laid down there; corrections were made. His position was, 'Don't offend orthodoxy—convert them.' In every respect, Gandhi considered the Vykom satyagraha an experiment."[23] Gandhi's efforts to formulate a means of winning over the high castes were based on his view that social change should preferably come from internal human processes rather than edicts. In effect, governments should not guide social change when ordinary mortals might lead it for themselves. The theoretical essence at that early stage of Gandhi's rising national authority was that if the morale of the antagonist could be touched through voluntary and uncomplaining acceptance of the ordeal that it had imposed on the petitioner, then self-sacrifice and suffering could pierce through what Joan Bondurant calls the opponent's rationalized defenses.[24]

Speaking from an ethical platform regarding caste represented a conscious choice for Gandhi, who viewed everything through his own moral framework. Yet as the almost chivalrous twenty-month Vykom struggle slowly hobbled forward, Gandhi adjusted some of his adamant constraints of the early months. By March 1925, with the campaign showing virtually no tangible results, Gandhi's views became more malleable because of the intransigence of the upper castes. He was skeptical of Pitt's concept of trading the removal of the barricades and pickets for the satyagrahis' standing or spinning while respecting the boundaries, but thought that it should be attempted as a way to insert the thin end of a wedge that could be pried open for further alterations.

Gandhi was aware of the squandering of the human resources of the volunteers, as maintaining their vigil during the great flood of 1924 took a toll in lives lost and health, and as smallpox infected some among them. He knew they endured reproach and disgrace. The "determined opposition," as Gandhi in 1908 called the satyagrahis, had not achieved its desired end. He knew that no British fiat could grant temple entry. Only the maharaja of Travancore could take this action and have it endure. With regard to Vykom, he began speaking of compulsion in pressuring the prince and orthodoxy: "I ask you, the Savarna Hindus of

---

[23] N. N. Pillai, interview (March 12, 2009).

[24] Joan V. Bondurant, *Conquest of Violence: The Gandhian Philosophy of Conflict* (Berkeley: University of California Press, 1965), 228.

Trivandrum and through you the whole of the Hindu community of Travancore, to insist to break down the prejudice of orthodoxy in Vaikom and to compel, by pressure of public opinion, . . . the opening of these roads to the untouchables and the unapproachables."[25] To *compel* through the *pressure* of public opinion reveals a sophisticated grasp of social and political power for a technique, rather than emphasizing moral suasion, even though ethical considerations may be involved.

With benefit of retroactive analysis, when the satyagraha eventually began to see some oblique effects, they did not come from the volunteers' incurring extreme self-sacrifice. The attempt to "glorify suffering" failed, as Ravindran put it, and in trying to "institutionalize suffering," the actors in Vykom used "mendacious and cheap propaganda," causing the suffering of the volunteers to lose its "ethical charm and glory."[26] The invoking of suffering had negative effects in some spheres. Sri Narayanan Guru is remembered as saying that there was no endurance, just empty stomachs. "Why not use an umbrella under downpours? Demand that injustice be addressed! Break the barricades! Go ahead and pollute the upper castes, and if the police beat you, that's a test of endurance, not standing in the rain."

Ayyankali, mentioned earlier, was a prominent leader of the Dalits in Travancore who defied the caste strictures and norms to ride his bullock cart and was an intrepid participant in several untouchable movements against the abuses of the caste system early in the twentieth century. Yet he did not actively participate in the Vykom satyagraha. The absence of Ayyankali from a major movement against the degradations of untouchability must be pondered. E. V. Ramasamy Naicker of Erode, the ardent speaker who outraged the governmental authorities, "was totally unhappy over the means adopted by Gandhiji in tackling the problem," according to V. Balambal. "He wanted both free movement in roads and temple entry; so he disliked the compromising attitude of Gandhiji. . . . Gandhiji's policy in the Vaikom satyagraha . . . made E. V. R. to resign from the Congress and concentrate on self-respect and other social reforms."[27]

[25] Gandhi, March 13, 1925, speech text, Trivandrum cantonment parade grounds, KSA: vol. 9, VSB, p. 5.

[26] T. K. Ravindran, *Vaikkam Satyagraha and Gandhi* (Trichur, India: Sri Narayana Institute of Social and Cultural Development, 1975), 117.

[27] V. Balambal. "E. V. R. and Vaikom Satyagraha," *Journal of Kerala Studies* 7 (March, June, September, December, 1980): 252–3.

A shortcoming in Gandhi's assumptions revealed itself when, in March 1925, he had given his third offer to the Vykom Nambudiris. In asking recognized pandits to examine the authenticity and authority of a scriptural mandate for unapproachability, he inadvertently legitimized the supremacy of the Brahmins' own ideological interpretation of their preeminence and grandeur. By effectively giving overweening authority to Vykom's high-caste officialdom and accepting its own textual interpretations of tradition, Gandhi disregarded the existence of a variety of bodies of precedents and precepts among the adherents of Hinduism. In all probability a majority of the Hindus was beyond the venerated traditions that rested on the ideologies of Brahmin dominion. The presence of reform movements posited on streams of unwritten religious precepts other than the Brahminical, such as that led by Narayana Guru, distinct from upper-caste reform efforts, warranted almost no attention from Gandhi. Moreover, he never sought to utilize potential splits among the multiple pathways of Hinduism to prod alterations for the avarnas.

Yet the accomplishments from the Vykom struggle, although they might preferably have addressed a larger circumference and been less illusory, were nonetheless important. To accept Ravindran's dismissal that "eight furlongs more were added to these free roads," Shreekumaran Nair analogized, would be like measuring the effect of Abraham Lincoln's Emancipation Proclamation by counting the number of slaves who were freed.[28] At Vykom, although the enunciated immediate goal was not straightforwardly realized, it should not be overlooked that a wave of ethical consideration was stimulated by the satyagraha, which would act as a preventive against violent social conflicts over untouchability in Travancore.

Viewed through a broader aperture, Gandhi's interest and commitment is revealed to have played a crucial role, regardless of the shortcomings of some of his actions and ideas. Adept in symbolic and psychological arts, and never attacking the orthodox opposition in Vykom or the maharaja, his effort to frame the struggle as socioreligious had a pragmatic component: limit the arena of conflict and minimize any deterioration of the already British-constrained powers of a princely state's maharaja. The way that he sought to draw parameters around the

---

[28] Shreekumaran Nair, review, Ravindran, *Vaikkam Satyagraha and Gandhi*, 766.

struggle, seeking simplification, led some to see the Vykom struggle as "one of the most successful of Gandhian campaigns."[29] The mind-set of Gandhi toward the untouchables, unapproachables, and unseeables had positive effects on the attitudes of some savarna Congress leaders. Even with the awkwardness of the so-called settlement, "It was his personal influence as well as the contribution of the savarnas, the upper-caste Hindus who were in support of the movement," as Kusuman assessed. "These two factors were important contributive factors for the success of the satyagraha. Anyone who has studied the situation must recognize the role of Gandhi. Those who look into the records and want to place the past cannot bypass Gandhi's part."[30]

Gandhi's commitment to eradication of untouchability traversed the decades of his return from South Africa and Vykom undeniably deepened his personal appreciation of the complexity of the issue. On no other matter, political philosopher Bhikhu Parekh asserts, was he as "viciously attacked" by his critics as on the question of untouchability.[31] His challenge from within Hinduism made him particularly dangerous in the eyes of Hindus who feared his influence over the popular mind. Many members of the Congress party were unpersuaded of the link between *swaraj* and untouchability. Meanwhile in Dalit politics, he was being attacked for upholding the established order. The Dalit leader Babasaheb Ambedkar's criticism that Gandhi would not oblige an oath repudiating untouchability as a qualification for membership in the Congress later became a caustic condemnation of resolutions on untouchability by the Congress as hypocritical.

The compromise that Gandhi and Pitt worked out for Vykom was truly that—a concession on both sides. Despite Gandhi's speaking and writing extensively on the objective of changing the hearts and minds of the upper castes, through a modification of their sensibilities, in this chronicle there is little evidence of the Nambudiris changing their attitudes or being converted—except if viewed in a long-term and metaphorical sense. Nevertheless, Gandhi's views were no longer flexible on

---

[29] Nair, review, Ravindran, *Vaikkam Satyagraha and Gandhi*, 764.

[30] Kusuman, interview (August 16, 2005).

[31] Bhikhu C. Parekh, *Colonialism, Tradition and Reform: An Analysis of Gandhi's Political Discourse* (New Delhi, Thousand Oaks, and London: SAGE Publications [1989] 1999), 228.

the goal. By 1934, he was calling for full eradication of untouchability. In Calcutta soon thereafter, he outrightly advocated the abolition of the caste system.[32]

Satyagraha and the Vykom Struggle

Having arrived in South Africa in 1893, Gandhi meant to stay for one year and remained for eight. In 1902 he returned for six months and stayed for twelve. Enrolling himself as an attorney in the Transvaal Supreme Court, he opened an office in Johannesburg that would become the center of his activities, as the Boer state of Transvaal would become his laboratory. Organized Indian political expression ante-dated Gandhi's arrival in South Africa by years, although in his own writings decades later Gandhi claims that the Indians in South Africa were incapable of amalgamating themselves into a unified group for pursuing common purposes. The Indian merchants there, however, had rarely been involved in politics. Gandhi would eventually represent the highest strata of the Indian communities and evolve into a full-time organizer, for which they had an acute need. He was especially suitable for that role, because as a lawyer fluent in Gujarati and English, he was ideologically compatible with the Indian traders, who came from his caste and milieu. They were averse, as was he, to pressing for drastic alterations of the social order.

Gandhi's initial approach in the Transvaal was based on compro-mise, along with using polite petitionary methods of letters, formal appeals, and special deputations, all of which characterized his politi-cal routine after he first became politically active in his early years there. Perhaps he thought that his only choice was conciliation. At first he would claim only limited protections and entitlements for his Indian constituents in South Africa, in what Maureen Swan calls a "timid strat-egy," for example, basing his argument for Indians' rights in the Transvaal on their being British subjects in a British colony.[33] Gandhi would not merit the label of leader until after 1906, and then with some qualification.

[32]   Sreedhara Menon, *Kerala and Freedom Struggle*, 141–2.
[33]   Maureen Swan, *Gandhi: The South African Experience* (Johannesburg: Ravan Press, 1985), 110.

That South Africa was inducing alterations in his philosophy is disclosed in his publication, *Indian Opinion*, which was initially to have served the function of informing white South Africans and Indians about each other. Yet it increasingly became a vehicle for the moral fortification of its Indian readers, as Gandhi sought to share with them the framework that he was developing for himself. The bulk of the satyagrahis in the Transvaal were humble Tamils, often merely hawkers rather than substantial merchants. In his columns, he undertook to tackle what he saw as the basic problem of a crisis in the Indians' politics, namely, their inability to unify and mobilize. He reiterated these concerns between 1904 and 1906, avidly sharing examples with his readers of how they could overcome the problems that he perceived were leading to disunity. During this period, Gandhi assertively presented examples to his readers to show them that internal disagreements and lack of a shared sense of duty were prohibiting their unification and their taking responsibility, both of which were prerequisites for political action. The examples that he chose to awaken his constituency were primarily drawn from what was happening internationally at that time.[34]

Gandhi's perception of a crisis originating with the individuals involved is characteristic of his pattern of thinking from his time in South Africa until his last breath. His explanations for failure or ineffectiveness virtually always redound to the individuals involved, rather than examining institutional limitations, ideological warping, the choice of the goal, or external forces and pressures. He devoted himself seriously to discerning lessons from his experiences, but autodidact that he was, he was not formally prepared for methodical, logical, and systematic analysis. He frequently lacked consistency and was changeable in his interpretations.

Still, Gandhi's writings in 1904–6 reveal that he was attentively watching and studying events around him in South Africa and elsewhere in Africa, as well as in Bengal, China, Ireland, and Russia. Having learned about the protracted 1849–67 national nonviolent struggle of the Hungarians against the Hapsburgs, he cited it as a lesson for the Indians in South Africa.[35] He scrutinized the suffragists' struggle in

[34] Swan, *Gandhi: South African Experience*, 111.

[35] Gandhi, "Benefits of Passive Resistance, Notable Instance" (from Gujarati, *Indian Opinion*, September 7, 1907), in *CWMG*, 7: 183–5.

Britain for the women's vote through news accounts. Monitoring the 1905 Russian revolution, which was overwhelmingly nonviolent and widely utilized the general strike as its method to bring all economic activity to a standstill, he propounded the events in Russia for his constituency as directly applicable to them, finding that it was "impossible to exact work from people by force." Not even the czar of Russia could force strikers to return to work at the point of the bayonet. In the context of seeking international examples to bolster the resolve of the politically inexperienced Indians and encourage them to overcome disagreements, Gandhi had discerned by 1905 a powerful insight that continues to animate contemporary nonviolent social movements: "For even the most powerful cannot rule without the co-operation of the ruled."[36] Thus, prior to his first major group action in Johannesburg in 1906, Gandhi's speeches and writings show that by following news reports and other study, he had become familiar with a concept of collective action as a method of political struggle.

Still in his early thirties at the time of this transcendent discernment in South Africa, Gandhi's watchful observations made him familiar with a concept of group action as a form of struggle and a technique, not a bricolage of personal beliefs or convictions. Although satyagraha as an ideal for him pertained to all dimensions of human life and activity, Gandhi's starting point is his own moral rectitude. His writings disclose awareness that the technique of civil resistance does not rely solely on an ethical or moral orientation of either the challengers or the target group. With his insight that any ruling power needs to secure cooperation and obedience, willing or coerced, from its subject population, he differentiated a foundational principle of power that would govern his experiments for the next forty-seven years. As revealed by his writings, the evidence is unmistakable that Gandhi was aware not only of dispersed cases in which forms of nonviolent action were being utilized as a technique of political struggle, but, while in South Africa, his theory of power evolved to an appreciation that all systems are *continuously* reliant on the cooperation and obedience of those in thrall to them. Just ten months later, he would take his first steps with the type of collective political action that now comprises the basic elements in what is globally recognized as nonviolent civil resistance.

[36] Gandhi, "Russia and India" (from Gujarati, *Indian Opinion*, November 11, 1905), in *CWMG*, 5: 8.

Gandhi was stunned to find in August 1906 that a proposed colonial Draft Asiatic Law Amendment Ordinance of the Transvaal Legislative Assembly, or so-called Black Act, would oblige every Indian man, woman, and child beginning at age eight to submit finger and thumb prints on a registration form. The existing laws on immigrants were already severe, but the new measure would humiliate and shame even the most prosperous Indian merchants, Gandhi's main constituency. Any Indian seeking to work and live in the Transvaal legally would have to have a registration certificate. Troubled by the treatment meted out to these traders, Gandhi's observation of struggles against oppression elsewhere was leading to his development of the concept of satyagraha. Lacking the vote and without parliamentary representation, Indians needed self-reliance and to depend on no one but themselves.

Never more than reformist in his goals, Gandhi's first active step in implementing ideas that he had been formulating began with a mass meeting of 3,000 Indians in Johannesburg's Empire Theatre on September 11. At the meeting, convened to discuss the Asiatic registration law, Abdul Gani, chairman of the British Indian Association, delivered a speech that reportedly ended with the words, "There is only one course open to the like[s] of me, to die but not to submit to the law."[37]

[37] Gandhi, "The Mass Meeting," September 11, 1906 (*Indian Opinion*, September 15, 1906), in *CWMG*, 5: 333, 335. Gandhi wrote weekly as the Johannesburg correspondent to *Indian Opinion*, or "From Our Johannesburg Representative," translated from Gujarati, with the first such despatch appearing on March 3, 1906, yet the record can be unclear due to translations. Gani's speech was apparently delivered in Urdu, after which it was translated by Dr. William Godfrey for the English-speakers present. This version is published in *Indian Opinion*, pp. 659–60. Gani (transliterated Ganie in *CWMG*) also stated, "I would ask you, in your demeanour and in your language, to be moderate. Our cause does not require any such props, but action is undoubtedly demanded of you. It will speak far more eloquently and appeal far more forcibly to the powers that be than any words however strong." Nothing is mentioned concerning nonviolence or nonviolent action.

The September 11, 1906, Johannesburg letter, later translated and published in *Indian Opinion* on September 15, 1906, states in Gujarati "narmash vaparvani che," literally meaning "make use of softness." The root of "narmash" is the noun "naram," meaning soft, smooth, gentle, tender, humble, weak, and effeminate. It strongly suggests passivity, if not meekness, of the sort that Gandhi would soon repudiate. David Hardiman, communication (December 19, 2013).

Reliance cannot be placed on the translated quotations from the September 11, 1906, Empire Theatre mass meeting that appear in the *Collected Works of Mahatma Gandhi*. As one example, Gandhi is quoted as saying, "This is for us the time for deeds, not words. We have to act boldly; and in doing so, we have to be humble and non-violent."[38] Those present passed a resolution comprised of five parts, avowing civil disobedience of the law requiring all "Asiatics" to carry registration cards, without which they risked imprisonment. The session closed when the participants took an oath not to submit to the ordinance and to defy it if enacted into law. According to Swan, the evidence shows that regardless of Gandhi's anticipated hopes for his constituents, the crowd at the Empire Theatre "represented a political rather than a moral response on the part of the Transvaal Indian merchants."[39] Thousands subsequently went to jail for refusing to register and disobeying the statute nonviolently. Acceptance of paying the penalty for breaking the law, including imprisonment, would become integral to Gandhi's method. In 1914 the government withdrew the act as a result of the civil disobedience campaign. The processes organized by Gandhi against the registration act and another bill on immigration to Natal were laborious and labyrinthine. He would spend 249 days in Transvaal jails.

In 1936, thirty years later, Gandhi told a group of visiting African Americans, "[N]on-violence is a term I had to coin in order to bring out the root meaning of ahimsa. In spite of the negative particle 'non', it is no negative force. . . . I was compelled to use the negative word. But it does not . . . express a negative force."[40] It is possible that Gandhi was

[38] Gandhi, "Johannesburg Letter" (from Gujarati, *Indian Opinion*, September 15, 1906), in *CWMG*, 5: 339. Gandhi is quoted as saying, "This is for us the time for deeds, not words. We have to act boldly; and in doing so, we have to be humble and non-violent." Instead, Gandhi had the speech by Abdul Gani translated into Gujarati, publishing it on pp. 664–5 of the same edition of *Indian Opinion*, which is the version that appears in *CWMG*. Only when the editors of *CWMG* translated Gandhi's Gujarati report into English did they use the term "non-violent." Gandhi, "Johannesburg Letter."

[39] Swan, *Gandhi: South African Experience*, 119.

[40] Mahadev Haribhai Desai, "A Talk on Non-violence" (*Harijan*, March 14, 1936), in Gandhi, *Non-violence in Peace and War*, vol. 1 (hereafter *NPW* [1]), ed. Mahadev Desai, 113.

using this term verbally in Johannesburg.[41] When he begins writing the term, he hyphenates the word in customary British spelling, a practice increasingly and consciously rejected internationally due to a perception that the English word is subtly inadequate by describing what it is not. Absent the hyphen, a contemporary reader can more readily understand the word as a forthright assertion.

For eight years following the formative events at the Empire Theatre, the young Indian worked to develop this new form of struggle. Thinking probingly about what he had discovered, ruminating about what he was learning through news reports, he was also studying writings from diverse systems of opinion and thought, including that of the Russian author Leo Tolstoy. Any form of power based on violence was considered by Tolstoy unethical, and equally, bloodshed in resistance to evil was corrupt, because it bred hatred and fear. His views on the violence of the modern nation-state and the right of citizens to noncooperation and civil disobedience affected Gandhi deeply, such that he and the Russian began corresponding, although they never met. Gandhi would test some of Tolstoy's ideas. Gandhi considered personal commitment to be the starting point for bringing about social alteration, including on a large scale. The conception that all change initially arises from the individual may be a comfortable psychological assumption in the twenty-first century, but Gandhi was subjected to intense criticism for this view of human agency throughout his life by Marxists, anarchists, and other critics.

By 1908, Gandhi was writing episodically about civil disobedience and would later demarcate its use with precision. Many believe that the term *civil disobedience* was first used by Henry David Thoreau. Widely cited for writing on "civil disobedience," in fact, Thoreau did not use the term, so far as anyone knows. In 1846 (possibly 1845), Thoreau was jailed for one night in Concord, Massachusetts, for refusing to pay

---

[41] Online *Oxford English Dictionary* cites first use of the word referring to a principle in the *London Medical Gazette*, August 6, 1831. It dates Gandhi's first use to 1920, in Nehru's *Autobiography* (1936), xii, 83, "I believe that non-violence is infinitely superior to violence, forgiveness is more manly than punishment." As an adjective, *OED* cites Gandhi, *Young India* (1922): 288—"We must not intend harm to the English or to our co-operating countrymen, if and whilst we claim to be non-violent."

the poll tax.[42] His resistance was intentional, he asserted, to show his refusal to support a government that he judged illegitimate because it condoned slavery and wanted to expand slave territory through the Mexican War. Thoreau was bailed out by a relative, unbeknown to him. His fleeting prison stay resulted in a lecture before the Concord Lyceum in mid-February 1848 called "The Rights and Duties of the Individual in Relation to Government."[43] It was first published as "Resistance to Civil Government."[44] His purposeful breaking of the law was, to Thoreau, a form of witness and remaining true to one's beliefs, mostly used in the nineteenth century by individuals or groups who had scant plans if any of producing major political modifications. In Gandhi's hands, six decades later, it was becoming an instrument of mass action aimed specifically at political change. Gandhi acknowledges Thoreau's lecture, referring to it as *The Duty of Civil Disobedience*, but pointedly states, "The statement that I had derived my idea of civil disobedience from the writings of Thoreau is wrong."[45] He subsequently acknowledged that Thoreau's essay had given him "scientific confirmation of what I was doing in South Africa."[46] With regard to noncooperation, Gandhi maintained that the concept originated with him: "The idea of noncooperation was conceived by me."[47]

A journalist from the United States, Webb Miller, associated with United Press International in the early 1930s, believed that Gandhi

[42] The poll tax would persist particularly in southern states of the United States for another century, disenfranchising African American and poor white voters, until the 1960s when Federal courts would rule it unconstitutional.

[43] Henry David Thoreau, "Familiar Letters of Henry David Thoreau," in *Writings of Henry David Thoreau*, vol. 11: *The Rights and Duties of the Individual in Relation to Government*, ed. F. B. Sanborn (Boston: Houghton Mifflin Company, 1894), 135.

[44] Henry David Thoreau, "Resistance to Civil Government," in *The Annals of America: 1841–1849*, vol. 7 (Chicago: *Encyclopædia Britannica*, 1976), 540–8. Originally Elizabeth P. Peabody (ed.), *Æsthetic Papers* (Boston: The Editor; New York: G. P. Putnam, 1849), 189–211.

[45] Gandhi, "Letter to P. Kodanda Rao" (September 10, 1935), in *CWMG*, 67: 400.

[46] Gandhi, "To American Friends" (August 3, 1942), in *CWMG*, 83: 163.

[47] Gandhi, "My Dharma" (from Gujarati, *Navajivan*, December 20, 1925), in *CWMG*, 33: 322.

resolved the matter in London, in 1931, when he asked Gandhi if he had read Thoreau. Gandhi replied:

> Why, of course I read Thoreau . . . first in Johannesburg in South Africa in 1906 and his ideas influenced me greatly. . . . I actually took the name of my movement from Thoreau's essay, "On the Duty of Civil Disobedience". . . . Until I read that essay I never found a suitable English translation for my Indian word, *Satyagraha*. . . . Thoreau's ideas greatly influenced my movement in India.[48]

In later years, Gandhi would circumscribe his view of the utility of civil disobedience. In the constructive program, he adduces a more limited role for this method, pressing for certain constraints and saying that civil disobedience would not be necessary to win freedom. The constructive program was more important to Gandhi than resistance for accomplishing his interlocking goals, although his presentation of it is sketchy and unsystematic. Its provision of alternative, or parallel, institutions represents a tangible means of offering people a way to liberate themselves and literally transform their condition by constructing independently organized and self-managed institutions, built on the very principles to be enacted, namely, decentralization, inclusion, mutual respect, participation, representation, self-governance, and Truth. Such parallel entities were to replace their antitheses—abusive, exploitive, corrupt, and depraved state (and market) forces.[49]

In maturity, Gandhi preferred that the energies of the entire nation should be invested in the constructive program. In other words, political independence would require a more comprehensive and complex undertaking involving millions, and the creation of decentralized institutions to serve as the infrastructure for a just society would make it possible to proceed toward a new social reality in the midst of the old.

---

[48] Webb Miller, *I Found No Peace: The Journal of a Foreign Correspondent* (New York: Simon and Schuster, 1936), 238–9.

[49] Sharp identifies three nonviolent methods that are based on the model of alternative, or parallel, institutions: alternative social institutions, alternative economic institutions, and dual sovereignty or parallel government (nos. 179, 192, and 198, respectively, of his 198 methods), with specific historical examples, although he does not emphasize the constructive program. Gene Sharp, *Politics of Nonviolent Action*, vol. 2, *The Methods of Nonviolent Action* (Boston: Porter Sargent Publishers, 1973), 398–400, 415–16, 423–33.

Writing in 1941, he makes a point of continuing relevance on civil disobedience for today's social movements: "Civil disobedience can never be directed for a general cause such as for independence." Instead of aiming for an abstract goal, fix on something "definite and capable of being clearly understood and within the power of the opponent to yield." It could be a factor in the "battle for freedom," if targeted to a specific issue, for example, free speech; yet merely breaking an unjust law would not be sufficient. He asks his reader to grasp that "civil disobedience in terms of independence without the co-operation of the millions by way of constructive effort is mere bravado and worse than useless." In other words, Indians should preferably be involved in constructing alternative, or parallel, institutions that they could control and through which, even if only partially realized, they could begin to realize their ideals. He was reckoning that the road to *poorna swaraj*, or complete independence, was "steep and narrow," with "slippery ascents and many deep chasms."[50] He speaks with such realism and lucidity that it is apparent that this is not someone who is reasoning from the ethical to the political. As Gene Sharp observes, Gandhi ventured from the political to the political.[51] Gandhi's formulation of satyagraha as a method of struggle, his "experiments with truth," his conviction that the means affect the end, and his multipronged constructive program for building swaraj and self-governing institutions were fundamental to his philosophy and theories and essentially comprised an independent phenomenon—a development stimulated by Gandhi's fund of experience, combined with observation and study of other historical and contemporary instances of nonviolent struggle.

Gandhi was secure in profound traditions of Indian thought that gave preference to nonviolent responses to the weary tribulations of

[50] Gandhi, "Constructive Programme: Its Meaning and Place" (December 13, 1941), in *CWMG*, 81: 354–74. Seeking to define "complete independence" and how to achieve it, he includes the ending of untouchability, and speaks of how "every Hindu should make common cause with [Harijans] and befriend them in their awful isolation—such isolation as perhaps the world has never seen in the monstrous immensity one witnesses in India. . . . It is part of the task of building the edifice of swaraj." Gandhi, "Constructive Programme: Its Meaning and Place," 357.

[51] Sharp, *Gandhi as a Political Strategist* (Boston: Porter Sargent Publishers, 1979), 25. See esp. "Origins of Gandhi's Use of Nonviolent Struggle," 23–41.

life. Yet his thinking diverged from ancient and contemporary usage that was otherworldly in its renunciation of this world and metaphysically seeking noninvolvement and detachment. Gandhi's nostrums may seem curious and quaint for present-day audiences, including his elevation of suffering, asceticism, rhapsodizing of poverty, celebration of celibacy, and infatuations with khadi and the perfect village. His regimented monastic simplicity of daily life and unceasing use of religious language when addressing political interventions can sometimes be an obstacle to understanding. His eccentricities often impede clear perception of his political significance. Yet his personal commitment to regimens of spirituality, meditation, and fasting made it possible for large numbers of Indian to identify with him and feel trust. While he readily saw himself as capable of error and possessed a mentality of experimentation with nonviolence, he could also be admittedly dictatorial.

Restlessly focused on tangible injustices, which he had himself experienced in South Africa and later observed all about him in India, Gandhi's voluminous writings reveal a revolutionary model that goes beyond a view based solely on moral principle. At the same time, he was not seeking a technique that was reducible to mere mechanics and logistics. He wanted to transform and overhaul Indian social structures, although he was not orderly or systematic in approaching them, and his constructive program lacked coherence and scale as a plan for building the nation. Asked in later years whether nonviolent rebellion was a program for the seizure of power, he replied, "A non-violent revolution is not a programme of 'seizure of power'. It is a programme of transformation of relationships ending in a peaceful transfer of power."[52] He emphasized the relational aspects of dealing with the adversary.

A fundamental choice for Gandhi was action versus inaction, rather than violent action versus nonviolent action, because inaction held little potential for change. Thinking that the Indians had been reduced "to a state bordering on cowardly helplessness,"[53] inaction held no

---

[52] Gandhi, "Non-violent Technique and Parallel Government," in *Non-Violence in Peace and War*, ed. Bharatan Kumarappa, vol. 2, 1st ed. (Ahmedabad: Navajivan Publishing House, 1949), 8. Hereafter, *Non-Violence in Peace and War*, vol. 2, is cited as *NPW* (2).

[53] Gandhi, "Letter to Lord Irwin" (March 2, 1930, Sabarmati), in *CWMG*, 48: 362.

potential for change to Gandhi. Leaving intact the status quo ante would not alter aggrieving circumstances. Inertness by individuals made it likely that the existing condition would remain intact. Action, on the other hand, offered a choice of violent or nonviolent means. For Gandhi, the latter was preferable and less likely to leave behind a quest for retaliation or revenge. If the only exertion an individual could make in the cause of social justice was violent, he favored that option to doing nothing. In 1932, he phrased this position thusly: "[V]iolence does not cease to be violence. It remains an evil. But cowardice is worse than violence."[54]

With his perception of *satya* as Truth, or the end, and *ahimsa*, non-injury, the means for searching for Truth, satyagraha was the tool by which to achieve Truth. It was the method for insisting on Truth and also realizing it, combining knowledge and action. In Hindu thought, Truth is the foundation of all existence. To Gandhi, Truth was God. At the conclusion of his autobiography, which discloses scant personal information, he says, "there is no other God than Truth."[55] In an expression of Hindu fusion, God, Truth, and Love were all-pervasive for Gandhi, and these are one. For Westerners, truth might be what can be authenticated, isolated, proved, quantified, replicated, or substantiated. Yet Gandhi's insistence on Truth and injunction to "hold on to truth" were familiar precepts for his audience, where folklore, dance, drama, and song also imparted the recognition of Truth or God as a fulfillment for which millions ached.

Gandhi's defining claim was that he could demonstrate a way to discover Truth by taking action in society. In other words, he sought God through action, giving further grounds for his dismay at inaction. Satyagraha for Gandhi represented a union of the ethical and the practical in deed, embodying his conviction that moral principles lack meaning unless they guide the daily endeavors of individuals. While for him satyagraha was produced from the clarity that comes from inner conviction, part of his uniqueness derived from combining nonviolence as a creed or principle with shrewd political forms of resistance to subjugation.

---

[54] Gandhi, "A Letter" (from Gujarati, April 18, 1932), in *CWMG*, 55: 248.

[55] Mohandas K. Gandhi, *An Autobiography: The Story of My Experiments with Truth*, trans. from Gujarati by Mahadev Haribhai Desai (Ahmedabad: Navajivan Publishing House, 1940; repr., Boston: Beacon Press, 1993), 503.

Given the relativity of Truth and myriad interpretations of it by those exploring it, the method of questing for Truth was essential. Determining how to pursue Truth was not a detached or esoteric query: how one fights for a goal is elemental and integral to its accomplishment. For Gandhi, the means and ends could not be severed: "The means may be likened to a seed, the end to a tree; and there is just the same inviolable connection between the means and the end as there is between the seed and the tree."[56] Rejecting as spurious any of the conventional suppositions that good ends can justify bad means, Gandhi thought it untenable to separate the means and ends. If one wanted a certain state of affairs, the process should exemplify the goal, and the measures taken to achieve it should embody and guide its implementation. The fight itself must be waged with truthful procedures.

What then were truthful means? Satyagraha proffers an answer. The means and ends may be drawn out and protracted over time, but cannot be detached from each other. Trial and error might be necessary to find a truthful course, but in Gandhi's eyes one should endeavor from the first step to act consistently with the goal, with each action revealing the ultimate purpose. In rejecting a difference between means and ends, he foresaw that even if enacting the goal today does not result in the desired effect later on, the goal has at least been lived, if only briefly. When the measures used are violent, the goal has not been realized, not even for an instant.

Thus, to act morally was to lead a life of Truth. Gandhi's theory of satyagraha is, in Bhikhu Parekh's succinct phrase, both epistemology and political enactment: a theory of knowledge and action. Furthermore, Parekh notes, analysts have neglected the fact that in Gandhi's first language, Gujarati, unlike in classical Sanskrit, *agraha* conveys insistence on something without being obstinate or unwilling to compromise. In other words, the action taker and the opponent may differ, but the satyagrahi will insist on a cooperative quest for the Truth. Hence, when satya and agraha are combined, the result has "a beautiful duality of meaning, implying both insistence *on* and *for* truth."[57] The once

[56] M. K. Gandhi, *Hind Swaraj or Indian Home Rule*, ed. Mahadev Haribhai Desai (South Africa, n. p., 1909; English edition repr., 1938; Ahmedabad: Jitendra T. Desai, Navajivan Mudranalaya, 1995), 64.

[57] Bhikhu C. Parekh, *Gandhi's Political Philosophy: A Critical Examination* (Houndsmill, Basingstoke, Hampshire, and London: Macmillan Press, 1989), 143.

philosophical precept of the connection between means and ends has in the years since Gandhi broadened, so that it is today also understood as strategically essential to the requirements for effective nonviolent civil resistance. In retrospect, Gandhi's emphasis on the inseparability of the measures used and the results obtained reveals the endowments that made him intuitively an inspired natural strategist.

When returning to India in 1915, Gandhi believed that he had fathomed a form of political defiance that the Indian émigrés in South Africa might effectively use in social self-defense from the predations of colonialism. In actual fact the circumstances faced by Indians in South Africa would worsen after his departure, but to his mind he was in possession of a technique that was practical, ethical, and effectual. He remained perturbed, nonetheless, by the ambiguous English phrase "passive resistance," vestigially in use today. Further exploration of the term *satyagraha* is thus justified.

By 1908, formally adopting satyagraha of Sanskrit and Gujarati derivation, Gandhi clarified in Johannesburg that "'resistance' means determined opposition to anything," which, he said, "rendered it as *agraha* [firmness, insistence]."[58] Two decades later, in 1928, asserting that none of those involved in South Africa knew what to name their movement, Gandhi explained that he had used the term *passive resistance* without understanding its implications. "I only knew that some new principle had come into being," he said.

> As the struggle advanced, the phrase "passive resistance" gave rise to confusion and it appeared shameful to permit this great struggle to be known only by an English name. . . . [T]hat foreign phrase could hardly pass as current coin among the community. A small prize was therefore announced in *Indian Opinion* to be awarded to the reader who invented the best designation for our struggle. . . .
>
> [T]he word sadagraha [was suggested], meaning "firmness in a good cause." I liked the word, but it did not fully represent the whole idea I wished it to connote. I therefore corrected it to "satyagraha." Truth (*Satya*) [*sic*] implies love, and firmness (*agraha*) engenders and therefore serves as a synonym for force. I thus began to call the Indian movement "Satyagraha," that is to say, the Force which is born of Truth and Love or non-violence, and gave up the use of the phrase "passive resistance," in

[58] Gandhi, "Johannesburg Letter" (from Gujarati, *Indian Opinion*, January 1, 1908), in *CWMG*, 8: 80.

connection with it, so much so that even in English writing we often avoided it and used instead the word "Satyagraha" itself or some other equivalent English phrase. This then was the genesis of the movement which came to be known as Satyagraha, and of the word used as a designation for it.[59]

Hence by 1928, satyagraha had become in Gandhi's eyes an engendering force. Concerned with producing substantive change, and with an eagerness to confront basic injustices, he infers that nonviolent resistance is the "force which is born of Truth." He is categorically not advocating passivity, cessation of activity, cowardice, non-resistance, or noninvolvement. Non-resistants have historically refused to participate in war, but also in matters concerning the nation-state, with emphasis on fidelity to their belief systems rather than attempting to shape social rebuilding or policy.[60]

Some Christian non-resistants and pacifists viewed Gandhi through the likeness of Jesus of Nazareth and found fault with Gandhi's nonviolent action as "militant" and possessing attributes of a state machinery of armed forces. More than one did not appreciate his speaking of the "weapon" of satyagraha or "non-violent warfare"; others did not welcome his vocabulary of "force" and "compulsion." For centuries, pacifism had been religiously constituted, rather than politically motivated, and was tightly connected to personal witness and moral codes of nonviolence. In the aftermath of World War I and as the twentieth century proceeded, pacifism would undergo its own permutations, as traditional moral opposition to war became melded with addressing the economic and political origins of militarism, eventually taking in the role of transnational corporations and the nation-state itself. Nevertheless, many worldwide have still not grasped Gandhi's major concentration on the force of social power, or perceived that his interest was not primarily in violence versus nonviolent action per se, but in the

---

[59] Gandhi, "The Advent of Satyagraha," trans. Valji Govindji Desai, in *Satyagraha in South Africa* (Ahmedabad: Navajivan Publishing House, rev. 2nd ed. [1928] 1950), 109–10.

[60] A précis of types of beliefs and action of pacifists, non-resistants, and other categories of adherents to principled nonviolence is found in Gene Sharp, "A Study of the Meanings of Nonviolence," in *Gandhi: His Relevance for Our Times*, ed. G. Ramachandran and T. K. Mahadevan, 2nd ed. (New Delhi, Bharatiya Vidya Bhavan, Bombay: Gandhi Peace Foundation, 1967), 23–42.

taking of action as opposed to inaction (although he appreciated that some action could be worse than none at all).

Social Constraints by Nonviolent Means

After 1922, the most successful local satyagrahas in India were generally the ones led by nationalists other than Gandhi, who were pragmatic rather than principled believers in nonviolent civil resistance.[61] At the peak of Gandhi's exertions and influence, two analysts were able to see what others missed. In 1923, one year before the start of the Vykom campaign, sociologist Clifford Marsh Case published his study on the "social psychology of passive resistance," which, importantly, saw that what was involved was the application of social constraints by nonviolent means. While recognizing early in the twentieth century that nonviolent action is an organized public undertaking in which average people can make collective claims on an oppressor or adversary, and despite using the term *passive resistance* interchangeably with *nonviolent resistance*, he deems boycotts, demonstrations, strikes, and noncooperation in general to entail what he calls *coerciveness*. With these methods employing coercive force in Case's mind, they are neither appeals nor protests. In his view, being a passive resistant originally meant merely one who submitted to personal abuse without retaliation, which he calls non-resistance, or no resistance at all, which he also sees as martyrdom. The term *passive resistance* then in use was later broadened to refer to the actions of conscripts who refused to bear arms when commanded by the state. To Case, both of these specific applications of resistance represented "nonconformity" and "passive endurance of the suffering inflicted," the refusal to obey in one instance and the failure to defend oneself in the other. In neither circumstance would the passive resistant be seeking to advance a "positive social policy, either by persuasion or coercion." Rather, the action taker or group asks only to be left alone.[62] Case anticipated by nearly a century

---

[61] As an example, Sardar Vallabhbhai Patel proved adept at deploying the method in a pragmatic way, as seen most notably in the Borsad (1923–4) and Bardoli satyagrahas (1928). See David Hardiman, *Peasant Nationalists of Gujarat: Kheda District, 1917–1934* (Delhi, New York: Oxford University Press, 1981).

[62] Clarence Marsh Case, *Nonviolent Coercion: A Study in Methods of Social Pressure* (New York: Century, 1923), 287, 301, on martyrdom, see 297.

the current broad understanding of nonviolent action as "methods of social pressure," while his term *nonviolent coercion* to portray the specific application of physical or moral force to induce change has been substantiated as an outcome in the voluminous literature of case studies and theory that has developed internationally particularly in the last five decades.[63]

In India in 1919, British officials insisted on statutes called the Rowlatt Bills, permitting incarceration without trial of anyone suspected of sedition and without right of appeal. Gandhi called for a *hartal*—an extensive demonstration or work stoppage to arouse consciousness that also intimated what an extended massive general strike might be like. Conceived of as a national day of "humiliation and prayer," with fasting, gatherings, and suspension of labor, it would display to the British the potential disruption of a mass program of noncooperation concerning the legislation. It also involved an act of civil disobedience, namely, the selling of banned literature in public, including Gandhi's *Hind Swaraj*. Hinting at what lay ahead if colonial authorities failed to show more sensitivity toward Indian opinion, the hartal was the start of Gandhi's first *nationwide* satyagraha campaign based on noncooperation, one of the few occasions on which Gandhi sanctioned mass countrywide civil disobedience (1930 and 1940–1 were others). Regarding the debates on the utilization of civil disobedience during 1919, Case wrote, "It is explicitly *non*-violent, and implicitly *coercive*, inasmuch as it is aimed to cause the Government to withdraw … legislation against its will or judgment. It is, therefore, a clear case of 'nonviolent coercion.'"[64]

Case was among a handful of analysts in the 1930s who used a "technique approach" in examining Gandhi's contributions, along with Krishnalal Shridharani, about whom more will be said. The Dutch anti-militarist Barthélemy de Ligt was also in the company of them. They shared an interest in discerning a realistic method that people in all walks of life could use, if necessary, to fight oppression with self-reliance. Richard Gregg was writing in the 1930s to explain Gandhi to readers beyond India. He introduced the concept of moral *jiu-jitsu* in explaining how nonviolent resistance can work

---

[63] Case, *Nonviolent Coercion*, 145.

[64] Case, *Nonviolent Coercion*, 379.

psychologically to affect the opponent's meting out of reprisals. Gregg wrote at great length about persuasion, akin to Gandhi's conversion, but in bending over backwards to elucidate the conversion of the opponent, his work in places is suggestive of religious pacifism. During the 1940s and 1950s, analysts looking at what had transpired in India tended not to focus on investigating and exploring the method, form, and technique of struggle that was being refined by Gandhi.[65] Instead, they accentuated Gandhi as a mahatma, a spiritual inspirer, whose accomplishments were attributable to personal charisma, and a leader whose thinking was limited solely to nonviolence as a matter of principle.[66]

The "mahatma perspective" emphasized biography. That Gandhi had been designated a mahatma contributed to his influence on the thinking of millions of Indians concerning untouchability, yet he disliked the homage of the title. Judith Brown notes his "pain and embarrassment in its connotations and the outward veneration that began to accompany it."[67] He favored the appellation *bapu*, or father. This school of research on Gandhi the man accelerated, sometimes hagiographically. Nehru, who had initially doubted the adequacy of Gandhi's method of nonviolent action if applied to the British and also had reservations about his colleagues' readiness for utilizing it for social change, pinpointed Gandhi's genius as "finding the real weak point

[65] While mindful of inner requirements of satyagraha, Gandhi frequently stressed it as a technique: "This process or method, which I have called nonviolent non-co-operation, is not without considerable success in its use in India." Gandhi, "To Every Briton" (*Harijan*, July 6, 1940), in *NPW* (1), ed. Mahadev Haribhai Desai, 3rd ed. (Ahmedabad: Navajivan Publishing House [1942], 1948), 280.

[66] On this point, see Sharp, "Shridharani's Contribution to the Study of Gandhi's Technique," in *Gandhi as a Political Strategist: With Essays on Ethics and Politics* (Boston: Porter Sargent Publishers, 1979), 315–23. The honorific *mahatma*, literally "great soul," may have been first bestowed on Gandhi by the poet Rabindranath Tagore, upon Gandhi's return to India in 1915.

[67] Judith M. Brown, *Modern India: The Origins of an Asian Democracy*, 2nd ed. (Oxford: Oxford University Press, 1994), 215.

which would shake up the foundation." What was "pivotal" is that "in military terms, it is the attack at the weakest point of the enemy" that counts. "You do that and the whole front goes."[68]

Shridharani's *War without Violence: A Study of Gandhi's Method and Its Accomplishments*, published in 1939, propitiously offers a firsthand interpretation of Gandhi's satyagraha. Born into a Brahmin family in Bhavnagar, Gujarat, Shridharani was graduated from Rabindranath Tagore's Shantiniketan school in 1934. Having become a newspaper journalist, he was among the original seventy-nine adherents who trained for months with Gandhi before the 1930 Salt March, practicing defiance of the law and forming a well-organized corps able to manage large throngs. Hailing from all walks of life, the adherents included male Dalits, editors, scholars, and weavers, ranging in age from 16 to 61 (though no women). Shridharani walked with Gandhi the 241 miles from Ahmedabad to Dandi on the west coast of Gujarat, at the Gulf of Cambay. After 24 days of marching on foot, with accompanying crowds swelling to thousands, Shridharani was on April 6 one of the "first batch" to break the Salt Law in an act of civil disobedience violating the government's salt monopoly. April 6 was the eleventh anniversary of Gandhi's 1919 call for national satyagraha against the Rowlett Bills, resulting in a major hartal.

The interpretations of Gandhian theories and techniques in *War without Violence* are valuable for having been written contemporaneously, relying on direct exposure. A 1962 paperback updates his book to the independence period and some later aspects of nonviolent struggle in India, yet his premature death at forty-nine years denies the field what might have been subsequent evaluations. Shridaharani's original insights deserve serious consideration, although they do not discuss the phenomenon of nonviolent action elsewhere in the world and understandably represent only one participant's narrative. He does not explicate the analysis of power underlying Gandhi's trenchant discernment of 1905 that all systems rely on the cooperation of the ruled.[69] Relatively

---

[68] Tibor Mende, *Conversations with Mr. Nehru* (London: Secker and Warburg, 1956), 28. Regarding Nehru's doubts, see p. 21.

[69] Gandhi, "Russia and India" (November 11, 1905), in *CWMG*, 5: 8.

unconcerned with complications brought by British colonialism and the scale of India's social movements for independence, the focus of Shridaharani's analysis is the materialization of a new resource, satyagraha, which he considers "a technique of concerted social action" to be equated with nonviolent direct action.[70] In not interrogating Gandhi's views on suffering with the exactitude warranted, he may have positioned satyagraha close to faith-based, principled reasoning.

Shridharani was perturbed about unsophisticated assumptions concerning violence, war, and pacifism as instruments for rectifying injustice and their ability to address both domestic and international conflict: "Conflict, competition, strife and struggle . . . are not the 'enemy' we are after . . . . It is war we are against; for as a means of settling our inevitable sporadic disputes, the institution of war has failed to fulfill its function."[71] War, he judged, tended to aggravate whatever the underlying problems and at a high price; without a better solution, the turn to warfare would persist. He saw the failure of pacifists, non-resisters, and conscientious objectors to alter the course of history as meaning that their positions had absented themselves from fighting the tyrannical and unscrupulous. The views of pacifists over centuries would comprise a cataloging of wide variation, at a minimum, generally meaning refusing to participate in international or civil warfare or violent revolutions because of ethical, moral, or religious principles, including principled nonviolence.[72]

---

[70] Krishnalal Shridharani, *War without Violence* (Bombay: Bharatiya Vidya Bhavan, 1962), 7.

[71] Shridharani, *War without Violence*, 4.

[72] Gandhi himself was not strictly a pacifist. In 1899 in South Africa, as the Boer War erupted, Gandhi thought Indians claiming citizenship in a British colony were obliged to defend it. He organized an Indian Ambulance Corps to support the British in the second Anglo-Boer War. Then viewing himself as a "citizen of the empire," he offered his services during the 1906 Zulu revolt against British rule and taxation in Natal, South Africa. During World War I, he raised recruits in India and an ambulance corps in London in 1914. Gandhi, "Why Did I Assist in the Last War?" *Young India*, November 17, 1921, in *NPW* (1), 22. He adds that experience taught him that the existing system was "wholly bad" and required a "special national effort to end or mend it," as it lacked the

Perceiving that sundry biographers had lost sight of the "hard-bitten realism" of Gandhi's process for seeking social reconstruction (in favor of appraising his individuality), Shridharani compares the technique of satyagraha to war, claiming that hostile contentions carried out with armed forces would furnish the yardstick for appraising satyagraha. Having worked with Gandhi from 1929 to 1933, along with scores of other satyagrahis, he declares Gandhi his principal source, including his writings, utterances, and meaningful silences. He credits methodical inspection of publications in Bengali, English, Gujarati, and Hindi, along with interactions with participating Indian leaders, for his being able to decipher a movement in the midst of action. Shridharani's contacts with police, magistrates, an English sergeant, native tax collectors, prison officials, and a spy helped him to grasp "satyagraha's neutralizing and paralyzing counter-action" against coercive agencies of power.[73]

In Shridharani's systematization, satyagraha can be organized mass action of national scope, which presumes that the grievance is deeply felt by a majority of the community, thus justifying the making of claims. Such mass actions were extralegal, extraconstitutional, and extraparliamentary, thus making them revolutionary (without connotations of violence). In his analysis, the campaign would proceed through a series of plateaus. In the first plateau, *negotiations* and *arbitration*, no avenue was left unexplored before embarking on nonviolent direct action. No one was viewed as beyond reclamation, but direct action should be used reluctantly, "only as the final weapon."[74] If negotiations and arbitration failed to bring redress, it was time for a campaign of *agitation* by those most directly affected by the dispute. The objective was "to disrupt the balance of personal and group loyalties in the opposition camp by psychological suggestions, by dramatizing

ability for self-correction. *Young India*, November 17, 1921, in *NPW* (1), 23. He would later revisit his 1914 "mentality," when "a believer in the Empire," explaining that as the "nonviolent rebel" that he had become by 1928, he would have nonviolently attempted to "defeat its purpose." Gandhi, "Still at It," *Young India*, March 15, 1928, in *NPW* (1), 71.

[73] Shridharani, *War without Violence*, 10.

[74] Shridharani, *War without Violence*, 17.

moral factors."[75] In the agitation phase, use of communications—through pamphlets, books, cinema, debates, discussions, meetings, news media, papers, personal contacts, radio, slogans, songs, and speeches—was critical to generate consciousness of the cause. Part of the reason for emphasizing means of communication, what would today be called messaging, in this period was to expose the moral weakness of the ruling group, or opponent. When no evidence was forthcoming of change from the adversary, various forms of *demonstrations* comprised the third phase, which with sequencing would grow larger, as public debates developed into mass meetings. Presentation of an *ultimatum* might follow, amounting to "a 'conditional declaration of war,' in this case a war without violence, at least on one side."[76]

When all constitutional and lawful attempts had failed, revolutionary activity was the sole alternative: "Moral suasion having proved ineffective, the Satyagrahis do not hesitate to shift their technique to compulsive force."[77] *Self-purification* is the fourth phase, in which the nonviolent actors take upon themselves some of the responsibility for the wrong that they oppose and identify ways to express their sincerity. The primary goal and direct result of Gandhi's self-purification is "paralysis of a government which lives on our vices and wickednesses." Shridharani's real-life exposition bares a non-sentimental appreciation of Gandhian reasoning, "For the tyrant has the power to inflict that which we lack strength to resist." Moreover, "submission is but a smaller crime than perpetration."[78] When all of these phases fail, the way is cleared for stronger sanctions, such as strikes and the general strike.

To Shridharani, satyagraha as a technique entails a process of conversion, which for him contains "the *compelling* element." Demoralizing the antagonist through voluntarily accepting suffering imposes distress and difficulty, a form of power akin to an engine being thrown into reverse. Nonviolent direct action "operates to compel not through

[75] Shridharani, *War without Violence*, 18. "In totalitarian countries and in colonies such as India once was, the battle begins at this early stage." Shridharani, *War without Violence*, 18.

[76] Shridharani, *War without Violence*, 20.

[77] Shridharani, *War without Violence*, 21.

[78] Shridharani, *War without Violence*, 22.

inflicting horrors and destruction as war does, but by disrupting the morale of the opponent by various psychological suggestions." Looked at in this way, he concedes that suffering generates social power. Welcoming its aspects of coercion and compulsion, yet without revenge or punishment, Shridharani expresses Gandhi's strategic thinking as war without violence, the eponymous source of his book's title, although he does not precisely equate satyagraha to war as a *coercive force*.[79] Shridharani can be faulted for oversimplifying the comparability of war and satyagraha, while the term *coercion* has numerous nuanced meanings, but at essence is his contemporaneous recognition that satyagraha possesses determinable power to compel assent when it makes claims; it does not work solely by exerting moral suasion. Some concepts of conventional warfare held the theory of breaking the will of one's opponent by inflicting suffering, but Gandhi inverted this notion and instead considered intentional self-suffering to be a formal declaration against the grievance, policy, or wrong. If the pain thus encumbered was greater than the original grievance, consciously accepting suffering becomes in his eyes a source of power for the reason that it confounds the foe. Also important to recognize is that with deliberate cultivation of no spirit of revenge, punishment, or retribution, Gandhi's compulsion does not seek the full extent of coercion. Rather, it seeks a change of heart and redressing the wrong, does not seek to inflict defeat, and holds potential for all parties to benefit—should that be beneficial. Indeed, victory might be shared.[80]

Shridharani considers Gandhi's "spasmodic fasts" to be patterned after the Jains' practice in their quest for enlightenment. Fasting anchored satyagraha with some Indians, whose customary beliefs held that through sacrifice the dedicated could achieve their desired ends when encountering a crisis, and for whom self-denial could prospectively become a way to realize goals. Fasting for Gandhi was part of his concept of satyagraha, including as an aspect of self-purification, yet he had scruples about recommending it as a wholesale policy. Gandhi admits, "[F]asting has not been accepted as a recognized part of *satyagraha*. It has only been tolerated by the politicians. I have however been driven to the conclusion that

---

[79] Shridharani, *War without Violence*, 263. Emphasis in original.
[80] Shridharani, *War without Violence*, 264.

fasting unto death is an integral part of *satyagraha* programme. . . . Not every one is qualified for undertaking it without a proper course of training."[81] Shridharani thought that the willingness to sacrifice entailed in fasting let onlookers know that satyagrahis were earnest. He describes it thusly: Self-purification persuades the opponent that the action takers "intend to struggle to the finish, and . . . are ready to make any sacrifice in order to achieve their ends."[82] Lest some Westerners think fasting and public prayers quaint, Shridharani cites Thomas Jefferson from June 1, 1774, when the port of Boston was to be closed by the British, saying that a day of general fasting and prayer was like a shock of electricity in the American colonies.[83] It could also work within a movement to strengthen morale. Gandhi's 1932 fast unto death to prevent what he saw as untouchables being segregated was perceived in many quarters as having worked. Therefore, fasting might indeed be applied as an instrument of satyagraha, yet it was a severe method with an uncertain effect. As time went on, eventually Gandhi came to view fasting as an exceedingly potent technique in which, due to an emotionally coercive impact, one's adversary was essentially obliged to change. Late in life, he reflects on having "had the temerity to claim that fasting is an infallible weapon in the armoury of Satyagraha. I have used it myself, being the author of Satyagraha." Yet he enunciated an accompanying proviso that one should "fast only as a last resort when all other avenues of redress have been explored and have failed."[84]

A Tool for Exerting Mass Political Force and Social Power

By the dawn of the twentieth century, Gandhi had perceived that human beings have at their disposal assured powers that can under particular circumstances be effective in settling group conflicts without armed violent struggle. He offered a theory about the use of social power along with methods for effecting it. Moreover, he believed that any person

---

[81] Gandhi, "Fasting in Non-violent Action" (*Harijan*, July 26, 1942), in *NPW* (1), 412.

[82] Shridharani, *War without Violence*, 23.

[83] Shridharani, *War without Violence*, 22.

[84] Gandhi, "Fasting in the Air" (*Harijan*, April 21, 1946), in *NPW* (2), 48.

could generally grasp the meaning of nonviolent action and on this presumption built it into a tool for exerting mass political force and social power. He saw nonviolent struggle as a practical and realistic alternative to the presumed efficacy of violence, and possessing greater reliability of outcome. In a way that modern conflict-resolution analysts sometimes fail to understand, Gandhi grasped that struggle presupposes conflict—incorrigibly a part of the human condition—and he understood that a solution would remain fixed only until it unraveled again.

With his experiments reflecting his perspective on the power of social action possessed by those living under oppressive machinery, and relishing the ability of ordinary people to act together, he was aware that the examination of the effectiveness of the use of nonviolent civil resistance was just beginning to take form. A virtually inexhaustible array of mass action was available, in Gandhi's eyes. In 1940, he wrote:

> [T]he way of violence is old and established. It is not so difficult to do research in it. The way of non-violence is new. The science of non-violence is yet taking shape. We are still not conversant with all its aspects. There is a wide scope for research and experiment in this field. You can apply all your talents to it.[85]

Indicative of the wide range for study and experimentation in the field for which Gandhi had constructed the foundation, by 1973, Gene Sharp had identified 198 discrete nonviolent methods, or sanctions.[86] Resulting from punctilious historical inquiry, Sharp ceased his tally with the realization that virtually every campaign and movement would devise new methods. A large number of infinitely varied nonviolent methods enjoy identifiable features that unite them. The recognition that popular consent can be proffered or withheld, as Gandhi had discerned in 1905, is enacted by strategies and tactics, which are implemented through nonviolent methods, which he also called sanctions. Each method stages and exerts pressure in an application of social, economic, political, psychological, and cultural power. Popular movements

---

[85] Gandhi, Speech, Gandhi Seva Sangh Meeting, Malikanda, Bengal (from Hindi), in *CWMG*, 77: 383.

[86] Sharp, *The Politics of Nonviolent Action*, 3 vols. (Boston: Porter Sargent, 1973).

have, since the time of Gandhi, and increasingly so, improvised or developed novel methods, yet in their exertion of pressure most fall into one of three broad categories: protest and persuasion, noncooperation, or nonviolent intervention.[87] Noncooperation is by far the largest of the three classes. Despite the seeming simplicity in such categorization, as Gandhi put it, we are still not conversant with all aspects of this science.

[87] *Waging Nonviolent Struggle: 20th Century Practice and 21st Century Potential*, ed. Gene Sharp (Boston: Porter Sargent Publishers, Inc., 2005), 51–65, updating Sharp, *The Politics of Nonviolent Action*, known as The Politics or Sharp's Trilogy, see esp. part 2, chapters 4–7, 183–356. "Overwhelmingly, the methods of nonviolent action involve noncooperation with the opponent." Sharp's Trilogy, 183. Based on extensive historical research and political theory, Sharp's classification of 198 nonviolent methods was a breakthrough in the appreciation that each method can exert particular forms of power and would fall into one of three categories of action, representing incremental stages of disruption: (*a*) the methods of protest and persuasion send messages (e.g., petitions, vigils, marches, processions); (*b*) the class of noncooperation methods is largest and entails suspending cooperation and assistance (e.g., boycotts, strikes, civil disobedience); (*c*) measures of nonviolent intervention disrupt and interrupt (e.g., sit-ins, fasts, hunger strikes, and parallel [alternative] institutions). Tactics, from the Greek *taktika*, meaning fit for arranging (Merriam–Webster Unabridged Dictionary) involve the grouping and planning for an engagement within a larger strategy; they are enacted by the choice and sequencing of methods.

7 Impact of Vykom on a Tool in International Theory

Gandhi deserves acknowledgment for nonviolent struggle being accepted as the chosen technique of fighting for India's independence, about which there was nothing inherent, innate, or natural. He had to persuade the Indian National Congress that this approach would be both practical and effective. India's first prime minister, Jawaharlal Nehru, who had held office as secretary and president of the Congress, makes this clear. When Gandhi "first brought this revolutionary idea of non-co-operation and all that, almost every leader in India opposed it. Even the most advanced leaders did not understand it."[1]

In seeking complex social reconstruction for India, Gandhi understood that most Indians would have trouble persevering with his catechism and was satisfied if they would simply adhere to its rules of action. A pragmatic viewpoint on the practice of nonviolent action was therefore acceptable for Gandhi, even if it did not accord with his profound personal canon: "I admit at once that there is 'a doubtful proportion of full believers' in my 'theory of nonviolence'. . . . [F]or my movement I do not at all need believers in the theory of nonviolence, full or imperfect. It is enough if people carry out the rules of nonviolent action."[2] Equally, Gandhi did not intend for his new form of struggle to

---

[1] Tibor Mende, *Conversations with Mr. Nehru* (London: Secker and Warburg, 1956), 23–4.

[2] Gandhi, *Correspondence with the Government, 1942–1944*, 2nd ed. (Ahmedabad, India: Navajivan Publishing Company, 1957), 138.

be merely tactical. He recognized peaceful resistance as less than his full meaning of satyagraha, in which the civil resisters concurred that non-violent methods were fundamentally preferable to the use of violence, but their commitment was not an all-pervasive philosophical attach-ment to his idiomatic doctrine of nonviolence.

Rather than adherence to a credo, a *policy* of nonviolent struggle is required by social movements seeking change without recourse to arms. B. R. Nanda emphasized that no mass movement in India could have been carried out on the basis of nonviolence as a creed or convic-tion.[3] Gandhi wanted unity on a policy of nonviolent action as a strat-egy. He accepted the fact that large numbers of those around him had adopted a tactical view of nonviolent action and did not view it as an all-embracing way of life. Nehru rejected belief in nonviolence as a doc-trine, but eventually accepted the necessity for noncooperation and civil disobedience as methods for fighting imperialism. "I have very little fault … with [Gandhi's] technique," Nehru said. "Where he has erred … is the unnecessary emphasis on certain personal aspects of nonviolence."[4] Surrounded by Congress members who did not share his dogma, Gandhi said, "With the Congress non-violence was always a policy. It was open to it to reject it if it failed. If it could not bring political and economic independence, it was of no use." Indeed, he thought that he had done "well to present to the Congress non-violence as an expedient. I could not have done otherwise, if I was to introduce it into politics. In South Africa too I introduced it as an expedient."[5] If anything, his overriding need was for agreement to a policy of nonvio-lent struggle by those who did *not* share his moralistic outlook, per-sonal spiritual beliefs, tenets, or way of life.

By the end of the twentieth century the use of nonviolent action as a technique was consolidating, yet rigorous theoretical analysis did not begin until the 1960s and 1970s. Most of this systematic pursuit of scholarly and practical understanding of the theory and practice of

---

[3] Balram R. Nanda, fax memorandum (New Delhi, October 6, 1995).

[4] Jawaharlal Nehru, *Selected Works of Jawaharlal Nehru*, ed. Chalapathi Rau et al. (New Delhi: Orient Longman, 1972–82), as cited in Judith M. Brown, *Nehru: A Political Life* (New Haven, Connecticut: Yale University Press, 2003), 145.

[5] Gandhi, "Question Box: Weakening Non-violence?" (*Harijan*, April 12, 1942), in Gandhi, *Non-violence in Peace and War*, vol. 1 (hereafter *NPW* [1]), 396.

waging struggle with civil resistance has in the contemporary era occurred outside of India. Within India, comprehension of other historical issues assumed priority, including the impact of colonialism and subaltern studies.[6] Both emphases are connected to India's growing role in the world and have vigorous constituencies, yet civil resistance as a field would benefit from robust Indian studies. As the undergirding research for theoretical studies in Europe and North America has grown, along with teaching material, myths and clichés have collapsed. It has become clear that nonviolent struggle as political action does not refer normatively to values of tolerance and the virtues of nonviolent interaction that in modern political thought constitute civil society. Rather, the organized collective actions undertaken by civil resisters define nonviolent struggle, not their convictions. Appreciation has grown that anarchism, idealism, pacifism, spirituality, or religious tenets are not requirements for participation in nonviolent struggle. Even the extreme right wing can be involved, as in ongoing challenges in Ukraine, where progressive liberals and rightist extreme nationalists allied themselves in struggle. In Thailand, the affluent pro-royalist middle classes brought down a democratically elected government. The Hindu right in India has also deployed nonviolent methods (alongside more violent ones). Social movements comprise people with immensely diverse beliefs and persuasions. Volume in numbers is often linked to success, hence the importance of including as broad a spectrum of population as possible. Nonviolent movements may include participants with a moral repugnance to violence, but they need equally action-takers who were formerly under arms, such as retired law enforcement officers, defectors from the security services, former soldiers and veterans of foreign wars, and even off-duty police.

[6] The term *subaltern* is often attributed to Antonio Gramsci, alluding to social groups that are excluded from established political structures. Closely related to post-colonial studies, a number of South Asian historians have importantly focused on members of mass populations, from the viewpoint of the subjugated, rather than the leadership of the social and economic elites, in the history of India and South Asia. See, for example, Ranajit Guha, ed., *Subaltern Studies: Writings on South Asian History and Society*, vols. 1–12 (Delhi: Oxford University Press, 1982–2005); David Hardiman, "Towards a History of Non-Violent Resistance," *Economic and Political Weekly* 48, no. 23 (June 8, 2013): 41–8.

Widespread Misperceptions of Vykom Then and Now Affect the "Mechanisms of Change"

The degradations from the Asiatic Registration Law in South Africa and other traumatic treatment of Indians led Gandhi toward the evolution of satyagraha, and he believed that he had conceived of a form of political struggle that would be a practical, ethical, and effective option for achieving a goal when thwarted by oppression. Despite the prescience of some of Gandhi's insights, and carefully self-taught as he was, he was not trained in systematic analysis. Although he mused deeply about his experiences, many of his insights are underdeveloped, immethodical, unreliable, and often inconsistent. He also lacked the tools that would later develop in the subject of political theory to help his scrutiny of such issues as consent, legitimacy, and obligation.

Making historical judgments about success or failure in specific campaigns of civil resistance is a sensitive matter, even when scrupulously constructing chronology from archival research in a place and time such as Travancore, where records of the royal palace and the British were preserved, and newspapers ardently reported events. Nevertheless, Gandhi's formulations that revealed themselves in Vykom have a number of distinctive failings and limitations that demand attention.

Converting Opponents with Self-Suffering?

A basic fault in Gandhi's reasoning was his certainty that if satyagraha failed, it meant that its practitioners had been insufficiently disciplined, even if other forces and social realities had intervened to affect the results. With his ideological certainty such that he vouched for the efficacy of satyagraha irrespective of the character of the opponent or its power bases, he claimed that the method could reform any adversary. He maintained from the onset of the Vykom struggle that it would achieve its reforms because the *satyagrahis* would convert the opponent "by sheer force of character and suffering," and "this silent and loving suffering ... will finally break the wall of prejudice."[7] Yet the evidence shows that Gandhi's confidence was woefully and painfully inadequate

---

[7] Gandhi, *Young India*, September 18, 1924, in *Collected Works of Mahatma Gandhi* (hereafter *CWMG*), 29: 172–3.

against the adamantine opposition faced by the satyagrahis in Vykom. The suffering of the Vykom volunteers abysmally failed to cut through the armaments of the upper-caste orthodoxy. The negative effects of Gandhi's myopia do not end there.

Gandhi could also misleadingly conflate the ideal with the reality. Throughout his working life, he confused aspirations with actuality. An early example of this bias is from South Africa, revealed in a 1910 letter to W. J. Wybergh, commissioner of mines in the Transvaal and among the initial figures to suggest segregating Indians into "locations." Gandhi decries the term *passive resistance* as a "misnomer" in a letter that asserts, "Violence ever fails; passive resistance is ever successful."[8]

In contrast to Gandhi's hope in Vykom that moral impulsion from the Nambudiris themselves would result from the suffering love of the volunteers, the recalcitrance of the orthodox deepened. He began, therefore, at that point to deliberate on how to compel the Travancore rulers to respond directly, if the temple authorities would not. Eventually, in other contexts, Gandhi would seek to create new forms of action, from an "armory," sometimes called by him "weapons," doing so with awareness that the powers wielded in noncooperation methods, such as the boycott and civil disobedience, do not work on moral supplication. By 1940, speaking of noncooperation and civil disobedience on a large scale, he was focused on its culmination in "mass refusal to pay rent and taxes."[9] His advocacy of handlooming khadi was partly intended to lessen India's imports of British-made materials, so as to free India from foreign capitalist dependency. Gandhi did not hesitate at other times to instigate resistance that would create administrative dilemmas for the British imperial government, by encouraging noncooperation in the civil service, courts of law, the judiciary, legislatures, police systems, and universities, to say nothing of rejecting honors and titles. While boycotts, strikes, and civil disobedience were not used in Vykom to manifest social opposition or constraint, and despite his habitually moralistic outlook, the measures that Gandhi advanced elsewhere would be capable of applying pressures of genuine disruption, hindrance, and obstruction. His national pan-Indian civil disobedience

---

[8] Gandhi, "Letter to W. J. Wybergh," May 10, 1910, in *CWMG*, 11: 39.

[9] Gandhi, "Democracy and Non-violence" (*Harijan*, May 18, 1940), in *NPW* (1), 270.

movements during 1920–2, 1930–4 (except portions of 1931), and 1940–2 were hardly based on humble appeals.

By 1925, as the Vykom struggle moved into its second year, Gandhi's writings begin to reference the need to *compel* justice, as a pressuring force. Nationally, he also sought to compel repentance on the part of the colonial government, having concluded that the system that he had hoped to mend was irreparable. While not seeking vengeance, retribution, or vanquishment, he spoke of the political compulsion inherent in nonviolent direct action. Only a portion of Gandhi's thinking accentuated persuasion and conversion, but well before the fields of psychology and the social sciences had gained the authority that would accrue to them as the twentieth century proceeded, he was devoting major contemplation to coercive social power and its instrumental measures. He had raised the issue of the citizen's responsibility and liability for the policies and actions of its government in early writings, based on his perception that the state is fundamentally reliant on the cooperation of the people. By 1940, he remained rooted in his 1905 discernment of popular consent as a basic framework: "No government, however powerful it may be, can [act] without the active co-operation of the people."[10] Still cautious, however, he was fearful of unleashing militant social-reform struggles that were not built on strong views of proscribing violence.

Was there ever a point in Vykom when the Brahmin ideology that bestowed massive entitlements and privileges to caste Hindus on the basis of birth would have been susceptible to the persuasive tactics of Gandhi, as he sought conversion? The evidence suggests not. He tried hard to narrow the pressures being applied in Vykom and to restrict the participants in what was probably the only circumscribed use of suffering in a satyagraha campaign of any length in India, but precise chronicling of Vykom shows that it did not work, unless assessed in a protracted and roundabout sense and in combination with other weighty factors.

Although Gandhi deliberated about how to compel social change in the face of continuing obstruction and oppression, the fact that he did not write or express himself so frequently on coercion as he did on persuasion has led to misperceptions. Gandhi was nothing if not

[10] Gandhi, "Panic" (*Harijan*, June 8, 1940), in *NPW* (1), 271.

acutely aware of the power potential of mass nonviolent action and spent years grappling with its practice and prospective powers, much less so on its limitations. Excessive emphasis on persuasion and conversion holds latent possibilities for harm. It could lead, for example, to accepting a deplorable situation on the grounds that the adversary has not yet been converted, resulting in acceptance of intolerable oppression.

The ethical and political import of satyagraha is undeniable if considered for its formative effect on a political method that has since become a more systematic and even intercontinental technique for challenging oppression, principally when institutionalized political remedies are unavailable or constitutional action is not possible. Gandhi can be credited with a contribution of inestimable value in a foundational understanding of a method for addressing conflict that is within the grasp of average persons. Yet with its constraints and inadequacies, it would be perilous to suppose that all conflicts can be tackled by attempting to win over the sensibilities of the adversary. The Vykom satyagraha was able to elaborate the cruelty of untouchability, unapproachability, and unseeability; project the facts under contestation, and weaken elements of the support for its continuation, including among some business leaders and figures in news media. It enlarged the willingness of a larger public to become involved in ending untouchability. Still, it was an overstatement for Gandhi to advocate a stance in which a preponderance of social conflicts could be resolved by seeking conversion and attempting to melt the hearts of the oppressor. Some disputes are so heinous and deep-seated that satyagraha cannot begin to resolve them. Besides, the involvement of other forms of power is often required for effective civil resistance. No one should assume that Gandhi's method can work universally, even though this is how he insisted on portraying it. Consider the impenetrable differences of viewpoints between him and Muhammad Ali Jinnah on the 1947 partition of India, with its accompanying horrific tragedies, considered by some scholars of genocidal proportion. Unmistakably, not all conflicts can be addressed by satyagraha.

The idea of self-suffering as a core, presumed aspect of nonviolent struggle has not survived the test of time. It may even have justified the repudiation of nonviolent strategies and made it acceptable to continue ignoring this significant modern development. If civil resistance is erroneously framed as suffering, submission, or non-action, it can render it unattractive to proper investigation and analysis. This may have reinforced the perception that while armed struggle is based on taking action, nonviolent struggle means shedding action. Such a misperception may have impeded the undertaking of serious analytical and historical study of this substantial form of engagement with conflict. Regardless, the notional objective of conversion remains a basic and attractive ideal in innumerable contexts for altering policies and bringing about social and political alterations. Is it worthy of being considered a mechanism of change?

The Elevation of Conversion: A Lasting Result of Erroneous Interpretations of Vykom

The legend of the Vykom struggle reinforced misjudgments about conversion. The question of whether the underlying attitudes of the higher castes could be punctured by the diligence, discipline, and restraint of the Vykom satyagrahis was topical in the 1920s and remained a persistent issue about this historical struggle until examined more closely here.

Gandhi may have been flexible regarding the ends that he sought, but he was extremely precise regarding the means, as suggested by his saying that "if one takes care of the means, the end will take care of itself."[11] As an ethical ideal to be desired, conversion may express an alluring goal, even if it is not definitively plausible to attain it. In the Vykom encounter, Gandhi constricted both the ends and means, in a doctrinaire manner, reflecting his strong judgment about how to bring about alterations in Brahminical attitudes. Leaders such as T. K. Madhavan were already organizing but sought to attach their cause to the momentum of the Congress party and Gandhi's singular leadership, understanding that he was pursuing a model in seeking to alter the attitudes of the high-caste temple authorities. Yet the early analyses of Vykom that reached audiences beyond India from 1934 onward did not comprehend that the local leaders had made a bargain: to harness Gandhi's prominence in fighting a grievance, one must accept his individualized and inimitable approach. The reports reaching the world

[11] Gandhi, "Working of Non-Violence," ed. Mahadev Haribhai Desai, in *NPW* (1), 199.

beyond India confused Gandhi's idiomatic aspirational goals with the outcome, misjudging the social realities that had prevailed. The spinmeisters of the day broadcast the motivating principle—altering the sensibilities of the target group—without examining what had actually occurred.

The perception of the Vykom struggle as an example of conversion completely lacks basis in fact, unless viewed as an oblique and elliptical sequence of events and performances, which culminated in the maharaja's opening of the Travancore temples to the "polluting castes" more than a decade later in 1936. Indeed the actual process involved in changing the existential and empirical situation of the outcastes gained ground largely because of the strength and breadth of anti-caste social reform movements in and around Travancore. The Vykom satyagraha was not about a change of hearts and minds; Gandhi was unable to persuade the oppositional local Nambudiri Brahmins, who, if they altered their thinking at all, did so due to local pressure. The princely state of Travancore reluctantly came to realize that it had to adjust to new circumstances.

Richard Gregg, a social philosopher, white southerner, and Quaker, traveled from the United States to India to seek out Gandhi and he spent nearly four years there, starting in 1925, scrutinizing his work while Gandhi was alive. For better or worse, his writings did as much as anyone to interpret Gandhi for Western audiences in the mid-twentieth century. His *Power of Nonviolence* appeared in 1934. He later corresponded with Martin Luther King Jr, who wrote the foreword to Gregg's 1960 edition of *Power of Nonviolence*, which was published in other editions, including a 1936 Swedish translation. Treading in the footsteps of Gandhi's thinking, Gregg stresses persuasion and attempting to convert the adversary. Unfortunately, he views persuasion as the primary method for success in nonviolent struggle and his pronounced emphasis on the conversion of the adversary often veers toward religious pacifism. Pacifism is not comparable to civil resistance, although innumerable nonviolent challengers have been pacifists, and nonviolent measures have long been methods of choice for pacifists who were seeking to take action. Of critical differentiation, however, is that Gandhi appreciated the difficulty of constructing a mass movement on the basis of a creed. His senior colleagues in the main, including Nehru and members of the Congress Working Committee, viewed a doctrine of nonviolence as anything but mystical—they did not even think of it as

an ethical principle—they saw in it a practical system for the realization
of their political quest for independence. This viewpoint was acceptable
to Gandhi, so long as they adhered to a policy of nonviolent action.

No one could have foreseen that Gregg's accentuation of persuasion
would create a torque in a portion of the international literature as it
emerged after the 1930s. By the 1960s, as a body of theory was developing outside India on the practice of nonviolent action, theoretician-
practitioner George Lakey began working on an analytical tool that
could be used prospectively by practitioners for planning purposes or
retroactively by analysts for research. Lakey's master's thesis, "The
Sociological Mechanisms of Nonviolent Action" (1962), for the first
time identifies conversion, persuasion, and coercion as mechanisms of
change, that is, categories of results that could be achieved by civil resistance or consequences for which it could aim.[12] Lakey's analyses later
served as the foundation for Gene Sharp's elaborations.

As scholars began classifying the main outcomes for how a struggle
can be won by a nonviolent mobilization, conversion was identified as
the first of the four mechanisms that explain how change occurs. The
mechanisms of change help to answer two questions: How does nonviolent action work? How can its strategy be aimed? The mechanisms comprise a theoretical model that is helpful in planning. They are also useful
in retroactively evaluating what happened in a particular or past struggle, serving as a practical and useful theoretical prototype for explaining
the workings of nonviolent struggle in order to comprehend it.[13]

In the first mechanism, *conversion*, the target group reacts to civil
resistance by accepting a new point of view. In a successful conversion,

[12] George Lakey, "The Sociological Mechanisms of Nonviolent Action"
(Master's thesis, University of Pennsylvania, 1962); Lakey, "The Sociological
Mechanisms of Nonviolent Action," *Peace Research Review* 2, no. 6 (1968): 1–
102; Lakey, *Nonviolent Action: How It Works* (Wallingford, Pennsylvania: Pendle
Hill, 1963).

[13] In the study of contentious politics (named for forms of contention that
include making claims on another party's interests, including social movements
using varying forms of collective action), *mechanisms* is part of the nomenclature, but has general meaning. Events that result in similar or the same effects
despite wide-ranging circumstances are referred to as mechanisms. This generic
term is not to be confused with the analytical instrument considered here,
which is located in the field of theory and praxis of nonviolent civil resistance.

the target group reacts to a campaign fought with nonviolent methods by adopting the goals of the nonviolent protagonists. That is, the opponents' belief systems are "converted." Conversion is still widely misperceived as the principal way in which nonviolent action brings about alterations—with the Vykom struggle erroneously corroborating this mechanism in the international literature—but, in fact, it is exceedingly rare. The second mechanism, *accommodation*, or what Lakey calls "persuasion," has historically occurred most frequently, with the target group choosing to yield to demands and adjust to the new conditions produced by the nonviolent challengers, though without necessarily changing positions on the underlying issues. The third mechanism, *nonviolent coercion*, transpires when members of the target group remain entrenched, their policies unchanged, but can no longer run their system without the cooperation of the nonviolent protagonists. In other words, their structure will not work without support from the challengers. Internal divisions may erupt among the adversary's power centers, which can happen without its will or consent. The opponent may retain control of the arrangements of power and the capability to use them, even as the capacity to contain the resisters wanes. The fourth mechanism, *nonviolent disintegration*, refers to bringing about the collapse of the opponent's power system. It, too, is uncommon.[14]

Conversion can occur through reasoning, presentation of arguments, or consequent to changes in the attitudes, beliefs, emotions, or moral and ethical outlook of the target group. The probability of conversion increases with lessening social distance between the oppressor and the oppressed. When, however, the opponent views the nonviolent challengers as being outside their moral order or of inferior status, the target of the action is more liable to feel indifference. Accordingly, social distances originating in caste, ethnicity, gender, language, race, or religion may allow dehumanizing ideologies to decrease the likelihood of conversion. In addition, cultural, social, and physical distances or poor communication between the oppressors and the oppressed may hinder conversion.

[14] Gene Sharp, *The Dynamics of Nonviolent Action*, vol. 3 of *The Politics of Nonviolent Action* (Boston: Porter Sargent, Inc., 1973), 707–68; Sharp, *Waging Nonviolent Struggle: 20th Century Practice and 21st Century Potential* (Boston: Porter Sargent, Inc., 2005). See Appendix II for a distillation of the mechanisms.

Beyond India, seeking to systematize outcomes that can be adopted and adapted for widely varying conflicts, the "mechanisms of change" were incorporated into scholarship, research, teaching, and training on how nonviolent action works and how it can be directed. Using Lakey's analyses in *The Politics of Nonviolent Action*, Sharp added to it in *From Dictatorship to Democracy: A Conceptual Framework for Liberation* (1994), originally prepared for activists in Burma's prodemocracy movement.[15] In *Dictatorship to Democracy*, and in a subsequent work, *Waging Nonviolent Struggle*, Sharp describes the mechanisms of change as four ways to achieve success.[16] In other words, depending on the specific goal, nonviolent action can aim to convert (conversion), persuade (accommodation), coerce (nonviolent coercion), or politically paralyze (disintegration) an opponent. A combination of mechanisms can be sought. It is sometimes necessary to adjust one's plan or goal in the midst of struggle, perhaps aspiring for conversion, but settling for accommodation. The mechanisms of change are not weighted equally. Nonviolent struggles are able to project vastly more potent pressure than anything suggested by conversion and accommodation. The potency of massive noncooperation manifested in, for example, strikes and civil disobedience can so alter social and political conditions, particularly the ability to wield power and effect decisions, that a ruler's ability to command the economic, social, political, parliamentary, and even security procedures of government and society at large is in actuality dissolved or collapses.

The fundamental error going back many decades in interpreting the Vykom struggle as a success of conversion may have prejudiced the perceived validity and employment of nonviolent action globally, if individuals and groups have turned away from the option of civil resistance because of a mistaken perception that they must be able to change and convert the hearts and minds of their opponents. The misconstrued

---

[15] Gene Sharp, *From Dictatorship to Democracy: A Conceptual Framework for Liberation*, monograph, 3rd ed. (Boston: Albert Einstein Institution, 2008). Also see Sharp, *There Are Realistic Alternatives*, monograph (Boston: Albert Einstein Institution, 2003), 13–14. Available at http://www.aeinstein.org/wp-content/uploads/2013/09/TARA.pdf (accessed January 30, 2014).

[16] Sharp, *Waging Nonviolent Struggle*, 45–6.

perception of conversion as a probable result from a nonviolent mobilization may also have been imputed as something that must be inspired by religious faith, belief in pacifism, or rejection of the use of violence, based on moral scruples or as an absolute creed. Academic or training programs that taught the mechanisms of change as a tool for planning strategy or making evaluations—to the extent that they drew on analysis of what had happened in Vykom—may have overemphasized persuasion and conversion as achievable states of being in realizing social and political change. The first mechanism is not always an appropriate aim. Vastly more is often required for whatever goal has been set. When conflict is regarded as a clash of contradictory interests, conversion of the target group's attitudes or beliefs should not even be contemplated. Aiming for other mechanisms of change would be more plausible, in which the purpose of mobilization would be to reduce the adversary's choices, create dilemmas, constrain its options, or weaken its power in order to ultimately produce alterations.

One possible explanation for misinterpretations in the published works of Gregg, Shridharani, and Bondurant is that although based on fieldwork in India, the authors were informed by sources who did not themselves understand the facts, but who may have heard Gandhi's preferred narrative. In 1934, when Gregg's first account reached the world beyond India, the fifty-year rule precluding release of British governmental records had not been reached. Under the regulations for review and declassification of official British documents, these authors would not have had access to British records from the 1920s for another fifty years, until 1997. (After World War II, classification was limited to 30 years.) Furthermore, they were at work before official archives in the capital of Travancore were opened to researchers. This meant that lionized accounts of Vykom, particularly by Gregg, Shridharani, and Bondurant, were influential with Western readers eager to learn from the Indian freedom struggles and comprehend Gandhi's strategic thinking.

Sharp's 1973 *Politics of Nonviolent Action* (The Trilogy) relied on available authors and would become the most influential single work in the twentieth century in the spread of ideas about nonviolent action worldwide. Both analytical and descriptive, it is based on historical research and accepted political theory. Its three volumes reached a world awash with ideological justifications for guerrilla warfare and armed national liberation insurrections—often Soviet- or

Chinese-inspired rationalizations for violent revolution and armed struggle—and so, in some ways, it did not receive the recognition it warranted in the 1970s. Its staying power since has more than compensated; it represented a quantitative and qualitative leap in knowledge on the neglected worldwide history of nonviolent struggle. Yet Sharp's reach also meant that although it forms only a small part of the Trilogy's 902 pages, still wider exposure was secondarily granted to Gregg and Shridharani's beguiling but mistaken interpretations of Vykom through his description, which relied on their accounts. Social scientist Brian Martin in 2005 stated, "Sharp is relentlessly thorough, most distinctively so in his epic book, *The Politics of Nonviolent Action*. . . . Sharp has had more influence on social activists than any other living theorist."[17] Paradoxically this factor may help to explain how a misinterpretation settled into a nook in the international study and practice of nonviolent resistance that Vykom was solved by the conversion of the upper castes. This overstated idea has reposed complacently and unchallenged until now, skewing reports of this particular historical struggle as well as affecting the global comprehension of the mechanisms of change in using nonviolent sanctions.

[17] Brian Martin, "Researching Nonviolent Action: Past Themes and Future Possibilities," *Peace and Change* 30, no. 2 (April 2005): 252–3.

8 An Historic Campaign Holds Contemporary Lessons

Civil resistance did not hold the capacity to make British rule impossible, although it may have sped its demise. In particular moments it posed serious contestations to the capacity of the Raj and its moral standing. More often, satyagraha slowed and rendered imperial governance arduous by, for example, pressuring village leaders to withdraw their cooperation, attacking key revenue sources, and filling prisons with agreeable civil disobedients. Britain could no longer uphold a far-reaching empire. The European imperial powers lost their ability to control global empires, to be replaced in some ways by the United States, and, to a lesser extent, the Soviet Union. With the end of World War II, Britain would essentially be driven to grant independence.

Gandhi's contribution to his nation and the world was nonetheless momentous, irrespective of quantifiable successes as well as failures. In important ways, he prepared India for self-rule, at least in a conventional sense. Gandhi's technique of nonviolent struggle, having greatly matured from its earliest developments in South Africa, proved its ability to unify a significant proportion of the population in exerting political pressures and forms of resistance. He had the perspicacity to see the training of an entire people in noncooperation as de facto training for self-rule.[1] The number jailed in his 1930–4 civil disobedience

---

[1] Asha Rani, *Gandhian Non-Violence and India's Freedom Struggle* (New Delhi: Shree Publishing House, 1981), 321.

campaigns is uncertain, but in the 1930 Salt Satyagraha, 60,000 suffered various terms of imprisonment.[2] Of these, 17,000 were women.[3] Judith Brown presents information for eleven states showing 71,041 men and 3,630 women, or a total of 74, 671 convictions, for the 1932–3 civil disobedience convictions alone.[4]

More likely, Gandhi's most significant contributions were changes in the ways that Indians thought of and felt about themselves. Onlookers of nonviolent mobilizations often gaze in wonderment, rendered speechless by the participants' apparent absence of fear. Nehru reveals with moving fluency, soon after becoming prime minister, the effect that Gandhi had on the Indian people:

> And then Gandhi came. He was like a powerful current of fresh air that makes us stretch ourselves and take deep breaths, like a beam of light that pierced the darkness and removed the scales from our eyes, like a whirl-wind that that upset many things but most of all the working of people's minds. He did not descend from the top; he seemed to emerge from the millions of India, speaking their language and incessantly drawing attention to them and their appalling condition. . . .
>
> . . . The essence of his teaching was fearlessness and truth and action allied to these, always keeping the welfare of the masses in view. . . . But the

---

[2] Dennis Dalton, *Mahatma Gandhi: Nonviolent Power in Action* (New York: Columbia University Press, 2012), 115. Dalton says this is a government estimate.

[3] Krishnalal Shridharani, *War without Violence* (Bombay: Bharatiya Vidya Bhavan, 1962), 126. Regarding the Salt March, Gandhi stated, "The Dandi March was entirely my conception. . . . I had to think in terms of millions. . . . [I]t was an almost magical awakening. Where in history shall we find parallels of the cool courage that our women displayed in such large numbers?" Gandhi, "An Interesting Discourse" (*Harijan*, August 25, 1940), in Gandhi, *Non-violence in Peace and War*, vol. 1 (hereafter *NPW* [1]), ed. Desai (1948), 326.

[4] Judith M. Brown, *Gandhi and Civil Disobedience: The Mahatma in Indian Politics, 1928–34* (Cambridge: Cambridge University Press, 1977), Table 8, 284–6. She also notes, "The peak figure of civil disobedience convicts actually in jail was 32,458 in April 1932" (p. 286n). On extensive mobilization by women, see Brown, *Gandhi and Civil Disobedience*, 136, 146, 291–2. On the "unexpected" participation of women, Dalton cites a government report, "India in 1930–31: A Statement Prepared for Presentation to Parliament," Government of India Central Publishing Branch, Calcutta, 1932, 73. Dalton, *Mahatma Gandhi*, 118, 255n103.

dominant impulse in India under British rule was that of fear, pervasive, oppressive, strangling fear; fear of the army, the police, the widespread secret service; fear of the official class; fear of laws meant to suppress, and of prison; fear of the landlord's agent; fear of the moneylender; fear of unemployment and starvation, which were always on the threshold. It was against this all-pervading fear that Gandhi's quiet and determined voice was raised: Be not afraid. . . . So, suddenly, as it were, that black pall of fear was lifted from the people's shoulders, not wholly, of course, but to an amazing degree. As fear is close companion to falsehood, so truth follows fearlessness. . . . [A] sea change was visible as the need for false-hood and furtive behavior lessened. It was a psychological change. . . . There was that psychological reaction also, a feeling of shame at our long submission to an alien rule that had degraded and humiliated us, and a desire to submit no longer, whatever the consequences might be.[5]

Meanwhile, on the other side of the globe, hunger for knowledge about the Indian struggles was growing in African American communities, which had themselves for generations felt fear and dread. By the 1920s, they were seeing in their own experiences of collective exclusion a form of casteism and were coming to believe that Gandhian strategies of resistance to oppression might be applicable in their situation.

African Americans Learn Gandhian Nonviolent Struggle

Reports about the struggles under way in India, including the battle against untouchability, were being directly dispatched to the black community in the United States through several avenues of communication. Historian Sudarshan Kapur shows that from 1919 to 1955, a significant interchange took place between individual African Americans and participants in the Indian independence struggles, well before the emergence of Martin Luther King Jr. For nearly four decades, ideas and thinking traveled 12,000 miles from the subcontinent in a great historical interaction that created links between two freedom movements, one in full throttle and the other incipient. Kapur's research in the morgues of twelve black-owned newspapers and journals in the United States for the period prior to 1955 discloses avid reporting on events and

[5] Jawaharlal Nehru, *The Discovery of India* (London: Meridian Books Limited, 1951), 334–5.

resistance actions in India that might apply in the U.S. context and on the increasing familiarity of the black community with the measures being utilized in India.

Starting in the 1930s, a time of extended ocean voyages, a steady stream of leaders from the U.S. black community was traveling to India before the onset of World War II. The voyagers held pivotal positions as heads of universities or seminaries, university professors, and clergy with influential congregations. In India, they learned about the Gandhian theories and methods directly, through personal encounters, from individuals who had contributed to that country's struggles. Returning to the United States, this respected elite spread word about the logic and meaning of what they had encountered by giving lectures, writing essays and articles, preaching sermons, and debating publically. They employed news coverage and networks of friendships that spanned church, academia, and social service organizations, while passing from hand to hand the few books available on Gandhi's rationale and strategies. Pockets of the black community became intensely aware of what was happening in India, indicating how oftentimes knowledge is transmitted about nonviolent action. Even today, it is frequently passed literally person to person. In Kapur's assessment, "Gandhi's very strong stand against untouchability was one of the key reasons why so many African Americans were drawn to him."[6]

On February 21, 1936, near Bardoli, Gujarat, a small group of black educators and clergy met for three hours with Gandhi under a mango tree.[7] Gandhi asked numerous questions. One of those present, Edward G. Carroll, later recalled, "Gandhi wanted to know why we hadn't tried civil disobedience. He asked why all the black people in America didn't stay home from work on a certain day."[8] Upon returning home, the

---

[6] Sudarshan Kapur, *Raising Up a Prophet: The African-American Encounter with Gandhi* (Boston: Beacon Press, 1992), 60.

[7] Kapur, *Raising Up a Prophet*, 87–8. Also see Gandhi, "Interview to American Negro Delegation," February 21, 1936, *Harijan* (March 14, 1936), in *Collected Works of Mahatma Gandhi* (hereafter *CWMG*), 68: 234–8.

[8] John Habner, "Faith, Hope and Bishop Carroll," *Boston Phoenix*, May 13, 1980, 10, as cited in Mary King, *Mahatma Gandhi and Martin Luther King Jr: The Power of Nonviolent Action*, 2nd ed. (New Delhi: Indian Council for Cultural Relations and Mehta Publishers, 2002), 179 n10. Carroll was a Methodist bishop from the Baltimore–Washington area.

leaders did not enact Gandhi's recommendation for a massive, national stay-at-home action. Yet they would become part of a broader, decade-long process of transmitting knowledge from India to the U.S. black community such that they were able to enlarge the scope for the success of the Montgomery bus boycott during 1955–6.

In retrospect it is possible to see that a diffuse black leadership was preparing for the emergence of Martin Luther King Jr, as expressed in the phrase "raising up a prophet." As these leaders traveled to India, they forged personal bonds with individuals working alongside Gandhi, and prominent Indians visited the United States to lecture and create connections with the nascent civil rights movement. Benjamin Mays, some ten years after meeting with Gandhi at Wardha, in India in 1936, would in his regular chapel lectures as president of Atlanta's Morehouse College open the eyes of a seventeen-year-old student named Martin Luther King Jr.[9]

Krishnalal Shridharani, discussed in Chapter 6, was among the Indians who lectured in the United States. During the 1940s, his *War without Violence* (1939) was eagerly studied by African American figures and passed around hand to hand. A. Philip Randolph of the Brotherhood of Sleeping Car Porters and James L. Farmer, who helped to found the Congress of Racial Equality (CORE), are among those who studied the volume. Farmer consulted with Shridharani, then at Columbia University, and explicitly premised CORE on what he learned from Shridharani. "In this book," Farmer later said, "Shridharani had outlined Gandhi's steps of investigation, negotiation, publicity, and then demonstration. . . . [W]e adopted these steps as our method of action."[10] As early as 1942, CORE began initiating sit-ins and freedom rides by the black community, two potent methods that would be revived and extensively used

[9] An account of Mays's meeting with Gandhi, by Mahadev Haribhai Desai, appears in *Harijan*, March 20, 1937; *vide* Gandhi, "Interview to Prof. Mays," dated "before January 10, 1937," 70: 261–4. King had initially been named Michael Luther King Jr, but a more prophetic name was bestowed on him at age six, when his father changed his name.

[10] In 1941, Farmer, then with the pacifist organization the Fellowship of Reconciliation (FOR), consulted with Shridharani, whose personal memories of the Salt March motivated him and others at FOR. James Farmer, prelude, "On Cracking White City," in Howell Raines, *My Soul Is Rested: Movement Days in the Deep South Remembered* (New York: G. P. Putnam's Sons, 1977), 28.

during the 1960s civil rights movement. For his part, Shridharani formed key working relations between Indian and U.S. organizers through his participation in several campaigns for racial justice while in the United States, including CORE's actions in the 1940s.[11]

Soon after Rosa Parks and the black Women's Political Council in Montgomery had begun the bus boycott against the city's racially segregated bus system in Alabama on December 1, 1955, experienced professional trainers arrived in town. They began intensive tutoring in nonviolent action of King, the new pastor of the Dexter Avenue Baptist Church, who, despite his reluctance to become involved in political action, had been enlisted to lead the Montgomery Improvement Association. Bayard Rustin, a black socialist and seasoned professional affiliated with the War Resisters League (WRL) and FOR, arrived on February 21, 1956. FOR asked a veteran organizer, Glenn E. Smiley, to go to Montgomery and explore whether FOR could be of help.[12] By February 27, Smiley, a white Texas-born Methodist minister, had relocated. Sitting with King nightly in his Montgomery parsonage, first Rustin and then Smiley coached him on the Indian struggles, plying him with books and interrogating him on the readings. Smiley noticed that King used "almost entirely" the nineteenth-century term "passive resistance" found wanting by Gandhi.[13] He recollected that King asked him to "teach him everything [Smiley] knew about nonviolence, since by his own admission he had only been casually acquainted with Gandhi and his methods."[14] Eventually Rustin—who had become a friend of Shridharani's, would visit India before the decade was out, and subsequently work for King full time—introduced the young pastor to War without Violence. King also studied Gandhi's autobiography,

[11] Kapur, Raising Up a Prophet, 8.

[12] Paul R. Dekar, "Forging Bonds and Obligations: The Fellowship of Reconciliation, Nonviolence, and Martin Luther King, Jr," in "In an Inescapable Network of Mutuality": Martin Luther King, Jr. and the Globalization of an Ethical Ideal, eds. Lewis V. Baldwin and Paul R. Dekar (Eugene, Oregon: Cascade Books, 2013), 124.

[13] David J. Garrow, Bearing the Cross: Martin Luther King, Jr., and the Southern Christian Leadership Conference (New York: William Morrow, 1986), 72.

[14] Glenn Smiley, Nonviolence: The Gentle Persuader (Nyack, New York: Fellowship of Reconciliation, 1991), 5, as cited in King, Mahatma Gandhi and Martin Luther King Jr, 126.

translated into English in 1940, and Gregg's *Psychology and Strategy of Gandhi's Nonviolent Resistance* (1929) and *Power of Nonviolence* (1934).[15]

On December 5, 1955, at the Holt Street Baptist Church in Montgomery, King convened the first major mass meeting after the launch of the boycott of the capital city's racially segregated bus system. He said to those assembled:

> We are not here advocating violence. There will be no crosses burned at any bus stops in Montgomery. There will be no white persons pulled out of their homes and taken on some distant road and murdered. There will be nobody among us who will stand up and defy the Constitution of this nation. . . . Our method will be that of persuasion, not coercion.[16]

Within Montgomery's black community, these allusions conjured the vigilante and terror groups that had long oppressed African American neighborhoods and rural hamlets in the South, including by burning crosses. King chose to repudiate violent retaliation in a way that had exact meaning. The world would soon through him hear more of Gandhi's terminology of nonviolent action. At the December 5 meeting, King did not use the terms "nonviolence" or "nonviolent action." As the boycott cohered into a disciplined and unified campaign, and his nightly tutorials accelerated, however, King's wording altered. Among his most transcendent contributions is his adoption several weeks into the Montgomery boycott of the lexicon of nonviolent civil resistance as coined by Gandhi. By February 1956, King had established the framework for what would ultimately become the U.S. civil rights movement, designating it "nonviolent."

City authorities and journalists estimated that 90 percent of Montgomery's black populace of 50,000 refused to ride the buses at the height of the boycott, but this is probably an underestimation. Bus stops were vacant. One man rode a mule to work, another his horse-drawn cart. Most walked to their jobs. The faultlessly sustained unanimity was aided by an efficient carpool of drivers, donated and private cars, and dispatch stations for transportation. Success came after 381 days. On June 13,

---

[15] Richard B. Gregg, *The Psychology and Strategy of Gandhi's Nonviolent Resistance*, ed. Charles A. Baker (Madras: S. Ganesan, 1929; repr., New York: Garland Publishing, Inc., 1972); Gregg, *The Power of Nonviolence*, 2nd rev. ed. (New York: Schocken Books, 1966; orig. 1934).

[16] As cited in Dalton, *Mahatma Gandhi*, 180.

a three-judge district court ruled, two to one, in the case of Browder v. Gayle that segregation on Montgomery's buses was unconstitutional. Following appeals by Alabama officials, the lower court's ruling was upheld by the Supreme Court on December 17, 1956, in a landmark decision.

King was the individual chiefly responsible for presenting the technique of nonviolent resistance in understandable and graspable terms in the United States. He was able, despite considerable ambivalence in the black community, to persuade innumerable African Americans that ideas and methods from India could be effective for attacking the structures of white racial supremacy in their own country. King's study of Shridharani's book, from which he adopted Gandhi's phraseology verbatim (often without attribution), makes it one of the critical works in the sharing of knowledge about the technique of civil resistance from India to the United States. Smiley in 1989 called Shridharani's work "a tiny pebble . . . thrown into the pond," whose "resulting ripples and waves have not . . . reached the distant shores of our planet."[17] After King's death, Smiley hand-carried King's writings to Latin America, sharing them with groups probing the use of nonviolent action. With the keen interest accompanying the U.S. civil rights movement, its application of concrete forms of nonviolent action adopted from India began to spread to continents beyond. In retrospect, Gandhi had foreseen the prospect of the U.S. black community's awakening to civil resistance when he ended his February 1936 meeting near Bardoli, saying that "it may be through the Negroes that the unadulterated message of nonviolence will be delivered to the world."[18]

Montgomery's boycott had an impact exponentially larger than its municipal setting. As a result of its success, black observers across the South who had followed the campaign came to believe that nonviolent direct action could work. In Nashville, for example, a group of ministers and laity concluded that what had happened in Montgomery was the most significant advance that had occurred for African Americans since the U.S. Civil War and 1863 Emancipation Proclamation to free the slaves, and that it must be repeated. They determined that it should be done again in Nashville, then elsewhere, and yet again.[19]

[17]   Glenn Smiley, "A Pebble Thrown into the Pond," *Fellowship*, June 1989, 8.

[18]   Gandhi, "American Negro Delegation," March 14, 1936, in *CWMG*, 68: 237–8.

[19]   James M. Lawson Jr, communication (May 3, 2013).

In 1957, King brought south the Reverend James M. Lawson Jr, a black Methodist minister who had spent three years teaching at Hislop College in Nagpur in Maharashtra, India, now affiliated with Nagpur University. While there, Lawson traveled to meet individuals who had worked with Gandhi in various satyagrahas, gaining knowledge from firsthand participants as he visited sites of struggles. He met with Nehru more than once. Upon his return to the United States, Lawson encountered King at Oberlin College, Ohio, where he was studying and King was speaking. Both were twenty-eight years of age. King exclaimed, "Don't wait! Come now! You're badly needed. We don't have anyone like you!"[20] Lawson became FOR's representative in Nashville, where in 1959 he began introducing the local clergy and student leaders to the theories and methods he had studied in India. On February 1, 1960, in Greensboro, North Carolina, four black students began to sit at a "whites only" lunch counter, requesting service, and remained in position if refused. When asked to leave, they would stay. Although they were unaware of the term, their "sit-in" was among the most disruptive nonviolent methods.

Unknown until after the start of the Greensboro sit-ins, students in other places were also preparing themselves for action. The Nashville Christian Leadership Conference, the first affiliate of the Southern Christian Leadership Conference (SCLC), established in 1957 by King after success in Montgomery, had in winter 1958 and spring 1959 commenced major nonviolent direct action targeted at discrimination in downtown Nashville restaurants and stores. Throughout autumn 1959, Lawson led weekly Monday-evening sessions, schooling participants in a profound interpretation of what it means to take nonviolent action and guiding them in understanding strategy and discipline. He systematically analyzed the Gandhian theories and techniques in which he had immersed himself at Nagpur. The group, encouraged by local clergy, launched several test cases, including small sit-ins for practice and role-playing. Lawson's workshops lasted for several months before the news broke from Greensboro. Upon receiving a telephone call from North Carolina notifying him of events there, seventy-five Nashville students moved to action. Within two months, student sit-ins blazed across the Southland (except for Mississippi), with thousands of

---

[20] Lawson, interview, Los Angeles, February 27, 1996; King, *Mahatma Gandhi and Martin Luther King Jr*, 132.

students engaged in nearly seventy-five cities, as if by spontaneous combustion.[21] Newspapers reporting sit-ins in distant cities created an impression of ubiquity and harmonization.

Eventually in more than a hundred southern cities, discrete student sit-in campaigns against segregated lunch counters became the prows for local struggles of nonviolent resistance. As understanding and knowledge was shared of applicable Gandhian insights, those sitting in resolutely faced burning cigarettes ground into their arms; ketchup and mustard poured on their heads; chewing gum stuck in their hair; spittle, insults, and punches hurled at them; and being knocked off stools. Remaining consciously restrained, many went limp in total noncooperation when arrested by police.

By the end of 1960, approximately 70,000 young people, primarily blacks, had sat in, along with an increasing number of whites. Some 3,600 of them had gone to jail. Speedily but silently, the signs demarcating "Whites Only" started to come down, intentionally without news conferences or announcements. This was a deliberate tactic. King had explained in Montgomery, "We are out to defeat injustice and not white persons who may happen to be unjust."[22] Having internalized Gandhi's reasoning on the connection between means and ends, King also adopted his separation of the antagonist from the antagonism as a matter of moral scruples, practicality, and strategy to enhance the possibility for reconciliation. Each stride, King believed, should reveal the goal and the future community envisioned. Worrying that success might lead to gloating, as early as 1957, he had warned against developing an attitude of triumphalism: "We must ... avoid the temptation of being victimized with a psychology of victors."[23]

King was not involved in the sit-ins, but he articulated support for them. As he, his advisers, and allies had hoped, a movement was

[21] See "Special Report: The Student Protest Movement," winter 1960, tech. rept. no. SRC–13, Atlanta, Southern Regional Council, 1960.

[22] King Jr., "Nonviolence and Racial Justice," *Christian Century*, February 6, 1957, as cited in King, *Mahatma Gandhi and Martin Luther King Jr*, 248.

[23] King Jr., "Give Us the Ballot—We Will Transform the South," in *A Testament of Hope: The Essential Writings and Speeches of Martin Luther King, Jr.*, ed. James Melvin Washington (San Francisco: Harper, 1991), 200.

cohering and becoming a mass phenomenon. The sit-ins' youthful leaders demonstrated that both students and nonviolent direct action could be effective. Lawson's impact through the Nashville workshops prepared the activists who would become the largest, most disciplined, and influential contingent of the 1960 student sit-in movement, which would by April 1960 give rise to the Student Nonviolent Coordinating Committee (SNCC, pronounced snick), the student wing of the civil rights movement.[24] Based in Atlanta, it was initially formed to coordinate among the leaders of disparate sit-in campaigns, which provided a mass base and Southwide reach, materially weaving the web of a regional movement. The Nashville component was largely responsible for SNCC's nonviolent militancy. Moreover, at the behest of King, Lawson ran workshops for each meeting of the SCLC, of which King was president until his death. Hence, the two main southern civil rights organizations of the 1960s explicitly benefited from Lawson's three years of firsthand exposure to Gandhian thinking and the Indian experience, whereas CORE, the key northern association, had been shaped by Farmer on the basis of his personal contact with Shridharani and his analyses of Gandhi.

Knowledge from India reached secluded, rural hamlets in the Deep South through FOR and WRL personnel, along with staff from the aforesaid civil rights organizations—also taught by Lawson, Rustin, or Smiley—training communities during nocturnal mass meetings held in churches. In this movement of movements, these professionals and the others that they had prepared helped the leaders of local resistance campaigns to grasp the logic of nonviolent action and especially the necessity for discipline. Such mass meetings occurred episodically, based on localized priorities, and precise training content was time and again selected from the Indian experience.

In typically twice-weekly mass meetings, local people participated in setting objectives, goals, and strategies, while readying themselves for beatings, arrests, prison, injuries, or worse, without retaliating in kind. What was simply called "the Movement" included the diverse and

---

[24] See Mary King, *Freedom Song: A Personal Story of the 1960s Civil Rights Movement* (New York: William Morrow and Company, 1987), 277–9. The author served on SNCC staff for four years in Atlanta and Jackson, and was herself taught by Lawson and Rustin.

differing priorities of local movements. The continuous, pinpointed process of training at the community level helps to explain how tens of thousands of isolated rural folk during the 1960s came to comprehend the use of nonviolent direct action and noncooperation in compelling county, state, and federal power structures to shift, beginning the process of bringing down racial barriers. That the U.S. civil rights movement unequivocally borrowed from the Indian struggles is evident in the way it analyzed power and consent, organized campaigns, stressed strategy, sequenced methods from persuasion to noncooperation to more disruptive measures, and emphasized communications and getting out the news.

King Travels to India

In 1959, King traveled to India for a study tour at the invitation of the Gandhi National Memorial Fund (Gandhi Smarak Nidhi).[25] The invitation read, "We expect you would be particularly interested to know how Gandhiji wrestled with the problem of untouchability in India and succeeded in showing the [way] out against the heaviest odds."[26] King, accompanied by his wife, Coretta Scott King, and the history professor Lawrence Reddick of Montgomery's Alabama State University, a King biographer, began his trip on February 10. For four weeks, they were the guests of Prime Minister Nehru. They met Chakravarti Rajagopalachari, encountered in Chapter 3; studied Gandhi with Pyarelal [Nayyar], personal secretary to Gandhi in his later years; and met Vinoba Bhave, social reformer and advocate for nonviolent action,

[25] Rustin served on an ad hoc committee that facilitated arrangements for the Kings to go to India and raised $4,000 from the Christopher Reynolds Foundation, New York. Harris L. Wofford also helped. The grant was administered by the American Friends [Quakers] Service Committee (AFSC). The invitation was proffered by the Gandhi National Memorial Fund, signed by G. Ramachandran and issued through diplomatic channels. Also see Martin Luther King Jr, "My Trip to the Land of Gandhi,"*Ebony*, July 1959, in *Testament of Hope*, 24–5.

[26] G. Ramachandran to King (letter), December 27, 1958, in Clayborne Carson, Susan Carson, Adrienne Clay, Virginia Shadron, and Kieran Taylor (eds), *Papers of Martin Luther King, Jr* (*Symbol of the Movement, January 1957–December 1958*), 4: 552–3 (Berkeley, Los Angeles, London: University of California Press).

the founder of the Bhoodan Yajna ("Land-Gift Movement"). Everywhere they went, Indians wanted to hear King speak. Coretta's professionalism as a concert singer made her solos as appealing as his lectures. Traveling by car, truck, rail, and plane, they went to New Delhi, Patna, Gaya, Burdwan, Shantiniketan (the school founded by Rabindranath Tagore), Calcutta, Madras (Chennai), Mahabalipuram, Gandhigram, Madurai and Gramdan villages (including to a Dalit community), Trivandrum (Kerala), Cape Comorin (Tamil Nadu), Bangalore (Karnataka), Bombay (Mumbai), Ahmedabad (Sabarmati ashram), and Kishingarh (Rajasthan). In Trivandrum and elsewhere, King pleaded for nonviolent applications to international disagreements and conflicts and voiced concerns about nuclear war.[27]

Intrigued to find that his skin color was an asset, his exposure to the struggles of non-Westerners led King to conclude that the "strongest bond of fraternity was the common cause of minority and colonial peoples in America, Africa and Asia struggling to throw off racialism and imperialism." He was surprised to learn that the Montgomery bus boycott was well known in India: "Indian publications perhaps gave a better continuity of our 381-day bus strike than did most of our papers in the United States. . . . [R]eporters . . . were scrupulously fair with us and in their editorials showed an amazing grasp of what was going on in America and other parts of the world." He judged that the "aftermath of hatred and bitterness that usually follows a violent campaign was found nowhere in India." He indicated that he had become more persuaded than ever of the validity of nonviolent resistance as a "potent weapon available to oppressed people in their struggle for freedom." The Gandhians "praised our experiment" in Montgomery, he said, using Gandhi's word *experiment*, viewing it as an example of possibilities for use in Western civilization. He concluded, "Nonviolent resistance *when planned* and *positive in action* can work effectively even under totalitarian regimes." Perceiving that India was at the time approximately one-third the size of the United States, with a population three times greater, he was attentive to the country's poverty, yet quick to say that India had "made greater progress in the fight against caste 'untouchability' than we have made . . . in our own country against

[27] "Notes from the Tour Diary of James Bristol" (New Delhi: Quaker Centre, dated June 10, 1959). Bristol was Director, Quaker Centre, New Delhi, and coordinated with the AFSC on in-country arrangements. Author's collection.

race segregation."[28] From reading his comments, King was given a blissful picture of how untouchability had been eradicated, or at least addressed, in India. As untouchabilty had been made illegal in India's constitution, few would want to incriminate themselves with him, and he was unable to view for himself the large numbers of caste Hindus in villages and towns alike who routinely discriminate against Dalits, something that has not abated to this day as anthropologists have observed. Pernicious forms of discrimination have a similar quality everywhere regardless of sociological classifications; in this respect there is a strong parallel between racism and casteism, often including pervasive denial.

King's party departed India on March 10, and soon after returning home, he preached what is now called the "untouchability sermon," at the Dexter Avenue Baptist Church. He described Gandhi to the congregation as being "able to mobilize and galvanize more people than, in his lifetime, than any other person in the history of this world [sic]," terming it a significant development in world history. With liberal storytelling license he told of the impact of Gandhi's 1932 fast unto death in Pune, claiming that as a result, priests in temples across India opened them to untouchables, while Brahmins were embraced by untouchables.[29] Obviously, efforts were made to persuade King that Gandhian actions had led to a widespread change of heart throughout India, resulting in this extravagant and unsubstantiated narrative.

Within four years, in 1963, King's "Letter from the Birmingham City Jail" would proffer a major justification for civil disobedience, which would subsequently move into the mainstream of political thought. His letter is permeated by the concept that cooperation must be withheld from unjust government, laws, or customs, a concept he first encountered while reading Thoreau at Morehouse College and was subsequently reinforced by studying Gandhi. Upon receiving the 1964 Nobel Peace Prize in Oslo, King asserted, "I venture to suggest [above all] . . . that . . . nonviolence become immediately a subject for study and for serious experimentation in every field of human conflict, by no means excluding relations between nations . . . which [ultimately] make war."

[28] King Jr., "My Trip to the Land of Gandhi," 24–9. Emphasis in original.

[29] Martin Luther King Jr., "Palm Sunday Sermon on Mohandas K. Gandhi," March 22, 1959, in *"In a Single Garment of Destiny": A Global Vision of Justice*, ed. Lewis V. Baldwin (Boston: Beacon Press, 2012), 90, 95–6.

Conclusion

Travancore had been known for a particular form of religious tolerance, due to the diversity of its religious traditions, with Christian, Jewish, and Muslim minorities living alongside the more prevalent Hindus. Throughout the centuries, its people had both professed and practiced a principle of accepting coexistence of many faiths. In contradiction, however, the state had also become known for some of the most extreme, religiously justified practices of severe exclusion and degradation in the modern period of human history. The story of how the people of Travancore changed this situation is one of epic proportions.

The 1924–5 Vykom satyagraha was a watershed in the political and social development of Travancore. There satyagraha had an initial test as a model action program for achieving social justice, notwithstanding its limits and the fact that Gandhi had to adjust it subsequently. Given the continuing influence of Gandhi's insights into the power of nonviolent action, the Vykom experiment with satyagraha, for all its vulnerabilities, was important for the development of the technique of nonviolent civil resistance. If anything, the trend is toward greater worldwide use of this method for fighting oppression, as more and more are unwilling to remain passive in the face of oppression and denial of rights. The Vykom struggle retained its nonviolent parameters throughout its twenty months' duration, despite the violence commissioned against it. Vykom foretold the future, in the sense of disclosing

an increasing turn to popular mobilization. Whether the Vykom settlement was a "bedrock of freedom," as Gandhi claimed in Alleppey, it
made the elimination of untouchability and issue of temple entry a
national concern, for the first time divulging the depth and extent of the
determination of a Hindu theocracy to repress, based on perceptions of
purity.

Strong democratic yearning is revealed in this chronicle as the
Ezhavas and those sympathetic to their strivings confronted the
hereditary powers of the raja. The respect, legitimacy, and traditional
esteem bestowed by the people of Travancore on the dynastic royal
house were transposed by them, as they flexed a democratic spirit, of
which the emergence of independent caste associations played a
major role. Although it took time, the palace eventually responded, in
1936, when, nearly twelve years after the Vykom struggle ended, the
new maharaja of Travancore and his *dewan* issued the temple-entry
proclamation. Due to the satyagraha, untouchability ceased to be a
source of acute misery in what is now Kerala, more than a decade
before it was constitutionally ended by free India. Ambedkar would
pilot India's constitution through the Constituent Assembly, with
Article 17 abolishing untouchability. Article 23 declared illegal hard
labor and forms of often hereditary servitude to which Dalits were
often subjected.

Gandhi's quest for social change through appealing to the con-
sciences of the upper castes was not achieved, notwithstanding the exuberant reports that reached the rest of the world. New ideas, processes,
methods, secularization, and even technology would weaken perceptions of "pollution" and potentiate the ability of caste associations to
seek other forms of honor, privilege, and social change. Rather, Gandhi's
bid "to march with the times," along with the self-transformation led
by caste associations and pressure exerted by upper-caste sympathizers,
would over time and in a circuitous way bring about material alterations to the social realities of Travancore.

Despite its technical shortcomings, blunders, leadership deficits,
and failure to exploit all of the opportunities available, the Vykom satyagraha brought untouchability, unapproachability, and unseeability to
the forefront of political issues in India. Several leaders of the satyagraha gained increased notoriety and prestige, such as the Ezhava leader

N. Kumaran, who went on to become a judge. The Ezhavas would become one of present-day Kerala's five main societal groups, joining the Harijans, Nairs, Christians, and Muslims.

It was necessary to revisit Vykom, in part, because of poor historical analysis, but also because Gandhi's own sometimes inexplicable and idiosyncratic attributes can impede interpretation. The role of Gandhi has thus been justifiably criticized, but undoubtedly he and the Congress added scale, scope, and clout to the effort. Heft from the foremost political organization in India helped to focus national and international consideration on the plight of the untouchables. It is more than conjecture to say that without the patronage of the Congress, the satyagraha would have been diminished to a merely local, if not an unheard-of, event in the history of modern India. Even with erroneous interpretations of what happened at Vykom during 1924–5 as the basis for the first mechanism of change—a utensil within the growing international theory on nonviolent civil resistance—this chronicle suggests that Vykom can continue to be a source of real-life lessons in addressing deep political, social, and cultural inequities—albeit what not to do.

Lessons Shared across Time and Place

In chronicling the Vykom encounter for purposes of expanding the understanding of nonviolent action, this case study has pursued an inquiry to present a supportable narrative of its 604 days. It illustrates dangers and impediments that have been regularly faced in nonviolent struggles. Without wishing to engage in "presentism" or filter an interpretation of the occurrences of the past through the thinking of today, it is possible to discern and learn from some of Vykom's quandaries.

Dilemmas of leadership are widespread, if not typical, in nonviolent movements. Sacrificing the key leaders to imprisonment, based upon an ill-formed idea that their suffering behind bars would appeal and change attitudes, was specious. It was a grave misstep in the Vykom campaign to suppose that their early imprisonment would penetrate the opposition of the privileged, cut through the density of Brahmin ideology, and overcome the maharaja's support for their justifications.

It created a state of vulnerability that weakened the movement and from which it was never to regain strength.

Inadequate or overly optimistic planning can undermine any movement. This is a recurrent error of groups seeking change through nonviolent struggle. The stagnation of the Vykom campaign in its early stages reinforces the need to prepare properly.

Movements must sometimes operate clandestinely and, therefore, intentionally destroy their internal materials. Generally, however, clear explanations of the purpose and goal of the mobilization are essential for recruitment and fundamental to the opponent understanding the sought-after change.

Social movements are not amenable to containment and often have a transformational effect in opening political space for others. One normally cannot predict their continuing impact. Gandhi's stipulations halted the evolution of Vykom into a broader democratic mobilization and constrained what the erstwhile untouchables could do for themselves.

The building of capacity at the local level and preparing for the future is an outcome from almost any campaign of civil resistance that merits contemplation, if not planning. Gandhi's overriding of the local leaders may have given national echo to the Vykom satyagraha, but it compromised the possibilities for vicinal direction. Vykom was not bereft of insights from local leaders, who also possessed imagination and experience.

Religiously justified opprobrium, especially when correlated with political power, can occasionally be targeted, or religious custodians may sometimes be enlisted to help the nonviolent protagonists. Along with other deeply powerful cultural, symbolic, and societal forces, religion can be a constructive or destructive factor in civil resistance, historically playing a part in its evolution as a method for securing social justice and political change. In the case of Vykom, the Travancore government had not in the past hesitated to apply its power for socially and religiously connected reforms, yet regarding the opening of temple roads to the untouchables, it selectively maintained a position of adamantine opposition, until the Maharaja Sri Mulam Thirunal died.

Errors in strategy are exceedingly common. In the case of Vykom, there was no exploitation of its power asymmetries and contradictions.

Whether more might have been done to cause splits or divisions, encourage defections from among the Nambudiris, or to break the ranks of the temple authorities and their supporters has been lost.

Nonviolent struggles often end in jaggedly abrupt dissolutions, which unravel due to insufficient clarity of goals, failure to anticipate fatigue and burnout, and downfalls in planning transitions. Although the conclusion of the Vykom struggle has been made clearer by this case study, after 604 days of diligence and discipline, the volunteers were in some ways back where they started. Genuine positive effects of their satyagraha would not become tangible until 1936.

The trajectory to be followed by a capacitating idea is impossible to predict. Observing Indians on the subcontinent building national focus on untouchability, prodded by Vykom, another people far away traveled to India looking for knowledge on how to change what they regarded as comparable to a caste system. African Americans would adopt critical elements of the theories and methods of nonviolent struggle, developed and experimented with by Gandhi, in their own quest for full democratic participation. With momentum from the U.S. civil rights movement, knowledge and awareness from India would be amplified and cross the world, encouraging waves of decolonizing movements to fight with primarily nonviolent methods to end European imperialism. The diffusion of knowledge about the technique of civil resistance from India to the United States would reverberate to the entire globe.

Gandhi and Beyond

Gandhi was center stage in the most important drama in the history of the twentieth century, the story of how people living under imperialism, institutionalized racism, and systematized exclusions of caste, gender, and creed were able to achieve basic human and civil rights without bloodshed. This was not mere absence of violence. Gandhi deserves the credit for articulating a method of projecting collective group action for manifesting social power that an unarmed people could use, inverting it to make the proscription of violence intentional. The anti-colonial movements that drew methods and thinking from Gandhi would culminate in the 1950s and 1960s, and the strategies and tactics that they adopted and refined have ricocheted and influenced subsequent social justice struggles across the world, into the twenty-first century. Gandhi was the most significant leader of his century, unique among leaders of mass popular movements, because his wielding of power was more than testamentary. He was the first non-Western figure of the modern era to capture worldwide attention.

Gandhi combined principled creedal nonviolence with shrewd methods, techniques, and strategies of resistance; a broad program for social reconstruction; and a process vastly more potent and effective than individual witness for attacking social ills through mass enlistment and exertion of social power. In so doing, he formulated an original method of action and the first comprehensive theory and praxis of nonviolent struggle. Creating a singular mode of political struggle in which from 1906 to 1948 his ideas were effectuated—thought transformed into action—Gandhi was able to galvanize millions for a sequence of historical interventions, which, with intentional discipline, rejected violent means for a number of reasons. With a basic view of civil resistance as a practical alternative to violence that all people could use, his political thought on noncooperation and the power held by the governed are rudimentary for comprehension of the field. He originated and honed a new, living political language for the English-speaking world and today's movements, coining or appropriating terms of enduring currency like *civil disobedience, civil resistance, noncooperation, nonviolence, nonviolent conflict, nonviolent methods, nonviolent revolution, sanctions, techniques of struggle,* and *transformation of conflict.* Pioneering in developing indispensable organizational and communications instruments for building mass mobilizations, he showed how it is possible to fight concurrently for fundamental justice in moral, political, social, religious, economic, and cultural spheres of contention.

Of continuing originality and relevance is Gandhi's conception of constructive programs, where the building of truthful, decentralized, noncoercive, and democratic institutions can serve as the infrastructure of a just society in the process of becoming, while remaining beyond the range of state-run and market forces. Alternative institutions can prepare the ground for transforming and liberating a society without, at least in the short term, undertaking the disintegration of oppressive structures. They can change a society from within, without openly challenging the control of authorities.

Although sometimes awkwardly planned, managed, and executed, contemporary countrywide movements have consciously confronted oppression, challenged discrimination, alleviated injustice, and achieved political liberation or other similar outcomes through the technique of nonviolent action. An argument long lodged that this method cannot work against a ruthless despot is no longer credible. It has evaporated in light of major, often national, struggles of civil resistance in the last two decades of the twentieth century and first two decades of the twenty-first in which significant political alterations resulted.

Indeed, the growth of understanding of civil resistance is a notable development of the twentieth and twenty-first centuries, to the extent that it is no longer possible to consider geopolitics without reckoning with such political action. Gandhi is to a degree responsible for this, even though the use of nonviolent action arises from divergent cultural and political traditions, histories, and sources worldwide. Contemporary struggles often build on basics from Gandhi, but have also surpassed him in identifiable ways. Gandhi's discernments about popular power and consent, and his ground-breaking development of what he called a technique, process, and method for addressing acute conflict and oppression remain foundational. With their nomenclature largely coined by him, for both philosophical *and* strategic reasons they seek to connect means and ends—although they may not be as skimping on rigor concerning the ends in favor of the means as was he. It is now generally considered self-evident that results are influenced by how one fights. Either implicitly or explicitly today's nonviolent mobilizations operate on Gandhi's 1905 supposition that even the most powerful cannot rule without the cooperation of the ruled.

Against this backdrop, Gandhi's notion that suffering and uncritical belief that nonviolent action never fails and can melt even the stoniest heart is a hazardous article of faith. Although Gandhi talked of suffering love in the process through which he sought conversion, he discerned at an early stage that this was of limited efficacy. Clinging to the aspiration, he was circumspect in evincing this view. In Vykom, he cherished the hope that appeals to the upper-caste orthodoxy would be tangibly persuasive, saying in April 1924 with his proclivity for over-confidence: "The [Vykom] Satyagrahis are certain to break down the wall of prejudice, no matter how strong and solid it may be if they continue firm, but humble, truthful and nonviolent. They must have faith in these qualities to know that they will melt the stoniest hearts."[1] In actuality, his years of struggle in South Africa had led him to conclude that supplication and entreaty also need to be accompanied by the exertion of power, although he did not always articulate this conclusion. By 1925—following his November 10 three-hour encounter with the Namburidi Brahmin elite's obduracy—melting hearts had come to require force, in the form of action, which he admitted:

> I do not believe in making appeals when there is no force behind them whether moral or material. Moral force comes from the determination of the appellants to do something, to sacrifice something for the sake of making their appeal effective. . . . Unless we recognize and are prepared to reduce to practice this principle we can but expose the Congress and ourselves to ridicule, if not worse.[2]

All this is not to say that there had been no efforts to put conversion in a more reasonable light. In his 1936 autobiography, Nehru probes some of the issues of conversion and coercion contemplated in these pages, in his chapter "Conversion or Compulsion." Until approximately 1928, Nehru was still persuaded that India would need to use violence in order to end the British Raj. In the mid-1930s he commented:

> To think . . . in terms of pure conversion of a class or nation or of the removal of conflict by rational argument or appeals to justice, is to delude oneself. It is an illusion to imagine that a dominant imperialist Power will give up its domination over a country, or that a class will give up its superior position and privileges, unless effective pressure, amounting to coercion, is exercised. Gandhiji obviously wants to apply that pressure, although he calls it conversion.

Conceding that the rapidity with which noncooperation and civil disobedience spread in India proves that a nonviolent movement can exercise a potent effect on huge numbers and convert innumerable

[1] Gandhi, *Young India*, April 17, 1924, in *Collected Works of Mahatma Gandhi* (hereafter *CWMG*), 27: 263.

[2] Gandhi, "Our Impotence," *Young India*, November 12, 1925, in *CWMG*, 33: 211.

waverers, Nehru acknowledges that Gandhi's method can powerfully influence and unnerve the adversary, appeal to its higher sentiments, and offer some prospect of conciliation. He concludes that the nonviolent technique's greatest potential for impact is on those who are indifferent, but may become "converted" to its use. He rejects a hard-and-fast line between violent struggle and nonviolent action, or coercion and conversion. With low tolerance for Gandhi's self-suffering, he believes that only a thin line exists between suffering for an ideal and suffering for the sake of suffering, which is apt to become "morbid" and "degrading."[3]

As another example of challenging simplistic thinking about conversion, in 1951, four years after India's independence and four years prior to the start of the Montgomery bus boycott, Rammanohar Lohia, a Gandhian socialist, gave twenty addresses during a six-week lecture tour in the United States. He traveled the country, advocating civil disobedience, meeting with activists, and spoke on national radio. He had been recently jailed in India for organizing a march in Delhi to contest landlords' evicting tillers. He visited Highlander Folk School in Monteagle, Tennessee, where a black seamstress from Montgomery, Alabama, named Rosa Parks, would, a few years later, receive a systematic orientation to nonviolent resistance. Lohia was part of a concerted effort, through face-to-face encounters, by Indian visitors to the United States to encourage African Americans actively to confront inequitable treatment by the methods used in India, chiefly by courting arrest and civil disobedience. In an article published in *Mankind* magazine in 1952, Lohia despairs of hearing about conversion of the opponent and about melting the hearts of the oppressor. Instead, he wants to hear about the hearts of the oppressed, so that they can rise up to help themselves. In Lohia's eyes the greater part of Gandhi's followers had become complacent and settled down to enjoying the fruits of his labor: "They have no need to change the hearts of the oppressed and to put courage into them. They find it easiest to take to the cosy activity of changing the heart of the oppressor and the exploiter." Enthusiasts as well as opponents of Gandhi have, he contends, "reduced the phrase 'change

[3] Jawaharlal Nehru, *An Autobiography* (Delhi, Oxford, New York: Oxford University Press, 1989 [orig. 1936]), 544–6.

of heart' to such mimic proportions that it bears no relationship what-soever to Mahatma Gandhi's own conception of life." In Lohia's view, Gandhi "devoted over forty years to putting courage into and thereby changing the hearts of tens of millions of people all over the world," but converting the viewpoints of the oppressed was more crucial than altering the perspectives of the oppressors.[4]

Did reform come in "driblets," as Mahadev Desai phrased it? A more accurate interpretation of the settlement of the Vykom satya-graha would be to see it as an example of the management of conflict. Actual resolution or solution of an acute conflict remains rare (most severe examples are temporal and are reduced, demoted, or con-tained). Where both parties are embittered by disagreement, and acute discontent has resulted from harm, no solution may be possible until the causal origins of the conflict have been fully faced. Peace can remain unfit for mention until the depths of despair, humiliation, and anguish have been addressed to the satisfaction of the aggrieved, which may be one or both or several parties. Intense conflicts may require the pursuit of intermediate results along a pathway to an eventual goal. In such a case, the push to accomplish a transitional objective may demand its own sub-strategy. The grand strategy for the ultimate pur-pose may need several sub-strategies. Aiming for a transitory stage in addressing an enduring wrong may be advantageous, unless the midway phase were to be confused with the ultimate goal. A theoreti-cal argument can be made that the Vykom struggle ended with a tem-porary arrangement that, in its most optimistic interpretation, managed the situation so as to secure time for accommodation, the second mechanism to occur. "Gandhi often pursued management of problems rather than deep change," Jnaneswaran commented, citing as an example how, without subsidies, the hand-looming sector would have crashed.[5]

Unless conversion is defined as an ideal, excessive zeal for the objec-tive of converting the opponent's hearts and minds can encourage a

---

[4] Rammanohar Lohia, "Gandhi and Socialism (speech, Hyderabad, August 1952)," in *Collected Works of Dr. Rammanohar Lohia: Marx, Gandhi and Socialism*, ed. Mastram Kapoor (New Delhi: Anamika Publishers and Distributors, 2010), 27, 47–8.

[5] Jnaneswaran, interview (March 25, 2009).

tendency to impute supernatural or superhuman properties to nonviolent action, implying that serious, elemental power relationships are not involved. Such perceptions can also be encouraged by advocacy efforts that urge the shedding of violence without offering a concrete alternative. This inclination can be dangerous because loose notions of being able to change an adversary's normative values, attitudes, and beliefs so that the persons involved come to sympathize with and cohere with the nonviolent protagonists' objectives can impede acknowledgment of nonviolent struggle as a practical and effective technique for seeking social justice that might gradually and incrementally be substituted for violence. Multiple forms of power are usually involved.

Conversion remains exceedingly infrequent. Any presumption that the antagonists' viewing of suffering self-inflicted by the action takers will bring about a change of attitude is a dangerous basis for planning strategy. Movements today make claims, rather than invoking appeals, supplications, or suffering. While operating on the basis of strategies and tactics that were in many instances tested by Gandhi, they now seek to undermine the bases of power of the institutions and sectors that enable the target group to persist with its policies and practices. Movements have become modular, in the sense that they possess common features of theory and methods, whose chosen measures can be applied to a broad variety of circumstances and needs. By dissociating requirements of belief or spiritual affiliation, and by not screening participants for their personal beliefs, present-day campaigns can recruit with the broadest appeal. Participants may view themselves as realists; take stands on the basis of philosophical idealism; or be motivated by strong personal moral values, faiths, and beliefs. In their choice of civil resistance, however, they may be equally, or more so, acting from pragmatism. Without assuming that they can change the attitudes of the opponent, they seek to alter its policies, practices, and structures.

The two most significant democratic reconstructions in two generations worldwide have resulted from civil resistance—in combination with other factors and forces—as seen in the national nonviolent revolutions of Eastern Europe and the former Eastern bloc of the 1980s–90s that led to the dissolution of the Soviet Union, and the 2010–12 Arab Awakening, which was in several countries interrupted. Healthy

democratic formation is underway in Tunisia, notwithstanding the dis-
rupted tragic outcomes in Syria, Egypt, and Bahrain, and the violence in
Libya. Girders for these exertions against dictatorships may have been
partially built by Gandhi, but work is required on a scale greater than
anything heretofore undertaken to investigate what makes for success
through nonviolent struggle—along with interrogation of major disap-
pointments. Aspects of theory need grounding through research and
documentation, while some deficits remain unstudied. A virtually
unlimited need exists for continuing to build knowledge on nonviolent
means for addressing persistent conflict. A poverty of efforts to research
the theory and practice of civil resistance is disclosed whenever present-
day journalists label a complex nonviolent mobilization of social
power as "protest," report on a demonstration as a "riot," or persist in
using the term "passive resistance" that Gandhi found compromising
while still in South Africa.

The abolition of untouchability, to the extent that it has proceeded
in India, has occurred primarily through resolute actions taken by and
within castes, which were the primary source of human agency,
although Gandhi's efforts to induce changes in upper-caste perspectives
certainly cannot be dismissed. Hence the import of making the technique of civil resistance more comprehensible, so that it can potentially
strengthen its reliability as a system that can enhance the possibilities
for groups and societies to achieve positive results in acute conflicts
with self-reliance and without resort to violence. Understanding the
many facets involved in nonviolent struggle is important, if for no
other reason than the judgments and choices made by the protagonists
can have life-and-death consequences for themselves and entire populations. It is, thus, critical to continue to improve understanding of the
workings and history of civil resistance.

De facto freedom for India arrived on September 2, 1946, when the
interim national government was installed under the leadership of
Jawaharlal Nehru. After India became independent in a formal transfer
of power on August 15, 1947, India's Constituent Assembly passed a
resolution outlawing the practice of untouchability, declared illegal
in the constitution. The *New York Times* wryly stated in its editorial,
"The idea of caste is not an Indian copyright," noting that 40 million
Indians were now legally able "leave their ghettos, use the village wells,

bathe in the rivers and enjoy the privileges of citizenship denied them by obscure tradition for centuries."[6] Moreover, passing laws against discrimination was only a first step, as well known in the United States. It was an historic decision, which the *Times* and other news media compared with the abolition of trans-Atlantic slavery.

India's emergent democracy has presented a structural opening for caste to become incorporated into its nationhood, within a political context, at least in a transitional sense. Caste, in many ways still a feature of Indian society even while being integrated into democratic electoral politics, has become a pathway for the Indian electorate to involve itself in democratic politics. Political parties and electioneering can sometimes be driven by caste advocacy or retribution. Sensitivities about whether the government should ask for identifying data have confounded official efforts to undertake corrective governmental measures to fight discrimination. With little data, 60-odd years of advancing democratic governance have sought to redress the slings and arrows of the past, with reservation of school and job placements for the Dalits and others—even if with mixed results. Countless Indians still discriminate against Dalits. As with prejudice anywhere, they may no longer refuse to sit at the next table in restaurants, accept contact in trains and buses, allow them in many (though not all) temples, yet would react aggressively toward any act of self-assertion, as seen in murders and rapes of Dalits who "get above themselves." The idea that Gandhi brought a "change of heart" in India is only partly true. Well-educated and sophisticated high-caste Indians can discriminate in subtle ways, as with the sort of discrimination faced all too often by African Americans in the United States and Afro-Caribbeans in Britain. Yet forces of globalization, technology, and travel are altering the picture. Caste allegiances as expressed in voting preferences increasingly possess the utility of ethnic voting in Chicago, Boston, and New York City. Although of uncertain destiny, the religious identification of caste has become secondary to its ability to act as a political driver.

In June 1947, Dewan Ramaswami Iyer had predicted that Travancore would become an independent state after the British departed. Representative government became visible in Travancore in 1948 with

---

[6] "Editorial: India's Untouchables," *New York Times*, December 17, 1948.

a three-person ministry of C. Kesavan (an Ezhava), Pattam Thanu Pillai (a Nair), and T. M. Varghese (a Syrian Christian). In 1891, Ezhavas had been ineligible for government jobs, but approximately six decades later a member of that community was chief minister of Travancore–Cochin. In 1891, Ezahavas had been ineligible for government jobs, but approximately six decades later a member of that community was chief minister of Travancore–Cochin. Another, Raman Shankar, rose to become leader of the Congress Party in the Kerala Legislative Assembly and in 1962 assumed office, becoming the first Ezhava chief minister for Kerala, after it became a state in 1956. This was not the result of sops being thrown—the Ezhavas had organized and waged disciplined non-violent struggle for what they had won.

Glossary

ahimsa	concept of noninjury and non-killing of any living being
ashram	Hindu religious community
*avarna*s	people who held no caste and fell outside the four main caste groups (collectively referred to as *savarna*s); from Sanskrit, one who does not have a *varn*, or an "outcaste," "untouchable," or Dalit; formerly meant "unclean," referring to those who were outside the caste system and would therefore "pollute" *savarna*s
Brahmins	priestly caste, customarily considered the most "pure"
caste system	a Hindu hierarchical social structure in which one's position is related to theoretical degrees of purity, with social and literal distances identified in terms of pollution versus purity
charka	spinning wheel for hand-looming khadi
Dalits	another name for so-called untouchables or *avarna*s; means "broken men" in the Marathi language of Maharashtra
devasam	temple property
dewan	chief executive minister; in effect, the prime minister for the maharaja
dharma	Sanskrit word for knowing and obeying the law (of God); in Hindu religious thought it is considered one's religious duty, one's allotted role in life

durbar	the court of a raja, executive government for a princely state, and also an audience or reception at the maharaja's palace in Travancore
Ezhavas	largest and highest-ranking group among Travancore's *avarna* Hindus; pron. Iravas or Erhavas
gaddi	plush pillow on which ruling sovereigns of Travancore sat
guru	spiritual teacher
Harijans	"children of God," Gandhi's chosen name for so-called untouchables
jati	localized caste groups
khadi	hand-loomed homespun; part of Gandhi's constructive program to unite all social groups and ranks in supporting the nationalist movement, while lessening imports of cloth from British mills would weaken Britain's desire to hold India
maharaja	head of state for a princely state; raja, or king, with the appendage *maha* means "great king"
maharani	head of Travancore's royal family; the senior rani, or queen, with the appendage *maha* signifies "great queen"
Nairs	also Nayars; in Travancore the warriors, militiamen, and chieftain *savarna* caste
Nambudiri Brahmins	Brahmins were called Nambudiris in Travancore, and in the districts of Cochin and Malabar
poorna swaraj	also *purna swaraj*; narrowly defined as self-rule, but more broadly means "complete independence"
princely state	nominally sovereign units not directly administered by the British; remained under traditional heriditary Indian rulers in a form of indirect rule under the British Raj; called "native" states, or Indian states, by the British
raj, the Raj	"rule"; frequently denotes British imperial rule

sabha	association
satyagraha	Gandhi's term for a then new technique of social action equivalent in present-day usage to nonviolent civil resistance; literally means holding on to Truth, firmness in Truth, or relentless insistence on Truth
satyagrahi	person who believes in satyagraha as a matter of principle or who practices it
*savarna*s	members of the four main castes, consisting of Brahmins; Kshatriyas—the ruler, warrior, or military caste; Vaisya (also Vaishya)—the merchant caste; and Sudra—laborers and artisans
SNDP Yogam	Sri Narayana Dharma Paripalana Yogam, an association for the propagation of dharma and an organized force behind Ezhava activism
swadeshi	self-reliance in a sense of simplification of material needs; using goods produced in one's own country
swaraj	self-rule, home rule; independence
*teendal palaka*s	notice boards maintained by Travancore's government to display prohibitions against the polluting strata entering onto the forbidden roads surrounding the Brahmin temple
temple entry	concept advancing the claim of Ezhavas and other so-called untouchables to enter any Hindu temple, a more maximalist demand than walking on the roads surrounding the Brahmin temple
unapproachability	also *doorata* (remoteness); prescribed distances imposed for certain groups without caste in Travancore; for example, members of these groups were expected to step off the road when members from a superior cluster approached, to avoid inadvertently polluting them
unseeability	a condition in which the Pulayas, Purayas, Panans, and other unseeables in Travancore lived in ditches

	and had to move about at night, emerging after dark to remain unseen
untouchability	Hindu concept that certain strata of society should not be touched; even their shadow could pollute upper castes; reflection of Hindu theocracy's determination to repress, based on perceptions of purity
untouchables	see under *avarnas*; among Travancore's untouchables, in descending status, were Ezhavas, Channans, Cherumas, Pulayas, Parayas, and Nayadis
upper castes	loosely refers to *savarnas*
varna	Sanskrit for "caste," literally means "color"

Appendix I
Timeline

Events: 604 Days[1]

March 30, 1924–November 23, 1925

February 6, 1924: The Anti-Untouchability Committee adopts a resolution to eradicate untouchability through peaceful opposition, and decides to launch the campaign in Vykom. Efforts had been underway since the late nineteenth century to reform the extreme practices of untouchability, unapproachability, and unseeability, particularly with regard to bans on all untouchables and outcastes from the roads immediately surrounding the Shiva temple. This lengthened the way home for the excluded groups.

March 26: In anticipation of a forthcoming march in Vykom, the police erect barriers around the restricted temple roads and post guards at the notice boards that declare the prohibited areas.

March 30: The Vykom satyagraha begins as three men of different caste strata approach the restricted roads surrounding the Shiva temple, seeking passage. After a one-hour standoff with police, all three are arrested and sentenced to six months' imprisonment.

---

[1] The struggle persisted for 604 days, from its first nonviolent action on March 30, 1924, until its end on November 23, 1925.

March 31: A Nair and two Ezhavas approach the barricade, are arrested, and sentenced to four months in the Trivandrum jail.

April 1: Gandhi writes to suggest that the satyagraha be temporarily suspended due to intense opposition from orthodox upper-caste Hindus. After meeting with representatives of the upper-caste elites, Gandhi advises the *satyagrahi*s in Travancore to try for a compromise.

April 7: As the campaign moves toward resumption after its temporary suspension, and more leaders arrive at Vykom, the district magistrate moves to incarcerate the senior figures. By early April, T. K. Madhavan and K. P. Kesava Menon, two of the critical leaders of the satyagraha, had defiantly walked to the prohibited area, only to be arrested and jailed.

April 10: Orders are issued by the British Police Commissioner, W. H. Pitt, to stop arresting satyagrahis and their leaders in order to avoid an escalation. Volunteers begin fasting at the barriers.

April 18: The *dewan* (similar to a maharaja's prime minister) visits Sri Narayana Guru at his ashram and offers to provide more convenient roads for the public, including for untouchables. His compromise is rejected.

June 19: With the key leadership behind bars, creating a vacuum, police and volunteers clash in a minor incident, revealing that the struggle has moved toward directionless drift.

June 21: Frustrated police seize the spinning wheels of the protesters and beat some volunteers with wooden batons.

June–August: Severe flooding in the great flood of 1924 intensifies the stalemate between police and the satyagrahis. As police take to row-boats and challengers stand in neck-deep water, public sympathy turns in favor of the satyagraha. National interest increases.

August 5: The district magistrate in Kottayam invokes the Criminal Procedure Code and bans supporters from coming to Vykom or visiting Kottayam District.

August 7: Maharaja Sri Mulam Thirunal dies; the Vykom satyagraha is suspended for three days of mourning.

September 1: Sethu Lakshmi Bayi is installed as the maharani regent, acting in lieu of the young heir. One of the maharani's first official acts is to release the prisoners associated with the satyagraha.

October 2: N. Kumaran—an Ezhava, leader of an important caste association, and a nominated member of the Travancore Legislative Council—introduces a resolution in the council calling for the opening of every Vykom temple road to all castes.

November 1: A *savarna jatha*, a grand procession of approximately 100 upper-caste participants, sets out at dawn from Vykom, marching in military fashion, having collected signatures for a "monster petition" to be submitted to the maharani. Wearing yellow headpieces and regalia, banners billowing, pipes and drums, their signs display the purposes of the jatha. Participants from all caste strata watch the procession. A Pulaya rice dish is eaten by the high-caste marchers, breaking the rules against inter-dining. A second jatha of 500 upper-caste marchers leaves from Suchindram, south Travancore. En route to the capital, their numbers swelled to a thousand, despite pouring rains.

November 11: The two jathas unite in Trivandrum at the completion of their marches, as 5,000 convene on the beach for a convocation.

November 14: A twelve-member deputation presents the monster petition to the maharani, signed by more than 25,000 caste Hindus.

November 21: A temporary truce is called as the annual Ashtami Hindu temple festival is celebrated at Vykom's Shiva temple, and 50,000 caste Hindus participate.

February 7, 1925: The resolution of October 2, 1924, is defeated in a 22–21 vote within the Legislative Council, with suspicions rising of governmental intrusion.

March 9: Gandhi arrives in Vykom to speak out against untouchability and promote the nationalist program of the Indian National Congress party.

March 10: Gandhi visits the satyagraha ashram and meets approximately fifty satyagraha volunteers. He also meets for three hours with high-level members of the orthodox opposition, possibly the first face-to-face encounter of his life with the entrenched prejudice of the upper castes. He offers three proposals for settlement, each of which is rejected.

March 12: Gandhi meets semi-privately with the leading spiritual and reform leader of Travancore, Sri Narayana Guru, an Ezhava, to relate the importance of nonviolent strategies in social movements. Guru gives him his assent.

March 18: Gandhi departs from Vykom by motorboat, as he arrived. As a state guest of the maharaja, Gandhi has been accompanied throughout his visit by the British Police Commissioner W. H. Pitt. He leaves a letter for Pitt proffering a compromise, based on their discussions during his visit to south India: the government would remove the barricades around the roads that had been erected in March 1924 in anticipation of demonstrations, and the satyagrahis would refrain from entering the forbidden roads.

March 25: Pitt replies to Gandhi, stating that the maharaja's government has accepted the suggestion.

April 4: The government formally withdraws its March 1924 prohibitory order. The agreement is enacted on April 8.

June 21: Three of the roads surrounding the temple are walked upon by members of lower excluded groups after a government order opens three of the four roads to all members of the populace.

June 23: A telegram from Gandhi instructs volunteers to take "no forward step" without his permission. Access to only three of the four roads is a capitulation that may defeat the purpose of the satyagraha. The satyagrahis are disheartened.

October 8: Gandhi receives details of what is being called a settlement; he authorizes the withdrawal of the satyagrahis.

October 31: A social conference of Nairs passes a resolution approving the expansion of access to the temple roads to all castes.

November 17: The Kerala Congress Untouchability Committee passes resolutions approving the opening of the temple roads.

November 23: During the preceding months, the government has come up with a concept of opening three of the four roads surrounding the temple and creating a secondary path, a diversion. This is presented as a "solution." A compromise is effected: a small portion of the road at the eastern gate of the Vykom temple is reserved for the temple authorities' exclusive use in entering the temple compound, alongside of which is created a separate variation pathway, upon which the so-called untouchables can walk.

November 24: The police inspector in Vykom notifies Pitt in Trivandrum that the standoff has ended.

December 7, 1925: K. Kelappan, steadfast in his leadership of the Anti-Untouchability Committee, sends the dewan a handwritten letter on committee stationery from Vykom. His letter contains the same resolutions written out by hand, referencing a "fact" that all roads in Vykom have been thrown open to all citizens. Thus begins a century of misinterpretation of the resolution of the Vykom struggle and what had happened there in 1924–5.

Appendix II
Mechanisms of Change

Four different "mechanisms of change," a description of possible outcomes, have evolved as an analytical tool to explain how nonviolent action can work and what may be the aim of its strategy.[1]

It is possible with careful planning for a campaign or movement to seek the most suitable mechanism.

In explaining how a nonviolent campaign can achieve its results, or deciding how to plan a group's strategy, a number of conditions determine what mechanism can be reached, including, "the specific conflict situation, the issues at stake, the social structure of the resisting population, the nature of the opponents ... the specific methods used, and the skill, discipline, and tenacity of the resisters."[2]

---

[1] The germinal work discerning ways in which nonviolent civil resistance could operate, and how its strategy could be targeted, was done by George Lakey, "The Sociological Mechanisms of Nonviolent Action" (Master's degree thesis, University of Philadelphia, 1962); Lakey, "The Sociological Mechanisms of Nonviolent Action," *Peace Research Review* 2, no. 6 (1968): 1–102. While Richard Gregg wrote extensively about conversion, the other three mechanisms, which occur more frequently, have been analyzed by scholars Clarence Marsh Case, George Lakey, and Gene Sharp, whose work builds on Lakey's.

[2] Gene Sharp, *There Are Realistic Alternatives*, monograph (Boston: Albert Einstein Institution, 2003), 13–14. Downloadable at http://www.aeinstein.org/wp-content/uploads/2013/09/TARA.pdf (accessed January 22, 2014).

1. *Conversion*: The target group reacts to nonviolent civil resistance by accepting a new point of view and adopts the goals of the nonviolent protagonists. The "hearts and minds" of the opponent are altered. Power transfers to the movement. Historically, this mechanism occurs rarely.
2. *Accommodation*: The target group chooses to yield to demands and adjusts to the new circumstances produced by the nonviolent challengers, but without necessarily changing positions on the underlying issues. This is historically the most frequent outcome between two contending parties in successful mobilizations. The shifts in policy or power from the adversary or target group to the nonviolent action takers may be unannounced, even when occurring.
3. *Nonviolent Coercion*: This mechanism transpires when the members of the target group remain in their stations and situations, policies unchanged, yet can no longer manage their own system without the cooperation of the nonviolent protagonists. This can happen without the will or consent of the opponent, which may retain control of the structures of power and the capability to use them, even as its capacity for containing the civil resisters wanes. As the nonviolent movement pulls away the opponent's bulwarks of support, isolating the adversary from its sources of power, it is forced to yield to the demands of the movement.
4. *Disintegration*: In extremely rare cases, the power system of the opponent completely collapses, as its bulwarks of support with their sources of power are pulled away by the nonviolent mobilization.

Select Bibliography

Books

Aiyappan, Ayinipalli. 1965. *Social Revolution in a Kerala Village: A Study in Culture*. London: Asia Publishing House.

Ambedkar, Babasaheb B. 1987. "Caste in India," *Caste and Democratic Politics in India*, in series, *Essential Writings in Politics*, eds. Rajeev Bhargava and Partha Chatterjee, extracted from Babasaheb Ambedkar, *Writings and Speeches*, vol. 3. Bombay: Government of Maharashtra.

Chandramohan, P. 1981. "Social and Political Protest in Travancore: A Study of the Sree Narayana Dharma Paripalana Yogam (1900–1938). " M.A. diss., Centre for Historical Studies, School of Social Sciences, Jawaharlal Nehru University.

Bondurant, Joan V. (1958) 1988. *Conquest of Violence: The Gandhian Philosophy of Conflict*. Princeton, New Jersey: Princeton University Press.

Brown, Judith M. 1977. *Gandhi and Civil Disobedience: The Mahatma in Indian Politics, 1928–34*. Cambridge: Cambridge University Press.

———. 1994. *Modern India: The Origins of an Asian Democracy*, 2nd ed. Oxford: Oxford University Press.

———. 2003. *Nehru: A Political Life*. New Haven, Connecticut: Yale University Press.

———. 2009. "Gandhi and Civil Resistance in India, 1917–47: Key Issues." In *Civil Resistance and Power Politics: The Experience of*

Non-violent Action from Gandhi to the Present, eds. Adam Roberts and Timothy Garton Ash, 43-57. Oxford: Oxford University Press.

Case, Clarence Marsh. 1923. *Nonviolent Coercion: A Study in Methods of Social Pressure.* New York: Century.

Dalton, Dennis. 2012. *Mahatma Gandhi: Nonviolent Power in Action.* New York: Columbia University Press.

Desai, Mahadev Haribhai. 1937. *The Epic of Travancore.* Ahmedabad: Navajivan Karyalaya.

Diwaker, Ranganath Ramachandra. 1946. *Satyagraha: Its Technique and History.* Bombay: Hind Kitabs.

_____. 1969. *Saga of Satyagraha.* New Delhi, Bombay: Gandhi Peace Foundation.

Gandhi, Mohandas K. 1948. *Constructive Programme: Its Meaning and Place* (pamphlet, orig. 1941). Ahmedabad: Navajivan Publishing House.

_____. (1942) 1948. *Non-violence in Peace and War*, ed. Mahadev Desai, vol. 1, 3rd ed. Ahmedabad: Navajivan Publishing House. Cited as *NPW* (1).

_____. 1949. *Non-violence in Peace and War*, ed. Bharatan Kumarappa, vol. 2, 1st ed. Ahmedabad: Navajivan Publishing House. Cited as *NPW* (2).

_____. (1928) 1950. *Satyagraha in South Africa*, 2nd ed., trans. by Valji Govindji Desai. Ahmedabad: Navajivan Publishing House.

_____. (1940) 1993. *An Autobiography: The Story of My Experiments with Truth*, trans. from Gujarati by Mahadev Desai. Ahmedabad: Navajivan Publishing House, repr., Boston: Beacon Press.

_____. 1958–99. *Collected Works of Mahatma Gandhi*, ed. K. Swaminathan, 100 vols. New Delhi: Ministry of Information and Broadcasting, Government of India.

_____. 1995. *Hind Swaraj or Indian Home Rule*, ed. Mahadev Desai (South Africa, n.p., 1909; English edition repr., 1938). Ahmedabad: Jitendra T. Desai, Navajivan Mudranalaya.

_____. 1997. *Hind Swaraj and Other Writings*, ed. Anthony J. Parel. Cambridge: Cambridge University Press.

Gregg, Richard B. (1934) 1960. *The Power of Nonviolence.* London: James Clarke and Company.

Hardiman, David. 2003. *Gandhi in His Time and Ours: The Global Legacy of His Ideas.* London: Hurst and Company.

Hardtmann, Eva-Maria. 2009. *The Dalit Movement in India: Local Practices, Global Connections.* Oxford and New York: Oxford University Press.

Hough, James. 1839. *History of Christianity in India from the Commencement of the Christian Era*, 5 vols. (1599–1830). London: R. B. Seeley and W. Burnside.

Hunt, William Saunders. 1924. *India's Outcastes: A New Era.* London: Church Missionary Society.

Jaffrelot, Christophe. 2005. *Dr Ambedkar and Untouchability: Analysing and Fighting Caste.* London: Hurst and Company.

Jeffrey, Robin. 1978. "Travancore: Status, Class and the Growth of Radical Politics, 1860–1940, the Temple-Entry Movement." In *People, Princes and Paramount Power: Society and Politics in the Indian Princely States*, ed. Robin Jeffrey. New Delhi: Oxford University Press.

_____. (1976) 1994. *The Decline of Nayar Dominance: Society and Politics in Travancore, 1847–1908.* New Delhi: Manohar Publications.

Joseph, George Gheverghese. 2003. *George Joseph: The Life and Times of a Kerala Christian Nationalist.* Hyderabad: Orient Longman.

Kapur, Sudarshan. 1992. *Raising Up a Prophet: The African-American Encounter with Gandhi.* Boston: Massachusetts: Beacon Press.

Kawashima, Koji. (1965) 1998. *Missionaries and a Hindu State: Travancore 1858–1936.* New Delhi: Oxford University Press.

King, Mary Elizabeth. (1999) 2002. *Mahatma Gandhi and Martin Luther King, Jr: The Power of Nonviolent Action*, 2nd ed. New Delhi: Indian Council for Cultural Relations and Mehta Publishers.

Mankekar, D. R. 1965. *The Red Riddle of Kerala.* Bombay: Manaktala.

Mende, Tibor. 1956. *Conversations with Mr. Nehru.* London: Secker and Warburg.

Menon, A. Sreedhara. 1967. *A Survey of Kerala History.* Kottayam, Kerala: Sahitya Pravarthaka Co-operative Society.

_____. 1997. *Kerala and Freedom Struggle.* Kottayam: D C Books.

Menon, K. P. Kesava. 1977. *The Vaikkom Satyagraha*, ed. K. P. Kesava Menon. Calicut: K. P. Kesava Menon 90th Birthday Celebration Committee.

Menon, P. K. Karunakara. 1970. *The History of the Freedom Movement in Kerala*, 2 vols. (1600–1885; 1885–1938). Trivandrum: Regional Records Survey Committee, Government of Kerala.

Nanda, B. R. 1958. *Mahatma Gandhi: A Biography.* Delhi: Oxford University Press.

Nanda, B. R. 1985. *Gandhi and His Critics*. Bombay, Calcutta, Madras: Oxford University Press.

Omvedt, Gail. 1994. *Dalits and the Democratic Revolution: Dr. Ambedkar and the Dalit Movement in Colonial India*. New Delhi, Thousand Oaks, and London: SAGE Publications.

Ouwerkerk, Louise. 1945. *The Untouchables of India*. London: Oxford University Press.

_____. 1994. *No Elephants for the Maharaja: Social and Political Change in the Princely State of Travancore, 1921–1947*. New Delhi: Manohar.

Panikkar, K. N. 1995. *Culture, Ideology and Hegemony: Intellectuals and Social Consciousness in Colonial India*. New Delhi: Tulika.

_____. 1995. "Vaikkam Satyagraha: The Struggle against Untouchability." In *We Fought Together for Freedom: Chapters from the Indian National Movement*, ed. Ravi Dayal. Delhi: Oxford University Press and Indian Council of Historical Research.

Raghunandan, Lakshmi. 1995. *At the Turn of the Tide: The Life and Times of Maharani Setu Lakshmi Bayi, the Last Queen of Travancore*. Bangalore: Maharani Setu Lakshmi Bayi Memorial Charitable Trust.

Rangaswami, Vanaja. 1981. *The Story of Integration: A New Interpretation in the Context of the Democratic Movements in the Princely States of Mysore, Travancore and Cochin 1900–1947*. New Delhi: Manohar.

Rao, M. S. A. 1987. *Social Movements and Social Transformation: A Study of Two Backward Classes Movements in India*. New Delhi: Manohar Publications.

Rao, N. Sudhakar. 2001. "The Structure of South Indian Untouchable Castes." In *Dalit Identity and Politics: Cultural Subordination and the Dalit Challenges*, vol. 2, ed. Ghanshyam Shah. New Delhi, Thousand Oaks, and London: SAGE Publications.

Ravindran, T. K. 1973. *Asan and Social Revolution in Kerala: A Study of His Assembly Speeches*. Travandrum: Kerala Historical Society.

_____. 1975. *Vaikkam Satyagraha and Gandhi*. Trichur, India: Sri Narayana Institute of Social and Cultural Development.

Sharp, Gene. 1973. *The Politics of Nonviolent Action*, 3 vols. Boston: Porter Sargent Publishers.

_____. 1979. *Gandhi as a Political Strategist*. Boston: Porter Sargent Publishers.

_____. 2005. *Waging Nonviolent Struggle: 20th Century Practice and 21st Century Potential*. Boston: Porter Sargent Publishers.

Shridharani, Krishnalal. 1962. *War without Violence*. Bombay: Bharatiya Vidya Bhavan.

Sobhanan, B. 1978. *Dewan Velu Tampi and the British*. Trivandrum: Kerala Historical Society.

Zelliot, Eleanor. 1996. *From Untouchable to Dalit: Essays on the Ambedkar Movement*. New Delhi: Manohar.

Journal Articles and Theses

Balambal, V. 1980. "E. V. R. and Vaikom Satyagraha." *Journal of Kerala Studies* 7 (March, June, September, December): 245–53.

Houtart, François and Geneviève Lemercinier. 1978. "Socio-Religious Movements in Kerala: A Reaction to the Capitalist Mode of Production." *Social Scientist* 6, no. 11, part one (June): 3–34; no. 12, part two (July): 25–43.

Jeffrey, Robin. 1974. "The Social Origins of a Caste Association, 1875–1905: The Founding of the SNDP Yogam." *South Asia* 4 (October): 39–59.

_____. 1976. "Temple-Entry Movement in Travancore, 1860–1940." *Social Scientist* 4, no. 8 (March): 3–43.

Lakey, George. 1968. "The Sociological Mechanisms of Nonviolent Action." *Peace Research Review* 2, no. 6: 1–102.

Mohan, P. Sanal. 2005. "Imagining Equality: Modernity and Social Transformation of Lower Caste in Colonial Kerala." Ph.D. Diss., Mahatma Gandhi University, Kottayam.

Nair, K. Ramachandran. 2006. *The History of the Trade Union Movement in Kerala*. Thiruvananthapuram: Kerala Institute of Labour and Employment.

Nair, M. P. Sreekumaran. 1976. "Review of *Vaikkom Satyagraha and Gandhi*," by T. K. Ravindran. *Journal of Indian History* 54 (December): 761–6.

Nair, P. R. Gopinathan. 1976. "Education and Socio-Economic Change in Kerala, 1793–1947." *Social Scientist* 4, no. 8 (March): 33–7.

Narayanan, M. G. S. 1975. "Historical Perspectives in Ancient India." *Social Scientist* 4, no. 3 (October): 9–10.

Radhakrishnan, P. 1976. Review of Robin Jeffrey's *The Decline of Nayar Dominance: Society and Politics in Travancore, 1847–1908*. *Social Scientist* 5, no. 12 (July): 76–9.

Raimon, Sundarannadar, ed. 2006. *Selected Documents on Vaikom Satyagraha.* Thiruvananthapuram: Kerala State Archives.

Rudolph, Lloyd I. and Suzanne Hoeber Rudolph. 1965. "The Modernity of Tradition: The Democratic Incarnation of Caste in India." *American Political Science Review* 59, no. 4 (December–January): 975–89.

Srinivas, M. N. 1957. "Caste in Modern India." *Journal of Asian Studies* 16, no. 4 (August): 529–48.

Primary and Archival Documents

Government of Kerala. 1924. *Proceedings of the Twentieth Session of the Sri Mulam Popular Assembly of Travancore.* Trivandrum: Superintendent, Government Press.

————. August 4, 1924–February 7, 1925. *Proceedings of the Travancore Legislative Council.* Trivandrum: Government of Kerala.

————. 1999. "The Growth of Political Consciousness among Women in Modern Kerala." In *Kerala State Gazetteer*, ed. P. J. Cherian, vol. 2, part 2: 486–510.

Government Secretariat. 1924–5. *English Records,* 5 vols. Trivandrum: Government Secretariat.

Palpu, Padmanabhan. *Dr. Padmanabhan Palpu Papers.* New Delhi: Nehru Memorial Library.

Vaikkom Satyagraha Bundle, 10 vols. Trivandrum: Kerala State Archives, Government of Kerala.

Newspapers

Malayala Manorama Daily (Kottayam). "Mahatma Gandhi's Visits to Kerala: 1924, 1925, 1927, 1934, 1937," Compendium, 1924–1925 (2009).

The Hindu

Mathrubhumi, Kozhikode, April 1924–November 1925

The Times (India)

Travancore Government Gazette

Trivandrum Daily News

Interviews

Devika, J. March 23, 2009. Trivandrum.

Gopalankutty, K. August 11, 2005. Kozhikode (formerly Calicut).

Jose, N. K. August 14, 2005. Vykom.

Jnaneswaran, Suresh. March 25, 2009. Trivandrum.

Kusuman, K. K. August 16, 2005. Trivandrum.

Lawson, James M. February 27, 1996. Los Angeles.

————. May 3, 2013. Telephone.

Maliakan, Joseph. March 12, 2009. New Delhi.

Mohan, Sanal. August 14, 2005. Vykom.

Narayanan, M. G. S. August 12, 2005. Kozhikode.

Panikkar, K. N. August 15, 2005. Trivandrum.

Philip, A. J. March 12, 2009. New Delhi.

Pillai, N. N. March 12, 2009. New Delhi.

Ramakrishnan, A. K. March 12, 2009. New Delhi.

Sebastian, Gilbert. March 12, 2009. New Delhi.

Sharp, Gene. February 18, 2010. Telephone.

Thilleri, Vasu. August 11, 2005. Kozhikode.

————. March 17 and 19, 2009. Kozhikode.

Index

Achuta Menon, V. 82
adversaries 73, 83, 145, 155, 160, 247, 252, 258, 260, 269, 271
African Americans 116, 242, 279–80, 284, 295, 299, 304; learn Gandhian Nonviolent Struggle 279–88; theories and methods of nonviolent struggle 280, 285, 295
agitations 52, 52n71, 59, 68, 109n56, 175, 189, 219–20, 257, *see also* satyagraha; nonviolent struggle); denial of civil rights and 224; Kusuman on 229
ahimsa 63, 68, 242, 248, *see also* nonviolence, nonviolent action
Ahmedabad (Sabarmati ashram) 289
Aiyappan, Ayinipalli 6, 62
Aiyappan, K. 128–9, 205
Aiyar, Subba 180
Akalis 124–5

al-Amin 100
Aleppo 12
Ali, Maulana Muhamed 88
Alwaye Union Christian College 194
Ambedkar, Bhimrao Ramji (Babasaheb) 17–18, 120, 200–1, 206, 226, 237, 292; on Broken Men 18n31; on Gandhi 237
Andrews, C. F. 61, 115, 118, 179, 221–2
Antioch 12
anti-satyagraha movement 152–3
anti-untouchability 88; movement of 96
Anti-Untouchability Committee 88–97, 102–3, 106, 135, 167, 194, 210, 309
Arab Awakening 302
Arab traders 12
arbitration 187, 257
arrest, courting 112, 144, 299; of key leaders 293

Student Nonviolent Coordinating
Committee (SNCC/ pro-
nounced *snick*) 287
subaltern studies 265
subcastes 17, 20, 80, see also
under *separate names*
Sudras 17
suzerainty 6, 64
swadeshi 66, 82
Swan, Maureen 238
swaraj/ swarajya 65–6, 70, 71, 75,
76, 116, 131, 153–4, 158, 182,
195, 237; defining 71; 306
Swati Thirunal 8
Syrian Christianity in Kerala, like
Hinduism 31
Syrian Christians 12–13, 22,
30–1, 36, 41, 52–3, 58, 117–8,
162, 303; had Hindu names
31; as Nambudiri Brahmins
36; ritual pollution and 31

taxation 19, 24, *see also* refusal to
pay rent and taxes *under*
Gandhi; nonviolence, nonviolent action
*teendal palaka*s 30, 43, 58, 91,
197, 224, 230
temple custodians 145, 199, 202,
228
temple entry 44, 53–5, 59–60,
74, 77, 87, 89, 93, 119, 216,
230–1, 234–5, 138, 190;
elsewhere 214; Gandhi on 76,
77, *see also* Ramasamy
Naicker, E. V. (Periyar);
proclamation on 229–31, 292
Temple Entry Enquiry Committee
216

temple roads 51–2, 54–5, 74,
86–7, 93–6, 99–100, 136–7,
154–5, 174–5, 193–4, 211–14;
elsewhere 214; opening of
136, 165, 294; untouchables
using 95, *see also* proclamation of opening princely state
roads *under* Maharaja of
Travancore
Temple Sivalingam 46
temple-building campaign, of
Guru 46
Temple-Entry Movement in
Travancore, 1860–1940 8–10,
20, 38, 54, 56, 58, 60, 96,
136, 139
temples 45–8, 52–5, 73–7, 86,
91–3, 102–3, 138–40, 178–
80, 202–7, 209–12, 214–16;
desertion of 52, see also under
individual names; entering 53,
54, 73, 75, 76, 86; land
owned by 19; *savarna*
52, 55
temple-entry proclamation, 1936
229–31, 292
Thilleri, Vasu 92, 204
Thirunal, Ayilyam 9
Thiruvarappu temple 215
Thomas the Apostle 12
Thoreau, Henry David 243
Tiruvarpu satyagraha 229
Tiyas 22*n*40, 23
Tolstoy, Leo 243
traders 22, 36, 66, 241
Travancore Criminal Procedure
Code 95, 198
Travancore government 14, 30,
48, 59, 113, 136–7, 153–4,

342 Index

About the Author

Mary Elizabeth King is Professor of Peace and Conflict Studies for the UN-affiliated University for Peace, main campus, Costa Rica; and Distinguished Fellow of the Rothermere American Institute, University of Oxford, UK. Some of her publications include: *Freedom Song: A Personal Story of the 1960s Civil Rights Movement* (1987), *Mahatma Gandhi and Martin Luther King Jr: The Power of Nonviolent Action* ([1999] 2002), *A Quiet Revolution: The First Palestinian Intifada and Nonviolent Resistance* (2007), *The New York Times on Emerging Democracies in Eastern Europe* (2009). She has also been the editor and co-author for several volumes for the University for Peace Africa Programme.